CONSUMER GUIDE®

1983 CARS

GW00771751

Contents

Introduction

Should you buy a new 1983 car? If you're not afflicted with "sticker shock" and can budget the monthly payments comfortably, the answer is yes. In fact, the U.S. market's current sales slump works in your favor. Both domestic and foreign automakers are desperate to get sales moving again. This means you can expect to see—and save money with—more rebates, low-interest-rate loan deals, and other buyer incentives of the sort we saw during the 1982 model year. Of course, prices are higher than ever and—inevitably—won't go any lower. But right now you can probably swing a more attractive deal than you think.

Naturally, the automakers will be trying harder than ever to lure you into their showrooms—and to plunk down for a new '83. Spending your hard-earned money wisely is what *1983 Cars* is all about. Here you'll find clear, concise reviews of what's new or what's different about all the models on the market, plus all the vital statistics you'll need to compare various models. Each report includes the expert evaluation of CONSUMER GUIDE® magazine's automotive staff in both words and an easy to read "box score" evaluation checklist.

In short, *1983 Cars* puts everything you need to know right at your fingertips. By checking here first, you'll have an easier time wading through advertising hype and sales double-talk at the showrooms. And once you're there, you can use our exclusive discount price lists to save money. The lists show you retail and dealer costs for the various models in each line and available factory options, plus our calculated low price that serves as your guide to a fair deal. Note that the column headed "Dealer Cost" refers to the dealer's *invoice* price. This figure includes delivery and handling charges (but not freight), a "holdback" amount to cover dealer interest charges, and miscellaneous fees, all of which are added to the factory's wholesale price. Thus, "Dealer Cost" is what the dealer actually pays to buy the vehicle from the factory and to keep it in his inventory until it's sold.

Buying a new car can still be fun and exciting. And like many things in life it's more pleasurable when you know what you're doing. That's also what *1983 Cars* is all about.

CONSUMER GUIDE®

AMC Concord

AMC Concord Limited 5-door wagon

WHAT'S NEW FOR '83

Once thought of as a compact, AMC's mid-size line returns
for '83 with fewer model choices and minus one engine. The
rear-drive Concord will be available only as a 4-door sedan
and 5-door wagon; the slow-selling 2-door sedan was
dropped during the '82 model year. Trim levels also have
been reduced from three to two. The lone engine available is
AMC's 258-cid straight six that was optional last year.
Compression ratio on this hardy powerplant is raised from
8.6 to 9.2:1, and AMC says it's more efficient because of a
new fuel feedback system and knock sensor. AMC has
stopped buying the carbureted version of the Pontiac 2.5-liter
four, and is tooling up to produce its own four, which will
actually be a cutdown version of the six. As of now, there are
no plans to offer the new engine in the Concord, which is due
to be replaced by 1985 at the latest.

EVALUATION

Since the basic design of the Concord goes back to the 1970
Hornet, it looks dated next to many contemporary mid-size
cars. It's not nearly as spacious inside as modern front-drive
competitors. It's also heavier, so mileage isn't as good.
Trusty old six is peppy enough, but you pay for the performance at the gas pump. On the plus side, Concord is a known
quantity and the assembly quality is usually among the best
in Detroit. The ride is pretty good, and overall the car offers a

high level of refinement. It's available with enough power options and comfort features to suit many confirmed big-car buyers. AMC's 24-month/24,000-mile powertrain warranty and 5-year no-rust-through warranty are value pluses. Strong competition from front-drive mid-size models makes this a poor choice for space or fuel-efficiency, but attractively priced.

EVALUATION CHECKLIST

Fuel economy	2	Cargo room	4
Driveability	4	Serviceability	3
Acceleration	3	Standard equipment	3
Braking	3	Body construction	4
Handling/roadholding	3	Paint/exterior finish	4
Driving position	3	Interior finish	4
Instruments/control	3	TOTAL POINTS	66
Visiblity	3		
Heating/ventilation	4		
Seat comfort	3	**RATING SCALE**	
Passenger room	3	5 = Excellent	
Ride	3	4 = Very Good	
Noise	4	3 = Average/Acceptable	
Exit/entry	3	2 = Fair	
		1 = Poor	

SPECIFICATIONS

	4-door sedan	5-door wagon
Wheelbase (in.)	108.0	108.0
Overall length (in.)	185.0	185.0
Overall width (in.)	71.0	71.0
Overall height (in.)	50.9	51.2
Track front (in.)	57.6	57.6
Track rear (in.)	57.1	57.1
Curb weight (lbs.)	2983	3022
Max. cargo vol. (cu. ft.)	12.2	57.0
Fuel tank capacity (gal.)	22.0	22.0
Seating capacity	5	5
Front headroom (in.)	38.1	38.1
Front shoulder room (in.)	54.0	54.0

SPECIFICATIONS	4-door sedan	5-door wagon
Front legroom, max. (in.)	40.8	40.8
Rear headroom (in.)	37.5	37.9
Rear shoulder room (in.)	53.4	53.4
Rear legroom, min. (in.)	36.1	36.1

BODY/CHASSIS

Drivetrain layout: longitudinal front engine/rear-wheel drive. **Suspension front:** independent, upper and lower control arms, coil springs, telescopic shock absorbers, anti-roll bar. **Suspension rear:** rigid axle, semi-elliptic leaf springs, telescopic shock absorbers. **Steering:** recirculating ball. **Turns lock-to-lock:** 6.0 manual, 3.4 power. **Turn diameter (ft.):** NA. **Brakes front:** 10.8-in. discs. **Brakes rear:** 9.0 × 2.0-in. drums (10.0 × 1.75 wagon). **Construction:** unit.

POWERTRAINS	ohv I-6
Bore × stroke (in.)	3.75× 3.90
Displacement (liters/cu. in.)	4.2/258
Compression ratio	9.2:1
Fuel delivery	2bbl.
Net bhp @ rpm	NA
Net torque @ rpm (lbs/ft)	NA
Availability	S/All
Final drive ratios	
4-speed manual	2.35:1
5-speed manual	2.73:1
3-speed automatic	2.35:1

KEY **bbl.** = barrel (carburetor); **bhp** = brake horsepower (advertised); **Cal.** = California only. **Fed.** = Federal/49 state; **FI** = fuel injection; **ohv** = overhead valve; **ohc** = overhead cam; **I** = inline engine; **V** = V engine; **D** = diesel; **T** = turbocharged; **OD** = overdrive transmission; **S** = standard engine; **O** = optional engine.

PRICES

CONCORD

	Retail Price	Dealer Cost	Low Price
4-door sedan	$6724	$6052	$6452
5-door wagon	7449	6704	7204
DL 4-door sedan	6995	6156	6646
DL 5-door wagon	7730	6802	7302
Limited 5-door wagon	8117	7143	7643

STANDARD EQUIPMENT (included in above prices):

4.2-liter (258-cid) 6-cylinder engine, 4-speed manual transmission w/
floorshift, front disc brakes, single horn, stowaway spare tire, front and rear
armrests, lighter, carpet (including cargo area on wagon), inside hood
release, bench seats, folding rear seat on wagon, rear bumper guards,
moldings (drip, wheellip, hood front edge, windshield surround, rear
window surround, rocker panel, bodyside scuff), wheel covers, P195/
75R14 BSW glass-belted radial tires. **DL** adds: individual reclining seats,
custom door panels, day/night mirror, custom steering wheel, cargo area
skid strips, electric clock, trunk carpet, landau vinyl roof (ex. wagon),
striping, front bumper guards, woodgrain side panels (wagons), color-
keyed wheel covers, WSW tires, dual horns, additional sound insulation.
Limited adds: premium seat trim, premium door trim, upgraded carpet,
luxury woodgrain steering wheel, styled wheel covers, visibility group, light
group.

OPTIONAL EQUIPMENT:

3-speed automatic transmission	$423	$351	$355
5-speed manual transmission w/floorshift	125	104	106
Twin-grip differential	82	68	69
Optional axle ratio	30	25	26
Power steering	212	176	178
Power brakes	100	83	84
Power door locks (NA base models)	170	141	143
Power decklid release	40	33	34
Power driver seat (NA base models)	189	157	159
Power left & right seats	302	251	254
Power windows & door locks (NA base)	425	353	357
Convenience group	73	61	62
Cruise control (auto. trans. req.)	170	141	143
Radio equipment			
AM	83	69	70
AM/FM stereo	199	165	167
AM/FM stereo w/cassette tape	329	273	276
Air conditioning	725	602	610
Tinted glass, all windows	105	87	88
Tilt steering wheel	106	88	89

	Retail Price	Dealer Cost	Low Price
Digital electric clock	61	51	52
Dual horns	17	14	15
Rear window wiper/ washer, wagon	124	103	106
Electric rear window defroster	135	112	114
Roof rack, wagon	115	96	97
Sunroof	295	245	248
Halogen headlamps	20	17	18
Tilt steering wheel	106	88	89
Leather-wrapped steering wheel			
DL.	60	50	51
Limited	24	20	21
Luxury steering wheel.	36	30	31
Custom wheel covers, base models	42	35	36
Styled wheel covers, base models	87	72	73
Wire wheel covers, base models	160	133	135
Spoke-style wheels			
Base models.	178	148	150
Others	136	113	115
Turbo cast aluminum wheels			
Base models.	411	341	345
Others	251	208	211
Extra-quiet insulation package	61	51	52
Protection group			
Base models.	132	110	112
Others	81	67	68
Bumper guards.	52	43	44
Heavy-duty engine cooling system	77	64	65
Heavy-duty battery.	26	22	23
Cold climate group	58	48	49
Handling package	48	40	41
Automatic load leveling	169	140	142
Trailer-towing package	104	86	87
Woodgrain delete, wagons	(71)	(65)	(71)
Cloth upholstery, DL (incl. individual front seats	67	56	57
Two-tone paint	135	112	114

AMC Eagle

WHAT'S NEW FOR '83

AMC's 4-wheel-drive passenger-car line is clipped to three models. Gone are the Spirit-based Kammback sedan and the long-wheelbase notchback 2-door. This leaves the short-

AMC Eagle Limited 5-door wagon

wheelbase SX/4 3-door coupe and the "senior" Eagle 4-door sedan and 5-door wagon. The sedan is now available only in DL trim, while the SX/4 and wagon are offered in three trim levels. AMC's Select-Drive System, which allows changing between 2- and 4-wheel drive from inside, is standard on all models. The 2.5-liter Pontiac four (without the fuel injection used on GM cars) is standard across the board, as is a 4-speed manual transmission. The optional 258-cid AMC six now has a higher compression ratio (to 9.2:1) and a new fuel feedback system and knock sensor. A 5-speed overdrive manual gearbox is optional with all engines. Automatic is available on the SX/4 with either engine, but only with the six on other models. Automatic is listed with an optional 2.73 final drive ratio for better acceleration. The SX/4 gets shorter 3.54 gearing with the 4-cylinder engine, also to improve performance.

EVALUATION

Eagle is still unique among domestics with its full-time 4wd capability, which makes it easier to overlook the shortcomings of its near-antique body/chassis design. The interior is crowded and the control layout is dated. Mileage also is disappointing even with Select-Drive, especially with the six. On the SX/4, the standard four gives surprisingly lively pickup and decent mileage. You're better off with the six on bigger models because of its greater power. AMC's extended powertrain warranty covers it for 2 years/24,000 miles, however, and body has 5-year no-rust-through protection. Remains an enigma: advanced engineering in an old-fashioned package. Slated to be marketed as a Jeep in another year or so.

EVALUATION CHECKLIST
(except SX/4)

Fuel economy	2	Cargo room	4
Driveability	4	Serviceability	3
Acceleration	3	Standard equipment	4
Braking	3	Body construction	4
Handling/roadholding	3	Paint/exterior finish	4
Driving position	3	Interior finish	4
Instruments/control	3	TOTAL POINTS	67
Visiblity	3		
Heating/ventilation	4		
Seat comfort	3		
Passenger room	3		
Ride	3		
Noise	4		
Exit/entry	3		

RATING SCALE
5 = Excellent
4 = Very Good
3 = Average/Acceptable
2 = Fair
1 = Poor

SPECIFICATIONS

	3-door coupe	4-door sedan	5-door wagon
Wheelbase (in.)	97.2	109.3	109.3
Overall length (in.)	166.6	183.2	183.2
Overall width (in.)	73.0	72.3	72.3
Overall height (in.)	55.0	54.4	54.6
Track front (in.)	59.6	59.6	59.6
Track rear (in.)	57.6	57.6	57.6
Curb weight (lbs.)	3038	3269	3284
Max. cargo vol. (cu. ft.)	25.0	12.2	57.0
Fuel tank capacity (gal.)	21.0	22.0	22.0
Seating capacity	4	5	5
Front headroom (in.)	38.1	38.1	38.1
Front shoulder room (in.)	53.9	54.0	54.0
Front legroom, max. (in.)	40.8	40.8	40.8
Rear headroom (in.)	35.6	37.5	37.9
Rear shoulder room (in.)	53.2	53.4	53.4
Rear legroom, min. (in.)	26.2	36.1	36.1

BODY/CHASSIS

Drivetrain layout: longitudinal front engine/selectable 2/4-wheel drive. **Suspension front:** independent, upper and lower control arms, coil springs, telescopic shock absorbers, anti-roll bar. **Suspension rear:** rigid axle, semi-elliptic leaf springs, telescopic shock absorbers. **Steering:** recirculating ball. **Turns lock-to-lock:** 3.0 power. **Turn diameter (ft.):** 33.8 **Brakes front:** 11.0-in. discs. **Brakes rear:** 10.0 × 1.75-in. drums. **Contruction:** unit.

POWERTRAINS	ohv I-4	ohv I-6
Bore × stroke (in.)	4.00× 3.00	3.75× 3.90
Displacement (liters/cu. in.)	2.5/ 151	4.2/ 258
Compression ratio	9.6:1	9.2:1
Fuel delivery	2bbl.	2bbl.
Net bhp @ rpm	NA	NA
Net torque @ rpm (lbs/ft)	NA	NA
Availability	S/All	O/All
Final drive ratios		
4-speed manual	3.54:1	2.73:1[1]
5-speed manual	3.54:1	2.73:1[1]
3-speed automatic		2.35:1

1. 2.35:1 on SX/4

KEY **bbl.** = barrel (carburetor); **bhp** = brake horsepower (advertised); **Cal.** = California only. **Fed.** = Federal/49 state; **FI** = fuel injection; **ohv** = overhead valve; **ohc** = overhead cam; **I** = inline engine; **V** = V engine; **D** = diesel; **T** = turbocharged; **OD** = overdrive transmission; **S** = standard engine; **O** = optional engine.

PRICES

EAGLE	Retail Price	Dealer Cost	Low Price
SX/4 3-door coupe	$ 7697	$ 6927	$ 7427
SX/4 DL 3-door coupe	8164	7184	7884
4-door sedan.	9162	8063	8763

	Retail Price	Dealer Cost	Low Price
5-door wagon	9882	8696	9396
Limited 5-door wagon	10343	9102	9902

STANDARD EQUIPMENT (included in above prices):

2.5-liter (151-cid) 4-cylinder engine, 4-speed manual transmission, power steering, power brakes, front bucket seats, vinyl upholstery, glass-belted radial tires, single-note horn. **SX/4 DL** adds: reclining bucket seats, dual horns, electric clock, left and right remote-control mirrors, day/night interior mirror, styled wheel covers, extra-quiet insulation package, WSW tires. **Limited** adds: leather seat trim, parcel shelf, luxury steering wheel, upgraded trim.

OPTIONAL EQUIPMENT

4.2-liter (258-cid) 6-cylinder engine	$155	$129	$131
3-speed automatic transmission w/floorshift	437	363	366
5-speed manual transmission w/floorshift..	219	182	184
Air conditioning			
SX/4	670	556	562
Eagle	725	602	609
Heavy-duty battery	26	22	23
Bumper guards	52	43	44
Cold climate group	58	48	49
Electric clock, SX/4 (std. DL)	61	51	52
Convenience group	73	61	62
Heavy-duty cooling system	67	56	57
Maximum cooling system	70	58	59
Cruise control	164	136	138
Console (incl. w/sport pkg.).........	65	54	55
Rear window defroster............	135	112	114
Eagle Sport Package			
SX/4	516	428	433
SX/4 DL	407	338	342
Others	344	286	289
Fog lamps, halogen (incl. w/sport pkg.) ..	82	68	69
Locking gas cap.................	10	8	9
Gauge package (console req.)			
Base SX/4	152	126	128
Others	91	76	77
Tinted glass			
SX/4	95	79	80
Others	105	87	88
Halogen headlamps (incl. w/sport pkg.)...	20	17	18
Dual horns, base SX/4	17	14	15
Insulation package, Eagle 50 (std. DL) ...	61	51	52
Light group....................	61	51	52

CONSUMER GUIDE®

	Retail Price	Dealer Cost	Low Price
Automatic load-leveling system,			
Eagle 30	169	140	142
Power decklid/liftback release	40	33	34
Power door locks			
Eagle exc. sedan	170	141	143
SX/4 DL	120	100	102
Power door locks & windows			
Eagle exc. sedan	425	353	357
SX/4 DL	300	249	252
Protection Group			
SX/4 w/o/Sport Package	72	60	61
SX/4 w/Sport Package.	20	17	18
Others w/o/Sport Package	75	62	63
Others w/Sport Package.	23	19	20
Radio equipment			
AM	83	69	70
AM/FM stereo	199	165	167
AM/FM stereo w/cassette	329	273	276
Roof rack, wagon	115	96	97
Power 6-way driver seat (NA SX/4)	189	157	159
Power 6-way driver & passenger seat	302	251	254
Front skid plate	77	64	65
Rear spoiler, SX/4.	104	86	87
Steering wheels			
Leather-wrapped			
All ex. Limited or SX/4 Sport	60	50	51
Limited	24	20	21
SX/4 DL	20	17	18
Luxury woodgrain	36	30	31
Vinyl sport, SX/4.	40	33	34
Tilt	106	88	89
Sunroof (NA wagon)	295	245	248
Extra-duty suspension, SX/4	65	54	55
Extra-duty suspension, others	77	64	65
Trailer-towing package A, exc. SX/4	104	86	87
Trailer-towing package B, exc. SX/4	222	184	186
Rear window wiper/washer (NA sedan) . . .	124	103	105
Woodgrain bodyside panels, wagon	144	120	122

AMC Spirit

WHAT'S NEW FOR '83

The Spirit lives on with a new GT offering and without the 2-door sedan from the old Gremlin days. The only body style

AMC Spirit GT 3-door coupe

is now the 3-door coupe. The GT includes black exterior trim, handling package, steel-belted radial tires, aluminum wheels, fog lamps, tachometer, gauge package, and other items to warm the hearts of the sport minded. Similar equipment was available on last year's options list. The only engine listed is AMC's 4.2-liter six, which gets a fuel feedback system, knock sensor, and a boost in compression ratio from 8.6 to 9.2:1 for '83. The 2.5-liter Pontiac-built four has been dropped. Trim levels comprise DL and GT, replacing last year's base and DL offerings. AMC's '82 cars were given revised drivetrains and gear ratios aimed at increasing mileage. For '83, gearing is shuffled slightly in the interest of better performance.

EVALUATION

Remember the Gremlin? It's still here, but what was once an acceptable small car is now something of a relic. Size puts Spirit in same league with Honda Accord, Ford Escort, Mazda GLC, VW Rabbit, and other more modern, high-mileage minicars with more interior room. Spirit has marginal space for four people, an old-fashioned driving position and dashboard, limited cargo space, and poor mileage by today's standards. Rear-drive layout hurts bad weather traction and cuts interior space, but service costs should be lower than for some front-drive cars. Price is still low, and Spirit is backed by AMC's comprehensive powertrain and rust warranties. However, the new domestically built Renault Alliance now sold through AMC dealers is in the same price range, and offers much better space and fuel efficiency.

EVALUATION CHECKLIST

Fuel economy	3	Cargo room	2
Driveability	4	Serviceability	3
Acceleration	3	Standard equipment	3
Braking	3	Body construction	4
Handling/roadholding	3	Paint/exterior finish	4
Driving position	2	Interior finish	4
Instruments/control	3	TOTAL POINTS	59
Visiblity	4		
Heating/ventilation	4		
Seat comfort	2		
Passenger room	1		
Ride	3		
Noise	2		
Exit/entry	2		

RATING SCALE
5 = Excellent
4 = Very Good
3 = Average/Acceptable
2 = Fair
1 = Poor

SPECIFICATIONS

	3-door coupe
Wheelbase (in.)	96.0
Overall length (in.)	167.2
Overall width (in.)	71.9
Overall height (in.)	51.5
Track front (in.)	57.6
Track rear (in.)	57.1
Curb weight (lbs.)	2809
Max. cargo vol. (cu. ft.)	25.3
Fuel tank capacity (gal.)	21.0
Seating capacity	4
Front headroom (in.)	38.1
Front shoulder room (in.)	53.9
Front legroom, max. (in.)	40.8
Rear headroom (in.)	35.6
Rear shoulder room (in.)	53.2
Rear legroom, min. (in.)	26.2

BODY/CHASSIS

Drivetrain layout: longitudinal front engine/rear-wheel drive.

Suspension front: independent, upper and lower control arms, coil springs, telescopic shock absorbers, anti-roll bar. **Suspension rear:** rigid axle, semi-elliptic leaf springs, telescopic shock absorbers. **Steering:** recirculating ball. **Turns lock-to-lock:** 6.0 manual, 3.4 power. **Turn diameter (ft.):** NA. **Brakes front:** 10.8-in. discs. **Brakes rear:** 9.0 × 2.0-in. drums. **Construction:** unit.

POWERTRAINS

	ohv I-6
Bore × stroke (in.)	3.75× 3.90
Displacement (liters/cu. in.)	4.2/ 258
Compression ratio	9.2:1
Fuel delivery	2bbl.
Net bhp @ rpm	NA
Net torque @ rpm (lbs/ft)	NA
Availability	S/All
Final drive ratios	
4-speed manual	2.35:1
5-speed manual	2.35:1
3-speed automatic	2.35:1

KEY bbl. = barrel (carburetor); **bhp** = brake horsepower (advertised); **Cal.** = California only. **Fed.** = Federal/49 state; **FI** = fuel injection; **ohv** = overhead valve; **ohc** = overhead cam; **I** = inline engine; **V** = V engine; **D** = diesel; **T** = turbocharged; **OD** = overdrive transmission; **S** = standard engine; **O** = optional engine.

PRICES

SPIRIT	Retail Price	Dealer Cost	Low Price
DL 3-door Liftback	$ 5995	$ 5336	$ 5686
GT 3-door Liftback	6495	5716	6116

STANDARD EQUIPMENT (included in above prices):

4.2 liter (258-cid) 6-cylinder engine, 4-speed manual transmission, front disc brakes, glass-belted radial tires, full carpeting, front bucket seats, vinyl upholstery, vinyl spare tire cover, rear bumper guards, wheel covers, AM radio. **GT adds:** steel belted radial tires, leather wrapped steering wheel,

Prices are accurate at time of printing; subject to manufacturer's change

center console, gauge package, parcel shelf, turbocast aluminum wheels, handling package.

OPTIONAL EQUIPMENT:	Retail Price	Dealer Cost	Low Price
3-speed automatic transmission (NA GT) . .	423	351	355
5-speed manual transmission	125	104	106
Power assists			
Steering	212	176	178
Brakes	100	83	84
Door locks.	120	100	102
Liftback release	40	33	34
Window & door locks	300	249	252
Air conditioning system	670	556	561
Heavy-duty battery	26	22	23
Cold climate group	58	48	49
Console w/armrest	92	76	77
Convenience group	73	61	62
Heavy-duty cooling system	77	64	65
Cruise control (auto trans. req.)	170	141	143
Rear window defroster	135	112	115
Twin-grip differential	82	68	69
Gauge package (std. GT).	91	76	77
Tinted glass.	95	79	80
Halogen headlamps	20	17	18
Light group.	61	51	52
Sunroof	295	245	248
Two-tone paint.	135	112	115
Protection group			
DL	40	33	34
GT	30	25	26
Radio equipment			
AM (standard DL)	82	68	69
AM/FM stereo			
DL	117	97	98
GT	199	165	167
AM/FM stereo w/CB			
DL	389	323	327
GT	471	391	395
AM/FM stereo w/cassette tape			
DL	247	205	208
GT	329	273	276
Handling package (std GT).	48	40	41
Rear spoiler	104	86	87
Rally tape stripes	88	73	74
Vinyl-wrapped steering wheel (NA GT). . . .	40	33	34
Woodgrain steering wheel (NA GT).	36	30	31
Leather-wrapped steering wheel (std. GT).	60	50	51

Prices are accurate at time of printing; subject to manufacturer's change

	Retail Price	Dealer Cost	Low Price
Tilt steering wheel.	106	88	89
Wire wheel covers (NA GT)	119	99	100
Spoke-style wheels (NA GT)	136	113	115
Rear window wiper/washer	124	103	105
Cloth upholstery	39	32	33

Audi Coupe & Quattro

Audi Quattro 2-door coupe

WHAT'S NEW FOR '83

The high-style coupes from Bavaria's other automaker stay largely the same this year. Introduced in mid-1981, the front-drive Coupe is basically a 2-door fastback derivative of the 4000 sedan body/chassis design, but is powered by the normally aspirated 2.1-liter (131-cid) 5-cylinder gasoline engine from the larger 5000 series. The Quattro, launched here in early 1982 as an '83 model, uses the Coupe bodyshell, front suspension, and interior package, but has full-time 4-wheel drive, all-disc brakes, independent rear suspension, and the turbo version of the Audi five aided by an air-to-air intercooler. Drivetrain and mechanical differences apart, the big difference between these two is price: the Quattro costs more than twice as much as the Coupe. Standard transmission in both is a 5-speed overdrive manual, with front/rear differential locking control on the Quattro. A 3-speed automatic is optional on the Coupe only.

Prices are accurate at time of printing; subject to manufacturer's change

EVALUATION

Despite very different characters, these cars share many of the same strengths and weaknesses. The former include a sporty, take-charge driving position, above-average workmanship, eager handling and roadholding, and a firm but not harsh ride with excellent bump control. Both are also easy to maneuver in tight spaces, and both offer spirited performance. Drawbacks are a high fastback tail that restricts driver vision astern, limited cargo space (aggravated by an oddly shaped trunklid), and marginal headroom for six-footers. The Coupe is a very nice car and a fine buy. We're much less enthusiastic about the Quattro, mainly because its extra capabilities just don't come into play in the sort of routine driving most people do.

EVALUATION CHECKLIST
(Coupe)

Fuel economy	3	Cargo room	3
Driveability	4	Serviceability	3
Acceleration	4	Standard equipment	4
Braking	4	Body construction	4
Handling/roadholding	4	Paint/exterior finish	4
Driving position	4	Interior finish	3
Instruments/control	4	TOTAL POINTS	72
Visiblity	3		
Heating/ventilation	3	**RATING SCALE**	
Seat comfort	4	5 = Excellent	
Passenger room	3	4 = Very Good	
Ride	4	3 = Average/Acceptable	
Noise	4	2 = Fair	
Exit/entry	3	1 = Poor	

SPECIFICATIONS

	Quattro 2-door coupe	(2-door) coupe
Wheelbase (in.)	99.5	99.8
Overall length (in.)	178.2	177.0
Overall width (in.)	67.9	66.3
Overall height (in.)	52.0	53.1

SPECIFICATIONS

	Quattro 2-door coupe	(2-door) coupe
Track front (in.)	56.0	55.1
Track rear (in.)	57.4	55.9
Curb weight (lbs.)	2838	2507
Max. cargo vol. (cu. ft.)	12.0	17.0
Fuel tank capacity (gal.)	23.8	15.8
Seating capacity	5	5
Front headroom (in.)	35.2	35.2
Front shoulder room (in.)	54.0	54.0
Front legroom, max. (in.)	42.0	42.0
Rear headroom (in.)	33.9	33.9
Rear shoulder room (in.)	54.6	54.6
Rear legroom, min. (in.)	35.2	35.2

BODY/CHASSIS

Drivetrain layout: longitudinal front engine/front-wheel drive (four-wheel drive on Quattro). **Suspension front:** independent, MacPherson struts, coil springs, telescopic shock absorbers, anti-roll bar. **Suspension rear:** Quattro: independent, coil spring/struts, telescopic shock absorbers; Coupe: "torsion-crank" beam axle, coil spring/struts, panhard rod, telescopic shock absorbers, anti-roll bar. **Steering:** rack-and-pinion, power-assisted. **Turns lock-to-lock:** 3.4. **Turn diameter (ft.):** 34.0/32.5. (Quattro/Coupe). **Brakes front:** 11.0-in. discs (Quattro), 9.4-in. discs (Coupe). **Brakes rear:** 9.4-in. discs (Quattro), 7.9-in. drums (Coupe). **Construction:** unit

POWERTRAINS

	ohc I-5T	ohc I-5
Bore × stroke (in.)	3.13× 3.40	3.13× 3.40
Displacement (liters/cu. in.)	2.1/ 131	2.1/ 131

POWERTRAINS

	ohc I-5T	ohc I-5
Compression ratio	7.0:1	8.2:1
Fuel delivery	FI	FI
Net bhp @ rpm	156@ 5500	100@ 5100
Net torque @ rpm (lbs/ft)	181@ 3000	112@ 3000
Availability	S/All[1]	S/All[2]

1: Quattro only 2: Coupe only

Final drive ratios

5-speed OD manual	3.89:1	4.46:1
3-speed automatic		3.45:1

KEY bbl. = barrel (carburetor); **bhp** = brake horsepower (advertised); **Cal.** = California only. **Fed.** = Federal/49 state; **FI** = fuel injection; **ohv** = overhead valve; **ohc** = overhead cam; **I** = inline engine; **V** = V engine; **D** = diesel; **T** = turbocharged; **OD** = overdrive transmission; **S** = standard engine; **O** = optional engine.

PRICES

AUDI QUATTRO & COUPE	Retail Price	Dealer Cost	Low Price
(1982 prices shown; 1983 prices not available at time of publication.)			
2-door Coupe, 5-speed.	$12370	$10673	$12100
2-door Coupe, automatic.	12775	11028	12500
Quattro 2-door coupe, 5-speed	35000	30100	35000

Note: Prices above do not include $280 freight charge, $75 dealer preparation charge, or $85 California warranty (Coupe).

STANDARD EQUIPMENT (included in above prices):

Coupe: 2.1-liter (131-cid) 5-cylinder fuel-injected engine, 5-speed manual overdrive or 3-speed automatic transmission, special handling suspension, low-profile 185/60R-14 radial tires, electrically heated driver's seat, power steering, power brakes, light alloy wheels, halogen headlamps, full instrumentation including tachometer, reclining front sport bucket seats with driver's side tilt/height adjuster, full carpeting, intermittent wipers, cloth upholstery, sports steering wheel, electric rear-window defroster, tinted glass, dual remote-control mirrors. **Quattro** adds: 2.1-liter (131-cid) turbocharged 5-cylinder engine with electronic fuel injection, 4-wheel drive with differential lock-outs, 5-speed overdrive manual transmission, power 4-wheel disc brakes, 205/60HR-15 steel-belted radial tires, air conditioning, power door locks, electric front window lifts, cruise control, AM/FM stereo radio with cassette player.

OPTIONAL EQUIPMENT	Retail Price	Dealer Cost	Low Price
Air conditioning, Coupe (std. Quattro)....	$ 725	$ 609	$ 620
Power door locks, Coupe (std. Quattro). . .	175	140	165
Metallic paint, Coupe	285	228	231
AM/FM stereo radio w/cassette player & electric antenna, Coupe (std. Quattro) . .	635	508	514
Passenger's seat height adjuster, Coupe . .	70	56	57
Speakers (4) & suppression, Coupe w/ electric antenna.	270	216	219
Power windows, Coupe (std. Quattro). . . .	280	224	270
Rear window wiper/washer, Coupe (std. Quattro)	210	168	171

Audi 4000

Audi 4000 2-door sedan

WHAT'S NEW FOR '83

The main news this year for Audi's smaller front-drive car line is a turbocharger for the optional 1.6-liter four-cylinder diesel engine. It comes from sister division Volkswagen and is, in fact, the same unit VW will offer in the '83 Quantum and Rabbit. Addition of the turbo necessitated a good deal of re-engineering on the familiar VW block. Horsepower goes up by 16 compared to the normally aspirated diesel, and torque is up by a healthy 27 lbs/ft. Otherwise, the 4000 is little changed from its 1982 specifications. Carried over from mid-1982 is the new "E-Mode" 3-speed automatic transmission for diesel models. This has a special economy position that shuts off fuel flow to the cylinders and allows the car to freewheel when the driver lifts off the accelerator. The model lineup is shuffled slightly, and starts with a base 2-door powered by the familiar fuel-injected 1.7-liter gasoline four. A normally aspirated diesel 4-door is also available. All other models, including the new turbodiesels, carry the "S" equipment package, with air conditioning, opening vent windows, wider wheels and tires, rear headrests, and height-adjustable driver's seat.

EVALUATION

As before, the 4000 is an upmarket small sedan that will appeal primarily to those who appreciate German engineering and craftsmanship and don't mind paying for it. We have yet to test either the turbo or non-turbo diesels. Based on our experience with various VWs the unblown engine should provide adequate acceleration allied to amazing mileage in the 4000. The turbodiesel should be on a performance par with the gasoline four. Crisp handling, fine grip, excellent front seating and driving position, and a smooth, supple ride make the 4000 a practical choice for the enthusiast. Negatives include interior furnishings that are too plain for most buyers, confined rear seat accommodations, steep initial price for what is basically a compact, and higher-than-average maintenance costs. The VW diesel engine also has a poor reliability reputation, mainly due to a history of oil leaks. This may or may not be solved on '83s. With those caveats, the 4000 seems well worth the money in driving pleasure if not prestige.

EVALUATION CHECKLIST

Fuel economy	4	Cargo room	3
Driveability	4	Serviceability	4
Acceleration	3	Standard equipment	3
Braking	4	Body construction	4
Handling/roadholding	4	Paint/exterior finish	4
Driving position	4	Interior finish	4
Instruments/control	4	TOTAL POINTS	75
Visiblity	4		
Heating/ventilation	3	**RATING SCALE**	
Seat comfort	4	5 = Excellent	
Passenger room	4	4 = Very Good	
Ride	4	3 = Average/Acceptable	
Noise	4	2 = Fair	
Exit/entry	3	1 = Poor	

SPECIFICATIONS

	2-door sedan	4-door sedan
Wheelbase (in.)	99.8	99.8
Overall length (in.)	176.6	176.6
Overall width (in.)	66.2	66.2
Overall height (in.)	53.8	53.8
Track front (in.)	55.1	55.1
Track rear (in.)	55.9	55.9
Curb weight (lbs.)	2150[1]	2200[1]
Max. cargo vol. (cu. ft.)	12.0	12.0
Fuel tank capacity (gal.)	15.8	15.8
Seating capacity	5	5
Front headroom (in.)	37.0	37.0
Front shoulder room (in.)	49.2	49.2
Front legroom, max. (in.)	42.0	42.0
Rear headroom (in.)	34.2	34.2
Rear shoulder room (in.)	54.6	54.6
Rear legroom, min. (in.)	35.2	35.2

1: estimated

BODY/CHASSIS

Drivetrain layout: longitudinal front engine/front-wheel drive. **Suspension front:** independent, MacPherson struts, coil springs, telescopic shock absorbers, anti-roll bar. **Suspension rear:** "torsion-crank" beam axle, coil springs/struts, panhard rod, telescopic shock absorbers, integral anti-roll bar. **Steering:** rack-and-pinion. **Turns lock-to-lock:** 3.9 manual, 3.4 power. **Turn diameter (ft.):** 32.5. **Brakes front:** 9.4-in. discs. **Brakes rear:** 7.9-in. drums. **Construction:** unit

POWERTRAINS	ohc I-4	ohc I-4D	ohc I-4TD
Bore × stroke (in.)	3.13× 3.40	3.01× 3.40	3.01× 3.40

POWERTRAINS

POWERTRAINS	ohc I-4	ohc I-4D	ohc I-4TD
Displacement (liters/cu. in.)	1.7/ 105	1.6/ 97	1.6/ 97
Compression ratio	8.2:1	23.0:1	23.0:1
Fuel delivery	FI	FI	FI
Net bhp @ rpm	74@ 5000	52@ 4800	68@ 4500
Net torque @ rpm (lbs/ft)	89@ 3000	72@ 2000	98@ 2800
Availability	S/All	S/All	S/All
Final drive ratios			
5-speed OD manual	4.11:1	4.11:1	4.11:1
3-speed automatic	3.73:1		NA

KEY bbl. = barrel (carburetor); **bhp** = brake horsepower (advertised); **Cal.** = California only. **Fed.** = Federal/49 state; **FI** = fuel injection; **ohv** = overhead valve; **ohc** = overhead cam; **I** = inline engine; **V** = V engine; **D** = diesel; **T** = turbocharged; **OD** = overdrive transmission; **S** = standard engine; **O** = optional engine.

PRICES

AUDI 4000	Retail Price	Dealer Cost	Low Price
(1982 prices shown; 1983 prices not available at time of publication.)			
4E 2-door sedan, 5-speed	$ 9755	$ 8424	$ 9424
Diesel 4-door sedan, 5-speed	10515	9069	9969
S 4-door sedan, 5-speed.	10865	9377	10577
S 4-door sedan, automatic	11270	9732	10932

Note: Prices above do not include $280 freight charge, $75 dealer preparation charge, or $85 "California equipment" charge.

STANDARD EQUIPMENT (included in above prices):

1.7-liter (105-cid) 4-cylinder engine with fuel injection or 1.6-liter (97-cid) 4-cylinder diesel engine, 5-speed overdrive manual or 3-speed automatic transmission as above, power brakes, electric rear window defroster, intermittent windshield wipers, quartz crystal clock, remote-control left door mirror, remote-control right door mirror (4E 2-door), trip odometer, passenger visor vanity mirror, halogen headlamps, dual-note horn, upshift indicator light (manual shift only), bodyside protection moldings, full carpeting, reclining front bucket seats, door storage pockets, locking gas cap, tinted glass, full wheel covers (Diesel) or hubcaps and wheel trim rings

Prices are accurate at time of printing; subject to manufacturer's change

(4E), voltmeter, oil temperature gauge. **S** adds: opening front ve
rear seat headrests, light-alloy wheels, air conditioning, manual
height adjuster.

OPTIONAL EQUIPMENT

S Package, Diesel sedan only	$ 995	$ 836	$ 875
Comfort Package			
4E and Diesel	600	480	525
S models	650	520	585
Air conditioning	690	581	586
Cruise control	195	164	166
Right door mirror, Diesel only	40	32	33
Heated door mirrors, L&R	190	152	155
Metallic paint	285	228	231
AM/FM stereo radio w/cassette player &			
automatic antenna	690	552	558
Sport seats	195	156	158
Speakers (4) & suppression	210	168	170
Power steering	390	328	335
Power sunroof	475	399	403
Tachometer, 4-doors	90	72	73
Alloy wheels			
2-door	595	476	481
4-doors	365	292	295
All models	230	184	186

Audi 5000

WHAT'S NEW FOR '83

The current version of Audi's senior series is in its final season. Coming to America by next fall (and arriving in Europe this winter) is a much sleeker rebodied successor boasting an unbelievably low 0.30 coefficient of drag, but retaining much of the current 5000's mechanical and chassis components. As a preview of the second-generation model, Audi adds a turbocharger to the 5000's 2.0-liter (121-cid) five-cylinder diesel and discontinues the normally aspirated 5000D for the '83 model year. The turbo boosts output by 17 horsepower and a significant 42 lbs/ft of torque. Only one transmission will be available, the "E-mode" 3-speed automatic with the fuel cutoff and engine freewheeling features described in the 4000 report. Returning from '82 are the fuel-injected turbo and non-turbo gasoline 5000s with the

Prices are accurate at time of printing; subject to manufacturer's change

Audi 5000 Turbodiesel 4-door sedan

spark-ignition version of this basic engine but with slightly more displacement. As before, the 5000 Turbo is limited to automatic transmission. The basic 5000 comes with a 5-speed overdrive manual as standard.

EVALUATION

Regardless of engine, a sophisticated, well-mannered machine offering a roomy interior, high-quality craftsmanship, and un-sedan-like handling and roadholding. Performance is adequate with the normal gasoline engine, very quick and smooth if you opt for the turbo version. Turbocharging has lifted the diesel engine's performance considerably, and despite what you may have read elsewhere this car is not a slug, even saddled with automatic. At this writing, we're completing our first test of the 5000 Turbodiesel, and its mileage potential appears almost as good as the unblown diesel's. All 5000s have austere interior furnishings by U.S. standards, but are nicely put together with top-rate materials. As before, complex mechanical layout discourages home maintenance, and dealer service can cost a mint. Although the repair record for all 5000 models appears good so far, several isolated cases we know of make us wonder about the model's long-term reliability, particularly the highly tuned gas turbo. Also, expensive compared to most domestics, though reasonably priced against similar upscale European sedans. Judgment: Not engineered to take abuse like a Chevy, but should hold up well with proper care and still as rewarding to drive as ever.

EVALUATION CHECKLIST
(5000 Turbodiesel)

Fuel economy	4	Cargo room	3
Driveability	4	Serviceability	3
Acceleration	4	Standard equipment	4
Braking	4	Body construction	4
Handling/roadholding	4	Paint/exterior finish	4
Driving position	4	Interior finish	4
Instruments/control	4	TOTAL POINTS	77
Visiblity	4		
Heating/ventilation	4		
Seat comfort	4		
Passenger room	4		
Ride	4		
Noise	3		
Exit/entry	4		

RATING SCALE
5 = Excellent
4 = Very Good
3 = Average/Acceptable
2 = Fair
1 = Poor

SPECIFICATIONS

	4-door sedan
Wheelbase (in.)	105.5
Overall length (in.)	188.9
Overall width (in.)	69.6
Overall height (in.)	54.7
Track front (in.)	57.9[1]
Track rear (in.)	56.9[1]
Curb weight (lbs.)	2703[2]
Max. cargo vol. (cu. ft.)	15.0
Fuel tank capacity (gal.)	19.8
Seating capacity	5
Front headroom (in.)	38.0
Front shoulder room (in.)	52.0
Front legroom, max. (in.)	44.0
Rear headroom (in.)	35.0
Rear shoulder room (in.)	56.0
Rear legroom, min. (in.)	37.0

1: 58.1/57.2 5000 Turbo
2: 2997 lbs. 5000 Turbodiesel, 3042 lbs. 5000 Turbo

BODY/CHASSIS

Drivetrain layout: longitudinal front engine/front-wheel drive. **Suspension front:** independent, MacPherson struts, coil springs, lower control arms, telescopic shock absorbers, anti-roll bar. **Suspension rear:** "torsion-crank" beam axle, coil spring/struts, panhard rod, telescopic shock absorbers, integral anti-roll bar. **Steering:** rack-and-pinion power-assisted. **Turns lock-to-lock:** 3.8. **Turn diameter (ft.):** 34.3. **Brakes front:** 10.2-in. discs (11.0-in. discs 5000 Turbo). **Brakes rear:** 9.0-in. drums (9.4-in. discs 5000 Turbo). **Construction:** unit

POWERTRAINS	ohc I-5TD	ohc I-5	ohc I-5T
Bore × stroke (in.)	3.01× 3.40	3.13× 3.40	3.13× 3.40
Displacement (liters/cu. in.)	2.0/ 121	2.1/ 131	2.1/ 131
Compression ratio	23.0:1	8.2:1	7.0:1
Fuel delivery	FI	FI	FI
Net bhp @ rpm	84@ 4500	100@ 5100	130@ 5400
Net torque @ rpm (lbs/ft)	127@ 2800	112@ 3000	142@ 3000
Availability	S/All[1]	S/All[2]	S/All[3]

1: Turbodiesel only   2: 5000 only   3: 5000 Turbo only

Final drive ratios

5-speed OD manual		4.11:1	
3-speed automatic	3.08:1	3.91:1	3.73:1

KEY bbl. = barrel (carburetor); **bhp** = brake horsepower (advertised); **Cal.** = California only. **Fed.** = Federal/49 state; **FI** = fuel injection; **ohv** = overhead valve; **ohc** = overhead cam; **I** = inline engine; **V** = V engine; **D** = diesel; **T** = turbocharged; **OD** = overdrive transmission; **S** = standard engine; **O** = optional engine.

PRICES

	Retail Price	Dealer Cost	Low Price
AUDI 5000			

(1982 prices shown; 1983 prices not available at time of publication.)

Diesel 4-door sedan, 5-speed	$12390	$10629	11729

Prices are accurate at time of printing; subject to manufacturer's change

	Retail Price	Dealer Cost	Low Price
S 4-door sedan, 5-speed.	13665	11123	12223
S 4-door sedan, automatic	14070	12074	13174
S Diesel 4-door sedan, 5-speed	13990	11997	13097
Turbo 4-door sedan, automatic	18490	15844	16944

STANDARD EQUIPMENT (included in above prices):

2.1-liter (131-cid) 5-cylinder engine with fuel injection or 2.0-liter (121-cid) 5-cylinder diesel engine, 5-speed overdrive manual or 3-speed automatic transmission as above, power brakes, power steering, cruise control, tinted glass, intermittent wipers, quartz clock, manual left and right remote-control door mirrors, full wheel covers, passenger vanity mirror, bodyside protection moldings, cut-pile carpeting, reclining front bucket seats, center console, rear-seat center armrest, passenger assist handles, lockable gas cap. **S** adds: air conditioning, driver seat tilt adjuster (manual), central locking system, power windows, opening front vent windows, rear-seat headrests. **Turbo** adds: 4-wheel disc brakes, front spoiler, black-out grille, halogen high-beam headlamps, digital clock, 4-spoke sports steering wheel, tachometer, turbo boost gauge, oil and water temperature gauges, AM/FM stereo cassette/radio with power antenna, wide lower bodyside moldings, special suspension.

OPTIONAL EQUIPMENT

Tachometer (std. Turbo, NA Diesel)	$ 90	$ 72	$ 73
Metallic paint.	325	260	265
Power seats (NA Diesel)	500	400	425
Heated front seat (NA Diesel)	140	112	114
Heated door mirrors	190	152	155
Leather trim, 5.	1025	820	900
Turbo	1205	964	1100
S Diesel, 5000.	750	600	675
Radio—AM/FM stereo radio w/cassette &			
power antenna	325	260	265
Sunroof	805	676	725

BMW

WHAT'S NEW FOR '83

At press time, Bavarian Motor Works hadn't released details of its 1983 U.S. models, but a number of revisions are known to be coming. Production of the firm's volume model, the 320i, has been halted in Germany and it will be sold only as

Prices are accurate at time of printing; subject to manufacturer's change

BMW 633CSi 2-door coupe (1982 model)

long as supplies last. The all-new 3-series, now slated to arrive here at mid-model year, will be about the same size outside, but is said to be considerably roomier. A 4-door will be offered in addition to a 2-door sedan for the first time. Power is likely to remain the 1.8-liter (110-cid) fuel-injected four from the current 320i. More immediately, BMW will introduce the 533i. This is essentially the current 528e (new last year and which continues unchanged for '83) powered by the larger 3.2-liter straight six from the 633CSi coupe and 733i sedan. The coupe, based on the 5-series chassis, will be updated with a revised nose, restyled dash, and a reworked front suspension incorporating the double-pivot geometry introduced with the 7-series. The 733i also comes in for a minor facelift this year in an attempt to lower its high drag coefficient and improve mileage. A long shot for '83 but definite for '84 is a 2.4-liter (145-cid) six-cylinder turbodiesel engine for yet another 5-series derivative to be called 524TD.

EVALUATION

We're eager to see the new 3-series, mainly because the old 320i had become dated compared to the Audi 4000, Volkswagen Quantum, and Honda Accord. As for BMW's other models, we like 'em all, and look forward to assessing changes in the '83s. Of this trio, the 528e is perhaps the least impressive, though it's still a very fine car in most respects. Essentially an updated version of the previous 528i, this 4-door is an excellent driver's car, but its new high-torque/low-revving "eta" engine is noisier and harsher than the "big-block" six used in the 6- and 7-series models. Road and wind noise control also seem to have slipped, and our test car wasn't as easy to drive or as well put together as the last 528i we drove. And though it felt nearly as strong, the "eta" failed to significantly improve on the older engine's mileage, but it's still very good considering the brisk performance. The 633CSi drives much like the 5-series, though its lower driving stance didn't appeal to our testers. It's also less practical, especially rear seat accommodation, which is marginal for adults. The big 733i is a classy car—quiet, surprisingly peppy, meticulously crafted, and roomy, but is let down by too-firm front seats and a ride that turns jiggly on patchwork city streets. All BMWs are solidly built, offer thoroughly well-sorted minor controls and exceptionally clear instruments, and nimble handling that belies their size (though BMW's customary semi-trailing arm rear suspension can mean sudden rear-end breakaway in fierce cornering or on slippery surfaces). Sophisticated mechanicals, so parts and service are costly. Overall, luxury in the German manner with more than a dash of sport. Shrewdly priced way below comparable Mercedes-Benz models.

EVALUATION CHECKLIST
(528e)

Fuel economy	4	Cargo room	4
Driveability	4	Serviceability	3
Acceleration	4	Standard equipment	4
Braking	4	Body construction	4
Handling/roadholding	4	Paint/exterior finish	5
Driving position	4	Interior finish	4
Instruments/control	4	TOTAL POINTS	78
Visiblity	4		
Heating/ventilation	4	**RATING SCALE**	
Seat comfort	4	5 = Excellent	
Passenger room	4	4 = Very Good	
Ride	3	3 = Average/Acceptable	
Noise	3	2 = Fair	
Exit/entry	4	1 = Poor	

SPECIFICATIONS (1982 models)	633CSi 2-door coupe	733i 4-door sedan	528e 4-door sedan
Wheelbase (in.)	103.4	110.0	103.3
Overall length (in.)	193.8	197.4	189.0
Overall width (in.)	67.9	70.9	66.9
Overall height (in.)	53.7	56.3	55.7

SPECIFICATIONS

	633CSi 2-door coupe	733i 4-door sedan	528e 4-door sedan
Track front (in.)	56.0	59.1	56.3
Track rear (in.)	58.5	59.7	57.9
Curb weight (lbs.)	3340	3440	2960
Max. cargo vol. (cu. ft.)	18.7	22.6	22.6
Fuel tank capacity (gal.)	16.6	22.5	16.6
Seating capacity	4	5	5
Front headroom (in.)	NA	37.1	36.7
Front shoulder room (in.)	56.5	57.7	54.3
Front legroom, max. (in.)	40.9	42.1	40.9
Rear headroom (in.)	NA	36.1	36.0
Rear shoulder room (in.)	55.5	57.2	53.9
Rear legroom, min. (in.)	NA	35.2	34.8

BODY/CHASSIS

Drivetrain layout: longitudinal front engine/rear-wheel drive.
Suspension front: independent, double-pivot MacPherson struts, lower lateral links, drag struts, coil springs, telescopic shock absorbers, anti-roll-bar (633CSi/733i), double-pivot struts, coil springs, anti-roll-bar, telescopic shock absorbers (528e). **Suspension rear:** independent semi-trailing arms, coil springs, telescopic shock absorbers; anti-roll bar on 633CSi and 528e. **Steering:** recirculating ball, variable power assist. **Turn diameter (ft.):** 33.1/34.8/32.8 (633CSi/733i/528e). **Brakes front:** 11.0-in. discs (11.8-in. 528e). **Brakes rear:** 10.7-in. discs (11.8-in. 528e). **Construction:** unit

POWERTRAINS	ohc I-6	ohc I-6
Bore × stroke (in.)	3.50× 3.39	3.31× 3.19
Displacement (liters/cu. in.)	3.2/ 196	2.7/ 164

POWERTRAINS

	ohc I-6	ohc I-6
Compression ratio	8.8:1	9.0:1
Fuel delivery	FI	FI
Net bhp @ rpm	181@ 6000	121@ 4250
Net torque @ rpm (lbs/ft)	195@ 4000	170@ 3250
Availability	S/All[1]	S/All[2]

1: 633CSi/733i only 2: 528e only

Final drive ratios

5-speed OD manual	3.25:1[1]	2.93:1
3-speed automatic	3.25:1[1]	2.93:1

1: 3.45:1 on 733i

KEY bbl. = barrel (carburetor); **bhp** = brake horsepower (advertised); **Cal.** = California only. **Fed.** = Federal/49 state; **FI** = fuel injection; **ohv** = overhead valve; **ohc** = overhead cam; **I** = inline engine; **V** = V engine; **D** = diesel; **T** = turbocharged; **OD** = overdrive transmission; **S** = standard engine; **O** = optional engine.

PRICES

BMW	Retail Price	Dealer Cost	Low Price*
(1982 prices shown; 1983 prices not available at time of publication.)			
320i 2-door sedan..............	$13290	$11170	$12170
528e 4-door sedan	23325	18900	21900
633CSi 2-door coupe............	36995	29985	33985
733i 4-door sedan..............	33315	27000	30000

*estimated; these models customarily sell at or above retail price in most locations. Prices shown do not include $175-$200 dealer preparation charge (depending on model) or $215 destination and handling charge. 320i is carryover 1982 model.

STANDARD EQUIPMENT (included in above prices):

320i: 1.8-liter (108-cid) 4-cylinder engine with electronic fuel injection, 5-speed overdrive manual transmission, power brakes, full carpeting including trunk, electric rear window defroster, tinted glass, reclining front bucket seats, trip odometer, tool kit, undercoating, intermittent windshield wipers. **528e** has: 2.7-liter (164-cid) 6-cylinder "eta" engine with electronic fuel injection, 5-speed overdrive, manual transmission, power steering, power 4-wheel disc brakes, air conditioning, tinted glass, electric rear-

Prices are accurate at time of printing; subject to manufacturer's change

window defroster, AM/FM stereo radio with cassette player, quartz digital clock, power door windows, central locking system, electrically adjustable door mirror, integral fog lamps, "active check control" warning light panel, intermittent wipers, cruise control, electric sliding sunroof, metallic paint (no charge option), light-alloy wheels, fuel economy indicator, tool kit. **633CSi and 733i** have: 3.2-liter (196-cid) 6-cylinder engine with electronic fuel injection, 5-speed manual transmission, air conditioning, AM/FM stereo cassette radio, electrically operated sunroof, electric rear-window defroster, leather upholstery, light-alloy wheels, power steering, power 4-wheel disc brakes, adjustable steering column, power windows, central locking system, quartz clock, electric remote-control left side door mirror, driver's seat tilt/height adjuster, full carpeting, rear headrests, tinted glass, warning light monitor system, halogen headlamps, intermittent wipers, tool kit.

OPTIONAL EQUIPMENT:

Luxus Touring Group, 320i[1]	$ 1685	$ 1115	$ 1300
"S" Package, 320i[2]	2620	2020	2300
On-board computer, 733i	635	515	575
Cruise control, 633CSi w/auto. trans.	310	255	260
Limited-slip differential, exc. 320i	390	337	350
Leather upholstery, 528e (std. 733i, 633CSi)	1090	916	1000
Metallic paint, 320i	420	365	385
Sliding steel sunroof (std. 733i, 633CSi)			
Manual, 320i only	555	500	530
Electric, 528e	745	665	700
3-speed automatic transmission			
320i	620	530	560
Others	775	630	700
Light-alloy wheels, 320i	500	415	450

1: incl. air conditioning, AM/FM stereo radio with cassette player and 2 speakers, fog lights.
2: incl. special alloy wheels, manual sunroof, Recaro front bucket seats, sport steering wheel, limited-slip differential, sport suspension, electric remote-control right door mirror, front air dam, halogen high-beam headlamps, deluxe tool kit, AM/FM stereo radio with cassette player, fog lights.

Buick Century

WHAT'S NEW FOR '83

Introduced in the middle of the '82 model run, Century is part of GM's front-drive A-body intermediate family based on the X-car platform (Skylark is Buick's member of that group). For '83, Century gains new T Type coupe and sedan models.

Buick Century Limited 2-door coupe

The package includes the division's "Gran Touring" suspension, 3.0-liter gas V-6 with 2.97 final drive ratio, heavy-duty brakes, special wheels and tires, sporty interior, and Euro-look exterior treatment. Buick intends to offer a 4-speed overdrive automatic transmission as a mid-year option for gas and diesel V-6s. The new transmission will pull a shorter first gear for quicker acceleration and a taller cruising gear for fuel economy. New options include front lamp monitors and a lighter wire wheel cover that is supposed to look more like the real thing. Engine choices are the same as last year. The on-board computer that comes with the 3.0-liter engine gets an additional task for '83, regulating the flow of exhaust gases into the intake manifold, a step that Buick says enhances drivability.

EVALUATION

Still mainly a quieter, plusher offshoot of the X-car. Compares favorably for interior space with the older, G-body rear-drive Regal, which still enjoys better sales, however. Ride is floaty with standard suspension, so we prefer the optional Gran Touring setup, which is firmer, but not harsh, and reduces vertical body motion on long-wave undulations and sway in turns. The new T Type is a good tourer, but lacks pep. The standard four and optional gas V-6 are smooth operators, but neither shows much strength off the line or returns great mileage. The Olds-built diesel V-6 is surprisingly peppy for an oil-burner, and runs with less clatter than other GM diesels we've tried. The driver gets a pleasant, upright seating position and a well-planned, if slightly glitzy, dash. Like most GM cars, power steering has too much assist and not enough feel. The engine bay is crowded with either V-6, and some service jobs look like they'll require a lot of costly mechanic time. GM reverts to its traditional "step-up" pricing this year, so you'll pay more for a Century than a Pontiac 6000 or Chevrolet Celebrity even though they're all basically the same. Summary: capable new-wave family car offering solid construction, fine accommodation, and luxury for those who'd really rather have an Electra.

EVALUATION CHECKLIST

Fuel economy	3	Cargo room	3
Driveability	4	Serviceability	2
Acceleration	3	Standard equipment	3
Braking	4	Body construction	4
Handling/roadholding	4	Paint/exterior finish	3
Driving position	4	Interior finish	3
Instruments/control	3	TOTAL POINTS	69
Visiblity	4		
Heating/ventilation	4	**RATING SCALE**	
Seat comfort	4	5 = Excellent	
Passenger room	4	4 = Very Good	
Ride	3	3 = Average/Acceptable	
Noise	4	2 = Fair	
Exit/entry	3	1 = Poor	

SPECIFICATIONS

	2-door coupe	4-door sedan
Wheelbase (in.)	104.9	104.9
Overall length (in.)	189.1	189.1
Overall width (in.)	66.8	66.8
Overall height (in.)	54.6	54.6
Track front (in.)	58.7	58.7
Track rear (in.)	57.0	57.0
Curb weight (lbs.)	2561	2694
Max. cargo vol. (cu. ft.)	16.2	16.2
Fuel tank capacity (gal.)	15.7[1]	15.7[1]
Seating capacity	6	6
Front headroom (in.)	38.6	38.6
Front shoulder room (in.)	56.2	56.2
Front legroom, max. (in.)	42.1	42.1
Rear headroom (in.)	37.9	38.0

CONSUMER GUIDE®

SPECIFICATIONS

	2-door sedan	4-door sedan
Rear shoulder room (in.)	57.0	56.2
Rear legroom, min. (in.)	36.1	35.9

1: 16.6 w/diesel engine

BODY/CHASSIS

Drivetrain layout: transverse front engine/front-wheel drive.
Suspension front: independent, MacPherson struts, lower control arms, coil springs, telescopic shock absorbers, anti-roll bar. **Suspension rear:** beam "twist" axle with integral anti-roll bar, trailing arms, panhard rod, coil springs, telescopic shock absorbers. **Steering:** power-assisted rack and pinion. **Turns lock-to-lock:** 3.1. **Turn diameter (ft.):** 38.5. **Brakes front:** 9.7-in. discs (10.2-in. T Type) **Brakes rear:** 8.9-in. drums. **Construction:** unit

POWERTRAINS

	ohv I-4	ohv V-6	ohv V-6D
Bore × stroke (in.)	4.00× 3.00	3.80× 2.66	4.06× 3.39
Displacement (liters/cu. in.)	2.5/ 151	3.0/ 181	4.3/ 262
Compression ratio	8.2:1	8.45:1	21.6:1
Fuel delivery	FI	2bbl.	FI
Net bhp @ rpm	90@ 4000	110@ 4800	85@ 3600
Net torque @ rpm (lbs/ft)	132@ 2800	145@ 2600	165@ 1600
Availability	S/All	O/All	O/All
Final drive ratios			
3-speed automatic	2.39:1	2.53:1	2.39:1
4-speed OD automatic		3.06:1	3.06:1

KEY bbl. = barrel (carburetor); **bhp** = brake horsepower (advertised); **Cal.** = California only. **Fed.** = Federal/49 state; **FI** = fuel injection; **ohv** = overhead valve; **ohc** = overhead cam; **I** = inline engine; **V** = V engine; **D** = diesel; **T** = turbocharged; **OD** = overdrive transmission; **S** = standard engine; **O** = optional engine.

PRICES

CENTURY	Retail Price	Dealer Cost	Low Price
Custom 2-door coupe	$ 8841	$ 7770	$ 8270
Custom 4-door sedan.	9002	7631	8131
T Type 2-door coupe	10017	8785	9285
T Type 4-door sedan	10178	8646	9146
Limited 2-door coupe.	9261	7994	8494
Limited 4-door sedan	9425	8135	8635

STANDARD EQUIPMENT (included in above prices):

2.5-liter (151-cid) fuel-injected 4-cylinder engine, 3-speed automatic transmission, power brakes, power steering, AM radio, full carpeting, P185/80R-13 fiberglass-belted radial tires. **Limited** adds: dual horns, lower bodyside moldings, hood ornament and wind split moldings, upgraded interior trim. **T Type** adds over base: 3.0 liter V-6 engine, left remote control mirror, gran touring suspension, styled aluminum wheels (4), sports steering wheel.

OPTIONAL EQUIPMENT:

Engines			
3.0-liter (181-cid) V-6	$ 150	$ 128	$ 130
4.3-liter (262-cid) diesel V-6 (incl. cold climate pkg.)	599	509	515
Air conditioning	725	616	623
Heavy-duty battery			
Gasoline engines	25	21	22
Diesel engine	50	43	44
Electric analog clock	35	30	31
Cold climate pkg. delete (credit)	(99)	(84)	(84)
Center console (w/o shift lever).	57	48	49
Center console (w/shift lever)	75	64	65
Heavy-duty cooling system			
w/air conditioning	40	34	35
w/o air conditioning	70	60	61
Cruise control	170	145	147
Electric rear-window defroster.	135	115	117
Electric power door locks			
Coupes.	120	102	104
Sedans	170	145	147
Tinted glass, full.	105	89	90
Engine block heater	18	15	16
Headlamp-on indicator	16	14	15
Auxiliary instrumentation.	48	41	42
Digital electronic instruments	299	254	257
Radio equipment			
AM delete (credit)	(56)	(48)	(48)

Prices are accurate at time of printing; subject to manufacturer's change

	Retail Price	Dealer Cost	Low Price
AM/FM stereo ETR	138	117	119
AM/FM stereo w/digital clock ETR.	177	150	152
AM/FM ETR stereo	302	257	260
AM/FM ETR stereo w/cassette & graphic equalizer	505	429	434
AM/FM ETR stereo w/cassette	277	235	238
Seat recliner, passenger only (NA T Type)	45	38	39
Seat recliners, dual (NA T Type)	90	77	78
6-way power seat (driver)	210	179	181
45/45 front seat	158	134	136
Lear Siegler bucket seats, T Type	600	510	516
Sport steering wheel (std. T Type)	50	43	44
Tilt steering wheel.	105	89	90
Flip-open glass sunroof	295	251	254
Automatic level control	175	149	150
Firm ride & handling package	27	23	24
Gran touring suspension (std. T Type) . . .	27	23	24
Theft deterrent system	159	135	137
Landau vinyl top.	181	154	156
Full vinyl top	155	132	134
Electric trunklid release.	40	34	35
Power windows			
Coupes.	180	153	155
Sedans.	255	217	220
Intermittent wipers	49	42	43

Buick Electra & LeSabre

Buick Electra Park Avenue 2-door coupe

WHAT'S NEW FOR '83

Buick's full-size cars will be the same for '83 with one exception. The standard 3.8-liter gas V-6 on the LeSabre now has an aluminum intake manifold to reduce weight and

Prices are accurate at time of printing; subject to manufacturer's change

improve cold-start drivability and an electric "early fuel evaporation system," also supposed to aid drivability. Buick has been concentrating its efforts on its smaller cars the past few years, so the C-body Electra and B-body LeSabre have received only minimal changes. Yet, they still sell well (LeSabre was the only Buick line to show a sales increase in '82) despite virtually no advertising.

EVALUATION

A fine choice for those who want big-car virtues and can live with (and afford) the vices. Main attractions are ride comfort, mechanical refinement, and plush accommodations. Interiors are roomy enough for six, and the trunk will take their luggage with ease. Size and weight look more conspicuous with each passing year, however. Not very practical for city use because of bulk and large turning circle. Performance is just adequate with the gas engines, and borders on sluggish with the diesel. Mileage is what you would expect: usually under 20 mpg with the gas engines, maybe up to 25 overall with the diesel. Can be expensive to maintain because of numerous standard power assists. GM's diesel V-8 continues to be plagued by a checkered repair history, and can be an expensive headache. In our book, there's not as much value for money here as in the cheaper Chevrolet Caprice/Impala or Ford LTD Crown Victoria. Verdict: something of a relic, but a nice one.

EVALUATION CHECKLIST

Fuel economy	2	Cargo room	4
Driveability	4	Serviceability	3
Acceleration	3	Standard equipment	4
Braking	4	Body construction	4
Handling/roadholding	3	Paint/exterior finish	4
Driving position	3	Interior finish	4
Instruments/control	3	TOTAL POINTS	74
Visiblity	3		
Heating/ventilation	4	**RATING SCALE**	
Seat comfort	4	5 = Excellent	
Passenger room	5	4 = Very Good	
Ride	4	3 = Average/Acceptable	
Noise	5	2 = Fair	
Exit/entry	4	1 = Poor	

SPECIFICATIONS	Electra 2-door coupe	Electra 4-door sedan	LeSabre 2-door coupe	LeSabre 4-door sedan	5-door wagon
Wheelbase (in.)	118.9	118.9	115.9	115.9	115.9
Overall length (in.)	221.3	221.3	218.4	218.4	220.5
Overall width (in.)	76.2	76.2	78.0	78.0	79.3
Overall length (in.)	56.8	56.9	56.0	56.7	59.1
Track front (in.)	61.8	61.8	61.8	61.8	62.2
Track rear (in.)	60.7	60.7	60.7	60.7	64.0
Curb weight (lbs.)	3686	3846	3604	3633	4228
Max. cargo vol. (cu. ft.)	20.8	20.8	20.8	20.8	87.9
Fuel tank capacity (gal.)	22.0	22.5[1]	25.0[1]	25.0[1]	22.0
Seating capacity	5	5	5	5	5
Front headroom (in.)	38.5	39.5	38.8	39.5	39.6
Front shoulder room (in.)	59.9	59.8	60.6	60.3	60.4
Front legroom, max. (in.)	42.2	42.2	42.2	42.2	42.2
Rear headroom (in.)	37.8	38.1	38.3	38.2	39.3
Rear shoulder room (in.)	59.0	59.8	58.9	61.0	60.9
Rear legroom, min. (in.)	41.3	41.7	38.3	38.2	39.3

1: 26.0 gal. w/diesel engine

BODY/CHASSIS

Drivetrain layout: longitudinal front engine/rear-wheel drive.
Suspension front: independent, unequal-length upper and lower A-arms, coil springs, telescopic shock absorbers, anti-roll bar. **Suspension rear:** rigid axle, four links, coil spring, telescopic shock absorbers (anti-roll bar optional). **Steering:** recirculating ball, power-assisted. **Turns lock-to-lock:** 3.4. **Turn diameter (ft.):** 40.3. **Brakes front:** 11.9-in. discs (11.0 LeSabre exc. wagon). **Brakes rear:** 11.0-in. drums (9.5-in. LeSabre exc. wagon). **Construction:** body-on-frame

POWERTRAINS	ohv V-6	ohv V-6	ohv V-8	ohv V-8D
Bore × stroke (in.)	3.80× 3.40	3.97× 3.40	3.80× 3.39	4.06× 3.39
Displacement (liters/cu. in.)	3.8/ 231	4.1/ 252	5.0/ 307	5.7/ 350
Compression ratio	8.0:1	8.0:1	8.0:1	21.6:1
Fuel delivery	2bbl.	4bbl.	4bbl.	FI
Net bhp @ rpm	110@ 3800	125@ 4000	140@ 3600	105@ 3200
Net torque @ rpm (lbs/ft)	190@ 1600	205@ 2000	240@ 1600	200@ 1600
Availability	S/All[1]	S/All[2]	O/All[3]	O/All

1: std. LeSabre, exc. wagon 2: std. Electra, opt. LeSabre exc. wagons 3: std. LeSabre/ Electra wagons

Final drive ratios

3-speed automatic	2.73:1[1]		2.41:1[2]	2.41:1
4-speed OD automatic		3.23:1	2.73:1[3]	2.93:1

1: 3.23:1 opt.
2: 3.08:1 opt.
3: 3.08:1, 3.23:1 opt. Fed.

KEY bbl. = barrel (carburetor); **bhp** = brake horsepower (advertised); **Cal.** = California only. **Fed.** = Federal/49 state; **FI** = fuel injection; **ohv** = overhead valve; **ohc** = overhead cam; **I** = inline engine; **V** = V engine; **D** = diesel; **T** = turbocharged; **OD** = overdrive transmission; **S** = standard engine; **O** = optional engine.

PRICES

LESABRE	Retail Price	Dealer Cost	Low Price
Custom 4-door sedan.	$ 9394	$ 8108	$ 9108
Custom 2-door coupe	9292	8021	9021
Limited 4-door sedan.	9990	8622	9622
Limited 2-door coupe.	9836	8490	9490
5-door Estate Wagon	11187	9656	10656
ELECTRA			
Limited 4-door sedan.	12586	10863	11863
Limited 2-door coupe.	12415	10716	11716
Park Avenue 4-door sedan.	14245	12295	13295
Park Avenue 2-door coupe	14094	12165	13165
5-door Estate Wagon	13638	11771	12771

STANDARD EQUIPMENT (included in above prices):

3.8-liter (231-cid) V-6 engine, (5.0-liter V-8 on wagon), 4-speed automatic transmission (ex. w/diesel engine), power steering & brakes, radial-ply whitewall tires, tinted glass, air conditioning (wagon), bumper guards, carpeting, deluxe wheel covers. **LeSabre Limited** adds: Limited-level notchback trim, woodgrain door trim, custom steering wheel. **Electra Limited** adds over LeSabre: 4.1-liter (252-cid) V-6 engine, 6-way power seat, remote-control left mirror, 55/45 cloth notchback seat, power windows, air conditioning, quartz digital clock. **Electra Park Avenue** adds: 50/50 seats, tilt steering wheel, cruise control, remote-control trunklid release, power door locks, AM/FM stereo radio, electric remote-control left mirror, dome reading light.

OPTIONAL EQUIPMENT:

Engines			
4.1-liter (252-cid) V-6 4-bbl.			
LeSabres ex. wagon	$ 150	$ 128	$ 130
5.0-liter (307-cid) V-8 4-bbl.			
LeSabres ex. wagon	225	191	193
Electras ex. wagon	745	64	65
5.7-liter (350-cid) diesel V-8	799	679	686
Accessory group			
Electra Limited	70	60	61
Electra Park Avenue	46	39	40
Electra wagon	70	60	61
Air conditioning, LeSabre (std. wag.)	725	616	623
Touch climate control air conditioning			
LeSabres ex. wagon	875	744	752
LeSabre wagon	150	128	130
Electras	150	128	130

Prices are accurate at time of printing; subject to manufacturer's change

	Retail Price	Dealer Cost	Low Price
Limited-slip differential	95	81	82
Heavy-duty battery, each.	25	21	22
Electric clock, LeSabre	60	51	52
Heavy-duty cooling			
w/o air conditioning	70	60	61
w/air conditioning	40	34	35
Cruise master cruise control.	170	145	147
Rear window defogger	135	115	117
Power door locks			
Coupes.	120	102	104
Sedans, wagons	170	145	147
Automatic power door locks			
Coupes.	200	170	172
Sedans, wagons	250	213	216
Engine block heater	18	15	16
Electric fuel cap lock (NA wagon)	44	37	38
85-amp generator			
w/o air conditioning or HD cooling	85	72	73
w/air conditioning or HD cooling	35	30	31
Tinted glass	105	89	90
Four-note horn.	28	24	25
Halogen high-beam headlamps	22	19	20
Cornering lamps	57	48	49
Door courtesy & warning lights (std. Park Avenue)			
Coupes.	44	37	38
Sedans, wagons	70	60	61
Front lamp monitor, ex. Electras	37	31	32
Front & rear lamp monitor, Electras	74	63	64
Mirrors			
Left remote, LeSabre (std. wag.)	24	20	21
Remote right			
LeSabre ex. wag., Electra Limited sed.	48	41	42
LeSabre wagon	24	20	21
Remote left w/thermometer			
LeSabre ex. wagon	62	53	54
LeSabre wag., Electra Limited & wagon	38	32	33
Sport, dual remote			
LeSabre ex. wagon	88	75	76
LeSabre wagon	40	34	35
Electra Limited, Estate Wagon	40	34	35
Electric control, left, right remote (add to sport mirror prices)	49	42	43

Prices are accurate at time of printing; subject to manufacturer's change

	Retail Price	Dealer Cost	Low Price
Electric control left w/thermometer, Remote right (add to sport mirror prices)	87	73	74
Lighted visor vanity, left or right	58	49	50
Designers' accent paint, LeSabre ex. wagon	215	183	185
Special color paint	200	170	172
Firemist paint	210	179	181
Radio equipment			
AM, LeSabre	112	95	96
AM/FM stereo (std. Park Avenue)	198	168	170
AM/FM stereo delete (credit), Park Avenue	(153)	(130)	(130)
AM/FM stereo ETR			
LeSabre ex. Estate Wagon	402	342	346
LeSabre Estate Wagon	377	320	324
Electra Limited	363	309	313
Electra Estate Wagon	338	287	290
Electra Park Avenue	165	140	142
AM/FM stereo w/cassette tape			
All ex. Park Avenue	298	253	256
Electra Park Avenue	100	85	86
AM/FM stereo ETR w/cassette tape			
LeSabre ex. wagon	555	472	477
LeSabre wagon	530	451	456
Electra Limited	516	439	444
Electra wagon	491	417	422
Electra Park Avenue	319	271	274
Power AM/FM Antenna			
w/radio	60	51	52
w/o radio	95	81	82
Astroroof (NA wagons)	1195	1016	1027
Power seat, driver or passenger			
LeSabre	210	179	181
Electra	180	153	155
Power seat, driver & passenger			
LeSabre	420	357	361
Electra	390	332	336
Power seatback recliner, left or right	139	118	120
Third seat, wagon	215	183	185
Sport steering wheel, LeSabre	50	43	44
Tilt steering wheel (std. Electra Wagon)	105	89	90
Tilt & telescope steering wheel			
LeSabre, Electra Limited	160	136	138
Electra Park Avenue	55	47	48

Prices are accurate at time of printing; subject to manufacturer's change

	Retail Price	Dealer Cost	Low Price
Electra wagon.	55	47	48
Automatic level control suspension.	175	149	151
Firm ride & handling suspension	27	23	24
Gran touring suspension, LeSabre ex. wag.	49	42	43
Remote-control tailgate lock.	50	43	44
Theft deterrent system (NA wagon)	159	135	137
Full vinyl top			
LeSabre ex. wagon.	180	153	155
Electra limited.	185	157	159
Full vinyl top, heavily padded, Electra	240	204	207
Landau vinyl top, LeSabre coupe	240	204	207
Landau vinyl top, heavily padded, Electra Limited	240	204	207
Trim			
Custom, 55/45 seat, LeSabre	125	106	108
Leather & vinyl, Park Ave.	525	446	451
Trunk carpeting, Electra	65	55	56
Trunk trim, LeSabre	53	45	46
Electric trunk lock, Electra	80	68	69
Electric trunk release	40	34	35
Power windows (std. Electra)			
Coupes.	180	153	155
Sedans, wagons	255	217	220
Controlled-cycle wipers.	49	42	43
Woodgrain vinyl applique, LeSabre wagon	345	293	296

Buick Regal

WHAT'S NEW FOR '83

Buick's rear-drive mid-size cars are mostly the same for '83. Last year's high performance Regal Sport Coupe is renamed T Type, and gets refinements on its standard 3.8-liter turbocharged V-6 plus GM's 4-speed overdrive automatic transmission (previously available only in the Riviera and the full-size Buicks). All Regals receive a new grille and wheel covers (except T Type). The base non-turbo gas V-6 picks up an aluminum intake manifold and an electric "early fuel evaporation system" for better drivability. The turbo V-6's microcomputer now regulates a revised exhaust gas recirculation system, and controls timing and exhaust flow for better

Prices are accurate at time of printing; subject to manufacturer's change

CONSUMER GUIDE®

Buick Regal T Type 2-door coupe

full-throttle performance. A refined electronic spark control system for the turbo gets an electric knock sensor. The T Type's final drive is a performance-oriented 3.42.

EVALUATION

Plans for discontinuing the Regal line in favor of the new front-drive Century are being pushed back because the Regals keep selling so well. Still basically the same car it has been since GM downsized its intermediates for 1978. With comfortable accommodations for four (five if you squeeze), Regal is a reasonably sized, well-built package for those buyers who aren't excited about front-wheel drive or transverse-mounted engines. The turbocharged T Type claims most of the excitement in the Regal line, and it has the best road manners. The Buick-built V-6s are sturdy and reliable. Acceleration isn't quick but at least it's smooth, and mileage is acceptable given the car's size and weight. Better economy is available from the V-6 and V-8 diesels but is offset by a poor service record on the V-8.

EVALUATION CHECKLIST

Fuel economy	3	Cargo room	3
Driveability	3	Serviceability	3
Acceleration	3	Standard equipment	3
Braking	3	Body construction	4
Handling/roadholding	3	Paint/exterior finish	4
Driving position	3	Interior finish	4
Instruments/control	3	TOTAL POINTS	67
Visiblity	3		
Heating/ventilation	4	**RATING SCALE**	
Seat comfort	4	5 = Excellent	
Passenger room	3	4 = Very Good	
Ride	4	3 = Average/Acceptable	
Noise	4	2 = Fair	
Exit/entry	3	1 = Poor	

SPECIFICATIONS

	2-door coupe	4-door sedan	4-door wagon
Wheelbase (in.)	108.1	108.1	108.1
Overall length (in.)	200.6	196.0	196.7
Overall width (in.)	71.6	71.1	71.2
Overall height (in.)	55.3	56.2	57.1
Track front (in.)	58.5	58.5	58.5
Track rear (in.)	57.7	57.7	57.8
Curb weight (lbs.)	3245	3261	3410
Max. cargo vol. (cu. ft.)	16.2	15.6	71.8
Fuel tank capacity (gal.)	18.1[1]	18.2	25.0[2]
Seating capacity	5	5	5
Front headroom (in.)	37.9	38.5	38.8
Front shoulder room (in.)	56.8	57.4	57.2
Front legroom, max. (in.)	42.8	42.8	42.8
Rear headroom (in.)	38.1	37.8	38.8
Rear shoulder room (in.)	56.1	57.1	57.1
Rear legroom, min. (in.)	36.3	36.3	35.9

1: 19.8 gal. w/diesel engine 2: 26.0 gal. w/diesel engine

BODY/CHASSIS

Drivetrain layout: longitudinal front engine/rear-wheel drive.
Suspension front: independent, unequal-length upper and lower A-arms, coil springs, telescopic shock absorbers, anti-roll bar. **Suspension rear:** rigid axle, four links, coil springs, telescopic shock absorbers; anti-roll bar on T Type. **Steering:** recirculating ball, power-assisted. **Turns lock-to-lock:** 3.6. **Turn diameter (ft.):** 38.6 (39.0 wagon). **Brakes front:** 10.5-in. discs. **Brakes rear:** 9.5-in. drums. **Construction:** body-on-frame.

POWER-TRAINS	ohv V-6	ohv V-6T	ohv V-6	ohv V-6D	ohv V-8D
Bore × stroke (in.)	3.80× 3.40	3.80× 3.40	3.97× 3.40	4.06× 3.39	4.06× 3.39

POWER- TRAINS	ohv V-6	ohv V-6T	ohv V-6	ohv V-6D	ohv V-8D
Displacement (liters/cu. in.)	3.8/ 231	3.8/ 231	4.1/ 252	4.3/ 262	5.7/ 350
Compression ratio	8.0:1	8.0:1	8.0:1	21.6:1	21.6:1
Fuel delivery	2bbl.	4bbl.	4bbl.	FI	FI
Net bhp @ rpm	110@ 3800	180@ 4000	125@ 4000	85@ 3600	105@ 3200
Net torque @ rpm (lbs/ft)	190@ 1600	290@ 2400	205@ 2000	165@ 1600	200@ 1600
Availability	S/All[1]	S/All[2]	O/All[3]	O/All[4]	O/All[3]

1: except T-Type 2: T-Type only; NA others 3: NA T-Type

Final drive ratios

3-speed automatic	2.41:1[1]		2.41:1[2]	2.41:1	2.29:1[4]
4-speed OD automatic		3.42:1	3.08:1[2]		

1: 3.08:1, 3.23:1 opt.
2: 3.23:1 opt.
3: 2.56:1 opt.
4: 2.73:1 opt.

KEY bbl. = barrel (carburetor); **bhp** = brake horsepower (advertised); **Cal.** = California only. **Fed.** = Federal/49 state; **FI** = fuel injection; **ohv** = overhead valve; **ohc** = overhead cam; **I** = inline engine; **V** = V engine; **D** = diesel; **T** = turbocharged; **OD** = overdrive transmission; **S** = standard engine; **O** = optional engine.

PRICES

REGAL	Retail Price	Dealer Cost	Low Price
4-door sedan.	$ 9279	$ 8009	$ 8759
2-door coupe.	9100	7855	8605
T Type 2-door coupe	10366	8947	9697
Limited 4-door sedan.	9856	8507	9257
Limited 2-door coupe.	9722	8100	8850
4-door Estate Wagon	9550	8243	8993

STANDARD EQUIPMENT (included in above prices):

3.8-liter (231-cid) V-6 engine, automatic transmission, power steering, power brakes, notchback seat, dual mirrors, deluxe steering wheel, whitewall steel-belted radial tires. **T Type** has: 3.8-liter (231-cid) turbo-

Prices are accurate at time of printing; subject to manufacturer's change

charged engine, quick-ratio power steering, halogen high-beam headlamps, instrumentation group, sport mirrors w/left remote control. **Limited** has (over base models): 55/45 notchback seat, custom steering wheel, upgraded trim and exterior moldings.

OPTIONAL EQUIPMENT:

Engines	Retail Price	Dealer Cost	Low Price
4.1-liter (252-cid) V-6 (NA T Type)	150	128	130
4.3-liter V-6 Diesel (NA T Type, Wagon)	599	509	515
5.7-liter (350-cid) V-8 Diesel (NA T Type)	799	679	686
Air conditioning	725	616	623
Automatic air conditioning	875	744	752
Limited-slip differential	95	81	82
Heavy-duty battery (each)	25	21	22
Electric clock	35	30	31
Console	82	70	71
Heavy-duty cooling			
w/o air conditioning	70	60	61
w/air conditioning	40	34	35
Cruise master	170	145	147
T Type decor pkg.	365	310	314
Rear window defogger	135	115	117
Power door locks			
2-door	120	102	104
4-door	170	145	147
Engine block heater	18	15	16
Tinted glass			
All	105	89	90
Windshield only	80	68	69
Halogen headlamps (std. T Type)	48	41	42
Headlamps-on indicator	16	14	15
Trip odometer instrumentation	16	14	15
Instrument gauges (std. T Type)	48	41	47
Cornering lights	57	48	49
Dome reading light	24	20	21
Radio Equipment			
AM	112	95	96
AM/FM stereo	198	168	170
AM/FM stereo electronic tune	402	342	346
AM/FM stereo electronic tune w/cassette	555	472	477
Dual rear speakers	30	26	27
Astroroof	895	761	769
Hatch roof	825	701	709
Power seat, 6-way	210	179	181

Prices are accurate at time of printing; subject to manufacturer's change

	Retail Price	Dealer Cost	Low Price
Passenger seat recliner............	75	64	65
Seats/trim			
55/45 bench (std. Limited)........	133	113	115
Buckets, ex. Limited............	195	166	168
Sport steering wheel	50	43	44
Tilt steering wheel................	105	89	90
Automatic level control suspension......	175	149	151
Firm ride & handling suspension	27	23	24
Gran touring suspension (std. T Type) ...	49	42	43
Theft deterrent system	159	135	137
Landau vinyl top			
Base	181	154	156
Heavily padded	240	204	206
Electric trunk release	40	34	35
Trunk trim	47	40	41
Power windows			
2-door	180	153	155
4-door	255	217	220
Power windows-front only, 4-door......	180	153	155
Wiper delay feature	49	42	43
Woodgrain bodyside applique, wagon	355	302	306

Buick Riviera

Buick Riviera 2-door coupe

WHAT'S NEW FOR '83

Buick's front-drive personal-luxury offering rolls into '83 with the convertible introduced during the '82 model year, the T Type coupe with revised turbocharged V-6, and the familiar standard coupe. The Riviera ragtop, Buick's first since 1975, is available in either white or red firemist. The top with either color is white. Engine choices on the convertible are Buick's 4.1-liter gas V-6 or the Oldsmobile 307-cid gas V-8. Standard are 4-wheel disc brakes, 4-speed overdrive automatic transmission, and red leather upholstery. The T Type is offered with an expanded range of colors. A digital instrument cluster is optional on all Rivieras, and there's a new premium sound system option that results from collaboration between GM's Delco Electronics Division and Bose Corporation.

EVALUATION

Not the best example of front-drive efficiency. Posh and a little pretentious, but well able to accomplish what it was designed for. A handsome, quiet car that's surprisingly competent on winding roads. Handling is better with the optional "Gran Touring" suspension, but the standard chassis isn't bad aside from marked body roll in tight turns. It's a big, heavy car, so mileage and performance are both weak. The exception is the turbo engine, which has good straight-line acceleration and plenty of reserve power for passing. All-independent suspension absorbs rough roads easily. Interior comfort is high despite a confined rear seat area (especially the convertible). Upkeep can be expensive, especially the turbo. The optional diesel V-8 gives the best mileage, but you'll have to do a lot of driving to make up for its high initial price and a long list of reliability woes makes it seem like false economy. Convertible adds more elegance, some flash, and carries an even heftier price tag.

EVALUATION CHECKLIST

Fuel economy	3	Cargo room	3
Driveability	4	Serviceability	2
Acceleration	3	Standard equipment	4
Braking	3	Body construction	4
Handling/roadholding	3	Paint/exterior finish	4
Driving position	4	Interior finish	4
Instruments/control	3	TOTAL POINTS	69
Visiblity	3		
Heating/ventilation	4	**RATING SCALE**	
Seat comfort	4	5 = Excellent	
Passenger room	3	4 = Very Good	
Ride	4	3 = Average/Acceptable	
Noise	4	2 = Fair	
Exit/entry	3	1 = Poor	

SPECIFICATIONS

	2-door coupe	conv.
Wheelbase (in.)	114.0	114.0
Overall length (in.)	206.6	206.6
Overall width (in.)	72.8	72.8
Overall height (in.)	54.3	54.3
Track front (in.)	59.3	59.3
Track rear (in.)	60.0	60.0
Curb weight (lbs.)	3697	3864
Max. cargo vol. (cu. ft.)	15.8	12.7
Fuel tank capacity (gal.)	21.1	21.1
Seating capacity	5	4
Front headroom (in.)	37.9	39.4
Front shoulder room (in.)	56.5	56.5
Front legroom, max. (in.)	42.8	42.9
Rear headroom (in.)	37.9	38.5
Rear shoulder room (in.)	55.9	44.6
Rear legroom, min. (in.)	39.2	35.6

BODY/CHASSIS

Drivetrain layout: longitudinal front engine/front-wheel drive. **Suspension front:** independent, torsion bars, unequal-length upper and lower control arms, telescopic shock absorbers, anti-roll bar. **Suspension rear:** independent, semi-trailing arms, coil springs, telescopic shock absorbers with electronic level control, anti-roll bar. **Steering:** recirculating ball, power-assisted. **Turns lock-to-lock:** 3.0. **Turn diameter (ft.):** 39.6. **Brakes front:** 10.5-in. discs. **Brakes rear:** 9.5-in. drums (10.5-in. discs opt.). **Construction:** body-on-frame

POWERTRAINS	ohv V-6	ohv V-8	ohv V-6T
Bore × stroke (in.)	3.97× 3.40	3.80× 3.39	3.80× 3.40

POWERTRAINS

	ohv V-6	ohv V-8	ohv V-6T
Displacement (liters/cu. in.)	4.1/ 252	5.0/ 307	3.8/ 231
Compression ratio	8.0:1	8.0:1	8.0:1
Fuel delivery	4bbl.	4bbl.	4bbl.
Net bhp @ rpm	125@ 4000	140@ 3600	180@ 4000
Net torque @ rpm (lbs/ft)	205@ 2000	240@ 1600	290@ 2400
Availability	S/All	O/All[1]	S/All[2]

1: no charge convertible   2: T-Type only; NA others

Final drive ratios

4-speed OD automatic	3.15:1	2.73:1	3.36:1

KEY bbl. = barrel (carburetor); **bhp** = brake horsepower (advertised); **Cal.** = California only. **Fed.** = Federal/49 state; **FI** = fuel injection; **ohv** = overhead valve; **ohc** = overhead cam; **I** = inline engine; **V** = V engine; **D** = diesel; **T** = turbocharged; **OD** = overdrive transmission; **S** = standard engine; **O** = optional engine.

PRICES

RIVIERA	Retail Price	Dealer Cost	Low Price
2-door coupe.	$15238	$13152	$14652
2-door T Type coupe	15906	13728	15228
2-door convertible.	24960	21542	24900

STANDARD EQUIPMENT (included in above prices):

4.1-liter (252-cid) V-6 engine, 4-speed automatic overdrive transmission, power steering, power brakes, whitewall tires, 45/45 front seat, power windows, tinted glass, quartz-digital clock, AM/FM ETR stereo radio w/automatic power antenna, electric door locks, power driver's seat, air conditioning, auto level control, cruise control. **T Type** adds: 3.8-liter turbocharged V-6 engine, tungsten headlamps, gran touring suspension, sport steering wheel. **Convertible** adds over base: 4-wheel disc brakes, Firemist paint, 45/45 leather w/vinyl front seat, trunk carpeting, custom locking wire wheel covers.

OPTIONAL EQUIPMENT:

Engines
5.0-liter (307-cid) V-8 4-bbl.
(NA T Type) . . . . $ 75 $ 64 $ 65

Prices are accurate at time of printing; subject to manufacturer's change

	Retail Price	Dealer Cost	Low Price
5.7-liter (350-cid) V-8 diesel (NA T Type or conv.)	799	679	686
Automatic air conditioning	150	128	130
Heavy-duty battery			
w/gas engine	25	21	22
w/diesel engine (2).	50	43	44
4-wheel disc brakes.	235	200	203
Heavy-duty cooling	40	34	35
Rear window defogger	135	115	117
Automatic electric door locks	80	68	69
Engine block heater	18	15	16
Electric fuel cap lock (NA w/diesel).	44	37	38
Halogen headlamps	22	19	20
Four-note horn.	28	24	25
Low-fuel indicator	16	14	15
Digital inst. cluster	238	202	205
Coach lamps (NA conv.).	102	87	88
Courtesy/reading lamp (NA conv.)	48	41	42
Fuel usage light	16	14	15
Illuminated door lock & interior light control	72	61	62
Front & rear light monitors	74	63	64
Designers' accent paint.	235	200	203
Special color paint	210	179	181
Radio equipment			
ETR AM/FM stereo, full-feature	125	106	108
Above w/8-track tape	278	236	239
ETR AM/FM stereo cassette	100	85	86
ETR AM/FM stereo w/cassette tape & graphic equalizer.	308	279	282
Above w/Dolby & Bose speakers	895	761	769
Astroroof	1195	1016	1027
Seat adjusters			
Power passenger 6-way.	210	179	181
Electric recliner, left or right	139	118	120
Two-position memory power seat (left) .	178	151	153
Sports steering wheel, Riviera, conv.	40	34	35
Tilt & telescope steering wheel	55	47	48
Bodyside stripe	42	36	37
Gran touring suspension (std. T Type) . . .	27	23	24
Theft deterrent system	159	135	137
Landau heavily padded vinyl top (incl. coach lamps)	325	276	279
Interior trim			
45/55 notchback front seat, leather w/ vinyl (std. conv.).	405	344	348

Prices are accurate at time of printing; subject to manufacturer's change

	Retail Price	Dealer Cost	Low Price
Trunk carpeting & trim (std. conv.)	30	26	27
Electric trunk release	40	34	35
Electric trunk lock (electric release required).	80	68	69
Wipers w/low-speed delay	49	42	43

Buick Skyhawk/ Oldsmobile Firenza

Buick Skyhawk Limited 2-door coupe

WHAT'S NEW FOR '83

After disappointing sales in its maiden run, the front-drive compacts are bolstered for '83 with a new engine lineup, optional 5-speed overdrive manual transmission, and a 5-door wagon body style to supplement the coupe and sedan introduced in early '82. Buick's J-car also gets a sporty T Type model, available in 2-door form only. The thrashy 1.8-liter Chevy-built overhead-valve four that returned uninspired performance and unexceptional mileage has been considerably re-engineered. It's now 2.0 liters due to a stroke increase, has electronic throttle-body fuel injection instead of last year's 2-barrel carburetor, plus reshaped combustion chambers, all intended for more pep and economy. Standard for T Type and optional elsewhere is a 1.8-liter overhead-cam four imported from GM's subsidiary in Brazil. The ohc four also has electronic fuel injection plus an aluminum crossflow cylinder head. The new 5-speed manual gearbox is available only with this engine. The 5-door wagon features a standard split folding rear seatback. The 2-door now has a front seat that slides forward for easier entry to the rear. Hoods on all Skyhawks lose their prop rod in favor of self-propping gas struts.

EVALUATION

Good materials and fine assembly in early J-cars were overshadowed by lackluster performance and mileage. High prices didn't help, either. Sales lagged accordingly. For '83 we're taking a wait-and-see attitude about the new J-car engines and the optional 5-speed. Based on initial, brief drives, the 2.0 Chevy engine is a bit stronger and quieter than last year's version, but it may not be that much better by the stopwatch or at the gas pumps. The Brazilian 1.8 looks like a better bet, though we'll await more experience with it before passing judgment. Like the other Js, these have a fine ride for small cars, and handling is almost athletic on the T Type. A handy car for urban dwellers, and has good visibility to all quarters. Comes with a fair number of standard features, but the price is correspondingly high. Early engines sounded like overworked food processors and acceleration was leisurely, so GM is working on these problems first. Still to be solved is the puzzle of how to boost J-car sales when the larger X-body compacts are available for the same or, in some cases, less money.

EVALUATION CHECKLIST

Fuel economy	4	Cargo room	3
Driveability	3	Serviceability	3
Acceleration	3	Standard equipment	3
Braking	3	Body construction	4
Handling/roadholding	3	Paint/exterior finish	4
Driving position	4	Interior finish	4
Instruments/control	4	TOTAL POINTS	70
Visiblity	4		
Heating/ventilation	4	**RATING SCALE**	
Seat comfort	3	5 = Excellent	
Passenger room	3	4 = Very Good	
Ride	4	3 = Average/Acceptable	
Noise	4	2 = Fair	
Exit/entry	3	1 = Poor	

Oldsmobile Firenza SX 3-door coupe

SPECIFICATIONS

	2/3-door coupe	4-door sedan	5-door wagon
Wheelbase (in.)	101.2	101.2	101.2
Overall length (in.)	175.3	175.3	177.1
Overall width (in.)	62.0	62.0	65.0
Overall height (in.)	54.0	54.0	54.0
Track front (in.)	55.4	55.4	55.4
Track rear (in.)	55.2	55.2	55.2
Curb weight (lbs.)	2394	2451	2522
Max. cargo vol. (cu. ft.)	12.6	13.5	64.5
Fuel tank capacity (gal.)	13.6	13.6	13.6
Seating capacity	5	5	5
Front headroom (in.)	37.7	38.5	38.3
Front shoulder room (in.)	53.7	53.7	53.7
Front legroom, max. (in.)	42.1	42.2	42.2
Rear headroom (in.)	36.5	37.8	38.7
Rear shoulder room (in.)	52.5	53.7	53.7
Rear legroom, min. (in.)	31.2	34.3	33.1

BODY/CHASSIS

Drivetrain layout: transverse front engine/front-wheel drive. **Suspension front:** independent, MacPherson struts, lower control arms, coil springs, telescopic shock absorbers, anti-roll-bar. **Suspension rear:** semi-independent, beam axle, trailing arms, coil springs, telescopic shock absorbers; anti-roll bar on T-Type. **Steering:** rack-and-pinion (power-assisted on T-Type). **Turns lock-to-lock:** 4.0. **Turn diameter (ft.):** 34.7. **Brakes front:** 9.7-in. discs. **Brakes rear:** 7.9-in. drums. **Construction:** unit

POWERTRAINS

	ohv I-4	ohc I-4
Bore × stroke (in.)	3.50× 3.15	3.34× 3.13
Displacement (liters/cu. in.)	2.0/ 121	1.8/ 112
Compression ratio	9.3:1	9.0:1
Fuel delivery	FI	FI
Net bhp @ rpm	86@ 4900	84@ 5200
Net torque @ rpm (lbs/ft)	110@ 3000	102@ 2800
Availability	S/All[1]	O/All[2]

1: NA T-Type 2: Std. T-Type, opt. others

Final drive ratios

4-speed OD manual	4.10:1	
5-speed OD manual		3.83:1
3-speed automatic	3.18:1[1]	3.18:1[1]

1: 3.33:1 opt.

KEY bbl. = barrel (carburetor); **bhp** = brake horsepower (advertised); **Cal.** = California only. **Fed.** = Federal/49 state; **FI** = fuel injection; **ohv** = overhead valve; **ohc** = overhead cam; **I** = inline engine; **V** = V engine; **D** = diesel; **T** = turbocharged; **OD** = overdrive transmission; **S** = standard engine; **O** = optional engine.

PRICES

SKYHAWK	Retail Price	Dealer Cost	Low Price
Custom 4-door sedan	$7166	$6400	$6800
Custom 2-door coupe	6958	6214	6614
Custom 5-door wagon	7492	6691	7091
T Type 2-door coupe	7961	7110	7610
Limited 4-door sedan	7649	6831	7331

Prices are accurate at time of printing; subject to manufacturer's change

	Retail Price	Dealer Cost	Low Price
Limited 2-door coupe...............	7457	6660	7160
Limited 5-door wagon	7934	7086	7586

STANDARD EQUIPMENT (included in above prices):

2.0-liter (121-cid) 4-cylinder engine w/fuel injection, 4-speed manual transmission, AM radio, power brakes, carpeting, P175/80 R13 fiberglass belted radial blackwall tires. **Limited** also has: instrument gauges, upgraded trim, acoustic package. **T Type** has over base Custom: 1.8-liter (112-cid) 4-cylinder fuel-injected engine, 5-speed manual transmission, instrument gauges, sport steering wheel, gran touring suspension, styled aluminum wheels (4), P195/70 R13 steel belted radial blackwall tires, left remote and right manual mirrors.

OPTIONAL EQUIPMENT:

	Retail	Dealer	Low
1.8-liter (112-cid) 4-cylinder engine (std. T Type)....	$ 50	$ 43	$ 44
Transmissions			
5-speed manual (std. T Type).......	75	64	65
Automatic			
T Type......	320	272	275
Custom, Limited...............	395	336	340
Accent stripe (NA T Type)............	195	166	168
Acoustic pkg. (std. Limited)...........	36	31	32
Air conditioning	625	531	537
Touch climate air conditioning	775	659	666
Heavy-duty battery	25	21	22
Elec. clock	35	30	31
Cruise control	170	145	147
Elec. rear defogger	125	106	108
Power door locks			
Coupes...................	120	102	104
Sedans, wagons	170	145	147
Tinted glass	90	76	77
Engine block heater	18	15	16
Dual horns, Cust. coupe, sedan	15	13	14
Headlamps-on indicator	15	13	14
Trip odometer, Custom..............	15	13	14
Instrument gauges, Custom...........	60	51	52
Instrument gauges & tachometer			
Custom (std. T Type)............	138	117	119
Limited.................	78	66	67
Dome reading light	30	26	27
Halogen headlamps	22	19	20
Decklid luggage rack (NA wagon)	105	89	90
Heavy-duty radiator			
w/o air conditioning	70	60	61

Prices are accurate at time of printing; subject to manufacturer's change

	Retail Price	Dealer Cost	Low Price
w/air conditioning	40	34	35
Radio equipment			
AM delete (credit)	(56)	(48)	(48)
AM/FM ETR stereo basic feature.	138	117	119
Above w/clock	177	150	152
AM/FM stereo ETR.	302	257	260
AM/FM ETR stereo basic feature w/ cassette	277	235	238
Flip-up sunroof (NA wagon)	295	251	254
Roof rack, wagons	105	89	90
Easy entry pass. seat, Custom coupe	16	14	15
6-way power left seat.	210	179	181
Power steering.	199	169	171
Sport steering wheel (std. T Type)	50	43	44
Tilt steering wheel.	99	84	85
Gran touring suspension (std. T Type) . . .	196	166	168
Remote tailgate elec. lock, wagons	35	30	31
Tailgate washer/wiper, wagons	120	102	104
Suede trim, bucket seats (NA T Type) . . .	295	251	254
Elec. trunk lock release.	40	34	35
Deluxe trunk trim	33	28	29
Power windows			
Coupes	180	153	155
Sedans, wagons	255	217	220
Intermittent wipers	49	42	43

OLDSMOBILE FIRENZA

	Retail Price	Dealer Cost	Low Price
S 3-door coupe	$7007	$6259	$6759
4-door sedan.	7094	6336	6836
Cruiser 5-door wagon	7314	6532	7032
SX 3-door coupe	7750	6922	7422
LX 4-door sedan.	7646	6599	7099
Cruiser Brougham 5-door wagon	7866	6789	7289

STANDARD EQUIPMENT (Included in above prices):

2.0-liter (121-cid) 4-cylinder fuel injected engine, 4-speed manual transmission, power brakes, AM radio, carpeting, P175/80R-13 fiberglass belted radial blackwall tires, floor console, reclining front bucket seats. **SX Coupe** adds: convenience group, rallye instrument cluster, custom sport steering wheel, remote control left rearview mirror, power steering. **LX Sedan** adds: deluxe steering wheel.

OPTIONAL EQUIPMENT:

	Retail Price	Dealer Cost	Low Price
1.8-liter (112-cid) 4-cylinder fuel injected engine	$ 50	$ 43	$44

Prices are accurate at time of printing; subject to manufacturer's change

	Retail Price	Dealer Cost	Low Price
5-speed manual transmission	75	64	65
3-speed automatic transmission	395	336	340
Air conditioning	625	531	537
Body accent stripe	42	36	37
High capacity battery	25	21	22
Cargo area cover (coupes).	60	51	52
Cruise control	170	145	147
Convenience group	54	46	47
Electric clock.	35	30	31
Roof luggage carrier (wagons)	98	83	84
Power door locks			
2-doors	120	102	104
4-doors	170	145	147
Electric rear window defroster.	125	106	108
Locking fuel filler door	10	9	9
Glass sunroof	295	251	254
Tinted glass	90	77	78
Custom interior (S Coupe)	250	213	216
Engine block heater.	19	16	17
Halogen headlamps	10	9	9
Dual horns	15	13	14
Rallye instrument cluster.	142	121	123
Radio Equipment			
Radio delete (credit).	(56)	(48)	(49)
AM/FM ETR stereo	138	117	119
AM/FM ETR stereo w/digital clock. . . .	177	150	152
AM/FM ETR stereo w/digital clock &			
cassette	277	235	238
Dual rear speakers	25	21	22
Power antenna	60	51	52
Power seat, driver side.	210	179	181
Split folding rear seat (coupes, wagons) . .	50	43	44
Custom sport steering wheel	50	43	44
Firm ride & handling suspension	30	26	27
Power tailgate release (wagons)	35	30	31
Power trunk release (coupes, sedans)	40	34	35
Power steering.	199	169	171
Tilt steering wheel.	99	84	85
Power windows			
2-doors	180	153	155
4-doors	255	217	220
Wood grain body panels (wagons)	275	234	237
Pulse wiper system	49	42	43
Rear window wiper/washer (coupes,			
wagons)	117	99	101
Rallye wheels	42	36	37

Prices are accurate at time of printing; subject to manufacturer's change

Buick Skylark/ Oldsmobile Omega

Buick Skylark T Type 2-door coupe

WHAT'S NEW FOR '83

The front-drive X-car from Flint heads into its fourth model year with a revised model lineup and minor equipment changes. Base models are redesignated Skylark Custom. Replacing last year's 2- and 4-door Sport offerings is the new T Type, offered only in 2-door form, powered by the H.O. (High-Output) version of the Chevy-built 2.8-liter 60-degree V-6. Other engine and transmission choices are the same as before. The T Type also gets standard 4-speed manual gearbox with a numerically higher final drive ratio for better off-the-line snap, plus the uprated "Gran Touring" suspension package (optional on other models). The Oldsmobile X-car heads into its fourth model year with only a few new appearance features. Door mirrors are now what Oldsmobile calls the aerodynamic "patch" type. Omega's dash has been brought into line with newer Olds models, and now has side window defroster vents, rocker-type (instead of push-pull) headlight switch, and a headlamps-on warning light. The standard bench seat now has a low-profile backrest, and on base models a fold-down center armrest is standard. A similar ES option group is available for both 2- and 4-door models, and can be teamed with either the standard four or the optional V-6 in standard or H.O. (High-Output) tune.

EVALUATION

The X-cars had great potential as fine smaller family cars, but

Oldsmobile Omega Brougham 4-door sedan

have been spoiled by persistent reliability and quality-control problems and too many recalls. Some of the bugs have been worked out and the Xs now benefit from chassis refinements adopted for their larger A-car relatives, but we still have nagging doubts about reliability. These cars appeal as before for interior room, decent mileage, fine ride, and capable road manners. The T Type with its strong V-6 and well-sorted chassis is one nifty car. Service access is a problem with the V-6, however, and the normal-tune version isn't as thrifty as the four. Drivability is still marred by balky shift action and a long-travel clutch with manual transmission. Workmanship has been spotty on the X-cars, so sometimes you get a good one, sometimes you don't. Still deserves consideration, but not as good a value in our eyes as Chrysler's K-cars.

EVALUATION CHECKLIST

Fuel economy 3	Cargo room. 3
Driveability. 4	Serviceability 2
Acceleration. 3	Standard equipment. 3
Braking 4	Body construction 4
Handling/roadholding 4	Paint/exterior finish 4
Driving position 4	Interior finish 4
Instruments/control. 3	TOTAL POINTS 70
Visiblity 4	
Heating/ventilation 4	**RATING SCALE**
Seat comfort 4	5 = Excellent
Passenger room 3	4 = Very Good
Ride 3	3 = Average/Acceptable
Noise 4	2 = Fair
Exit/entry. 3	1 = Poor

SPECIFICATIONS

	2-door coupe	4-door sedan
Wheelbase (in.)	104.9	104.9
Overall length (in.)	181.1	181.1
Overall width (in.)	69.1	69.1
Overall height (in.)	53.0	53.0
Track front (in.)	58.7	58.7
Track rear (in.)	57.0	57.0
Curb weight (lbs.)	2531	2561
Max. cargo vol. (cu. ft.)	14.3	14.3
Fuel tank capacity (gal.)	15.1	15.1
Seating capacity	5	5
Front headroom (in.)	38.2	38.2
Front shoulder room (in.)	55.7	55.6
Front legroom, max. (in.)	42.2	42.2
Rear headroom (in.)	37.4	37.4
Rear shoulder room (in.)	56.1	55.6
Rear legroom, min. (in.)	34.5	35.5

BODY/CHASSIS

Drivetrain layout: transverse front engine/front-wheel drive. **Suspension front:** independent, MacPerson struts, lower control arms, coil springs, telescopic shock absorbers, anti-roll bar. **Suspension rear:** beam "twist" axle with integral anti-roll bar, trailing arms, panhard rod, coil springs, telescopic shock absorbers. **Steering:** rack-and-pinion, power-assisted. **Turns lock-to-lock:** 3.1 **Turn diameter (ft.):** 39.4 **Brakes front:** 9.7-in. discs. **Brakes rear:** 7.9-in. drums. **Construction:** unit

POWERTRAINS

	ohv I-4	ohv V-6	ohv V-6[1]
Bore × stroke (in.)	4.00× 3.00	3.50× 2.99	3.50× 2.99

POWERTRAINS

	ohv I-4	ohv V-6	ohv V-6[1]
Displacement (liters/cu. in.)	2.5/ 151	2.8/ 173	2.8/ 173
Compression ratio	8.2:1	8.42:1	8.94:1
Fuel delivery	FI	2bbl.	2bbl.
Net bhp @ rpm	90@ 4000	112@ 5100	135@ 5400
Net torque @ rpm (lbs/ft)	132@ 2800	148@ 2400	145@ 2400
Availability	S/All	O/All	O/All

1: H.O. engine

Final drive ratios

4-speed OD manual	3.32:1	3.32:1	3.65:1
3-speed automatic	2.39:1	2.53:1	3.06:1

KEY bbl. = barrel (carburetor); **bhp** = brake horsepower (advertised); **Cal.** = California only. **Fed.** = Federal/49 state; **FI** = fuel injection; **ohv** = overhead valve; **ohc** = overhead cam; **I** = inline engine; **V** = V engine; **D** = diesel; **T** = turbocharged; **OD** = overdrive transmission; **S** = standard engine; **O** = optional engine.

PRICES

SKYLARK	Retail Price	Dealer Cost	Low Price
Custom 4-door sedan.	$7718	$6893	$7393
Custom 2-door coupe	7548	6741	7241
T Type 2-door coupe	9337	8339	9039
Limited 4-door sedan.	8150	7279	7779
Limited 2-door coupe.	7988	7134	7634

STANDARD EQUIPMENT (included in above prices):

2.5-liter (151-cid) 4-cylinder fuel-injected engine, 4-speed manual transmission, AM radio, power steering, power brakes, notchback bench seat, carpeting, roof drip and window moldings, glovebox lock, P185/80R-13 glass-belted tires. **Limited** adds: additional acoustic insulation, light group, belt reveal moldings, deluxe wheel covers, wheel opening moldings, hood ornament and windsplit moldings, wide rocker panel and rear quarter panel moldings, front fender moldings, pillar applique (sedan). **T Type** has: Skylark equipment plus bumper rub strips, instrument gauges w/trip odometer, rallye ride-and-handling suspension, sport wheels w/P205/70R-

Prices are accurate at time of printing; subject to manufacturer's change

13 steel-belted radial tires, sport mirrors (left remote), sport steering wheel, 2.8-liter (173-cid) H.O. V-6 engine.

OPTIONAL EQUIPMENT:

Engines	Retail Price	Dealer Cost	Low Price
2.8-liter (173-cid) V-6 (NA T Type)	150	128	130
2.8-liter (173-cid) H.O. V-6 (std. T Type)	300	255	258
3-speed automatic transmission	425	361	365
Acoustic package (std. Limited T Type) . . .	60	51	52
Air conditioning	725	616	623
Heavy-duty battery	25	21	22
Electric clock	35	30	31
Heavy-duty cooling			
w/o air conditioning	70	60	61
w/air conditioning	40	34	35
Console	100	85	86
Cruise master cruise control.	170	145	147
Rear window defogger	135	115	117
Power door locks			
Coupes	120	102	104
Sedans.	170	145	147
Engine block heater	18	15	16
85-amp. generator	85	72	73
Tinted glass	105	89	90
Special instrumentation.	48	41	42
Coach lamps (Limited)	102	87	88
Dome reading light	24	20	21
Designer accent paint (NA T Type)	210	179	181
Radio equipment			
AM delete (credit)	(56)	(48)	(48)
AM/FM ETR stereo basic feature w/o clock	138	117	119
Above w/clock	177	150	152
AM/FM ETR stereo full feature	302	257	260
AM/FM stereo basic feature w/cassette. .	277	235	238
Seat recliner, passenger or driver (each) . .	45	38	39
Power seat	210	179	181
Superlift rear shock absorbers	68	58	59
Sport steering wheel	50	43	44
Tilt steering wheel.	105	89	90
Sunroof, Vista-Vent	295	251	254
Firm ride & handling suspension	27	23	24
Gran Touring Suspension (Std. T Type) . . .	272	230	233
Vinyl top			
Landau, padded (coupes).	215	183	185
Long	155	132	134
Electric trunk release	40	34	35

Prices are accurate at time of printing; subject to manufacturer's change

	Retail Price	Dealer Cost	Low Price
Power windows			
Coupes	180	153	155
Sedans	255	217	220
Intermittent wiper system	49	42	43

OLDSMOBILE OMEGA

	Retail Price	Dealer Cost	Low Price
2-door coupe	$7478	$6679	$7179
4-door sedan	7676	6856	7356
Brougham 2-door coupe	7767	6937	7437
Brougham 4-door sedan	7948	7098	7598

STANDARD EQUIPMENT (included in above prices):

2.5-liter (151-cid) 4-cylinder fuel-injected engine, 4-speed manual transmission, AM radio with mast antenna, power brakes, power steering, full carpeting, front disc brakes, P185/80R-13 glass-belted radial tires. **Brougham** adds: rocker panel and wheel opening moldings, pillar applique (sedan), hood ornament and windsplit molding, wide belt moldings, lower rear-quarter moldings, wheel covers, upgraded interior trim.

OPTIONAL EQUIPMENT:

	Retail Price	Dealer Cost	Low Price
2.8-liter (173-cid) V-6 engine	$ 150	$ 128	$130
3-speed automatic transmission	425	361	365
Air conditioning	725	616	623
Heavy-duty battery	25	21	22
ES package			
w/4-cylinder engine	896	762	770
w/V-6 engine	1046	888	897
w/H.O. V-6 engine	1196	1012	1028
ESC Coupe package			
w/4-cylinder engine	851	724	732
w/V-6 engine	1001	850	859
w/H.O. V-6 engine	1196	1017	1028
Gauge package (inc. w/ES)	120	102	104
Tinted glass	105	89	90
Dual horns	15	13	14
Electric clock	35	30	31
Heavy-duty cooling			
w/o air conditioning	40	34	35
w/air conditioning	70	60	61
Console	100	85	86
Cruise control	170	145	147
Electric rear-window defroster	135	115	117
Power door locks			
2-doors	120	102	104
4-doors	170	145	147
Radio equipment			
AM/FM ETR stereo w/digital clock	177	150	152

Prices are accurate at time of printing; subject to manufacturer's change

	Retail Price	Dealer Cost	Low Price
AM/FM ETR stereo w/digital clock & cassette	455	387	391
Seat recliner, passenger or driver (each) . .	45	38	39
Power seat	210	179	181
Bucket seats	147	125	127
Custom sport steering wheel	50	43	44
Tilt steering wheel	105	89	90
Sunroof	295	251	254
Firm ride & handling package	30	26	27
Power trunklid release	40	34	35
Full vinyl top, sedans	155	132	134
Landau vinyl top, coupes	215	183	185
Power windows			
Coupes	180	153	155
Sedans	255	217	220
Intermittent wiper system	49	42	43

Cadillac Cimarron

Cadillac Cimarron 4-door sedan

WHAT'S NEW FOR '83

The luxury-class version of GM's front-drive J-car family was a slow seller in its first model year. Cadillac has reacted by matching Cimarron against proven European sedans like the Audi 5000S, BMW 320i, Volvo GL, and Saab 900S sedan. A new ad campaign is designed to make the smallest Caddy seem like a strong contender in the sports sedan market with "bold new performance" from a "snappy new 2.0-liter electronically fuel-injected engine." Gone is last year's 1.8-liter carbureted powerplant (all 1983 Cadillac engines have fuel injection). The 2.0 is the stroked version of the small four, built by Chevy. It has new "swirl" intake ports and cylinder head design, revised camshaft, and a higher compression ratio. A new 5-speed overdrive manual transmission is now standard. All this, Cadillac claims, results in quicker acceleration and improved drivability. On the outside, Cimarron sports a new grille with thin vertical bars. A new option is a sunroof that tilts at the rear as well as sliding open. Electronically tuned AM/FM stereo radios and fold-down center armrest are other standard equipment additions.

EVALUATION

The Cimarron has suffered the same performance and mileage maladies as the rest of the '82 J-car clan, and sales suffered accordingly. The new engine yields discernibly better performance than the old one, but Cimarron is still far from eager compared to its rivals. Cadillac also is making hay about the new 5-speed manual, but the fact is that nearly all Cimarrons will be sold with automatic. J-car virtues continue (fine ride, good driving position, competent handling), but whether the nameplate says Cadillac or a Chevrolet, it's still the same basic car. Cadillac dresses up its version with plusher appointments and more equipment to do battle with a group of roadworthy Euro sedans and charges a lofty price, but the car's basic engineering is hardly altered. We think Cadillac is still going to have a hard time convincing buyers that the Cimarron is that much different—or better—than a Cavalier or any of the other less expensive Js.

EVALUATION CHECKLIST

Fuel economy	3	Cargo room	3
Driveability	3	Serviceability	3
Acceleration	3	Standard equipment	5
Braking	3	Body construction	4
Handling/roadholding	3	Paint/exterior finish	3
Driving position	4	Interior finish	4
Instruments/control	4	TOTAL POINTS	68
Visiblity	4		
Heating/ventilation	3	**RATING SCALE**	
Seat comfort	3	5 = Excellent	
Passenger room	3	4 = Very Good	
Ride	3	3 = Average/Acceptable	
Noise	4	2 = Fair	
Exit/entry	3	1 = Poor	

SPECIFICATIONS

	4-door sedan
Wheelbase (in.)	101.2
Overall length (in.)	173.1
Overall width (in.)	65.0
Overall height (in.)	52.0
Track front (in.)	55.4
Track rear (in.)	55.2
Curb weight (lbs.)	2639
Max. cargo vol. (cu. ft.)	12.0
Fuel tank capacity (gal.)	13.6
Seating capacity	5
Front headroom (in.)	38.2
Front shoulder room (in.)	53.1
Front legroom, max. (in.)	42.2
Rear headroom (in.)	37.5
Rear shoulder room (in.)	53.1
Rear legroom, min. (in.)	34.3

BODY/CHASSIS

Drivetrain layout: transverse front engine/front-wheel drive. **Suspension front:** independent, MacPherson struts, coil springs, telescopic shock absorbers, anti-roll bar. **Suspension rear:** independent; beam axle, trailing arms, coil springs, telescopic shock absorbers, anti-roll bar. **Steering:** rack-and-pinion power-assisted. **Turns lock-to-lock:** 2.5. **Turn diameter (ft.):** 38.2. **Brakes front:** 9.7-in. discs. **Brakes rear:** 7.9-in. drums. **Construction:** unit

POWERTRAINS

	ohv I-4
Bore × stroke (in.)	3.50× 3.15
Displacement (liters/cu. in.)	2.0/ 121

POWERTRAINS

	ohv I-4
Compression ratio	9.3:1
Fuel delivery	FI
Net bhp @ rpm	88@ 4800
Net torque @ rpm (lbs/ft)	110@ 2400
Availability	S/All
Final drive ratios	
5-speed OD manual	3.83:1
3-speed automatic	3.18:1[1]

1: 3.43:1 high-altitude areas

KEY bbl. = barrel (carburetor); **bhp** = brake horsepower (advertised); **Cal.** = California only. **Fed.** = Federal/49 state; **FI** = fuel injection; **ohv** = overhead valve; **ohc** = overhead cam; **I** = inline engine; **V** = V engine; **D** = diesel; **T** = turbocharged; **OD** = overdrive transmission; **S** = standard engine; **O** = optional engine.

PRICES

CIMARRON

	Retail Price	Dealer Cost	Low Price
4-door sedan.	$12215	$10909	$11909

STANDARD EQUIPMENT (included in above prices):

2.0 liter (121-cid) 4-cylinder engine, 5-speed overdrive manual transmission, power brakes, power steering, controlled-cycle wipers, air conditioning, tinted glass, AM/FM ETR stereo radio, digital clock, leather-faced bucket seats, electric remote-control door mirrors, leather-wrapped steering wheel, trunk carpeting, full instrumentation including tachometer, halogen headlamps, fog lamps.

OPTIONAL EQUIPMENT:

3-speed automatic transmission	320	272	275
Heavy-duty battery	25	21	22
Cruise control	170	145	147
Garage door opener.	165	140	142
Power door locks	170	145	147
Luggage rack.	98	83	84
Heavy-duty radiator	40	34	35

Prices are accurate at time of printing; subject to manufacturer's change

Radio equipment	Retail Price	Dealer Cost	Low Price
AM/FM stereo w/cassette	203	173	175
AM/FM stereo delete (credit)	(151)	(128)	(128)
Power antenna	55	47	48
6-way power driver's seat	210	179	181
Dual 6-way power front seats	420	357	361
Tilt steering wheel.	99	84	85
Sunroof	295	251	254
Astroroof	915	778	786
Power trunklid release	40	34	35
Power windows	255	217	220

Cadillac DeVille & Fleetwood

Cadillac DeVille 2-door coupe

WHAT'S NEW FOR '83

The full-size Cadillac looks about the same this year, but gets a few subtle mechanical refinements. Last year's optional 4.1-liter Buick-built gasoline V-6 has been withdrawn. Standard power remains the division's 4.1-liter (249-cid) gas V-8 with all-aluminum construction and standard digital electronic fuel injection. Minor internal tweaks give the "HT 4100" powerplant 10 more horsepower and 10 extra lbs/ft of torque compared to last year. A new wrinkle is that the engine's electronic control module now has the capability of signalling when it's time for service via a warning light on the dash.

Prices are accurate at time of printing; subject to manufacturer's change

EVALUATION

The 4.1-liter V-8 introduced in '82 has so far proven to be more reliable and economical than the ill-fated "V-8-6-4" variable-displacement engine. The complex digital electronic fuel injection can be costly to fix if it malfunctions, but this new system has apparently been as reliable as previous simpler setups in customer use. This smooth engine has to haul a lot of weight, however, and its EPA city rating of 17 mpg seems optimistic to us. But that probably won't matter to most Cadillac buyers, for whom fuel economy usually isn't a big priority. Otherwise, the full-size Cadillacs remain what they've always been: roomy, quiet, comfortable, and luxurious, with tolerable road manners, a silky ride, and bulky dimensions. Workmanship may not be what it once was, but the Cadillac name still has much allure for those seeking comfort and especially prestige.

EVALUATION CHECKLIST

Fuel economy	2	Cargo room	4
Driveability	4	Serviceability	3
Acceleration	2	Standard equipment	5
Braking	3	Body construction	4
Handling/roadholding	2	Paint/exterior finish	4
Driving position	4	Interior finish	4
Instruments/control	3	TOTAL POINTS	71
Visiblity	3		
Heating/ventilation	4	**RATING SCALE**	
Seat comfort	5	5 = Excellent	
Passenger room	4	4 = Very Good	
Ride	3	3 = Average/Acceptable	
Noise	5	2 = Fair	
Exit/entry	3	1 = Poor	

SPECIFICATIONS

	DeVille 2-door coupe	Fleetwood Brougham 2-door coupe	DeVille 4-door sedan	Fleetwood Brougham 4-door sedan
Wheelbase (in.)	121.5	121.5	121.5	121.5
Overall length (in.)	221.0	221.0	221.0	221.0
Overall width (in.)	75.4	75.4	75.3	75.3

SPECIFI- CATIONS	DeVille 2-door coupe	Fleetwood Brougham 2-door coupe	DeVille 4-door sedan	Fleetwood Brougham 4-door sedan
Overall height (in.)	54.6	54.6	55.6	56.7
Track front (in.)	61.7	61.7	61.7	61.7
Track rear (in.)	60.7	60.7	60.7	60.7
Curb weight (lbs.)	3935	3986	3993	4029
Max. cargo vol. (cu. ft.)	19.6	19.6	19.6	19.6
Fuel tank capacity (gal.)	24.5[1]	24.5[1]	24.5[1]	24.5[1]
Seating capacity	5	5	6	6
Front headroom (in.)	38.1	38.1	39.0	39.0
Front shoulder room (in.)	59.4	59.4	59.4	59.4
Front legroom, max. (in.)	42.0	42.0	42.0	42.0
Rear headroom (in.)	37.8	37.8	38.1	38.1
Rear shoulder room (in.)	58.6	58.6	59.4	59.4
Rear legroom, min. (in.)	41.7	40.6	42.3	41.2

1: 26.0 gal. w/diesel engine

BODY/CHASSIS

Drivetrain layout: longitudinal front engine/rear-wheel drive. **Suspension front:** independent, unequal-length upper and lower A-arms, coil springs, telescopic shock absorbers, anti-roll-bar. **Suspension rear:** rigid axle, four links, coil springs, telescopic shock absorbers. **Steering:** recirculating ball, power-assisted. **Turns lock-to-lock:** 3.2. **Turn diameter (ft.):** 40.5. **Brakes front:** 11.7-in. discs. **Brakes rear:** 11.0-in. drums. **Construction:** body-on-frame

POWERTRAINS

	ohv V-8	ohv V-8D
Bore × stroke (in.)	3.46× 3.30	4.06× 3.39
Displacement (liters/cu. in.)	4.1/ 249	5.7/ 350
Compression ratio	8.5:1	22.7:1
Fuel delivery	FI	FI
Net bhp @ rpm	135@ 4400	105@ 3200
Net torque @ rpm (lbs/ft)	200@ 2200	200@ 1600
Availability	S/All	O/All
Final drive ratios		
4-speed OD automatic	3.42:1[1]	2.93:1

1: 3.73:1 high-altitude areas

KEY bbl. = barrel (carburetor); **bhp** = brake horsepower (advertised); **Cal.** = California only. **Fed.** = Federal/49 state; **FI** = fuel injection; **ohv** = overhead valve; **ohc** = overhead cam; **I** = inline engine; **V** = V engine; **D** = diesel; **T** = turbocharged; **OD** = overdrive transmission; **S** = standard engine; **O** = optional engine.

Prices follow Cadillac Seville

Cadillac Eldorado

Cadillac Eldorado 2-door Touring Coupe

WHAT'S NEW FOR '83

A new premium sound system, minor exterior trim changes, and a few more standard horsepower highlight Cadillac's personal-luxury coupe. A new option on Eldorado is a sound system developed by GM's Delco Electronics Division and the Bose Corporation. It's tuned to the interior acoustics of each model in which it's offered, and has four integrated speaker/amp units, 50 watts per channel, and built-in Dolby noise reduction. Other stereo options also have been added. A revised grille has a more vertical theme and Cadillac script nameplate. Aluminum wheels are a new option. Inside, the base Eldo gets a new type of cloth trim and more color choices for the optional leather upholstery. The Touring Coupe model, introduced at mid-1982, has saddle-tan leather and vinyl trim. It's now available in "Sonora Saddle Firemist" (light brown) in addition to "Sable Black." The standard Cadillac-built 4.1-liter aluminum V-8 has 10 more horsepower and an additional 10 lbs/ft torque over last year.

EVALUATION

For a luxury coupe, Eldorado offers surprising handling and roadholding ability, due mainly to front-wheel drive and a well-thought-out four-wheel independent suspension. Ride is in the Cadillac tradition, as are the plush interior furnishings and numerous comfort and convenience gadgets. In the Touring Coupe (or with the optional touring suspension), the Eldorado takes on an even more roadworthy character without suffering any loss in comfort. The Touring Coupe is an unusual product for Cadillac, and it's a direction the division seems willing to explore further. The 4.1-liter V-8 hasn't suffered the reliability problems the variable-displacement V–8–6–4 did—at least so far—and its complex digital electronic fuel injection system has also been bug-free. Cadillac is dropping the Buick V-6 as an option mainly for image reasons, we suspect. As in its other applications at GM, the 350 diesel V-8 has an indifferent reliability record; we remain leery of it for that reason. Overall, there isn't a big difference between the Eldorado and the less expensive Buick Riviera or Olds Toronado. They're all swanky, impressive-looking personal-luxury models and good at what they were designed for, but aren't really our sort of car.

EVALUATION CHECKLIST

Fuel economy	3	Cargo room	3
Driveability	4	Serviceability	2
Acceleration	3	Standard equipment	5
Braking	3	Body construction	4
Handling/roadholding	3	Paint/exterior finish	4
Driving position	4	Interior finish	4
Instruments/control	2	TOTAL POINTS	68
Visiblity	3		
Heating/ventilation	4		
Seat comfort	4	**RATING SCALE**	
Passenger room	3	5 = Excellent	
Ride	3	4 = Very Good	
Noise	4	3 = Average/Acceptable	
Exit/entry	3	2 = Fair	
		1 = Poor	

SPECIFICATIONS

	2-door coupe
Wheelbase (in.)	114.0
Overall length (in.)	204.5
Overall width (in.)	70.6
Overall height (in.)	54.3
Track front (in.)	59.3
Track rear (in.)	60.6
Curb weight (lbs.)	3748
Max. cargo vol. (cu. ft.)	14.9
Fuel tank capacity (gal.)	20.3[1]
Seating capacity	5
Front headroom (in.)	37.9
Front shoulder room (in.)	56.1
Front legroom, max. (in.)	42.8
Rear headroom (in.)	37.9
Rear shoulder room (in.)	54.1
Rear legroom, min. (in.)	39.1

1:22.8 gal. w/diesel engine

BODY/CHASSIS

Drivetrain layout: longitudinal front engine/front-wheel drive. **Suspension front:** independent, torsion bars, unequal-length upper and lower control arms, telescopic shock absorbers, anti-roll bar. **Suspension rear:** independent, semi-trailing arms, coil springs, telescopic shock absorbers with electronic level control, anti-roll bar. **Steering:** recirculating ball, power-assisted. **Turns lock-to-lock:** 3.0. **Turn diameter (ft.):** 38.4. **Brakes front:** 10.4-in. discs. **Brakes rear:** 10.4-in. discs. **Construction:** body-on-frame

POWERTRAINS	ohv V-8	ohv V-8D
Bore × stroke (in.)	3.46× 3.30	4.06× 3.39
Displacement (liters/cu. in.)	4.1/ 249	5.7/ 350
Compression ratio	8.5:1	22.7:1
Fuel delivery	FI	FI
Net bhp @ rpm	135@ 4400	105@ 3200
Net torque @ rpm (lbs/ft)	200@ 2200	200@ 1600
Availability	S/All	O/All
Final drive ratios		
4-speed OD automatic	3.15:1¹	2.93:1

1: 3.36:1 high-altitude areas

KEY bbl. = barrel (carburetor); **bhp** = brake horsepower (advertised); **Cal.** = California only. **Fed.** = Federal/49 state; **FI** = fuel injection; **ohv** = overhead valve; **ohc** = overhead cam; **I** = inline engine; **V** = V engine; **D** = diesel; **T** = turbocharged; **OD** = overdrive transmission; **S** = standard engine; **O** = optional engine.

Prices follow Cadillac Seville

Cadillac Seville

WHAT'S NEW FOR '83

A bit more power for the standard engine, minor appearance

Cadillac Seville Elegante 4-door sedan

changes, and an advanced new stereo system are the main news for Cadillac's bustleback front-drive sedan. The "HT4100" all-aluminum V-8 introduced last year is boosted 10 horsepower and 10 lbs/ft of torque by means of detail internal modifications. The 4.1-liter Buick V-6 optional last year is gone. Returning is Oldsmobile's 350-cid diesel V-8 as the only engine option. Like other Cadillacs, the Seville gets a minor front-end redo with Cadillac script on the grille, clear lenses for parking/turn signal lamps, and new optional aluminum wheels. The new Delco/Bose premium sound system optional on Seville (as well as GM's E-body personal-luxury coupes) has an electronically tuned receiver, four enclosures containing speakers and amplifiers, and Dolby noise reduction, and is specifically tailored to match the Seville interior's sound characteristics.

EVALUATION

Predictably, much like last year's model. Compared with the lookalike Lincoln Continental 4-door, Seville offers the traction and space advantages of front-wheel drive, but the Lincoln is easier and likely cheaper to maintain with its more conventional front-engine/rear-drive arrangement. Cadillac's all-aluminum V-8 has so far proven reliable, but then it's only been on the market a year. As in other Caddys, the fortified '83 version gives Seville leisurely acceleration, but it's quiet and unobtrusive in operation, which is probably what matters most to buyers in this class. We wonder about the complex digital electronic fuel injection, particularly what it would cost to fix it if it ever goes sour, but the HT4100 is built in a highly automated plant, and Cadillac is claiming high levels of assembly quality for this engine. Only time and more owner experience will tell. We've commented elsewhere on the service record of Oldsmobile's diesel V-8. There's some reason to think newer engines may be less troublesome than the early ones, but in view of its price and performance penalties we don't strongly recommend it. In brief: equipped to the hilt and plush as can be, though the styling remains controversial (due to be changed for '84). Rates about equally with the baby Lincoln in most respects, but we marginally prefer the Continental as a total package.

EVALUATION CHECKLIST

Fuel economy	2	Cargo room	3
Driveability	3	Serviceability	3
Acceleration	2	Standard equipment	5
Braking	3	Body construction	4
Handling/roadholding	3	Paint/exterior finish	4
Driving position	4	Interior finish	4
Instruments/control	3	TOTAL POINTS	71
Visiblity	3		
Heating/ventilation	4	**RATING SCALE**	
Seat comfort	5	5 = Excellent	
Passenger room	4	4 = Very Good	
Ride	4	3 = Average/Acceptable	
Noise	5	2 = Fair	
Exit/entry	3	1 = Poor	

SPECIFICATIONS

	4-door sedan
Wheelbase (in.)	114.0
Overall length (in.)	204.8
Overall width (in.)	70.9
Overall height (in.)	54.3
Track front (in.)	59.3
Track rear (in.)	60.6
Curb weight (lbs.)	3844
Max. cargo vol. (cu. ft.)	14.5
Fuel tank capacity (gal.)	20.3[1]

SPECIFICATIONS

	4-door sedan
Seating capacity	5
Front headroom (in.)	38.1
Front shoulder room (in.)	55.7
Front legroom, max. (in.)	42.8
Rear headroom (in.)	37.3
Rear shoulder room (in.)	56.8
Rear legroom, min. (in.)	39.1

1:22.8 gal. w/diesel engine

BODY/CHASSIS

Drivetrain layout: longitudinal front engine/front-wheel drive. **Suspension front:** independent, torsion bars, control arms, telescopic shock absorbers, anti-roll bar. **Suspension rear:** independent, trailing arms, coil springs, telescopic shock absorbers with electronic level control, anti-roll bar. **Steering:** recirculating ball, variable-ratio, power-assisted. **Turns lock-to-lock:** 3.0. **Turn diameter (ft.):** 38.4. **Brakes front:** 10.4-in. discs. **Brakes rear:** 10.4-in. discs. **Construction:** body-on-frame

POWERTRAINS

	ohv V-8	ohv V-8D
Bore × stroke (in.)	3.46× 3.30	4.06× 3.39
Displacement (liters/cu. in.)	4.1/ 249	5.7/ 350
Compression ratio	8.5:1	22.7:1
Fuel delivery	FI	FI
Net bhp @ rpm	135@ 4400	105@ 3200
Net torque @ rpm (lbs/ft)	200@ 2200	200@ 1600
Availability	S/All	O/All

POWERTRAINS

	ohv V-8	ohv V-8D
Final drive ratios		
4-speed OD automatic	3.15:1[1]	2.93:1

1: 3.36:1 high-altitude areas

KEY bbl. = barrel (carburetor); **bhp** = brake horsepower (advertised); **Cal.** = California only. **Fed.** = Federal/49 state; **FI** = fuel injection; **ohv** = overhead valve; **ohc** = overhead cam; **I** = inline engine; **V** = V engine; **D** = diesel; **T** = turbocharged; **OD** = overdrive transmission; **S** = standard engine; **O** = optional engine.

PRICES

	Retail Price	Dealer Cost	Low Price
DEVILLE			
Coupe Deville 2-door	$15970	$13624	$15124
Sedan Deville 4-door	16441	14026	15526
ELDORADO			
2-door coupe.	19334	16494	19000
FLEETWOOD			
Brougham 2-door coupe	18688	15943	17443
Brougham 4-door sedan	19182	16364	17864
Limousine	29323	25045	27545
Formal limousine	30349	25890	28390
SEVILLE			
4-door sedan.	21440	18290	20790

STANDARD EQUIPMENT (included in above prices):

DeVille: 4.1-liter (250-cid) V-8 engine with fuel injection, automatic transmission, power brakes, power steering, WSW steel-belted radial tires, automatic climate-control air conditioning, AM/FM stereo signal-seeking digital-display radio, corning lights, lamp monitors, power windows, power antenna, 6-way power seat, tinted glass, wheel covers, remote-control left mirror, right visor vanity mirror, automatic parking brake release, stowaway spare tire. **Fleetwood Brougham:** DeVille equipment plus 4-wheel power disc brakes, electronic level control, remote-control right mirror, 45/55 dual-comfort front seats, opera lamps, controlled-cycle wipers. **Fleetwood Limousines:** DeVille equipment less 6-way power seat on Formal Limousine, plus electronic level control, remote-control right mirror, accent striping, opera lamps. **Eldorado:** 4.1-liter (250-cid) V-8 engine with fuel injection, automatic transmission, 4-wheel power disc brakes, power steering, WSW steel-belted radial tires, electronic level control, automatic climate-control air conditioning, twilight sentinel, 55/45 dual-comfort front seats w/6-way driver's side power adjuster, side window defoggers, power door locks, power windows, illuminated entry system, controlled-cycle

Prices are accurate at time of printing; subject to manufacturer's change

wipers, AM/FM stereo signal-seeking digital-display radio, automatic power antenna, remote-control mirrors, electric trunklid release w/power pull-down, cornering lights, lamp monitors, seatbelt chimes, column-mounted headlamp dimmer, accent striping, tinted glass, automatic parking brake release, right vanity mirror, stowaway spare tire, carpeted trunk. **Seville:** 4.1-liter (250-cid) V-8 engine, automatic transmission, 4-wheel power disc brakes, power steering, padded vinyl roof, AM/FM stereo signal-seeking radio w/digital display & automatic power antenna, automatic climate control, electronic level control, dual remote-control mirrors, illuminated entry system, twilight sentinel, electric trunklid release w/power pull-down, power door locks, power windows, cornering lights, tilt/telescope steering wheel, controlled-cycle wipers, lamp monitors, passenger seat recliner, rear seat reading lamps, power seats (6-way driver, 2-way passenger), tinted glass, stowaway spare tire, fuel monitor system, carpeted trunk, rear window defogger.

OPTIONAL EQUIPMENT:

	Retail Price	Dealer Cost	Low Price
Accent striping Fleetwood Brougham,			
DeVille	$ 77	$ 65	$ 66
Astroroof	1225	1029	1040
d'Elegance package, Brougham			
Cloth upholstery	1250	1050	1061
Leather upholstery	1800	1512	1528
Cruise control	185	155	157
Rear window defogger (std. Seville)	160	135	137
DeVille d'Elegance package	1150	966	976
Automatic door locks	157	132	134
Dual-comfort front seats, DeVille	225	189	191
Biarritz package, Eldorado	3395	2852	2881
Eldorado cabriolet package	415	349	353
Electronic level control, DeVille	203	171	173
Engine block heater	27	23	24
Garage door opener	140	118	120
100-amp. generator	50	42	43
Headlamp control, Guidematic	93	78	79
Heavy-duty ride package, DeVilles,			
Brougham 4-Door	319	268	271
Illuminated entry system	76	64	65
Digital instrument cluster	238	200	203
Leather upholstery			
Seville	680	571	577
DeVille	515	433	438
Others ex. limousines	550	462	467
Memory seat (NA limousines)	185	155	157
Illuminated visor vanity mirrors	140	118	120
Electric power mirrors w/left thermometer,			
all ex. DeVille	99	83	84

Prices are accurate at time of printing; subject to manufacturer's change

CONSUMER GUIDE®

	Retail Price	Dealer Cost	Low Price
Two-tone paint			
Regular colors, ex. limousines, Seville..................	345	290	293
w/Firemist colors, ex. limousines, Seville....................	465	391	395
Standard radio plus			
8-track tape	299	251	254
Cassette tape	299	251	254
Cassette tape & CB	577	485	490
Cassette tape, Bose Spkrs	895	752	760
Power recliner			
Driver (w/dual-comfort seats)	155	130	132
Passenger, including power adjustment (w/Dual-comfort seats)	365	307	311
Passenger (w/notchback seat), DeVille ..	155	130	132
Padded vinyl roof, DeVilles	280	235	238
Elegante package, Seville	3879	3258	3291
Tilt & Telescope steering wheel	179	150	152
Theft deterrent system	185	155	157
Puncture sealing tires.............	135	113	115
Touring Cpe. Pkg., Eldorado	1975	1659	1676
Touring suspension, Eldorado, Seville	115	97	98
Trumpet horn (NA Seville)	38	32	33
Power trunklid release & pull-down, DeVille, Limousines	120	101	103
Twilight sentinel, DeVilles & Limousines ..	79	66	67
Controlled-cycle wipers, DeVille........	60	50	51

Chevrolet Camaro

WHAT'S NEW FOR '83

A sales winner in '82, this sexy third-generation ponycar heads into its first full model year with two new transmission choices and minor options changes. The three-model lineup spanning four engines is unchanged, but a 5-speed overdrive manual gearbox is a new extra for the base Sport Coupe, and is standard for the V-6 Berlinetta and V-8 Z-28. Also added is a 4-speed overdrive automatic with lockup torque converter effective in all ratios except first. It's standard on the Z-28 with the "Cross-Fire" fuel-injected V-8 and optional on other models. Other refinements include a matching front passenger's chair for the optional "Conteur" multi-adjustable driver's seat, new tri-tone upholstery with repeating Camaro

Prices are accurate at time of printing; subject to manufacturer's change

Chevrolet Camaro Z-28 2-door coupe

logo for Z-28s, and electronic tuning for all optional factory radios.

EVALUATION

Smaller and more agile than pre-1982 models, but still a fairly heavyweight "image" car in the American tradition. The base Sport Coupe and mid-range Berlinetta offer a comfortable ride for a live-axle design plus stable, predictable cornering response. The Z-28's very firm chassis delivers exceptionally high roadholding, but you pay for it with a stiff bucking-bronco ride over all but the smoothest pavement. Though once considered a "small-block," the Chevy 305 V-8 moves the Camaro along in fine style, but we prefer the Division's high-revving 2.8-liter V-6 as the best choice for performance with some semblance of economy. Revised shift linkage on both 4- and 5-speed manual transmissions make swapping gears a lot easier than on the '82s, but lever action is still notchy, and the high shifter placement can lead to a form of tennis elbow. We don't doubt most buyers will opt for automatic. Snug driving position and good control placement. Cabin space adequate in front, mostly for show in the back. Not much luggage room despite flip-down back seat, but it's styling that sells this car, not utility. Summary: genuine date bait, and about the hottest-looking car you can drive now apart from its Pontiac Firebird cousin or—when it arrives—the '83 Corvette. Despite its performance pretentions, Z-28 isn't as fast or as practical as the H.O. V-8 Ford Mustang/Mercury Capri, and it costs more, too.

EVALUATION CHECKLIST
(Z-28)

Fuel economy	2	Cargo room	2
Driveability	3	Serviceability	3
Acceleration	4	Standard equipment	4
Braking	4	Body construction	4
Handling/roadholding	4	Paint/exterior finish	4
Driving position	4	Interior finish	4
Instruments/control	4	TOTAL POINTS	65
Visiblity	3		
Heating/ventilation	3	**RATING SCALE**	
Seat comfort	3	5 = Excellent	
Passenger room	2	4 = Very Good	
Ride	2	3 = Average/Acceptable	
Noise	2	2 = Fair	
Exit/entry	3	1 = Poor	

SPECIFICATIONS

	2-door coupe
Wheelbase (in.)	101.0
Overall length (in.)	187.8
Overall width (in.)	72.0
Overall height (in.)	49.8
Track front (in.)	60.7
Track rear (in.)	61.6
Curb weight (lbs.)	3031
Max. cargo vol. (cu. ft.)	8.7/30.9
Fuel tank capacity (gal.)	16.0[1]
Seating capacity	4
Front headroom (in.)	37.0
Front shoulder room (in.)	57.4
Front legroom, max. (in.)	43.0
Rear headroom (in.)	35.6
Rear shoulder room (in.)	56.3
Rear legroom, min. (in.)	28.6

1: average all models w/base equipment

BODY/CHASSIS

Drivetrain layout: longitudinal front engine/rear-wheel drive. **Suspension front:** independent, modified MacPherson struts, lower control arms, coil springs, telescopic shock absorbers, anti-roll bar. **Suspension rear:** rigid axle, torque tube, longitudinal control arms, coil springs, panhard rod, telescopic shock absorbers, anti-roll bar. **Steering:** recirculating ball, power-assisted. **Turns lock-to-lock:** 2.5-3.0. **Turn diameter (ft.):** 36.9. **Brakes front:** 10.5-in. discs. **Brakes rear:** 9.5-in. drums (discs opt.). **Construction:** unit

POWERTRAINS	ohv I-4	ohv V-6	ohv V-8	ohv V-8
Bore × stroke (in.)	4.00× 3.00	3.50× 2.99	3.74× 3.48	3.74× 3.48
Displacement (liter/cu. in.)	2.5/ 151	2.8/ 173	5.0/ 305	5.0/ 305
Compression ratio	8.2:1	8.5:1	8.6:1	9.5:1
Fuel delivery	FI	2bbl.	4bbl.	FI
Net bhp @ rpm	90@ 4000	112@ 5100	150@ 4000	175@ 4200
Net torque @ rpm (lbs/ft)	132@ 2800	148@ 2400	240@ 2400	250@ 2800
Availability	S/All[1]	O/All[2]	O/All[3]	S/All[4]

1: opt. Berlinetta; NA Z-28
2: std. Berlinetta; opt. Sport coupe; NA Z-28
3: std. Z-28; opt. Berlinetta only
4: Z-28 only

Final drive ratios

4-speed manual	3.42:1			
5-speed OD manual	3.73:1	3.42:1	3.73:1	
3-speed automatic	3.08:1	3.08:1		
4-speed OD automatic	3.42:1	3.23:1	3.08:1[1]	2.93:1[2]

1: 3.23:1 on Z-28 2: 3.23:1 opt.

KEY bbl. = barrel (carburetor); **bhp** = brake horsepower (advertised); **Cal.** = California only. **Fed.** = Federal/49 state; **FI** = fuel injection; **ohv** = overhead valve; **ohc** = overhead cam; **I** = inline engine; **V** = V engine; **D** = diesel; **T** = turbocharged; **OD** = overdrive transmission; **S** = standard engine; **O** = optional engine.

PRICES

CAMARO	Retail Price	Dealer Cost	Low Price
2-door Sport Coupe.	$ 8036	$ 7177	$ 8000
Berlinetta 2-door coupe	9881	8825	9875
Z-28 2-door coupe	10336	9231	10300

STANDARD EQUIPMENT (included in above prices):

2.5 liter (151-cid) 4-cylinder engine with electronic fuel injection, 4-speed manual transmission, power steering, power brakes, center console, full carpeting, bucket seats, sport mirrors, fold-down rear seatback. **Berlinetta adds:** 2.8 liter (173-cid) V-6 engine, body color sport mirrors with left remote, full instrumentation, deluxe luggage compartment trim, quartz analog clock, Smooth-Ride suspension system, Custom interior trim, courtesy lights, Quiet Sound Group. **Z-28** has over base Sport Coupe: 5.0-liter (305-cid) V-8 engine, handling suspension, dual horns, leather wrapped steering wheel, full instrumentation, black exterior accents, front air dam, special hood, rear deck spoiler, dual resonators and tailpipes, body color sport mirrors with left remote, courtesy lights, quartz analog clock.

OPTIONAL EQUIPMENT:

Engines			
2.8-liter (173-cid) V-6, Sport Coupe . . .	$ 150	$ 128	$ 130
5.0-liter (305.cid) V-8 (std. Z-28)			
Sport Coupe	350	298	301
Berlinetta	225	191	193
5.0-liter (305-cid) V-8 with ''Cross-Fire''			
fuel injection, Z-28 only.	450	383	387
Transmissions			
5-speed manual			
Sport Coupe	125	106	108
Z-28 Berlinetta.	NC	NC	NC
3-speed automatic			
Sport Coupe	425	361	365
Berlinetta	195	166	168
4-speed automatic w/overdrive			
Sport Coupe	525	446	451
Z-28, Berlinetta	295	251	254
Air conditioning	725	616	623
Optional axle ratio	21	18	19
Locking rear axle	95	81	82
Heavy-duty battery	25	21	22
Four-wheel disc brakes (V-8s only)	179	152	154
Cargo Area cover	64	54	55
Quartz analog clock, Sport Coupe	35	30	31

Prices are accurate at time of printing; subject to manufacturer's change

	Retail Price	Dealer Cost	Low Price
Quartz digital clock (requires radio)			
Sport Coupe.	39	33	34
Heavy-duty cooling system			
w/o air cond.	70	60	61
w/air cond.	40	34	35
Electric rear-window defroster.	135	115	116
Power door locks	120	102	104
Tinted glass	105	89	90
Power hatch release	40	34	35
Halogen hi-beam headlamps.	10	9	10
Dual horns (std. Berlinetta)	12	10	11
Special instrumentation, Sport Coupe	149	127	129
Auxiliary lighting.	52	44	45
Deluxe luggage compartment trim			
(std. Berlinetta).	164	139	141
Sport mirrors, left remote, Sport Coupe . .	51	43	44
Dual electric remote-control sport mirrors			
Sport Coupe.	137	116	118
Berlinetta, Z-28.	89	76	77
Quiet sound group (std. Berlinetta)			
Sport Coupe.	82	70	71
Z-28	72	61	62
Radio equipment (stereos include extended-range speaker system)			
AM	112	95	96
AM/FM	171	145	147
AM/FM stereo ETR			
Sport Coupe	302	257	260
Z-28 or Berlinetta	267	227	230
AM/FM stereo cassette w/seek & scan, ETR, clock			
Z-28 Berlinetta	520	442	447
Sport Coupe	555	472	477
Removable glass roof panels	825	701	709
Power seat, 6-way driver's	210	179	181
Auto-speed control	170	145	147
Rear spoiler (std. Z-28)	69	59	60
Comfortilt steering wheel	105	89	90
F41 sport suspension, Sport Coupe	49	42	43
Seats/Trim			
Cloth bucket seat.	28	24	25
LS Conteur cloth bucket seats, Z-28 . . .	375	319	323
Custom trim (ex. Berlinetta)	299	254	257
Custom trim w/LS Conteur bucket seat. .	650	553	559
Power windows	180	153	155
Intermittent wipers	49	42	43
Rear window wiper/washer	120	102	104

Prices are accurate at time of printing; subject to manufacturer's change

CONSUMER GUIDE®

Chevrolet Caprice & Impala

Chevrolet Caprice 4-door sedan

WHAT'S NEW FOR '83

They're nearing the end of the road, but the B-body full-size Chevys are back with more and less of the same. In the "less" column, the Caprice coupe and Impala wagon are cancelled, as is the previously optional 267-cid Chevy-built V-8, which never found much customer favor. Styling, options, dimensions, and mechanicals are basically unchanged.

EVALUATION

Ties in virtually all respects with the full-size Ford (now called LTD Crown Victoria). Despite its size, Caprice/Impala can be surprisingly well-behaved off the straight and narrow when equipped with the low-cost F41 suspension package. Performance is lackluster with any available engine, especially the diesel, and mileage isn't miraculous, either. Reliability problems with GM's diesel V-8s continue to surface, and make us leery of recommending this engine to anyone except perhaps high-mileage owners who must have a car this large and want maximum fuel economy. Even then, you might be better off with the base V-6. Our view: the best big-car buy by a small margin, but aging just as rapidly as other members of this fast-dying breed.

EVALUATION CHECKLIST

Fuel economy 2
Driveability. 4
Acceleration. 3
Braking 3
Handling/roadholding 3
Driving position 4
Instruments/control. 3
Visiblity 3
Heating/ventilation 4
Seat comfort 4
Passenger room 5
Ride 3
Noise 4
Exit/entry. 4

Cargo room. 5
Serviceability 3
Standard equipment. 3
Body construction 4
Paint/exterior finish 4
Interior finish 4
TOTAL POINTS 72

RATING SCALE
5 = Excellent
4 = Very Good
3 = Average/Acceptable
2 = Fair
1 = Poor

SPECIFICATIONS

	4-door sedan	5-door wagon
Wheelbase (in.)	116.0	116.0
Overall length (in.)	212.1	215.1
Overall width (in.)	75.3	79.3
Overall height (in.)	56.4	58.1
Track front (in.)	61.8	62.2
Track rear (in.)	60.8	64.1
Curb weight (lbs.)	3663[1]	4215[2]
Max. cargo vol. (cu. ft.)	20.9	87.9
Fuel tank capacity (gal.)	25[2]	22
Seating capacity	5/6	5/6
Front headroom (in.)	39.2	39.6
Front shoulder room (in.)	60.9	60.9
Front legroom, max. (in.)	42.2	42.2
Rear headroom (in.)	38.0	39.3
Rear shoulder room (in.)	60.9	60.9
Rear legroom, min. (in.)	38.3	37.8

1: average all models w/base equipment
2: 27 gal. w/diesel engine

BODY/CHASSIS

Drivetrain layout: longitudinal front engine/rear-wheel drive. **Suspension front:** independent, unequal-length upper and lower A-arms, coil springs, telescopic shock absorbers, anti-roll bar. **Suspension rear:** rigid axle, four links, coil springs, telescopic shock absorbers (anti-roll bar optional). **Steering:** recirculating ball, power-assisted. **Turns lock-to-lock:** 3.2. **Turn diameter (ft.):** 39.2. **Brakes front:** 11.0-in. discs (11.9-in. wagon). **Brakes rear:** 9.5-in. drums (11.0-in. wagon). **Construction:** body-on-frame

POWERTRAINS	ohv V-6	ohv V-8	ohv V-8D	ohv V-6
Bore × stroke (in.)	3.74× 3.48	3.74× 3.48	4.06× 3.39	3.80× 3.40
Displacement (liter/cu. in.)	3.8/ 229	5.0/ 305	5.7/ 350	3.8/ 231
Compression ratio	8.6:1	8.6:1	22.1:1	8.0:1
Fuel delivery	2bbl.	4bbl.	FI	2bbl.
Net bhp @ rpm	110@ 4000	150@ 4000	105@ 3200	110@ 3800
Net torque @ rpm (lbs/ft)	190@ 1600	240@ 2400	200@ 1600	190@ 1600
Availability	S/Fed.	O/All[1]	O/All	S/Cal.

1: std. wagon; opt. Sedans

Final drive ratios

3-speed automatic	2.56:1[1]	2.41:1	2.41:1[2]	2.73:1
4-speed OD automatic		2.73:1	2.93:1	

1: 2.73:1 req. w/AC   2: 2.56:1 wagon

KEY bbl. = barrel (carburetor); **bhp** = brake horsepower (advertised); **Cal.** = California only. **Fed.** = Federal/49 state; **FI** = fuel injection; **ohv** = overhead valve; **ohc** = overhead cam; **I** = inline engine; **V** = V engine; **D** = diesel; **T** = turbocharged; **OD** = overdrive transmission; **S** = standard engine; **O** = optional engine.

PRICES

CAPRICE/IMPALA	Retail Price	Dealer Cost	Low Price
Impala 4-door sedan	$8331	$7191	$8191

Prices are accurate at time of printing; subject to manufacturer's change

	Retail Price	Dealer Cost	Low Price
Caprice Classic 4-door sedan	8802	7598	8598
Caprice Classic 5-door wagon	9518	8216	9216

STANDARD EQUIPMENT (included in above prices):

3.8-liter (229-cid) V-6 engine, 3-speed automatic transmission, power brakes, power steering, carpeting, knit cloth bench seat, lighter, P205/75R-15 BSW steel-belted radial tires. **Caprice Classic** adds: electric clock, dual horns, wheel opening moldings, quiet sound group, stand-up hood ornament, carpeted lower door panels. **Wagon** has Caprice Classic equipment, plus 5.0-liter V-8 2-bbl. engine, vinyl bench seats and interior, P225/75R-15 BSW steel-belted radial-ply tires.

OPTIONAL EQUIPMENT:

Engines			
5.0-liter (305-cid) V-8 4-bbl.			
Sedans	$ 225	$ 191	$ 193
Wagon	STD	STD	STD
5.7-liter (350-cid) V-8 diesel			
Sedans	700	595	601
Wagon	525	446	451
4-speed automatic overdrive transmission .	175	149	151
Vinyl bench seat, sedan	28	24	25
Knit cloth 50/50 seat			
Sedan	257	218	221
Wagon	285	242	245
Special custom cloth 50/50 seat	452	384	388
Four-season air conditioning	725	616	623
Limited-slip differential	95	81	82
Heavy-duty battery, gas engine	25	21	22
Heavy-duty battery, diesel engine (2)	50	43	44
Bumper guards	66	56	57
Roof carrier, wagon	150	128	130
Digital electric clock			
Impala	66	56	57
Caprice Classic	34	29	30
Electric clock, Impala	35	30	31
Cold-climate package	99	84	85
Heavy-duty cooling			
w/o air conditioning	70	60	61
w/air conditioning	40	34	35
Rear defogger	135	115	117
Power door locks	170	145	147
Estate equipment, wagon	307	261	264
Floor carpeting			
Load floor, wagon	89	76	77

Prices are accurate at time of printing; subject to manufacturer's change

	Retail Price	Dealer Cost	Low Price
Deluxe cargo area, wagon	129	110	112
Gauge package.	64	54	55
Tinted glass	105	89	90
Halogen high-beam headlamps	10	9	10
Cornering lamps.	55	47	48
Auxiliary lighting			
Impala sedan	42	32	33
Caprice Classic	32	36	37
Deluxe luggage compartment (ex. wagon) .	59	50	51
Custom two-tone paint	141	120	122
Quiet sound group, Impala	66	56	57
Radio equipment			
AM	112	95	96
AM/FM	171	145	147
AM/FM stereo	198	168	170
AM/FM stereo w/cassette tape	298	253	256
Power seat (50/50 seat required).	210	179	181
Automatic speed control	170	145	147
Comfortilt steering wheel	105	89	90
Superlift rear shock absorbers, wagon . . .	64	54	55
Heavy-duty suspension.	26	22	23
Sport suspension (ex. wagon), F41	49	42	43
Power tailgate lock	49	42	43
Puncture-sealant tires			
Wagon	132	111	113
Others	106	89	90
Power trunk opener.	40	34	35
Value appearance group, Impala	118	100	102
Vinyl top (ex. wagon)	180	153	155
Power windows	255	217	220
Intermittent wiper system	49	42	43

Chevrolet Cavalier

WHAT'S NEW FOR '83

A stronger engine, new 5-speed manual gearbox option, reduced equipment for more competitive prices, and a new convertible mark Chevy's front-drive subcompact in its sophomore year. The overhead-valve J-car four is stroked to 2.0 liters (121 cid) and gets higher compression, electronic throttle-body fuel injection to replace last year's carburetor, and a "cyclonic" cylinder head design said to promote faster

Prices are accurate at time of printing; subject to manufacturer's change

Chevrolet Cavalier CS 4-door sedan

fuel burning. The result is 10 percent more torque to answer complaints about the '82 Cavalier's sluggishness. The 5-speed overdrive manual transaxle, an extra-cost alternative to the standard 4-speed and supplied by Isuzu of Japan, is offered for the same reason. Otherwise, the Chevy J remains the same, except that some formerly standard equipment has been made optional to help hold the line on prices, another thing customers objected to last year. The upper series is renamed CS. The previous CL designation now applies to a package option that restores some, but not all, of the "lost" items. Coming in January is a 4-passenger drop-top model, a conversion carried out by the American Sunroof Corporation in Lansing, Michigan. Standard equipment includes power top, steering, brakes, and windows, plus the firmer F41 suspension package.

EVALUATION

More power, more models, and revamped equipment and pricing signal that GM is starting over with all the J-cars, not just Cavalier. The new 2.0-liter injected engine actually has marginally less rated horsepower than last year's 1.8-liter carbureted unit, but its greater torque gives Cavalier noticeably better pickup with either manual or automatic, especially from standstill. Even so, Chevy only claims 15.9 seconds in the 0–60 mph test (down from 17.5), which is hardly sparkling. The main problem is excess weight. The Js are heavy for their size next to competitors like the Honda Accord or Nissan Stanza, and feel heavier and far less agile in turns. Conversely, ride smoothness and noise isolation are both good for the class, which adds to the "little luxury car" feel, aided by tight construction and good use of sound-deadening materials. Assessment: performance more livable now, but still not tops in value for money. Scores mainly for refinement, fit and finish, and Chevy's huge dealer network.

EVALUATION CHECKLIST

Fuel economy	4	Cargo room	3
Driveability	3	Serviceability	3
Acceleration	3	Standard equipment	3
Braking	3	Body construction	4
Handling/roadholding	3	Paint/exterior finish	4
Driving position	4	Interior finish	4
Instruments/control	3	TOTAL POINTS	69
Visiblity	4		
Heating/ventilation	4	**RATING SCALE**	
Seat comfort	3	5 = Excellent	
Passenger room	3	4 = Very Good	
Ride	4	3 = Average/Acceptable	
Noise	4	2 = Fair	
Exit/entry	3	1 = Poor	

SPECIFICATIONS

	3-door coupe	2-door sedan	4-door sedan	5-door wagon
Wheelbase (in.)	101.2	101.2	101.2	101.2
Overall length (in.)	173.5	170.9	172.4	173.0
Overall width (in.)	66.0	66.0	66.3	66.3
Overall height (in.)	51.9	52.0	53.9	54.4
Track front (in.)	55.4	55.4	55.4	55.4
Track rear (in.)	55.2	55.2	55.2	55.2
Curb weight (lbs.)	2443	2381	2427	2486
Max. cargo vol. (cu. ft.)	16.0/ 38.5	13.2	13.6	34.1/ 64.4
Fuel tank capacity (gal.)	14.0	14.0	14.0	14.0
Seating capacity	4/5	4/5	4/5	4/5
Front headroom (in.)	37.6	37.7	38.5	38.4
Front shoulder room (in.)	53.7	53.7	53.7	53.7
Front legroom, max. (in.)	42.1	42.1	42.2	42.2
Rear headroom (in.)	36.5	36.5	37.8	38.9
Rear shoulder room (in.)	52.5	52.5	53.7	53.7

SPECIFICATIONS

	3-door coupe	2-door sedan	4-door sedan	5-door wagon
Rear legroom, min. (in.)	30.9	31.2	34.3	33.1

BODY/CHASSIS

Drivetrain layout: transverse front engine/rear-wheel drive. **Suspension front:** independent, MacPherson struts, lower control arms, coil springs, telescopic shock absorbers, anti-roll bar. **Suspension rear:** semi-independent, beam axle, trailing arms, coil springs, telescopic shock absorbers, anti-roll bar optional. **Steering:** rack-and-pinion. **Turns lock-to-lock:** 4.0 manual, 2.9 power. **Turn diameter (ft.):** 34.7. **Brakes front:** 9.7-in. discs. **Brakes rear:** 7.9-in. drums. **Construction:** unit

POWERTRAINS

	ohv I-4
Bore × stroke (in.)	3.50× 3.15
Displacement (liter/cu. in.)	2.0/ 121
Compression ratio	9.3:1
Fuel delivery	FI
Net bhp @ rpm	86@ 4900
Net torque @ rpm (lbs/ft)	110@ 3000
Availability	S/All
Final drive ratios	
4-speed OD manual	3.32:1
5-speed OD manual	2.83:1
3-speed automatic	3.18:1[1]

1: 3.73:1 opt.

KEY bbl. = barrel (carburetor); **bhp** = brake horsepower (advertised); **Cal.** = California only. **Fed.** = Federal/49 state; **FI** = fuel injection; **ohv** = overhead valve; **ohc** = overhead cam; **I** = inline engine; **V** = V engine; **D** = diesel; **T** = turbocharged; **OD** = overdrive transmission; **S** = standard engine; **O** = optional engine.

PRICES

CAVALIER	Retail Price	Dealer Cost	Low Price
2-door sedan	$5888	$5435	$5785
4-door sedan	5999	5531	5881
5-door wagon	6141	5669	6019
CS 2-door sedan	6363	5683	6083
CS 3-door coupe	6549	5847	6247
CS 4-door sedan	6484	5791	6191
CS 5-door wagon	6633	5924	6324

STANDARD EQUIPMENT (included in above prices):

2.0-liter (121-cid) 4-cylinder fuel-injected engine, 4-speed manual transmission, reclining front bucket seats, power brakes, electric rear-window defroster, remote trunk/hatchback/tailgate release, full carpeting, trip odometer, cigarette lighter, bumper rub strips. **CS adds:** AM radio, tinted glass, halogen headlights, auxiliary lighting, left remote & right mirror, intermittent wipers, gauge package, leather-wrapped steering wheel, Custom interior trim.

OPTIONAL EQUIPMENT:

	Retail	Dealer	Low
Air conditioning	$ 625	$ 531	$ 537
3-speed automatic transmission	395	336	340
Five-speed manual	75	64	65
Optional axle ratio	21	18	19
Heavy-duty battery	25	21	22
CS equipment pkg.			
CS coupe	696	592	598
CS wagon	657	558	564
CS 2-door	577	490	495
CS 4-door	607	516	522
Cargo area cover	64	54	55
Rear defogger	125	106	108
Power door locks			
2-door sedan, coupe	120	102	104
4-door sedan, wagon	170	145	147
Gauge package	69	59	60
Tinted glass	90	77	78
Halogen headlamps	10	9	10
Special instrumentation, CS	139	118	120
Heavy-duty radiator			
w/air conditioning	40	34	35
w/o air conditioning	70	60	61
Radio equipment			
AM (std. CS)	112	95	96

Prices are accurate at time of printing; subject to manufacturer's change

	Retail Price	Dealer Cost	Low Price
AM/FM			
Base models	171	145	147
CS models	82	70	71
AM/FM stereo ETR w/clock			
Base	277	235	238
CS	177	150	152
AM/FM stereo ETR w/cassette & clock			
Base	377	320	324
CS	277	235	238
Radio delete (credit)	(56)	(48)	(48)
Roof luggage carrier	98	83	84
Power 6-way driver's seat	210	179	181
Speed control	170	145	147
Power steering	199	169	171
Tilt steering wheel	99	84	85
Sunroof	295	251	254
Sport suspension	49	42	43
Power windows			
2-door sedan, coupe	180	153	155
4-door sedan, wagon	255	217	220
Rear washer/wiper	117	99	101
Intermittent wipers	49	42	43

Chevrolet Celebrity

Chevrolet Celebrity CL 4-door sedan

WHAT'S NEW FOR '83

Out last January, Chevy's member of the front-drive A-body intermediate quartet is a complete carryover into its first full model year. Although initially listed as an option, the Oldsmobile 4.3-liter (262-cid) V-6 diesel engine becomes officially available for Celebrity from the start of '83 production. Minor equipment changes since introduction include electronic instead of mechanical tuning for all extra-cost factory radios (a pushbutton AM set is standard) and deletion of the 8-track tape player option.

EVALUATION

Quieter, softer-riding, and altogether more big-car in feel than the X-body Citation even though it shares much under the skin. Not a strong performer with any of the three available engines, though the gas V-6 borders on peppy and the diesel V-6 is surprisingly refined for a compression-ignition engine. The standard chassis is set for the soft ride most big-car buyers like, but we'd prefer slightly tighter spring rates and shock damping to get rid of the front-end bobbing that can be set up by gently rolling waves taken quickly. Body lean is not excessive for a family car, and in general the Celebrity and its cousins are more capable than they have to be given their target market. The standard power steering is geared fairly high for minimal wheel flailing and is accurate, but effort is too light and lacks adequate feel in the straight-ahead position. Interior affords sufficient space for three adults in back provided front seaters compromise on leg space. Good outward vision, well-chosen driving position, tidy if uninspired dash all make you feel at home behind the wheel. Trunk is not as large as it looks from outside. Workmanship, especially paint finish, isn't the best, and the engine room is crowded with either V-6, which doesn't bode well for maintenance costs.

EVALUATION CHECKLIST

Fuel economy	3	Cargo room	3
Driveability	4	Serviceability	2
Acceleration	3	Standard equipment	3
Braking	4	Body construction	4
Handling/roadholding	4	Paint/exterior finish	3
Driving position	3	Interior finish	3
Instruments/control	3	TOTAL POINTS	69
Visiblity	4		
Heating/ventilation	4	**RATING SCALE**	
Seat comfort	4	5 = Excellent	
Passenger room	3	4 = Very Good	
Ride	4	3 = Average/Acceptable	
Noise	4	2 = Fair	
Exit/entry	4	1 = Poor	

SPECIFICATIONS

	2-door coupe	4-door sedan
Wheelbase (in.)	104.9	104.9
Overall length (in.)	188.3	188.3
Overall width (in.)	69.3	67.8
Overall height (in.)	53.7	53.7
Track front (in.)	58.7	58.7
Track rear (in.)	57.0	57.0
Curb weight (lbs.)	2796[1]	2839[1]
Max. cargo vol. (cu. ft.)	16.2	16.2
Fuel tank capacity (gal.)	15.7[2]	15.7[2]
Seating capacity	5/6	5/6
Front headroom (in.)	38.6	38.6
Front shoulder room (in.)	56.3	56.2
Front legroom, max. (in.)	42.1	42.1
Rear headroom (in.)	37.9	38.0
Rear shoulder room (in.)	57.1	56.2
Rear legroom, min. (in.)	36.1	36.4

1: average all models w/base equipment   2: I-4 engine; 16.4 w/gas V-6, 16.6 w/diesel

BODY/CHASSIS

Drivetrain layout: transverse front engine/front-wheel drive.
Suspension front: independent, MacPherson struts, lower control arms, coil springs, telescopic shock absorbers, anti-roll bar. **Suspension rear:** beam "twist" axle with integral anti-roll bar, trailing arms, panhard rod, coil springs, telescopic shock absorbers. **Steering:** rack-and-pinion power-assisted. **Turns lock-to-lock:** 3.0. **Turn diameter (ft.):** 36.9. **Brakes front:** 9.7-in. discs. **Brakes rear:** 8.9-in. drums. **Construction:** unit

POWERTRAINS

	ohv I-4	ohv V-6	ohv V-6D
Bore × stroke (in.)	4.00× 3.00	3.50× 2.99	4.06× 3.39

POWERTRAINS

	ohv I-4	ohv V-6	ohv V-6D
Displacement (liters/cu. in.)	2.5/ 151	2.8/ 173	4.3/ 262
Compression ratio	8.2:1	8.5:1	21.6:1
Fuel delivery	FI	2bbl.	FI
Net bhp @ rpm	90@ 4000	112@ 5100	85@ 3600
Net torque @ rpm (lbs/ft)	132@ 2800	148@ 2400	165@ 1600
Availability	S/All	O/All	O/All
Final drive ratios			
3-speed automatic	2.39:1	2.84:1	2.39:1
4-speed OD automatic			2.14:1

KEY bbl. = barrel (carburetor); **bhp** = brake horsepower (advertised); **Cal.** = California only. **Fed.** = Federal/49 state; **FI** = fuel injection; **ohv** = overhead valve; **ohc** = overhead cam; **I** = inline engine; **V** = V engine; **D** = diesel; **T** = turbocharged; **OD** = overdrive transmission; **S** = standard engine; **O** = optional engine.

PRICES

CELEBRITY	Retail Price	Dealer Cost	Low Price
2-door coupe.	$8059	$6954	$7704
4-door sedan.	8209	7085	7835

STANDARD EQUIPMENT (included in above prices):

2.5-liter (151-cid) fuel-injected 4-cylinder engine, 3-speed automatic transmission, power brakes, power steering, front bench seat, cloth upholstery, full carpeting, AM radio, P185/80R-13 fiberglass-belted radial tires, bodyside moldings, glovebox lamp and lock, day/night rearview mirror, black lefthand door mirror, dome and instrument panel courtesy lights.

OPTIONAL EQUIPMENT:

Engines:			
2.8-liter (173-cid) V-6	$ 150	$ 128	$ 130
4.3-liter (262-cid) diesel V-6	500	425	430
Air conditioning	725	616	623
Heavy-duty battery			
Diesel engine	25	21	22

Prices are accurate at time of printing; subject to manufacturer's change

	Retail Price	Dealer Cost	Low Price
Gasoline engines	50	43	44
Bumper guards, front or rear	56	48	49
Digital clock	39	33	34
Center console.	100	85	86
Heavy-duty cooling system			
w/air conditioning	40	34	35
w/o air conditioning	70	60	61
Electric rear window defroster.	135	115	117
Power door locks			
Coupes.	120	102	104
Sedans	170	145	147
Gauge package (incl. trip odometer)	64	54	55
Tinted glass	105	89	90
Halogen high beam headlamps	10	9	10
Engine block heater, diesel	49	42	43
Auxiliary lighting package	50	43	44
Radio equipment			
AM delete (credit)	(56)	(48)	(48)
AM/FM	82	70	71
AM/FM stereo ETR w/clock	177	150	152
AM/FM stereo ETR w/cassette &			
digital clock	277	235	238
Reclining front seatbacks	90	77	78
6-way power front seats	210	179	181
Cruise control	170	145	147
Tilt steering wheel.	105	89	90
Bodyside pinstriping	57	48	49
Heavy-duty suspension.	26	22	23
Sport suspension, F41	33	28	29
Puncture-sealant tires.	106	89	90
Interior trim/seats			
Cloth 45/45 front bench seat	100	85	86
Vinyl front bench seat	28	24	25
Custom cloth interior			
Coupes	109	93	94
Sedans	179	152	154
Custom vinyl interior			
Coupes	137	116	118
Sedans	207	176	178
Special custom cloth interior 45/45			
Coupes	250	213	216
Sedans	350	281	284
Vinyl top	155	132	134
Wheel cover locking package	39	33	34
Sport wheel covers	63	54	55

Prices are accurate at time of printing; subject to manufacturer's change

	Retail Price	Dealer Cost	Low Price
Wire wheel covers	153	130	132
Rally wheels	56	48	49
Power windows			
Coupes	180	153	155
Sedans	255	217	220
Intermittent wipers	49	42	43

Chevrolet Chevette/ Pontiac 1000

Chevrolet Chevette S 3-door sedan

WHAT'S NEW FOR '83

Now ousted as the country's top-seller by the front-drive Ford Escort, the aging rear-drive Chevette remains its familiar self for another year. Although advertised earlier, the Isuzu-built 5-speed overdrive manual transmission option can now actually be ordered with the standard gasoline four as well as the extra-cost four-pot diesel now that supply problems have cleared. New this year is the "S" exterior appearance package, consisting mainly of black-finish moldings set off by red accent stripes and decals. Models without this option come in for minor changes to exterior brightwork. Inside is a thicker headliner for lower noise levels. The bare-bones Scooter models acquire new door trim panels and reclining front seats as standard, and their passenger's seats can be adjusted fore and aft for the first time. Cars with automatic transmission, power steering, and air conditioning are equipped with a new idle speed control that stabilizes engine rpm to compensate for full load conditions. The most noticeable change for Pontiac's clone of the Chevette is the nameplate. This year it reads "1000" instead of "T1000" to bring nomenclature in line with other Pontiac models. The '83s are also marked by an integral front air dam, fluted taillight lenses, and black "Rally" hubcaps with exposed chrome lug nuts. Inside, there's a new instrument panel trim plate, and base trim is now a choice of vinyl or cloth. New options for '83 are limited to a black-finish roof luggage rack, revised tape striping, and a custom interior trim group. Other changes are shared with Chevette.

EVALUATION

Looks more antiquated every year, but still sells well mainly, we think, due to attractive pricing. Good mileage and sturdy simplicity are other virtues, and about the only ones. Ride is jiggly, interior space limited, and handling/roadholding only fair. Performance is dismal with the diesel, which is also very noisy. Driving position cramped for medium to large adults, aggravated by odd shift lever positioning and offset pedals. Not all that well equipped compared to most Japanese rivals (even less so in Scooter form), and finish is crude in places (we particularly dislike the very obvious painted metal visible inside). Makes some sense as knockabout, low-cost urban transport, but far from the best choice as a one-and-only small car suitable for all-around use.

EVALUATION CHECKLIST

Fuel economy	4	Cargo room	4
Driveability	3	Serviceability	3
Acceleration	3	Standard equipment	3
Braking	3	Body construction	4
Handling/roadholding	3	Paint/exterior finish	3
Driving position	2	Interior finish	3
Instruments/control	2	TOTAL POINTS	56
Visiblity	4		
Heating/ventilation	3	**RATING SCALE**	
Seat comfort	2	5 = Excellent	
Passenger room	2	4 = Very Good	
Ride	1	3 = Average/Acceptable	
Noise	2	2 = Fair	
Exit/entry	2	1 = Poor	

SPECIFICATIONS

	3-door sedan	5-door sedan
Wheelbase (in.)	94.3	97.3
Overall length (in.)	161.9	164.9
Overall width (in.)	61.8	61.8
Overall height (in.)	52.9	52.9
Track front (in.)	51.2	51.2
Track rear (in.)	51.2	51.2
Curb weight (lbs.)	2056	2119
Max. cargo vol. (cu. ft.)	9.3/ 27.0	9.3/ 28.6
Fuel tank capacity (gal.)	12.5	12.5
Seating capacity	4	4
Front headroom (in.)	37.8	38.3
Front shoulder room (in.)	50.1	49.8
Front legroom, max. (in.)	41.7	41.7
Rear headroom (in.)	37.3	37.4
Rear shoulder room (in.)	49.4	49.4
Rear legroom, min. (in.)	30.9	33.2

BODY/CHASSIS

Drivetrain layout: longitudinal front engine/rear-wheel drive.
Suspension front: independent, unequal-length upper and lower A-arms, coil springs, telescopic shock absorbers, anti-roll bar. **Suspension rear:** rigid axle, four links, panhard rod, torque tube, coil springs, telescopic shock absorbers. **Steering:** rack-and-pinion. **Turns lock-to-lock:** 3.6 manual, 3.0 power. **Turn diameter (ft.):** 30.6. **Brakes front:** 9.7-in. discs. **Brakes rear:** 7.9-in. drums. **Construction:** unit

POWERTRAINS

	ohc I-4	ohc I-4D
Bore × stroke (in.)	3.23× 2.98	3.31× 3.23

POWERTRAINS

	ohc I-4	ohc I-4D
Displacement (liters/cu. in.)	1.6/ 98	1.8/ 111
Compression ratio	9.2:1	22.0:1
Fuel delivery	2bbl.	FI
Net bhp @ rpm		
Net torque @ rpm (lbs/ft)		
Availability	S/All	O/All
Final drive ratios		
4-speed manual	3.36:1[1]	
5-speed OD manual	3.36:1	3.36:1
3-speed automatic	3.36:1[1]	3.36:1[1]

1: 3.62:1 opt.; std. Cal. w/4-speed

KEY bbl. = barrel (carburetor); **bhp** = brake horsepower (advertised); **Cal.** = California only. **Fed.** = Federal/49 state; **FI** = fuel injection; **ohv** = overhead valve; **ohc** = overhead cam; **I** = inline engine; **V** = V engine; **D** = diesel; **T** = turbocharged; **OD** = overdrive transmission; **S** = standard engine; **O** = optional engine.

PRICES

CHEVETTE-41 states	Retail Price	Dealer Cost	Low Price
Scooter 3-door sedan.	$4977	$4598	$4898
Scooter 5-door sedan.	5333	4907	5207
3-door sedan.	5469	4868	5269
5-door sedan.	5616	4999	5399
Diesel 3-door sedan.	6535	5817	6317
Diesel 5-door sedan.	6683	5949	6449
AK,AZ,CA,HI,ID,NV,OR,UT,WA			
Scooter 3-door sedan.	4977	4598	4898
Scooter 5-door sedan.	5333	4907	5207
3-door sedan.	5348	4760	5160
5-door sedan.	5495	4891	5291
Diesel 3-door sedan.	6414	5707	6207
Diesel 5-door sedan.	6582	5841	6341
1000			
3-door sedan.	5582	4969	5269
5-door sedan.	5785	5149	5449

Prices are accurate at time of printing; subject to manufacturer's change

STANDARD EQUIPMENT (included in above prices):

1.6-liter (98-cid) 4-cylinder 2-bbl. engine, 4-speed manual transmission, high-energy ignition, rack-and-pinion steering, front disc brakes, vinyl bucket seats, P155/80-13 BSW fiberglass-belted radial tires. **All except Scooter** add: deluxe bumpers, cigarette lighter, bodyside moldings, AM radio, WSW tires, wheel trim rings, reclining front seats. **Diesel** models have: 1.8-liter (111-cid) 4-cylinder diesel engine and 5-speed overdrive manual transmission, power brakes.

OPTIONAL EQUIPMENT	Retail Price	Dealer Cost	Low Price
5-spd. manual transmission (w/o diesel) . .	$ 75	$ 64	$ 65
3-speed automatic transmission	395	336	340
Air conditioning	625	531	537
Heavy-duty battery	25	21	22
Power brakes	95	81	82
Heavy-duty cooling			
w/air conditioning	40	34	35
w/o air conditioning	70	60	61
Rear window defogger	125	106	108
Deluxe exterior.	165	140	142
Tinted glass	90	77	78
Two-tone paint.	133	113	115
Radio equipment			
AM (Scooter)	83	71	72
AM/FM			
Scooter	165	140	142
Others	82	70	71
AM/FM stereo (ex. Scooter)	109	93	94
Custom cloth bucket seats.	130	111	113
Sport decor, exterior	95	81	82
Power steering.	199	169	171
Comfortilt steering wheel	99	84	85

Pontiac 1000 3-door sedan

Prices are accurate at time of printing; subject to manufacturer's change

	Retail Price	Dealer Cost	Low Price
Rear wiper/washer	117	99	101
Cargo cover, 1000	64	54	55
Lamp group, 1000	43	37	38
Luggage carrier, 1000	90	77	78
Cloth seat trim, 1000	28	24	25
Custom trim group, 1000	151	128	130

Chevrolet Citation

Chevrolet Citation 5-door sedan

WHAT'S NEW FOR '83

Unchanged in appearance, Chevrolet's variation on GM's front-drive X-car theme comes in for only a slightly reworked dash and revised powertrain chart. Contrary to earlier reports, the X-11 sports package is continued, but the H.O. (High-Output) V-6 that was previously limited to this option is now available for any Citation as a separate extra. The X-11 package is initially available on the 3-door hatchback sedan, and will be extended to the 2-door "slantback" coupe (revived as a price leader for mid-1982) later in the year. Exterior colors are shifted, and interiors are marked by dark silver paint on the dash and standard low-back front seats with adjustable headrests. Otherwise, Citation is a complete rerun.

EVALUATION

An admirably designed compact, but still hurt severely in our estimation by continuing owner complaints of mechanical problems that occasion recalls after more than three years of

Prices are accurate at time of printing; subject to manufacturer's change

production. It's unclear whether the X-cars' disappointing service history is the result of insufficient engineering development or sloppy workmanship, but it can't be ignored and is a big reason why we prefer the Dodge Aries/Plymouth Reliant K-cars as the best buys in this class. In other respects, Citation remains as before. It offers the traction and packaging advantages of front drive, good roadholding, easy handling, and ample interior room for its size just like the other X-cars. Economy is good, though not exceptional, and performance is sprightly with the optional V-6. The hatchback models are versatile, commodious load carriers compared to the notchback models at other GM divisions. Citation is also pleasant to drive, offers splendid outward vision, and doesn't bounce you around on rough roads. However, assembly quality is not consistent or consistently high, and the car comes off as taxicab-plain unless you pour a lot of dough into options. As GM's first fling with front drive, Citation and its siblings have taught the company a lot. Too bad it had to learn at the expense of thousands of disgruntled owners.

EVALUATION CHECKLIST

Fuel economy	3	Cargo room	4
Driveability	4	Serviceability	2
Acceleration	3	Standard equipment	3
Braking	4	Body construction	4
Handling/roadholding	4	Paint/exterior finish	4
Driving position	4	Interior finish	3
Instruments/control	3	TOTAL POINTS	69
Visiblity	4		
Heating/ventilation	4	**RATING SCALE**	
Seat comfort	3	5 = Excellent	
Passenger room	3	4 = Very Good	
Ride	3	3 = Average/Acceptable	
Noise	4	2 = Fair	
Exit/entry	3	1 = Poor	

SPECIFICATIONS

	2-door coupe	3-door sedan	5-door sedan
Wheelbase (in.)	104.9	104.9	104.9
Overall length (in.)	176.7	176.7	176.7
Overall width (in.)	68.3	68.3	68.3
Overall height (in.)	53.9	53.9	53.9

SPECIFICATIONS

	2-door coupe	3-door sedan	5-door sedan
Track front (in.)	58.7	58.7	58.7
Track rear (in.)	57.0	57.0	57.0
Curb weight (lbs.)	2495[1]	2526[1]	2551[1]
Max. cargo vol. (cu. ft.)	12.5	19.7/ 35.7	19.7/ 35.7
Fuel tank capacity (gal.)	15.9	15.9	15.9
Seating capacity	5	5	5
Front headroom (in.)	38.1	38.1	38.1
Front shoulder room (in.)	56.2	56.2	56.3
Front legroom, max. (in.)	42.2	42.2	42.2
Rear headroom (in.)	37.5	37.7	37.7
Rear shoulder room (in.)	56.2	56.2	56.3
Rear legroom, min. (in.)	34.5	34.5	35.5

1: average all models w/base equipment

BODY/CHASSIS

Drivetrain layout: transverse front engine/front-wheel drive.
Suspension front: independent, MacPherson struts, lower conrol arms, coil springs, telescopic shock absorbers, anti-roll-bar. **Suspension rear:** beam "twist" axle with integral anti-roll bar, trailing arms, panhard rod, coil springs, telescopic shock absorbers. **Steering:** rack-and-pinion. **Turns lock-to-lock:** 3.5 manual, 3.1 power. **Turn diameter (ft.):** 36.1. **Brakes front:** 9.7-in. discs. **Brakes rear:** 7.9-in. drums. **Construction:** unit

POWERTRAINS

	ohv I-4	ohv V-6	ohv V-6[1]
Bore × stroke (in.)	4.00× 3.00	3.50× 2.99	3.50× 2.99
Displacement (liters/cu. in.)	2.5/ 151	2.8/ 173	2.8/ 173
Compression ratio	8.2:1	8.5:1	8.9:1

POWERTRAINS

	ohv I-4	ohv V-6	ohv V-6[1]
Fuel delivery	FI	2bbl.	2bbl.
Net bhp @ rpm	90@ 4000	112@ 5100	135@ 5400
Net torque @ rpm (lbs/ft)	132@ 2800	148@ 2400	145@ 2400
Availability	S/All	O/All	O/All

1: H.O. engine

Final drive ratios

4-speed OD manual	2.42:1	2.69:1	2.96:1
3-speed automatic	2.39:1	2.53:1	3.06:1

KEY obl. = barrel (carburetor); **bhp** = brake horsepower (advertised); **Cal.** = California only. **Fed.** = Federal/49 state; **FI** = fuel injection; **ohv** = overhead valve; **ohc** = overhead cam; **I** = inline engine; **V** = V engine; **D** = diesel; **T** = turbocharged; **OD** = overdrive transmission; **S** = standard engine; **O** = optional engine.

PRICES

CITATION	Retail Price	Dealer Cost	Low Price
2-door coupe	$6333	$5846	$6246
3-door sedan	6788	6063	6563
5-door sedan	6934	6193	6693

STANDARD EQUIPMENT (included in above prices):

2.5-liter (151-cid) 4-cylinder fuel-injected engine, 4-speed manual transmission, front disc brakes, AM radio (ex. 2-door coupe), hubcaps, bright grille, wide rocker panel moldings and wheel opening moldings, styled steel wheels w/P185/80R-13 glass-belted radial tires, carpeting, bench seats, lighter, glovebox lock.

OPTIONAL EQUIPMENT:

2.8-liter (173-cid) V-6 2-bbl. engine	$ 150	$ 128	$ 130
2.8-liter (173-cid) V-6 HO engine	300	255	258
3-speed automatic transmission	425	361	365
Air conditioning	725	616	623
Heavy-duty battery	25	21	22
Power brakes	100	85	86
Bumper guards	56	48	49
Bumper rub strips	50	43	44

Prices are accurate at time of printing; subject to manufacturer's change

	Retail Price	Dealer Cost	Low Price
Electric clock	35	30	31
Heavy-duty cooling			
w/o air conditioning	70	60	61
w/air conditioning	40	34	35
Console	100	85	86
Rear window defogger	135	115	117
Power door lock system			
Coupe	120	102	104
Sedan	170	145	147
Deluxe exterior			
3-door w/o two-tone paint	157	133	135
3-door w/two-tone paint	118	100	102
5-door w/o two-tone paint	130	111	113
5-door w/two-tone paint	218	185	187
Gauge package	104	88	89
Tinted glass	105	89	90
Dual horns	12	10	11
Auxiliary lighting	50	43	44
Two-tone paint	176	150	152
Quiet sound/rear compartment decor	43	37	38
Radio equipment			
AM/FM	82	70	71
AM/FM stereo	109	93	94
AM/FM stereo w/cassette	209	178	180
Automatic speed control	170	145	147
Sport decor pkg	299	254	257
Power steering	210	179	181
Comfortilt steering wheel	105	89	90
Heavy-duty suspension	26	22	23
Sport suspension, F41	33	28	29
Trim/Interior			
Sport cloth bench seat	28	24	25
Sport cloth bucket seats			
Coupes	221	188	190
Sedan	250	213	216
Custom interior w/cloth bench seat	295	251	254
Custom interior w/cloth bucket seats			
Hatchback	467	397	401
Sedan	492	418	423
Power windows			
Coupes	180	153	155
Sedan	255	217	220
Remote swing-out rear side windows,			
3-door	108	92	93
Intermittent wiper system	49	42	43
X-11 sport equipment package	998	846	855

Prices are accurate at time of printing; subject to manufacturer's change

CONSUMER GUIDE®

Chevrolet Corvette

Chevrolet Corvette 2-door coupe (prototype)

WHAT'S NEW FOR '83

One of Detroit's worst-kept secrets should arrive in Chevy showrooms a month or two after you read this. At press time, Chevy hadn't released details on the all-new sixth-generation Corvette, but a good deal about it is already known. Our spy photo shows the final production-approved styling, which pretty much speaks for itself. The body is still made of fiberglass, but now sports a one-piece lift-off roof panel over the cockpit, and the curved back window functions like a hatchback for the first time. Power will be supplied by the 350-cid V-8 with Cross Fire throttle-body fuel injection introduced for 1982. The standard transmission will be GM's 4-speed overdrive automatic with lockup torque converter. Optional is a 4-speed manual with what is said to be a very complicated computer-controlled electronic overdrive that, in effect, provides seven forward speeds. Chassis features include a transverse leaf spring made of reinforced plastic for the front suspension; a new four-link geometry for the independent rear suspension, with a separate transverse link and another plastic spring; and a switch from recirculating ball steering to the more precise rack-and-pinion type. Brakes are still power-assisted discs at each corner. The new 'Vette is about the same size and weight as the old one, but is said to have a little more cockpit space. Six-way power bucket seats with reclining backrests will be standard, and the dash will pioneer use of liquid-crystal displays in a U.S. production car. Price is presently pegged at above $20,000.

Specifications, evaluations, and prices for 1983 Corvette not available at time of publication.

Chevrolet Malibu & Monte Carlo

Chevrolet Monte Carlo 2-door coupe

WHAT'S NEW FOR '83

You'll again have to look twice to spot the differences between this year's G-body intermediates from Chevy and their immediate predecessors. The '83 Malibu 4-door sedan and wagon look the same as the '82s, but lose the "Classic" part of their name and a few standard equipment items (full wheel covers, sound package, and some exterior moldings). These are now available either as separate extras or as part of a new "CL" package option. The companion Monte Carlo coupe gains a more open grille insert as its main identifying feature. Its equipment stays the same, and a CL option is available here, too, consisting mainly of fancier seat and door trim. Last year's 267-cid gasoline V-8 has been scratched. Standard gas V-6, optional gas V-8, and Oldsmobile diesel V-6 and V-8 return, all coupled to standard 3-speed automatic with lockup torque converter.

EVALUATION

A thoroughly time-tested design, and suffers by comparison to newer class rivals, including Chevy's own front-drive

Celebrity, because of it. Looked great in 1978, but seems outmoded five years later. Main pluses are relaxed highway performance, good comfort for front seaters, passable rear seat room (though not so hot relative to external size), and safe if soggy road manners. Performance sluggish with gas V-6 or either diesel, acceptable with optional 5.0-liter (305-cid) gas V-8. Diesel looks attractive because of its mileage ratings, but we'd think twice because of its drawbacks. These include messy refuelling, noisier operation (particularly at idle), a substantial price penalty, and a disturbing list of reliability and service problems (V-8 diesel, but may afflict its V-6 derivative, too). The F40 heavy-duty chassis option is cheap, and recommended for its more comfortable ride, especially with a full passenger and cargo load. Summary: Dullness with a capital "D," but should give reliable service over many miles with one of the sturdy gasoline engines.

EVALUATION CHECKLIST

Fuel economy	3	Cargo room	3
Driveability	4	Serviceability	3
Acceleration	3	Standard equipment	3
Braking	3	Body construction	4
Handling/roadholding	3	Paint/exterior finish	3
Driving position	4	Interior finish	4
Instruments/control	3	TOTAL POINTS	65
Visiblity	3		
Heating/ventilation	4	**RATING SCALE**	
Seat comfort	3	5 = Excellent	
Passenger room	3	4 = Very Good	
Ride	3	3 = Average/Acceptable	
Noise	3	2 = Fair	
Exit/entry	3	1 = Poor	

SPECIFICATIONS

	Monte Carlo 2-door coupe	Malibu 4-door sedan	Malibu 4-door wagon
Wheelbase (in.)	108.1	108.1	108.1
Overall length (in.)	200.4	192.7	193.3
Overall width (in.)	71.8	72.3	71.9
Overall height (in.)	54.3	55.7	55.8
Track front (in.)	58.5	58.5	58.5

SPECIFICATIONS

	Monte Carlo 2-door coupe	Malibu 4-door sedan	Malibu 4-door wagon
Track rear (in.)	57.8	57.8	57.8
Curb weight (lbs.)	3190	3190	3342
Max. cargo vol. (cu. ft.)	16.2	16.6	72.4
Fuel tank capacity (gal.)	18.1[1]	18.1[1]	18.2
Seating capacity	4/5	5/6	5/6
Front headroom (in.)	38.5	38.7	38.8
Front shoulder room (in.)	56.7	57.2	57.2
Front legroom, max. (in.)	42.8	42.8	42.8
Rear headroom (in.)	37.6	37.7	38.8
Rear shoulder room (in.)	57.1	57.1	57.1
Rear legroom, min. (in.)	38.0	38.0	35.5

1: 19.8 w/diesel engine

BODY/CHASSIS

Drivetrain layout: longitudinal front engine/rear-wheel drive. **Suspension front:** independent, unequal-length upper and lower A-arms, coil springs, telescopic shock absorbers, anti-roll bar. **Suspension rear:** rigid axle, four links, control arms, coil springs, telescopic shock absorbers, anti-roll bar optional. **Steering:** recirculating ball, power-assisted. **Turns lock-to-lock:** 3.3. **Turn diameter:** 37.1 (wagon:40.0). **Brakes front:** 10.5-in. discs. **Brakes rear:** 9.5-in. drums. **Construction:** body-on-frame

POWER TRAINS

	ohv V-6	ohv V-6D	ohv V-8	ohv V-8D	ohv V-6
Bore × stroke (in.)	3.74× 3.48	4.06× 3.39	3.74× 3.48	4.06× 3.39	3.80× 3.40
Displacement (liters/cu. in.)	3.8/ 229	4.3/ 260	5.0/ 305	5.7/ 350	3.8/ 231

POWERTRAINS

	ohv V-6	ohv V-6D	ohv V-8	ohv V-8D	ohv V-6
Compression ratio	8.6:1	22.8:1	8.6:1	22.1:1	8.0:1
Fuel delivery	2bbl.	FI	4bbl.	FI	2bbl.
Net bhp @ rpm	110@ 4000	85@ 3600	150@ 4000	105@ 3200	110@ 3800
Net torque @ rpm (lbs/ft)	190@ 1600	165@ 1600	240@ 2400	200@ 1600	190@ 1600
Availability	S/Fed.	O/Fed.	O/All	S/All	S/Cal.
Final drive ratios					
3-speed automatic	2.41:1	2.41:1	2.29:1[1]	2.29:1[2]	2.41:1[3]

1: 2.73:1 opt. Sedan, Monte Carlo; 2.41:1 wagon (3.08 opt.)
2: 2.73:1 opt.
3: 2.73:1 wagon

KEY bbl. = barrel (carburetor); **bhp** = brake horsepower (advertised); **Cal.** = California only. **Fed.** = Federal/49 state; **FI** = fuel injection; **ohv** = overhead valve; **ohc** = overhead cam; **I** = inline engine; **V** = V engine; **D** = diesel; **T** = turbocharged; **OD** = overdrive transmission; **S** = standard engine; **O** = optional engine.

PRICES

	Retail Price	Dealer Cost	Low Price
MALIBU			
4-door sedan....................	$8084	$6978	$7728
4-door wagon	8217	7093	7843
MONTE CARLO			
2-door coupe..................	8552	7382	8132

STANDARD EQUIPMENT (included in above prices):

3.8-liter (229-cid) V-6 engine, 3-speed automatic transmission, power steering, power brakes, bench front seat, carpeting.

OPTIONAL EQUIPMENT:

Engines			
5.0-liter (305-cid) V-8 4-bbl.........	$ 225	$ 191	$ 193
4.3-liter V-6 diesel	500	425	431
5.7-liter (350-cid) V-8 diesel	700	595	601
Custom cloth 55/45 bench seat, sedan			
Air conditioning	725	616	623

Prices are accurate at time of printing; subject to manufacturer's change

	Retail Price	Dealer Cost	Low Price
Rear window air deflector, wagon	36	31	32
Limited-slip differential	95	81	82
Performance axle ratio	21	18	19
Heavy-duty battery, each	25	21	22
Bumper guards	50	43	44
Bumper rub strips	56	48	49
Load floor carpet, wagon	84	71	72
Roof carrier, wagon	125	106	108
Electric clock	35	30	31
Cold climate package	99	84	85
Heavy-duty cooling			
w/o air conditioning	70	60	61
w/air conditioning	40	34	35
Electro-clear rear window defroster	135	115	117
Power door locks	170	145	147
Estate equipment, wagon	307	261	264
Gauge package	95	81	82
Tinted glass	105	89	90
Halogen headlamps	10	9	10
Auxiliary lighting			
Sedan, coupe	49	42	43
Wagon	56	48	49
Mirrors			
Left remote (ex. Monte Carlo)	22	19	20
Sport, left remote, right manual	59	50	51
Radio equipment			
AM	112	95	96
AM/FM	171	145	147
AM/FM stereo	198	168	170
AM/FM stereo w/cassette tape	298	253	256
Dual rear speakers	30	26	27
Power antenna	60	51	52
Removable glass roof panels, Monte Carlo	825	701	709
Cargo security package, wagons	44	37	38
Power seat, Monte Carlo	210	179	181
Automatic speed control	170	145	147
Comfortilt steering wheel	105	89	90
Pinstriping	57	48	49
Heavy-duty suspension (ex. wagons)	26	22	23
Sport suspension, Monte Carlo (F41)	49	42	43
Power tailgate window release	40	34	35
Wheel cover locking package	39	33	34
Power windows			
Coupe	180	153	155
Sedans, wagons	255	217	220
Intermittent wiper system	49	42	43

Prices are accurate at time of printing; subject to manufacturer's change

CONSUMER GUIDE®

Chrysler Cordoba/ Dodge Mirada

Chrysler Cordoba 2-door coupe

WHAT'S NEW FOR '83

The slow-selling personal-luxury coupes from Chrysler get only minor changes this year. The lower-priced Cordoba LS model is discontinued. A landau-style vinyl roof is standard, and the optional "Cabriolet" simulated convertible roof returns as an extra. Besides new exterior colors, Cordoba's only other changes are a standard 60/40 split-bench front seat with passenger backrest recliner, premium wheel covers, and a crystal pentastar standup hood ornament. The rear-drive chassis, engine/transmission choices, and familiar styling are all unchanged from '82. Other than new exterior colors, Dodge's companion Mirada is a rerun of the '82 which was essentially the same as the '81. Both personal-luxury entries have generated little buyer interest, and are being kept on the roster only because more contemporary front-drive replacements haven't arrived yet. Mirada is still available as a hardtop only. Mirada and Cordoba are built on same chassis as the 4-door Dodge Diplomat/Plymouth Gran Fury and Chrysler New Yorker Fifth Avenue.

EVALUATION

An aging design that looks less appealing as time goes by and Chrysler updates its other models. New-look Ford Thunderbird and Mercury Cougar could make Cordoba and stablemate Dodge Mirada even less attractive. Also contends with the high-volume Olds Cutlass Supreme, Buick Regal, Chevy Monte Carlo, and Pontiac Grand Prix from GM, but lacks their diesel option for economy-conscious buyers. These are capable long-distance cruisers for two with a roomy front seat, soft ride, and substantial sound insulation, but by today's standards they suffer in many areas. They're bulky, have a cramped rear seat and soggy handling, and mileage is poor. Dependable standard slant six is bogged down by emissions hardware and the hefty weight, so mileage and performance are both mediocre. The optional V-8 is equally reliable and has more power, but brings a further economy penalty. Pluses include thoroughly familiar design and workmanship that's now usually better than average. Also backed by Chrysler's 5-year/50,000 mile powertrain and rust warranties—a value bonus that may weigh more heavily with those buyers interested more in long-term ownership than in space- and fuel-efficiency.

EVALUATION CHECKLIST

Fuel economy	2	Cargo room	3
Driveability	4	Serviceability	3
Acceleration	3	Standard equipment	4
Braking	3	Body construction	4
Handling/roadholding	3	Paint/exterior finish	4
Driving position	4	Interior finish	4
Instruments/control	3	TOTAL POINTS	68
Visiblity	3		
Heating/ventilation	4	**RATING SCALE**	
Seat comfort	4	5 = Excellent	
Passenger room	3	4 = Very Good	
Ride	3	3 = Average/Acceptable	
Noise	4	2 = Fair	
Exit/entry	3	1 = Poor	

Dodge Mirada CMX 2-door coupe

SPECIFICATIONS	2-door coupe
Wheelbase (in.)	112.7
Overall length (in.)	209.5
Overall width (in.)	72.7
Overall height (in.)	53.2
Track front (in.)	60.0
Track rear (in.)	59.5
Curb weight (lbs.)	3467[1]
Max. cargo vol. (cu. ft.)	16.7[2]
Fuel tank capacity (gal.)	18.0
Seating capacity	5
Front headroom (in.)	37.5
Front shoulder room (in.)	58.8
Front legroom, max. (in.)	43.7
Rear headroom (in.)	36.5
Rear shoulder room (in.)	59.3
Rear legroom, min. (in.)	35.2

1: Base model 2: Manufacturer's estimate

BODY/CHASSIS

Drivetrain layout: longitudinal front engine/rear-wheel drive. **Suspension front:** independent, lateral non-parallel control arms, transverse torsion bars, telescopic shock absorbers, anti-roll bar. **Suspension rear:** rigid axle, semi-elliptic leaf springs. **Steering:** recirculating ball, power-assisted. **Turns lock-to-lock:** 3.5. **Turn diameter (ft.):** 40.7. **Brakes front:** 10.8-in. discs. **Brakes rear:** 10.0-in. drums. **Construction:** unit

POWERTRAINS	ohv I-6	ohv V-8
Bore × stroke (in.)	3.40× 4.12	3.91× 3.31

POWERTRAINS

	ohv I-6	ohv V-8
Displacement (liters/cu. in.)	3.7/ 225	5.2/ 318
Compression ratio	8.4:1	8.5:1
Fuel delivery	1bbl.	2bbl.
Net bhp @ rpm	90@ 3600	130@ 4000
Net torque @ rpm (lbs/ft)	165@ 1600	230@ 1600
Availability	S/All	O/All
Final drive ratios		
3-speed automatic	2.94:1	2.26:1

KEY bbl. = barrel (carburetor); **bhp** = brake horsepower (advertised); **Cal.** = California only. **Fed.** = Federal/49 state; **FI** = fuel injection; **ohv** = overhead valve; **ohc** = overhead cam; **I** = inline engine; **V** = V engine; **D** = diesel; **T** = turbocharged; **OD** = overdrive transmission; **S** = standard engine; **O** = optional engine.

PRICES

	Retail Price	Dealer Cost	Low Price
CHRYSLER CORDOBA			
2-door coupe.	$9580	$8241	$9141
DODGE MIRADA			
2-door coupe.	$9011	$7757	$8757

STANDARD EQUIPMENT (included in above prices):

3.7-liter (225-cid) 6-cylinder engine, 3-speed automatic transmission, power steering, power brakes, front and rear bumper guards, velour or cloth-and-vinyl upholstery, 60/40 split bench front seat with center armrest (Cordoba), full carpeting, luxury wheel covers (Cordoba) and steering wheel, AM radio, tinted glass, reading lamps, landau vinyl roof (Cordoba), dual remote-control door mirrors, electronic digital clock (Cordoba).

OPTIONAL EQUIPMENT:

Engines			
5.2-liter (318-cid) V-8 2-bbl.	$ 225	$ 191	$ 193
Light package (incl. w/Basic group)	168	143	145
Basic group			
w/o Sport equip. pkg.	1146	974	984
w/Sport equip. pkg.	1048	891	899
Protection group, Mirada	146	124	126

Prices are accurate at time of printing; subject to manufacturer's change

	Retail Price	Dealer Cost	Low Price
Protection package, Cordoba	114	97	98
CMX Package, Mirada	982	835	844
Sport equipment package, Mirada	1237	1051	1062
Cabriolet roof package, Cordoba	587	499	504
Air conditioning	787	669	676
500-amp. long-life battery	43	37	38
Electronic digital clock	64	54	55
Console (bucket seats, Light Pkg. req.)			
Mirada w/o CMX	124	105	107
Mirada w/CMX, Cordoba	75	64	65
Center armrest (incl. w/CMX)	49	42	43
Electric rear-window defroster	138	117	119
Triad horns	27	23	24
Cornering lamps	60	51	52
Illuminated entry system	75	64	65
Illuminated vanity mirror	61	52	53
Power assists			
Left bucket or 60/40 split bench seat ...	199	169	171
Windows	180	153	155
Door locks	120	102	104
Decklid release			
Mirada w/light pkg. or basic group ...	40	34	35
Mirada w/o light pkg. or basic group,			
Cordoba	58	49	50
Radio equipment			
AM, delete (credit)	(56)	(48)	(56)
AM/FM stereo, manual-tune (incl. w/			
Mirada Sport Equip. Pkg.)	109	93	94
AM/FM Stereo, electronic-tune			
w/o sport pkg.	263	224	227
w/sport pkg.	154	131	133
AM/FM stereo, electronic-tune w/cassette			
tape			
Mirada w/o sport pkg.	402	342	346
Mirada w/sport pkg., Cordoba	293	249	252
Seats/trim			
Leather buckets w/armrest & passenger			
recliner			
Mirada w/o CMX package	598	508	514
Mirada w/CMX package	549	467	472
Cordoba	529	450	455
60/40 split bench w/armrest &			
passenger recliner			
Mirada w/o CMX package	266	226	229
Mirada w/CMX package	217	184	187
Conventional spare tire	63	54	55

Prices are accurate at time of printing; subject to manufacturer's change

	Retail Price	Dealer Cost	Low Price
Automatic speed control	174	148	150
Tilt steering column (intermittent wipers req.)	99	84	85
Leather-wrapped steering wheel	53	45	46
Heavy-duty suspension	36	31	32
Rear sway bar	36	31	32
Bodyside, hood & decklid tape stripes, Cordoba	98	83	84
Trunk dress-up	48	41	42
Undercoating (incl. w/basic group)	41	35	36
Intermittent windshield wipers (req. w/tilt column; incl. w/basic group)	52	44	45

Chrysler LeBaron/ Dodge 400

Chrysler LeBaron 4-door sedan

WHAT'S NEW FOR '83

Chrysler's successful luxury versions of the front-drive K-car family were new last year. The 2-door coupe, 4-door sedan, LeBaron 5-door wagon, and the convertible all return. The last will be offered with the wagon's woody-look bodyside trim later in the year as a new option. The upper Medallion trim is dropped, but the Mark Cross option with leather seat inserts will be offered for LeBarons. New features include Electronic Voice Alert system (standard on Mark Cross convertibles and T & C wagons) described in the Chrysler E Class report. Another new option is an electronic travel computer. New standard features are a tethered gas cap, halogen headlamps, and an improved heat/vent system that

Prices are accurate at time of printing; subject to manufacturer's change

CONSUMER GUIDE®

adds "ram air" vent outlets to the dash. Brakes have been reworked with larger front rotors and rear drums for a claimed improvement in braking balance and pedal feel. The standard 2.2-liter K-car engine gains 10 horsepower. Fuel injection will be offered on the 2.2 in mid year.

EVALUATION

Higher-priced variants of the K-cars that combine the basic virtues of the lower-priced models with greater comfort and convenience. Both engines have proven to be smooth, dependable performers but the Mitsubishi 2.6-liter four seldom gets above 22 mpg (except in straight highway driving) with the required automatic transmission. The 2.2 delivers better mileage, and is a mechanic's dream for service access. Except for the convertible, all models have a comfortable, controlled ride and adequate (though uninspired) road manners. The snazzy convertible is a stylish success, but leaves much to be desired on the road. Our test ragtop felt bogged down by the added weight of the reinforcements added to maintain body rigidity, the transmission was slow to shift, the brakes felt overworked, and gas mileage was under 20 mpg. It certainly is nice-looking, though. One beef we have with all members of the K-car family is lack of engine instruments. Only alternative is the new talking dashboard. Generous factory warranty covers engine, drivetrain, and body rust for 5 years or 50,000 miles.

EVALUATION CHECKLIST
(except convertible)

Fuel economy	3	Cargo room	4
Driveability	4	Serviceability	5
Acceleration	3	Standard equipment	4
Braking	3	Body construction	4
Handling/roadholding	3	Paint/exterior finish	3
Driving position	4	Interior finish	4
Instruments/control	3	TOTAL POINTS	73
Visiblity	4		
Heating/ventilation	4	**RATING SCALE**	
Seat comfort	4	5 = Excellent	
Passenger room	4	4 = Very Good	
Ride	3	3 = Average/Acceptable	
Noise	4	2 = Fair	
Exit/entry	3	1 = Poor	

Chrysler Town & Country 2-door convertible

SPECIFICATIONS	2-door coupe	2-door convertible	4-door sedan	5-door wagon
Wheelbase (in.)	100.1	100.1	100.1	100.1
Overall length (in.)	181.2	181.2	181.2	179.8
Overall width (in.)	68.5	68.5	68.5	68.5
Overall height (in.)	52.5	NA	52.9	52.7
Track front (in.)	57.6	57.6	57.6	57.6
Track rear (in.)	57.0	57.0	57.0	57.0
Curb weight (lbs.)	2464[1]	2532[1]	2541[1]	2656[1]
Max. cargo vol. (cu. ft.)	15.0	13.1	15.0	68.6
Fuel tank capacity (gal.)	13.0	13.0	13.0	13.0
Seating capacity	5	4	5	5
Front headroom (in.)	38.2	38.4	38.6	38.5
Front shoulder room (in.)	55.5	55.2	55.7	55.7
Front legroom, max. (in.)	42.2	42.2	42.2	42.2
Rear headroom (in.)	37.0	34.6	37.8	38.4
Rear shoulder room (in.)	57.7	37.3	56.1	56.1
Rear legroom, min. (in.)	35.1	32.5	35.1	34.9

1: Base models

BODY/CHASSIS

Drivetrain layout: transverse front engine/front-wheel drive. **Suspension front:** independent, MacPherson struts, lower A-arms, coil springs, telescopic shock absorbers, anti-roll bar. **Suspension rear:** beam "flex" axle, trailing arms, coil springs, telescopic shock absorbers, anti-roll bar. **Steering:** rack-and-pinion, power-assisted. **Turns lock-to-lock:** 2.5/3.2. **Turn diameter (ft.):** 34.8. **Brakes front:** 10.0-in. discs. **Brakes rear:** 7.9-in. drums. **Construction:** unit

POWERTRAINS	ohc I-4	ohc I-4
Bore × stroke (in.)	3.44× 3.62	3.59× 3.86
Displacement (liters cu. in.)	2.2/ 135	2.6/ 156
Compression ratio	9.0:1	8.2:1
Fuel delivery	2bbl.	2bbl.
Net bhp @ rpm	94@ 5200	93@ 4500
Net torque @ rpm (lbs/ft)	117@ 3200	132@ 2500
Availability	S/All	O/All
Final drive ratios		
5-speed OD manual	2.57:1[1]	
3-speed automatic	2.78:1[2]	2.78:1

1: avail. 2-doors only exc. convertible   2: 3.02:1 opt.; std. convertible

KEY bbl. = barrel (carburetor); **bhp** = brake horsepower (advertised); **Cal.** = California only. **Fed.** = Federal/49 state; **FI** = fuel injection; **ohv** = overhead valve; **ohc** = overhead cam; **I** = inline engine; **V** = V engine; **D** = diesel; **T** = turbocharged; **OD** = overdrive transmission; **S** = standard engine; **O** = optional engine.

PRICES

CHRYSLER LEBARON	Retail Price	Dealer Cost	Low Price
2-door coupe	$ 8514	$ 7588	$ 8488
4-door sedan	8790	7831	8731

Prices are accurate at time of printing; subject to manufacturer's change

	Retail Price	Dealer Cost	Low Price
2-door convertible.	12800	11360	12460
Town & Country 5-door wagon	9731	8659	9559
Mark Cross 2-door convertible	15595	13820	14920

DODGE 400

	Retail Price	Dealer Cost	Low Price
2-door coupe.	$ 8014	$ 7148	$ 7748
2-door convertible.	12500	11096	12096
4-door sedan.	8490	7567	8267

STANDARD EQUIPMENT (included in above prices):

2.2-liter (135-cid) 4-cylinder engine, 4-speed manual transmission, AM radio, padded vinyl roof (exc. convertible and wagon), power steering, power brakes, cloth-and-vinyl or all-vinyl upholstery, front bench seat with center armrest or front bucket seats with dual seatback recliners, rear-seat fold-down center armrest (4-door), bodyside tape accent stripes, interior courtesy light package, full wheel covers, halogen headlamps. **Mark Cross** convertible adds: special leather interior trim, tinted glass, air conditioning, 2.6-liter/156-cid 4-cylinder engine, 3-speed automatic transmission, sill moldings, undercoating, trunk dress-up, cast-aluminum road wheels. **Town & Country** wagon has LeBaron equipment, plus: woodgrain bodyside and tailgate appliqués, rear window wiper/washer, fold-down back seat.

OPTIONAL EQUIPMENT:

2.6-liter (156-cid) 4-cylinder engine (incl. w/Mark Cross Edition)	$ 259	$ 226	$ 229
3-speed automatic transmission (required w/2.6 engine)	439	373	377
Bodyside tape striping (incl. w/Sport Appearance Pkg.)	42	36	37
Sport appearance package, coupe	218	185	187
Interior trim			
Cloth & vinyl bucket seats w/dual recliners, leather	160	136	138
Mark Cross Package			
T&C.	963	819	828
Others	1232	1047	1058
Two-tone paint.	176	150	152
Air conditioning (tinted glass req.; Std. Mark Cross Edition)	732	622	629
Armrest, center (bucket seats req.)	59	50	51
500-amp. maintenance free battery	43	37	38
Bumper guards, F or R.	23	20	21
Console (buckets seats req.)	100	85	86
Maximum engine cooling (NA w/AC).	141	120	122
Electric rear window defroster.	137	116	118

Prices are accurate at time of printing; subject to manufacturer's change

	Retail Price	Dealer Cost	Low Price
Tinted glass, all windows	105	89	90
Cornering lamps.	60	51	52
Reading lamps.	24	20	21
Luggage rack.	106	90	91
Electronic Voice Alert.	63	56	57
Mirrors			
Illuminated visor vanity, right	50	42	43
Dual remote-control, chrome.	57	48	49
Dual power remote-control, chrome			
T&C	47	40	41
Others	104	88	89
Moldings			
Door edge protectors	15	13	14
2-doors	25	21	22
4-doors	23	20	21
Power assists			
Decklid/Liftgate release	40	34	35
Door locks			
2-doors	120	102	104
4-doors	170	144	146
Seat, left or bench (auto. trans. req.			
w/bench on coupe)	210	178	180
Windows			
2-doors	180	153	155
4-doors	255	217	220
Radio & Speakers			
AM delete (credit)	(56)	(48)	(49)
AM/FM stereo, manual tune	109	93	94
AM/FM stereo, electronic tune	263	224	227
AM/FM stereo electronic tune w/cassette			
tape	402	342	346
Premium speaker system	126	107	109
Conventional spare tire	63	54	55
Automatic speed control (Intermittent			
wipers req.).	174	148	150
Steering wheels			
Sport.	50	42	43
Luxury leather-wrapped	50	42	43
Tilt steering column.	105	89	90
Sport suspension	55	47	48
Trunk dress-up (std. Cross Edition)	51	43	44
Undercoating (std. Mark Cross Edition) . . .	41	35	36
Intermittent wipers	52	44	45
Electronic travel computer	206	175	177
Vinyl lower bodyside protection.	39	33	34

Prices are accurate at time of printing; subject to manufacturer's change

Chrysler New Yorker Fifth Avenue

Chrysler New Yorker Fifth Avenue Edition 4-door sedan

WHAT'S NEW FOR '83

The name is longer and more cumbersome, but the car itself is basically the '82 New Yorker. It's now called the New Yorker Fifth Avenue to distinguish it from a new front-drive New Yorker to be introduced at mid-year. The rear-drive Fifth Avenue shares the same chassis as Chrysler's other rear-drive cars. Sales were surprisingly strong in '82, so much so that Chrysler decided to bring it back for an encore. A long list of standard equipment that helped spark sales can now be supplemented with a Luxury Equipment package that includes V-8 engine, leather seats, speed control, tilt steering wheel, premium sound system and other amenities. Four new colors have been added to the three offered last year. A power glass sunroof also is being considered by Chrysler as an option.

EVALUATION

You can call it a New Yorker, or you can call it a Fifth Avenue, but many buyers in '82 called it a bargain compared to some competitors. Luxurious and loaded with comfort and convenience equipment, it appeals to the traditional big-car buyer who wants to go in style. Price looks very attractive compared to smaller, less well-equiped front-drive rivals and against the much pricier, similarly equipped Cadillac Seville and Lincoln Continental. Though styling gives New Yorker the aura of a big car, its interior is cramped, and trunk space is merely adequate. The old-style chassis has trouble coping with bombed-out urban roads, resulting in a lumpy ride and excessive road noise for what's supposed to be a high-class luxury liner. Still, fit and finish is generally high, a benefit of working with a familiar design, and materials are of good quality. The standard slant six engine is overmatched by the 3600-pound weight, so the thirstier V-8 is a practical alternative. With either, you get 5-year/50,000 mile warranty against body rust and powertrain problems.

EVALUATION CHECKLIST

Fuel economy	2	Cargo room	3
Driveability	4	Serviceability	3
Acceleration	2	Standard equipment	5
Braking	3	Body construction	4
Handling/roadholding	3	Paint/exterior finish	4
Driving position	3	Interior finish	4
Instruments/control	3	TOTAL POINTS	66
Visiblity	2		
Heating/ventilation	4	**RATING SCALE**	
Seat comfort	4	5 = Excellent	
Passenger room	3	4 = Very Good	
Ride	3	3 = Average/Acceptable	
Noise	4	2 = Fair	
Exit/entry	3	1 = Poor	

SPECIFICATIONS

	4-door sedan
Wheelbase (in.)	112.7
Overall length (in.)	205.7
Overall width (in.)	74.2
Overall height (in.)	55.3
Track front (in.)	60.0
Track rear (in.)	59.5
Curb weight (lbs.)	3631
Max. cargo vol. (cu. ft.)	15.6
Fuel tank capacity (gal.)	18.0

SPECIFICATIONS

	4-door sedan
Seating capacity	5
Front headroom (in.)	39.3
Front shoulder room (in.)	55.8
Front legroom, max. (in.)	42.5
Rear headroom (in.)	37.7
Rear shoulder room (in.)	55.5
Rear legroom, min. (in.)	37.0

BODY/CHASSIS

Drivetrain layout: longitudinal front engine/rear-wheel drive. **Suspension front:** independent, lateral non-parallel control arms, transverse torsion bars, telescopic shock absorbers, anti-roll bar. **Suspension rear:** rigid axle, semi-elliptic leaf springs, telescopic shock absorbers. **Steering:** recirculating ball, power-assisted. **Turns lock-to-lock:** 3.5. **Turn diameter (ft.):** 40.7. **Brakes front:** 10.8-in. discs. **Brakes rear:** 10.0-in. drums. **Construction:** unit

POWERTRAINS

	ohv I-6	ohv V-8
Bore × stroke (in.)	3.40× 4.12	3.91× 3.31
Displacement (liters/cu. in.)	3.7/ 225	5.2/ 318
Compression ratio	8.4:1	8.5:1
Fuel delivery	1bbl.	2bbl.
Net bhp @ rpm	90@ 3600	130@ 4000
Net torque @ rpm (lbs/ft)	165@ 3600	230@ 4000
Availability	S/All	O/All
Final drive ratios		
3-speed automatic	2.94:1	2.26:1

PRICES

CHRYSLER NEW YORKER FIFTH AVENUE	Retail Price	Dealer Cost	Low Price
4-door sedan	$12487	$10712	$11812

STANDARD EQUIPMENT (included in above prices):

3.7-liter (225-cid) 6-cylinder engine, 3-speed automatic transmission, power steering, power brakes, 60/40 split front bench seat with center armrest, full carpeting including trunk, deluxe wheel covers, tinted glass, electric rear window defroster, WSW tires, halogen headlamps, padded vinyl roof, air conditioning, AM radio, cloth upholstery.

OPTIONAL EQUIPMENT:

	Retail	Dealer	Low
5.2-liter (318-cid) V-8 2-bbl. (incl. w/ Luxury Equipment Pkg.)	$ 225	$ 191	$ 193
Luxury Equipment Package (incl. V-8)	1870	1589	1605
Protection Group (incl. w/Luxury Pkg.)	70	59	60
500-amp maintenance-free battery	43	37	38
Power assists			
Power decklid release (incl. w/Luxury Pkg.)	40	34	35
Power door locks (incl. w/Luxury Pkg.)	159	135	137
Power seat, left (incl. w/Luxury Pkg.)	199	169	171
Power seat, left & right			
w/o Luxury Pkg	398	338	342
w/Luxury Pkg	199	169	171
Illuminated visor vanity, right (incl. w/ Luxury Pkg.)	61	52	53
Radio equipment			
AM/FM stereo, manual tune (incl. w/ Luxury Pkg.)	109	93	94
AM/FM stereo, electronic tune			
w/o Luxury Pkg.	263	224	227
w/Luxury Pkg.	154	131	133
AM/FM ETR stereo w/cassette tape			
w/o Luxury Pkg.	402	342	346
w/Luxury Pkg.	293	249	252
Conventional spare tire	63	54	55
Automatic speed control (incl. w/Luxury Pkg.)	170	144	146
Steering wheel, leather-covered (incl. w/ Luxury Pkg.)	53	45	46

Prices are accurate at time of printing; subject to manufacturer's change

	Retail Price	Dealer Cost	Low Price
Tilt steering column (incl. w/Luxury Pkg; Intermittent wipers req.)	99	84	85
Heavy-duty suspension	26	22	23
Power glass sunroof	1041	885	894
Undercoating (incl. w/Luxury Pkg.)	41	35	36
Intermittent wipers (incl. w/Luxury Pkg.) . .	49	42	43

Datsun Maxima

Datsun Maxima GL 4-door sedan

WHAT'S NEW FOR '83

Heading into its third season, Nissan's luxury leader retains its basic 1981 design but with a few notable refinements. Grille and taillights are reworked slightly, and accent moldings appear on bumpers, wheel arches, and the front of the hood. Geometry on the 5-door wagon's rear suspension is switched to the commonly used four-bar link type for better control of its live axle, the sedan retains its independent rear suspension. Engines are the same as last year's, but the optional automatic transmission is now a 4-speed overdrive unit with lockup torque converter, replacing last year's 3-speed. Optional for sedans only is a package consisting of leather upholstery and digital instrumentation.

EVALUATION

We've tested both gas and diesel Maximas, and are still disappointed with this car. The diesel proved a surprise in

Prices are accurate at time of printing; subject to manufacturer's change

some ways, being pretty quick for an oil-burner and exhibiting little vibration and tolerably low noise levels. Start-up waiting time is commendably brief in moderate temperatures. Perhaps because of its automatic, though, the Maxima Diesel wasn't all that frugal. The best we could average was the low 20s. This leaves us wondering why anyone would pay extra for less performance with no significant economy gain. Despite its extra horsepower, the gasoline model isn't all that peppy with automatic (3-speed on our test car), though again drivetrain refinement is high. And we couldn't achieve much over 19.5 mpg in routine city/suburban driving. With the standard 5-speed, however, the car is discernibly quicker and much more pleasant to drive. Maxima is a fairly large car and none too svelte. Even so, its passenger room is limited, particularly headroom, which is marginal for those over 5 ft. 10 in. on cars equipped with the space-robbing power sunroof. Sedan trunk space is also below par, and the ride is unexpectedly lumpy for a luxury model with all-independent suspension. Road manners are only fair, and the long snout and wide turning radius makes garage maneuvering tedious. The dash has too many pieces that Nissan workers can't seem to line up properly; it's a fault of every Maxima we've seen. This highlights workmanship that's generally below the usually high Japanese standards, something that now seems characteristic of all Nissan/Datsun products. Verdict: looks appealing, but average in too many areas for what it costs.

EVALUATION CHECKLIST

Fuel economy	3	Cargo room	2
Driveability	3	Serviceability	3
Acceleration	4	Standard equipment	5
Braking	3	Body construction	3
Handling/roadholding	3	Paint/exterior finish	3
Driving position	3	Interior finish	3
Instruments/control	4	TOTAL POINTS	65
Visiblity	3		
Heating/ventilation	4	**RATING SCALE**	
Seat comfort	3	5 = Excellent	
Passenger room	3	4 = Very Good	
Ride	3	3 = Average/Acceptable	
Noise	4	2 = Fair	
Exit/entry	3	1 = Poor	

SPECIFICATIONS

	4-door sedan	5-door wagon
Wheelbase (in.)	103.4	103.4
Overall length (in.)	183.3	186.8
Overall width (in.)	65.2	64.6
Overall height (in.)	54.5	55.7
Track front (in.)	54.7	54.3
Track rear (in.)	53.9	53.5
Curb weight (lbs.)	2794	2897
Max. cargo vol. (cu. ft.)	10.7	63.1
Fuel tank capacity (gal.)	16.4	15.9
Seating capacity	5	5
Front headroom (in.)	36.4	36.8
Front shoulder room (in.)	53.1	53.2
Front legroom, max. (in.)	41.6	41.9
Rear headroom (in.)	35.0	36.5
Rear shoulder room (in.)	53.5	53.4
Rear legroom, min. (in.)	30.8	31.2

BODY/CHASSIS

Drivetrain layout: longitudinal front engine/rear-wheel drive. **Suspension front:** independent, MacPherson struts, lower control arms, coil springs, telescopic shock absorbers, anti-roll bar. **Suspension rear:** independent, semi-trailing arms, coil springs, anti-roll bar (sedan); rigid axle, four trailing links, coil springs, anti-roll bar (wagon). **Steering:** rack-and-pinion, power-assisted. **Turns lock-to-lock:** NA. **Turn diameter (ft.):** 37.7. **Brakes front:** 9.8-in. discs. **Brakes rear:** 10.6-in. discs (9.0-in. drums on wagon). **Construction:** unit

POWERTRAINS

	ohc I-6	ohc I-6D
Bore × stroke (in.)	3.32× 2.94	3.39× 3.11

POWERTRAINS

	ohc I-6	ohc I-6D
Displacement (liters/cu. in.)	2.4/ 146	2.8/ 170
Compression ratio	8.9:1	22.7:1
Fuel delivery	FI	FI
Net bhp @ rpm	120@ 5200	80@ 4600
Net torque @ rpm (lbs/ft)	134@ 2800	120@ 2400
Availability	S/All	O/All
Final drive ratios		
5-speed OD manual[1]	3.55:1	3.55:1
3-speed automatic[2]	3.55:1	
4-speed automatic		3.36:1

1: Sedans only; NA wagons
2: Std. wagons; opt. sedans

KEY bbl. = barrel (carburetor); **bhp** = brake horsepower (advertised); **Cal.** = California only. **Fed.** = Federal/49 state; **FI** = fuel injection; **ohv** = overhead valve; **ohc** = overhead cam; **I** = inline engine; **V** = V engine; **D** = diesel; **T** = turbocharged; **OD** = overdrive transmission; **S** = standard engine; **O** = optional engine.

PRICES

DATSUN MAXIMA	Retail Price	Dealer Cost	Low Price
GL 4-door sedan, 5-speed	$10869	$ 9326	$10326
GL 5-door wagon, automatic	12159	10432	11432
GL Diesel 4-door sedan, 5-speed.	11719	10055	11055
GL Diesel 5-door wagon, automatic	12529	10777	11777

STANDARD EQUIPMENT (included in above prices):

2.4-liter (146-cid) 6-cylinder engine with electronic fuel injection or 2.8-liter (168-cid) Diesel engine, 5-speed overdrive manual or 4-speed overdrive automatic transmission as above, power brakes, power steering, wipers w/intermittent delay, tilt steering wheel, electric rear-window defroster, tinted glass, full carpeting, rear window washer/wiper (wagon), air conditioning, halogen high-beam headlamps, interior light package, full instrumentation, reclining front bucket seats, center console, map pockets, dual electric remote-control door mirrors, power windows, central locking system, illuminated entry system with fadeout lighting, rear-window defroster timer, driver's seat lumbar support adjuster, tilt-adjustable driver's seat cushion, rear-seat center armrest (sedan), carpeted lower door panels, cruise control with resume feature, remote trunklid/tailgate release, remote fuel filler door release, AM/FM stereo radio with cassette player and automatic antenna.

OPTIONAL EQUIPMENT	Retail Price	Dealer Cost	Low Price
4-speed overdrive automatic transmission, sedans only	$ 500	$ 435	$ 440
High-altitude emissions system	N/C	N/C	N/C
Leather package, sedans only (incl. leather seat upholstery and digital instrumentation)	800	640	647
Bodyside moldings, wagons only	51	38	39
Power sunroof, sedans (std. wagon, NA diesel wagon)	480	384	388
Two-tone paint	N/C	N/C	N/C

Datsun/Nissan Pulsar

Nissan Pulsar 3-door sedan

WHAT'S NEW FOR '83

Replacing the 310, this newly designed front-drive minicar is essentially a spinoff of the Nissan Sentra, introduced midway through the 1982 model year. Pulsar shares the Sentra's E-series four, which gets a slight displacement increase this year from 1.5 to 1.6 liters. Basic chassis dimensions, the all-independent suspension, and transmissions are also shared. Bodily, the two models are virtually the same from the B-pillar forward. Pulsar will initially be offered as a 2-door

Prices are accurate at time of printing; subject to manufacturer's change

notchback coupe dubbed NX, with pop-up headlights and rear-quarter styling not unlike that of the Ford EXP. Later, 3- and 5-door hatchback sedans go on sale. Pulsar boasts drag coefficient numbers that are fairly low for the class—0.38 for the sedans and 0.37 for the coupe. With standard 5-speed manual gearbox, Pulsar earns EPA ratings of 35/50 mpg city/highway; with optional lockup-converter automatic it's 31/39 mpg. There is no Pulsar equivalent to the Sentra MPG, nor will this year's new diesel four from the Sentra be offered, though it might appear later. Tinted glass, stereo radio, tachometer, adjustable steering column, and quartz clock are standard across the board.

EVALUATION

New or substantially changed model, and not available for assessment at time of publication.

SPECIFICATIONS	2-door coupe	3-door sedan	5-door sedan
Wheelbase (in.)	95.0	95.0	95.0
Overall length (in.)	162.4	162.0	162.0
Overall width (in.)	63.7	63.7	63.7
Overall height (in.)	54.1	54.3	54.3
Track front (in.)	54.9	54.9	54.9
Track rear (in.)	54.1	54.1	54.1
Curb weight (lbs.)	1907[1]	1895[1]	1907[1]
Max. cargo vol. (cu. ft.)	NA	NA	NA
Fuel tank capacity (gal.)	13.2	13.2	13.2
Seating capacity	4	4	4
Front headroom (in.)	NA	NA	NA
Front shoulder room (in.)	NA	NA	NA
Front legroom, max. (in.)	NA	NA	NA
Rear headroom (in.)	NA	NA	NA
Rear shoulder room (in.)	NA	NA	NA
Rear legroom, min. (in.)	NA	NA	NA

1: Base models

BODY/CHASSIS

Drivetrain layout: transverse front engine/front-wheel drive.
Suspension front: independent, MacPherson struts, lower lateral arms, coil springs, telescopic shock absorbers. **Suspension rear:** semi-trailing arms, coil springs, telescopic shock absorbers. **Steering:** rack-and-pinion (power-assisted on NX). **Turns lock-to-lock:** 3.3. **Turn diameter (ft.):** 30.2.
Brakes front: 9.5-in. discs. **Brakes rear:** 7.9-in. drums.
Construction: unit

POWERTRAINS	ohc I-4
Bore × stroke (in.)	NA
Displacement (liters/cu. in.)	1.6/97
Compression ratio	9.4:1
Fuel delivery	2bbl.
Net bhp @ rpm	69@ 5200
Net torque @ rpm (lbs/ft)	92@ 3200
Availability	S/All
Final drive ratios	
5-speed OD manual	3.79:1
3-speed automatic	3.60:1

KEY bbl. = barrel (carburetor); **bhp** = brake horsepower (advertised); **Cal.** = California only. **Fed.** = Federal/49 state; **FI** = fuel injection; **ohv** = overhead valve; **ohc** = overhead cam; **I** = inline engine; **V** = V engine; **D** = diesel; **T** = turbocharged; **OD** = overdrive transmission; **S** = standard engine; **O** = optional engine.

PRICES

PULSAR EQUIPMENT SUMMARY

(prices not available at time of publication)

STANDARD EQUIPMENT:

1.6-liter (97-cid) four-cylinder engine, 5-speed overdrive manual transmission, rear window wiper/washer, wheel trim rings, cargo area cover, AM/FM stereo radio, tinted glass, halogen headlamps, remote rear-door locks (5-door only), analog quartz clock, trip odometer, cargo area courtesy light, remote rear side window openers (3-door models), front bucket seats, split fold-down rear seatback, adjustable steering column, tachometer. **NX** coupe adds: sunroof, 175/70SR-13 RWL radial tires, full wheel covers, pop-up headlamps, trunk courtesy light.

OPTIONAL EQUIPMENT:

Power steering, manual sliding sunroof, air conditioning, 3-speed automatic transmission.

Datsun/Nissan Sentra

Nissan Sentra XE 3-door coupe

WHAT'S NEW FOR '83

Launched last spring to replace the old rear-drive Datsun 210, Nissan's front-drive subcompact line heads into '82 basically unchanged in design. However, the 1983 Sentra does get an extra 100cc displacement for its overhead-cam E-series four-cylinder engine, good for a slight gain in rated horsepower and torque. In an all-out assault on the EPA mileage crown, Nissan also offers a 1.5-liter four-cylinder diesel as a new option for the lightweight Sentra. The little smoker is available in the 2- and 4-door sedans and 5-door wagon. The sedan with standard 4-speed manual gearbox earns astounding ratings: 48 mpg city and 62 mpg highway, according to preliminary government figures. The miser-minded Sentra MPG 2-doors are continued for all but California buyers, and retain last year's 1.5-liter gas engine. The diesel Sentra is expected to be approved for full 50-state sale.

EVALUATION

Though we haven't had much long-term experience with it yet, we think Nissan is onto a winner with the Sentra. Its main problems right now are a soggy suspension that yields more body list in hard cornering than a sailboat in a hurricane, lightweight construction that makes us wonder about long-term durability (particularly rust resistance), and a too-obvious plasticky quality about the interior. On the plus side, mileage is excellent (35.4 mpg observed with our test 5-speed wagon), performance is adequate (though you have to work the little engine hard much of the time), noise levels are moderate (except when you do that), and there's passable room for four in the well-planned interior. The soft chassis detracts from handling, but does provide a very absorbent, comfortable ride for a small car. A very thoroughly developed econocar and excellent value for money, but a bit on the small side.

EVALUATION CHECKLIST

Fuel economy	5	Cargo room	3
Driveability	3	Serviceability	4
Acceleration	3	Standard equipment	3
Braking	3	Body construction	4
Handling/roadholding	4	Paint/exterior finish	3
Driving position	4	Interior finish	4
Instruments/control	3	TOTAL POINTS	70
Visiblity	4		
Heating/ventilation	4	**RATING SCALE**	
Seat comfort	3	5 = Excellent	
Passenger room	3	4 = Very Good	
Ride	4	3 = Average/Acceptable	
Noise	3	2 = Fair	
Exit/entry	3	1 = Poor	

SPECIFICATIONS

	3-door coupe	2-door sedan	4-door sedan	5-door wagon
Wheelbase (in.)	94.5	94.5	94.5	94.5
Overall length (in.)	167.3	167.3	167.3	172.2
Overall width (in.)	63.7	63.7	63.7	63.7
Overall height (in.)	NA	NA	NA	NA

SPECIFICATIONS

	3-door coupe	2-door sedan	4-door sedan	5-door wagon
Track front (in.)	54.9	54.9	54.9	54.9
Track rear (in.)	54.1	54.1	54.1	54.1
Curb weight (lbs.)	1920	1875	1895	1995
Max. cargo vol. (cu. ft.)	16.5	11.3	11.3	23.5
Fuel tank capacity (gal.)	13.2	13.2[1]	13.2	13.2
Seating capacity	4	5	5	5
Front headroom (in.)	37.3	38.3	38.3	37.6
Front shoulder room (in.)	52.6	52.6	52.6	52.6
Front legroom, max. (in.)	43.1	43.1	43.1	43.1
Rear headroom (in.)	36.7	36.7	36.7	36.1
Rear shoulder room (in.)	52.0	52.0	52.9	52.9
Rear legroom, min. (in.)	30.1	31.4	31.4	31.4

1: 10.5 gal. MPG models

BODY/CHASSIS

Drivetrain layout: transverse front engine/front-wheel drive.
Suspension front: independent, MacPherson struts, lower lateral arms, coil springs, telescopic shock absorbers. **Suspension rear:** semi-trailing arms, coil springs, telescopic shock absorbers. **Steering:** rack-and-pinion. **Turns lock-to-lock:** 3.3. **Turn diameter (ft.):** 29.5. **Brakes front:** 9.4-in. discs. **Brakes rear:** 7.1-in. drums. **Construction:** unit

POWERTRAINS	ohc I-4	ohc I-4D	ohc I-4
Bore × stroke (in.)	NA	NA	2.97× 3.23

POWERTRAINS

	ohc I-4	ohc I-4D	ohc I-4
Displacement (liters cu. in.)	1.6/ 97	1.7/ 103	1.5/ 91
Compression ratio	9.4:1	21.9:1	9.3:1
Fuel delivery	2bbl.	FI	2bbl.
Net bhp @ rpm	69@ 5200	55@ 4800	67@ 5200
Net torque @ rpm (lbs/ft)	92@ 3200	104@ 2800	90@ 3200
Availability	S/All	O/All	S/Fed[1]

1: Deluxe MPG model only

Final drive ratios

4-speed manual			3.55:1
5-speed manual	3.79:1[1]	3.79:1	
3-speed automatic	3.60:1	NA	

1: 3.55:1 MPG 5-speed

KEY bbl. = barrel (carburetor); **bhp** = brake horsepower (advertised); **Cal.** = California only. **Fed.** = Federal/49 state; **FI** = fuel injection; **ohv** = overhead valve; **ohc** = overhead cam; **I** = inline engine; **V** = V engine; **D** = diesel; **T** = turbocharged; **OD** = overdrive transmission; **S** = standard engine; **O** = optional engine.

PRICES

DATSUN/NISSAN SENTRA	Retail Price	Dealer Cost	Low Price
Standard 2-door sedan	$4949	$4454	$4754
Deluxe MPG 2-door sedan	5699	5129	5179
Deluxe 2-door sedan	5999	5195	5545
Deluxe 4-door sedan	6199	5368	5718
Deluxe 5-door wagon	6649	5738	6138
Deluxe 3-door coupe	6599	5695	6095

STANDARD EQUIPMENT (included in above prices):

1.6-liter (97-cid) four-cylinder engine (1.5-liter/89-cid on MPG), 5-speed overdrive manual transmission (4-speed manual on MPG). **Deluxe** adds: AM/FM stereo radio, remote locking fuel-filler door, halogen headlamps, tinted glass, trip odometer, trunk carpeting, visor vanity mirror, full door trim.

Prices are accurate at time of printing; subject to manufacturer's change

OPTIONAL EQUIPMENT:

	Retail Price	Dealer Cost	Low Price
Air conditioning (NA STD, MPG)	$ 610	506	512
3-speed automatic transmission (NA STD, MPG).	350	297	300
Bodyside moldings	60	40	41
Power steering, Deluxe exc. MPG (std. w/ XE package).	190	161	163
Protection Package (wheel lip & bodyside moldings)	110	80	81
Sports accent stripe, coupe only	94	66	67
Sunroof, coupe w/XE pkg., wagon	260	208	211
Deluxe woodgrain pkg., wagon only	324	233	236
XE pkg., coupe only	400	345	350

Datsun/Nissan Stanza

Nissan Stanza Deluxe 3-door sedan

WHAT'S NEW FOR '83

New last year, the middle model in the Nissan/Datsun range is a complete carryover for its encore season with a single exception. That involves the optional 3-speed automatic transmission, which now acquires a lockup torque converter for reduced internal frictional losses and better mechanical efficiency as an aid to mileage. Everything else stays the same, including the four-model lineup of 3- and 5-door sedans in base and better-equipped XE form.

EVALUATION

Vastly more capable and up-to-date than its rear-drive Dat-

Prices are accurate at time of printing; subject to manufacturer's change

sun 510 predecessor, the Stanza nevertheless needs refinement in several key areas. The driving position is curiously Italianate, and won't suit long-legged pilots. Drivability is marred by torque steer in hard acceleration, abrupt clutch take-up, and mushy brake feel. Tar patches and rough surfaces make the ride turbulent at times, and there's some fore/aft pitching over undulations. Rough pavement causes annoying tire roar, and engine/exhaust boom intrudes above 3500 rpm. The cloth uphostery in our test XE 3-door was coarse and scratchy, sort of like burlap, and there were enough fit-and-finish gaffes to make us think someone was sleeping in the quality control department. But the Stanza's strengths outnumber its weaknesses. The eager 2.0-liter engine delivers good off-the-line punch. Shift action is light and precise, the XE's standard power steering has excellent feel and isn't overassisted, and the car feels light and nimble in transient maneuvers. The heat/vent system works well, though we dislike its low-mounted controls. There's a surprising amount of rear seat room, almost enough for this to qualify as a genuine 5-seater. Our mileage figure fell 5 mpg short of the EPA estimate, but nearly 26 mpg in hard city/suburban running isn't shabby. Hatchback versatility is always a plus for us, but the two-piece parcel shelf and high rear sill detract from ease of loading. Verdict: a Japanese Ford Escort with a different set of virtues and vices. Needs better noise isolation, higher-grade fittings, more grip on wet and better control spacings.

EVALUATION CHECKLIST

Fuel economy	4	Cargo room	3
Driveability	3	Serviceability	4
Acceleration	4	Standard equipment	3
Braking	4	Body construction	4
Handling/roadholding	3	Paint/exterior finish	3
Driving position	3	Interior finish	3
Instruments/control	4	TOTAL POINTS	68
Visiblity	3		
Heating/ventilation	4	**RATING SCALE**	
Seat comfort	3	5 = Excellent	
Passenger room	4	4 = Very Good	
Ride	3	3 = Average/Acceptable	
Noise	3	2 = Fair	
Exit/entry	3	1 = Poor	

SPECIFICATIONS[1]

	3-door sedan	5-door sedan
Wheelbase (in.)	97.2	97.2
Overall length (in.)	170.9	173.4
Overall width (in.)	65.2	65.6
Overall height (in.)	53.9	54.7
Track front (in.)	56.5	56.5
Track rear (in.)	55.5	55.5
Curb weight (lbs.)	2152	2220
Max. cargo vol. (cu. ft.)	18.8	19.6
Fuel tank capacity (gal.)	14.3	14.3
Seating capacity	5	5
Front headroom (in.)	37.5[2]	38.1[3]
Front shoulder room (in.)	53.3	54.1
Front legroom, max. (in.)	40.9	40.9
Rear headroom (in.)	35.4	36.5
Rear shoulder room (in.)	52.2	53.8
Rear legroom, min. (in.)	32.9	33.3

1: Some dimensions may vary slightly depending on model
2: 36.3 in. w/sunroof
3: 37.6 in. w/sunroof

BODY/CHASSIS

Drivetrain layout: transverse front engine/front-wheel drive.
Suspension front: independent, MacPherson struts, lower A-arms, coil springs, telescopic shock absorbers. **Suspension rear:** independent, MacPherson struts, parallel lower lateral links, trailing arms, coil springs, telescopic shock absorbers. **Steering:** rack-and-pinion. **Turns lock-to-lock:** 2.9 **Turn diameter (ft.):** 32.1 **Brakes front:** 9.1-in. discs. **Brakes rear:** 8.0-in. drums. **Construction:** unit

POWERTRAINS

	ohc I-4
Bore × stroke (in.)	3.33×3.46

POWERTRAINS

	ohc I-4
Displacement (liters/cu. in.)	2.0/120
Compression ratio	8.5:1
Fuel delivery	2bbl.
Net bhp @ rpm	88@ 5200
Net torque @ rpm (lbs/ft)	112@ 2800
Availability	S/All
Final drive ratios	
5-speed OD manual	3.55:1
3-speed automatic	3.36:1

KEY bbl. = barrel (carburetor); **bhp** = brake horsepower (advertised); **Cal.** = California only. **Fed.** = Federal/49 state; **FI** = fuel injection; **ohv** = overhead valve; **ohc** – overhead cam; **I** = inline engine; **V** = V engine; **D** = diesel; **T** = turbocharged; **OD** = overdrive transmission; **S** = standard engine; **O** = optional engine.

PRICES

STANZA	Retail Price	Dealer Cost	Low Price
Deluxe 3-door sedan	$6999	$6040	6540
Deluxe 5-door sedan	7199	6213	6713

STANDARD EQUIPMENT (included in above prices):

2.0-liter (120-cid) four-cylinder engine, 5-speed overdrive manual transmission, power brakes, radial tires, styled steel wheels, tinted glass, halogen headlamps, quartz analog clock, full carpeting, electric rear window defroster, reclining front bucket seats, fold-down rear seatback, ashtray and cargo area lights, center console, passenger visor vanity mirror.

OPTIONAL EQUIPMENT:

Air conditioning			
Mechanical controls, Deluxe	$ 610	$ 506	$ 512
Vacuum controls, XE pkg.	640	525	531
3-speed automatic transmission	350	297	300
Bodyside moldings (incl. w/ XE pkg.)	70	49	50
Electric sliding sunroof (XE pkg. req.)	480	384	388
Two-tone paint.	160	128	130

Prices are accurate at time of printing; subject to manufacturer's change

	Retail Price	Dealer Cost	Low Price
XE pkg.			
w/manual transmission	900	777	785
w/automatic transmission (incl. cruise control)	1020	873	882
High-altitude emissions system	N/C	N/C	N/C

Datsun 200-SX

Datsun 200-SX 2-door and 3-door SL coupes

WHAT'S NEW FOR '83

Despite rumors of a new turbocharged model and optional digital instrument cluster, the compact sporty cars from Nissan/Datsun are almost exactly the same as before. The lower-priced Deluxe hardtop and hatchback have been upgraded with standard power steering, previously limited to the pricier SL versions. All models now have standard stereo sound system.

EVALUATION

We hate to say it but, after driving the '82, Datsun's personal-luxury sports car just isn't the same car anymore. Probably because of its extra displacement, the 2.2-liter engine is disappointingly harsher and noisier than the free-running 2.0-liter unit we remember from 1980. It emits an unpleasant-ly thrashy growl, yet feels lifeless when asked to put on some speed. As on other recent Nissan/Datsun products we've tried, workmanship seems to have slipped badly in two years, and what was once a nicely turned out cockpit now seems merely plasticky and a little careless. Our test car's shifter and clutch both had a more vague and somewhat

Prices are accurate at time of printing; subject to manufacturer's change

coarser action than in our earlier car. Why all this has happened or been allowed to happen is a mystery, but it takes a lot of enjoyment out of driving the SX. As for the rest, all is as before. Mileage is still quite good, as is overall outward vision, the driving position is comfortable if low relative to the beltline, and you still get those beautiful instruments to look at and loads of convenience features to play with. The SX is also still generally restful on the highway, though tiring engine drone sets in earlier than it used to. The high-geared power steering and compact size aid parking, even if the relatively long hood doesn't. Faults remain, too: puny fresh-air ventilation, extremely cramped back seat, and insufficient grip from the tires that leads to sudden rear-end breakaway in hard wet-weather cornering. Verdict: once our prize pick among sporty coupes, but has rested on its laurels too long. The comparably priced four-cylinder Toyota Celica is our hands down choice for 1983 in this class.

EVALUATION CHECKLIST

Fuel economy	4	Cargo room	2
Driveability	3	Serviceability	4
Acceleration	3	Standard equipment	5
Braking	4	Body construction	3
Handling/roadholding	3	Paint/exterior finish	3
Driving position	4	Interior finish	3
Instruments/control	5	TOTAL POINTS	64
Visiblity	4		
Heating/ventilation	2	**RATING SCALE**	
Seat comfort	3	5 = Excellent	
Passenger room	3	4 = Very Good	
Ride	3	3 = Average/Acceptable	
Noise	2	2 = Fair	
Exit/entry	2	1 = Poor	

SPECIFICATIONS

	2-door hardtop	3-door coupe
Wheelbase (in.)	94.5	94.5
Overall length (in.)	176.2	176.2
Overall width (in.)	66.1	66.1
Overall height (in.)	51.6	51.6
Track front (in.)	53.0	53.0

SPECIFICATIONS

	2-door coupe	3-door coupe
Track rear (in.)	53.7	53.7
Curb weight (lbs.)	2576	2603
Max. cargo vol. (cu. ft.)	8.6	19.6
Fuel tank capacity (gal.)	14.0	15.9
Seating capacity	4	4
Front headroom (in.)	37.1	36.5
Front shoulder room (in.)	51.8	51.7
Front legroom, max. (in.)	44.0	43.8
Rear headroom (in.)	35.4	33.5
Rear shoulder room (in.)	50.8	50.6
Rear legroom, min. (in.)	23.8	22.9

BODY/CHASSIS

Drivetrain layout: longitudinal front engine/rear-wheel drive. **Suspension front:** independent, MacPherson struts, lower lateral arms, compliance struts, coil springs, telescopic shock absorbers, anti-roll bar. **Suspension rear:** rigid axle, lower trailing arms, upper angled arms, coil springs, telescopic shock absorbers, anti-roll bar. **Steering:** recirculating ball, power-assisted. **Turns lock-to-lock:** 3.9. **Turn diameter (ft.):** 34.1. **Brakes front:** 10.0-in. discs. **Brakes rear:** 10.1-in. drums. **Construction:** unit

POWERTRAINS

	ohc I-4
Bore × stroke (in.)	3.43×3.62
Displacement (liters/cu. in.)	2.2/133
Compression ratio	8.5:1
Fuel delivery	FI
Net bhp @ rpm	102@ 5200
Net torque @ rpm (lbs/ft)	129@ 2800

POWERTRAINS

	ohc I-4
Availability	S/All
Final drive ratios	
5-speed OD manual	3.55:1
3-speed automatic	3.70:1

KEY bbl. = barrel (carburetor); **bhp** = brake horsepower (advertised); **Cal.** = California only. **Fed.** = Federal/49 state; **FI** = fuel injection; **ohv** = overhead valve; **ohc** = overhead cam; **I** = inline engine; **V** = V engine; **D** = diesel; **T** = turbocharged; **OD** = overdrive transmission; **S** = standard engine; **O** = optional engine.

PRICES

DATSUN 200-SX	Retail Price	Dealer Cost	Low Price
1982 prices shown; 1983 prices not available at time of publication.			
Deluxe 2-door hardtop	$7739	$6655	$7455
Deluxe 3-door coupe	7939	6830	7630

STANDARD EQUIPMENT (included in above prices):

2.2-liter (133-cid) 4-cylinder engine with fuel injection, 5-speed manual transmission, power brakes, electric rear-window defroster, AM/FM stereo radio, tinted glass, full carpeting, reclining front bucket seats, intermittent wipers, electric remote-control door mirrors, remote trunklid release, full instrumentation with tachometer.

OPTIONAL EQUIPMENT:

Air conditioning, manual	$ 620	$ 520	$ 526
3-speed automatic transmission	330	277	280
SL package			
Hardtop w/manual transmission	1350	1134	1146
Hardtop w/automatic transmission	1470	1235	1248
Hatchback w/manual transmission.	1450	1218	1231
Hatchback w/automatic transmission . . .	1570	1319	1333
Sport group (alloy wheels & sunroof)	510	418	433

Datsun 280-ZX

WHAT'S NEW FOR '83

Chassis tuning aimed at greater ride comfort and one new

Datsun 280-ZX Turbo 3-door coupe

option package are the main news concerning the Nissan/ Datsun sports car foursome. The 280-ZX line will again comprise 2-seat and 2+2 coupes powered by normally aspirated and turbocharged versions of the familiar fuel-injected 2.8-liter straight six. Standard with either is a 5-speed overdrive manual gearbox (introduced for the turbo engine last August), with 3-speed automatic at extra cost. Suspension settings are now the same for both turbo and non-turbo ZXs. The former used to have a firmer setup. Shock absorber rates have been softened, and the turbo models now get the lower spring rates of the non-turbo cars. Tire width has been upped by 10mm from 195 to 205 mm. Turbo ZXs continue on Bridgestone Potenza 60-series radials; unblown models have 70-series Goodyear Eagle GTs. Optional for all ZXs this year is a new equipment group. It includes leather upholstery with "nu-suede" side bolsters, plus a new digital instrument cluster. Automatic temperature control, bronze-tint glass, electric door mirror defoggers, and something called an "ambience" sound system are also included. Turbo models with solid-color exterior come with a standard blackout treatment with new bodyside tape striping.

EVALUATION

A very different car than the Zs of old, and rather incongruous. Despite racy looks, the ZX comes off more as a luxury cruiser for Interstate flying than as a sports car for exploring winding country lanes. The last ZX we tested, the Turbo 2-seater with automatic, was spoiled most by an annoyingly jiggly ride on patchwork city streets and by a cabin that is adequately spacious but feels cramped. This year's revised suspension settings may make the going smoother. We hope so. The turbocharged engine gives brilliant performance, which we think is an aid to avoiding accidents. Workmanship on the last few Datsuns we've sampled isn't as good as we've come to expect from this maker, paint finish in particular being rather tacky. Despite the turbo engine's greater complexity, service access is quite good. One of our testers described the ZX as "the Ford LTD of sports cars," and that still pretty well sums it up.

EVALUATION CHECKLIST

Fuel economy	2	Cargo room	3
Driveability	3	Serviceability	4
Acceleration	4	Standard equipment	5
Braking	3	Body construction	4
Handling/roadholding	3	Paint/exterior finish	3
Driving position	4	Interior finish	5
Instruments/control	5	TOTAL POINTS	67
Visiblity	3		
Heating/ventilation	2	**RATING SCALE**	
Seat comfort	3	5 = Excellent	
Passenger room	3	4 = Very Good	
Ride	2	3 = Average/Acceptable	
Noise	3	2 = Fair	
Exit/entry	3	1 = Poor	

SPECIFICATIONS

	3-door coupe	2 + 2 3-door coupe
Wheelbase (in.)	91.3	99.2
Overall length (in.)	174.0	181.9
Overall width (in.)	66.5	66.5
Overall height (in.)	51.0	51.0
Track front (in.)	54.9	54.9
Track rear (in.)	54.7	54.7
Curb weight (lbs.)	2860[1]	2958[1]
Max. cargo vol. (cu. ft.)	15.6	18.2
Fuel tank capacity (gal.)	21.1	21.1
Seating capacity	2	4

SPECIFICATIONS

	3-door coupe	2 + 2 3-door coupe
Front headroom (in.)	36.5	36.6
Front shoulder room (in.)	52.2	52.5
Front legroom, max. (in.)	43.3	44.0
Rear headroom (in.)	—	35.3
Rear shoulder room (in.)	—	50.0
Rear legroom, min. (in.)	—	23.8

1: Base models

BODY/CHASSIS

Drivetrain layout: longitudinal front engine/rear-wheel drive.
Suspension front: independent, MacPherson struts, lower lateral arms, compliance struts, coil springs, telescopic shock absorbers, anti-roll bar. **Suspension rear:** independent, semi-trailing arms, coil springs, telescopic shock absorbers, anti-roll bar. **Steering:** rack-and-pinion, power-assisted. **Turns lock-to-lock:** 2.7. **Turn diameter (ft.):** 32.2. **Brakes front:** 9.9-in. discs. **Brakes rear:** 10.6-in. discs. **Construction:** unit

POWERTRAINS

	ohc I-6	ohc I-6T
Bore × stroke (in.)	3.39× 3.11	3.39× 3.11
Displacement (liters cu. in.)	2.8/ 168	2.8/ 168
Compression ratio	8.3:1	7.4:1
Fuel delivery	FI	FI
Net bhp @ rpm	145@ 5200	180@ 5600
Net torque @ rpm (lbs/ft)	156@ 4000	202@ 2800
Availability	S/All	S/All¹

1: Turbo models only

POWERTRAINS

	ohc I-6	ohc I-6T
Final drive ratios		
5-speed OD manual	3.90:1	3.55:1
3-speed automatic	3.55:1	3.55:1

KEY bbl. = barrel (carburetor); **bhp** = brake horsepower (advertised); **Cal.** = California only. **Fed.** = Federal/49 state; **FI** = fuel injection; **ohv** = overhead valve; **ohc** = overhead cam; **I** = inline engine; **V** = V engine; **D** = diesel; **T** = turbocharged; **OD** = overdrive transmission; **S** = standard engine; **O** = optional engine.

PRICES

DATSUN 280-ZX	Retail Price	Dealer Cost	Low Price
1982 prices shown; 1983 prices not available at time of publication.			
3-door coupe.	$11299	$ 9548	$11048
3-door 2+2 coupe	14949	12557	14557
Turbo 3-door coupe.	16999	14249	16749
Turbo 3-door 2+2 coupe	18299	NA	NA

STANDARD EQUIPMENT (included in above prices):

2.8-liter (168-cid) 6-cylinder fuel-injected engine (turbocharged on Turbo), 5-speed overdrive manual transmission, power brakes, power steering, air conditioning, alloy wheels (except base coupe), full instrumentation including tachometer, remote hatchback release, reclining front bucket seats, lockable fuel filler door, engine compartment light, quartz clock, electric rear-window defroster, driver's seat lumbar support adjuster, halogen headlamps, front spoiler, interior light package, full carpeting, center console, AM/FM stereo radio with 4 speakers, front seat tilt adjusters. **2+2** adds: dual remote-control door mirrors, power windows, tinted glass, AM/FM stereo radio with cassette player and automatic antenna, cloth upholstery, lighted vanity mirror, passenger's seat lumbar support adjuster, warning light check system, split-back fold-down rear seat, cruise control, intermittent wipers. **Turbo** adds: uprated suspension, low-profile radial tires, headlight washers, turbo boost gauge, special nameplates, twin exhausts, engine oil cooler.

OPTIONAL EQUIPMENT:

3-speed automatic transmission	$ 320	$ 272	$ 275
Two-tone paint.	160	128	130
T-bar roof.	800	650	725
Leather package, 2-seaters	500	410	415
2+2 models.	600	510	515

Prices are accurate at time of printing; subject to manufacturer's change

Dodge Aries/ Plymouth Reliant

Dodge Aries Special Edition 4-door sedan

WHAT'S NEW FOR '83

Chrysler's successful front-drive K-car twins gain a 5-speed overdrive manual transmission as a new option and power brakes and self-adjusting rear brakes as standard equipment. Halogen headlamps, tethered gas cap, and maintenance-free battery are also new standards on all models. There are now two trim levels, one fewer than before. The familiar coupe and sedan are available in base and Special Edition trim, while the wagon comes in Custom and SE form. The 5-speed, available only with the standard 2.2 engine and bucket seats and center console, uses a cable shift linkage instead of the rod linkage on Chrysler's previous manual gearboxes. Chrysler claims this provides shorter shift strokes and crisper feel. The 2.2 gets higher compression, revised carburetor settings, and redesigned intake and exhaust manifolds that are supposed to improve economy and yield 10 extra horsepower over last year's engine. The throttle on the optional 2.6-liter engine has been revised for quicker engine response. The vent/heat system incorporates a new ram-air feature and adds one more dash vent. A bi-level setting is now provided with air conditioning. Sound deadening is improved on all models.

EVALUATION

Though the K-cars' basic design has stayed the same since

its 1981 debut, Chrysler has been refining it. The good news this year is the 5-speed option that should improve highway mileage. The bad news is you have to buy bucket seats and console to get it. With 2.2 and standard 4-speed, mileage is fine; less so with automatic and/or the 2.6 engine. Rates high for passenger and luggage space, quiet and smooth drivetrains, and a ride that is a nice compromise between mushy soft and rock hard. The 2.2 engine is a gem for servicing, and the 2.6 is fairly easy to work on also. Lacks sufficient instrumentation for those who like to keep an eye on engine performance. Real shortcoming is that no tachometer is available for manual shift fans. Neither engine is a hot performer, though both are capable and durable. Likewise, handling is more family car than road racer, in keeping with the mild-mannered nature of the K-cars. Overall, well-liked by us and recommended because of its competitive price and general competence. Chrysler's 5-year/50,000-mile warranty has been extended to '83 models, another plus point.

EVALUATION CHECKLIST

Fuel economy	3	Cargo room	4
Driveability	4	Serviceability	5
Acceleration	3	Standard equipment	3
Braking	3	Body construction	4
Handling/roadholding	3	Paint/exterior finish	4
Driving position	4	Interior finish	3
Instruments/control	2	TOTAL POINTS	73
Visiblity	4		
Heating/ventilation	4	**RATING SCALE**	
Seat comfort	3	5 = Excellent	
Passenger room	4	4 = Very Good	
Ride	3	3 = Average/Acceptable	
Noise	4	2 = Fair	
Exit/entry	3	1 = Poor	

SPECIFICATIONS

	2-door coupe	4-door sedan	5-door wagon
Wheelbase (in.)	100.1	100.1	100.1
Overall length (in.)	176.0	176.0	176.2
Overall width (in.)	68.6	68.6	68.6
Overall length (in.)	52.3	52.7	52.4

SPECIFICATIONS

	2-door coupe	4-door sedan	5-door wagon
Track front (in.)	57.6	57.6	57.6
Track rear (in.)	57.0	57.0	57.0
Curb weight (lbs.)	2317[1]	2323[1]	2432[1]
Max. cargo vol. (cu. ft.)	15.0	15.0	70.0
Fuel tank capacity (gal.)	13.0	13.0	13.0
Seating capacity	6	6	6
Front headroom (in.)	38.2	38.6	38.5
Front shoulder room (in.)	55.0	55.4	56.2
Front legroom, max. (in.)	42.2	42.2	42.2
Rear headroom (in.)	37.0	37.8	38.4
Rear shoulder room (in.)	58.8	55.9	56.7
Rear legroom, min. (in.)	35.1	35.4	35.0

1: Base models

BODY/CHASSIS

Drivetrain layout: transverse front engine/front-wheel drive. **Suspension front:** independent, MacPherson struts, lower A-arms, coil springs, telescopic shock absorbers, anti-roll bar. **Suspension rear:** beam "flex" axle, trailing arms, coil springs, telescopic shock absorbers, anti-roll bar. **Steering:** rack-and-pinion. **Turns lock-to-lock:** 4.0 manual, 3.2 power. **Turn diameter (ft.):** 34.8. **Brakes front:** 9.3-in. discs. **Brakes rear:** 7.9-in. drums. **Construction:** unit

POWERTRAINS

	ohc I-4	ohc I-4
Bore × stroke (in.)	3.44× 3.62	3.59× 3.86
Displacement (liters cu. in.)	2.2/ 135	2.6/ 156
Compression ratio	9.0:1	8.2:1
Fuel delivery	2bbl.	2bbl.

POWERTRAINS

	ohc I-4	ohc I-4
Net bhp @ rpm	94@ 5200	93 4500
Net torque @ rpm (lbs/ft)	117@ 3200	132@ 2500
Availability	S/All	O/All
Final drive ratios		
4-speed OD manual	2.69:1	
5-speed OD manual	2.20:1[1]	
3-speed automatic	2.78:1[2]	2.78:1

1: 2.57:1 opt.
2: 3.02:1 opt.

KEY bbl. = barrel (carburetor); **bhp** = brake horsepower (advertised); **Cal.** = California only. **Fed.** = Federal/49 state; **FI** = fuel injection; **ohv** = overhead valve; **ohc** = overhead cam; **I** = inline engine; **V** = V engine; **D** = diesel; **T** = turbocharged; **OD** = overdrive transmission; **S** = standard engine; **O** = optional engine.

PRICES

ARIES/RELIANT	Retail Price	Dealer Cost	Low Price
2-door coupe.	$6577	$6081	$6581
4-door sedan.	6718	6209	6709
Custom 5-door wagon	7636	6816	7316
Special Edition 2-door coupe	7260	6485	6985
Special Edition 4-door sedan	7417	6623	7123
Special Edition 5-door wagon	8186	7300	7900

STANDARD EQUIPMENT (included in above prices):

2.2-liter (135-cid) 4-cylinder engine, 4-speed overdrive manual transmission, power brakes, front bench seat w/center armrest, vinyl upholstery, dual horns, upper door frame and belt moldings, halogen headlamps, full carpeting, AM radio. **Special Edition** adds: remote-control door mirror, special sound insulation, wagon bodyside woodgrain applique, luxury steering wheel; cloth upholstery, carpeted lower door panels, woodtone dash and door panel appliqués, digital clock.

OPTIONAL EQUIPMENT:

2.6-liter (156-cid) 4-cylinder engine	$ 259	$ 220	223
3-speed automatic transmission	439	373	377

Prices are accurate at time of printing; subject to manufacturer's change

	Retail Price	Dealer Cost	Low Price
5-speed manual transmission (bucket seats req.)	75	64	65
Air conditioning (power brakes, tinted glass req.)	732	622	629
Performance axle ratio, 5-speed	22	19	20
500-amp. maintenance-free battery	43	37	38
Bumper guards front or rear	28	24	25
Door edge protectors			
Coupes	15	13	13
Sedans, wagons	25	21	21
Engine cooling package (incl. w/AC)	141	120	122
Power decklid or tailgate release	40	34	35
Electric rear window defroster	137	116	118
Power door locks (dual remote mirrors req.)			
Coupes	120	102	105
Sedans, wagons	170	145	147
Tinted glass	105	89	90
Light Package			
Coupes	93	79	80
Sedans, wagons	103	88	89
Luggage rack	106	90	91
Sill moldings	23	20	20
Radio equipment			
AM, base models	78	66	67
AM delete (credit), ex. base models . . .	(56)	(48)	(56)
AM/FM stereo, manual-tune			
Base models	187	159	161
Custom, Special Edition	109	93	94
AM/FM stereo, electronic-tune			
Base models	341	290	293
Custom, Special Edition	263	224	227
AM/FM stereo electronic-tune w/cassette			
Base models	480	408	413
Custom, Special Edition	402	342	346
Seats			
Bench, cloth & vinyl	31	26	27
Buckets, vinyl, cloth.			
(na base models)	156	13	135
Center armrest (bucket seats req.)	63	54	55
Power seat, left bucket	210	179	181
Special sound insulation	43	37	38
Conventional spare tire	63	54	55
Luxury steering wheel, base models	40	34	35
Power steering (std. Spl. Edn. wagon) . . .	214	182	185
Tilt steering column			
(intermittent wipers req.)	105	89	90

Prices are accurate at time of printing; subject to manufacturer's change

	Retail Price	Dealer Cost	Low Price
Heavy-duty suspension	26	22	23
Automatic speed control (intermittent wiper req.)	174	148	150
Rear tonneau cover, wagons	68	58	59
Trunk dress-up (na wagon)	51	43	44
Undercoating	41	35	36
Lower bodyside protection	39	33	34
Vinyl roof			
Full, 4-door sedans	172	146	148
Landau, coupes	177	150	152
Intermittent wipers	52	44	45
Tailgate wiper/washer, wagons	117	99	100
Bodyside tape stripe (NA w/two-tone paint)	48	41	42
Two-tone paint, coupes (NA w/vinyl roof) . .	176	150	152
Power windows			
Coupes	180	153	155
Sedans, wagons	255	217	220

Dodge Challenger/ Plymouth Sapporo

Dodge Challenger Technica 2-door coupe

WHAT'S NEW FOR '83

These rear-drive sporty coupes are built by Mitsubishi and sold in near-identical form. Unlike the front-drive Colt, which will be sold by Dodge and Plymouth dealers under the same name, the Challenger and Sapporo retain nominally separate identities. The reason, Chrysler insists, is that they appeal to different kinds of buyers. Both brands are offered with a new

Prices are accurate at time of printing; subject to manufacturer's change

"Technica" performance package. It's marked by silver paint, black hood and exterior trim, and a high-tech dashboard with digital speedometer and graphic display tachometer, 6-speaker stereo system, and speed control. Technica also has a vocal warning system. Challenger and Sapporo are offered in two versions. The S features black exterior moldings. The L has a dark argent grille, body color accents around dual-lens taillamps, and rear window louvers.

EVALUATION

Stylish, well-built, and well-equipped Oriental ponycar, but poorly promoted by Chrysler. Conventional front-engine/rear-drive layout, but front occupants are given first-class accommodations and ample room. Taller people might feel crunched by the low ceiling, although the driver's seat adjusts for height and rake to alleviate the snug fit. Competent on the road, though performance isn't thrilling with the mild 2.6-liter four, but roadholding is fine. Engine growls at higher rpm and tires roar over coarse surfaces. Front end tends to lift at higher speeds. The manual shift linkage is precise, and clutch action is light and smooth. Stylish dash ranks with competitors from Datsun and Toyota. Tight construction results in rattlefree body even without side pillars. Nice fit on upholstery and carpeting. Small trunk capacity reduces usefulness. Due to be discontinued after this year, a pity as it's really a much better car than most people think.

EVALUATION CHECKLIST

Fuel economy	3	Cargo room	2
Driveability	4	Serviceability	4
Acceleration	4	Standard equipment	5
Braking	4	Body construction	5
Handling/roadholding	3	Paint/exterior finish	4
Driving position	4	Interior finish	4
Instruments/control	5	TOTAL POINTS	75
Visiblity	4		
Heating/ventilation	3	**RATING SCALE**	
Seat comfort	4	5 = Excellent	
Passenger room	3	4 = Very Good	
Ride	3	3 = Average/Acceptable	
Noise	4	2 = Fair	
Exit/entry	3	1 = Poor	

SPECIFICATIONS

	2-door coupe
Wheelbase (in.)	99.6
Overall length (in.)	180.0
Overall width (in.)	65.9
Overall height (in.)	52.8
Track front (in.)	54.1
Track rear (in.)	53.3
Curb weight (lbs.)	2723[1]
Max. cargo vol. (cu. ft.)	12.4
Fuel tank capacity (gal.)	15.8
Seating capacity	5
Front headroom (in.)	36.8
Front shoulder room (in.)	51.8
Front legroom, max. (in.)	41.1
Rear headroom (in.)	35.4
Rear shoulder room (in.)	51.0
Rear legroom, min. (in.)	34.6

1: w/base equipment

BODY/CHASSIS

Drivetrain layout: longitudinal front engine/rear-wheel drive. **Suspension front:** independent, MacPherson struts, coil springs, telescopic shock absorbers, anti-roll bar. **Suspension rear:** rigid axle, upper and lower control arms, coil springs, telescopic shock absorbers. **Steering:** recirculating ball, power-assisted. **Turns lock-to-lock:** 3.4. **Turn diameter (ft.):** 32.8. **Brakes front:** 9.9-in. discs. **Brakes rear:** 9.0-in. drums (9.6-in. discs optional). **Construction:** unit

POWERTRAINS

	ohc I-4
Bore × stroke (in.)	3.59×3.86
Displacement	2.6/156

POWERTRAINS

	ohc I-4
Compression ratio	9.0:1
Fuel delivery	2bbl.
Net bhp @ rpm	93@ 4500
Net torque @ rpm (lbs/ft)	132@ 2500
Availability	S/All
Final drive ratios	
5-speed OD manual	3.31:1
3-speed automatic	3.31:1

KEY bbl. = barrel (carburetor); **bhp** = brake horsepower (advertised); **Cal.** = California only. **Fed.** = Federal/49 state; **FI** = fuel injection; **ohv** = overhead valve; **ohc** = overhead cam; **I** = inline engine; **V** = V engine; **D** = diesel; **T** = turbocharged; **OD** = overdrive transmission; **S** = standard engine; **O** = optional engine.

PRICES

DODGE CHALLENGER/ PLYMOUTH SAPPORO	Retail Price	Dealer Cost	Low Price

(1982 prices shown; 1983 prices not available at time of publication.)

	Retail Price	Dealer Cost	Low Price
2-door coupe.	$8043	$7295	$7985

(Note: vehicle and options prices identical regardless of nameplate.)

STANDARD EQUIPMENT (included in above prices):

2.6-liter (156-cid) 4-cylinder engine, 5-speed overdrive manual transmission, power steering, power brakes, tinted glass, electric rear-window defroster, dual remote-control door mirrors, tilt-adjustable steering column, full carpeting, dual horns, reclining front bucket seats, full instrumentation, intermittent wipers, digital clock, overhead console, door key-cylinder lamps, AM/FM stereo radio, locking fuel filler door, remote fuel filler and trunklid releases, right visor vanity mirror, trip odometer, full interior courtesy light package, wide bodyside moldings.

OPTIONAL EQUIPMENT:

Air conditioning	$ 620	$ 533	$ 539
AM/FM stereo radio w/cassette	197	169	171
Speed control	138	119	121

Prices are accurate at time of printing; subject to manufacturer's change

	Retail Price	Dealer Cost	Low Price
3-speed automatic transmission	303	261	264
Trunk dress-up	41	35	36
Road-wheel package[1]	382	329	333

1: incl. cast-aluminum wheels, 4-wheel disc brakes.

Dodge/Plymouth Colt

Dodge Colt 5-door sedan

WHAT'S NEW FOR '83

The front-drive Mitsubishi-built minicars sold through Dodge and Plymouth dealers receive only minor appearance and mechanical changes, but will be sold under a new marketing scheme. Previously sold by Plymouth dealers under the Champ name, both versions are now called Colt. Chrysler will actually be stressing that these are imports, trying to cash in on the lure that Made in Japan now has for many car buyers. Revised front end styling involves a redesigned hood, headlamps, and grille, all claimed to improve aerodynamics. A redesigned instrument panel groups heater controls higher on the dash and adds a fourth air vent. Deluxe and Custom Colts feature Mitsubishi's clever Twin-Stick dual-range manual gearbox, which lets the driver choose between economy and performance modes. Optional gear ratios will be available with automatic for the first time for greater highway fuel economy.

Prices are accurate at time of printing; subject to manufacturer's change

EVALUATION

These hatchbacks are attractively priced and return high mileage, even when driven briskly. The 5-door model added last year yields more interior space than the 3-door, but the rear seat in both is still no fit place for adults. It's most useful when folded down and used to enlarge the cargo space. Nimble size and agility make the Colt great for zipping around town aided by tight turn circle and fine visibility. On the highway, the engine sounds busy and road noise also picks up with speed. The larger engine is smoother and peppier, and doesn't lose much in mileage. It's a better bet for those who like to mix fun with frugality. Chrysler is pricing Colt to beat other low-end imports, which makes it a must to consider. A good alternative to the class-leading Honda Civic, though not as refined or stingy with gas.

EVALUATION CHECKLIST

Fuel economy	4	Cargo room	3
Driveability	3	Serviceability	4
Acceleration	3	Standard equipment	3
Braking	3	Body construction	4
Handling/roadholding	4	Paint/exterior finish	4
Driving position	4	Interior finish	4
Instruments/control	3	TOTAL POINTS	68
Visiblity	5		
Heating/ventilation	3	**RATING SCALE**	
Seat comfort	3	5 = Excellent	
Passenger room	2	4 = Very Good	
Ride	3	3 = Average/Acceptable	
Noise	3	2 = Fair	
Exit/entry	3	1 = Poor	

SPECIFICATIONS

	3-door sedan	5-door sedan
Wheelbase (in.)	90.6	93.7
Overall length (in.)	156.9	161.0
Overall width (in.)	62.4	62.6
Overall height (in.)	50.0	50.0
Track front (in.)	53.9	53.9

SPECIFICATIONS

	3-door sedan	5-door sedan
Track rear (in.)	52.8	52.8
Curb weight (lbs.)	1865[1]	1955[1]
Max. cargo vol. (cu. ft.)	22.9	22.9
Fuel tank capacity (gal.)	10.6	10.6
Seating capacity	4	4
Front headroom (in.)	36.8	36.8
Front shoulder room (in.)	51.0	51.0
Front legroom, max. (in.)	40.6	40.6
Rear headroom (in.)	36.0	36.0
Rear shoulder room (in.)	52.4	52.4
Rear legroom, min. (in.)	29.7	32.7

1: Base models

BODY/CHASSIS

Drivetrain layout: transverse front engine/front-wheel drive.
Suspension front: independent, MacPherson struts, lower
control arms, coil springs, telescopic shock absorbers, anti-
roll bar. **Suspension rear:** independent, full trailing arms,
coil springs, anti-roll bar optional. **Steering:** rack-and-pinion.
Turns lock-to-lock: 3.2/3.9. **Turn diameter (ft.):** 32.8.
Brakes front: 8.94-in. discs. **Brakes rear:** 7.1-in. drums.
Construction: unit

POWERTRAINS

	ohc I-4	ohc I-4
Bore × stroke (in.)	2.91× 3.23	3.03× 3.39
Displacement (liters/cu. in.)	1.4/ 86.0	1.6/ 98.0
Compression ratio	8.8:1	8.5:1
Fuel delivery	2bbl.	2bbl.
Net bhp @ rpm	64@ 5000	72@ 5000

POWERTRAINS

	ohc I-4	ohc I-4
Net torque @ rpm (lbs/ft)	78@ 3000	85@ 3000
Availability	S/All	O/All[1]

1: NA base models; std. Custom; opt. Deluxe

Final drive ratios

4-speed OD manual	3.17:1	
4 × 2-speed manual	3.47:1	3.47:1
3-speed automatic		2.80:1

KEY bbl. = barrel (carburetor); **bhp** = brake horsepower (advertised); **Cal.** = California only. **Fed.** = Federal/49 state; **FI** = fuel injection; **ohv** = overhead valve; **ohc** = overhead cam; **I** = inline engine; **V** = V engine; **D** = diesel; **T** = turbocharged; **S** = standard engine; **O** = optional engine; **OD** = overdrive transmission.

PRICES

DODGE/PLYMOUTH COLT

	Retail Price	Dealer Cost	Low Price
(1982 prices shown; 1983 prices not available at time of publication.)			
3-door sedan...............	$5443	$4999	$5299
Deluxe 3-door sedan	5800	5321	5671
Custom 3-door sedan.........	6122	5611	6011
5-door sedan..............	5710	5240	5590
Custom 5-door sedan.........	6153	5638	6038

(Note: vehicle and options prices identical regardless of nameplate.)

STANDARD EQUIPMENT (included in above prices):

1.4-liter (86-cid) 4-cylinder engine, 4-speed manual transmission, power brakes, reclining front bucket seats, carpeting, cigarette lighter, trip odometer. **Deluxe** adds: 4x2-speed Twin-Stick manual transmission, tinted glass, electric rear-window defroster. **Custom** adds: 1.6-liter (98-cid) engine, console, cargo area carpet, remote liftgate release, tape striping.

OPTIONAL EQUIPMENT:

1.6-liter (98-cid) 4-cylinder engine......	$ 88	$ 76	$ 77
Air conditioning	620	533	539
3-speed automatic transmission (w/1.6-liter engine)................	300	258	261
Digital clock	55	47	48
Electric rear-window defroster, base	103	89	90
13-gal. fuel tank...............	25	22	22

Prices are accurate at time of printing; subject to manufacturer's change

	Retail Price	Dealer Cost	Low Price
Tinted glass, base	56	48	49
Handling package			
Base	38	33	34
Others	32	28	29
Dual horns	18	15	16
LS/RS Package, Custom	571	491	496
Luggage rack	96	83	84
Radio equipment			
AM	89	77	78
AM/FM stereo			
Custom	212	182	184
Deluxe	247	212	215
Roadwheel package	295	254	257
Sunroof, glass flip-up	250	215	218
Rear-window wiper/washer	64	55	56
Wheel trim rings	49	42	43

Dodge Diplomat/ Plymouth Gran Fury

Dodge Diplomat Medallion 4-door sedan

WHAT'S NEW FOR '83

The only changes in these mid-size sedans are that new exterior colors are available and cancellation of the base Diplomat. Salon and Medallion Diplomats and the Gran Fury Salon return, all four-door sedans. They remain for big-car fans and fleet buyers looking for a longer wheelbase and plush interiors. The chassis is same one used for the

Chrysler New Yorker Fifth Avenue and Cordoba, and the Dodge Mirada.

EVALUATION

Boring, anonymous car with mid-'70s engineering. Okay as family transport on shopping trips and the occasional longer journey, though it possesses shortcomings because of its aged design. Because of high curb weight, the standard 6-cylinder engine has to work extra hard to give adequate performance. The optional V-8 is better, but uses more gas. The front cabin is roomy and plush, yet rear seat isn't exceptionally large for the car's size. Neither is the trunk. Tall drivers might feel cramped because the seat can't be pushed back far enough from pedals. Chassis settings are soft so handling is mushy, body lean marked. Rear axle tends to hop uncomfortably on rough patches. Familiarity with proven design means that most are turned out with good finish and few assembly problems, so this car is not without virtues. It's also covered for 5 years or 50,000 miles under factory powertrain and rust warranty. Assessment: the same as last year: outclassed as an intermediate, yet doesn't compare well as a full-size either.

EVALUATION CHECKLIST

Fuel economy	3	Cargo room	3
Driveability	3	Serviceability	3
Acceleration	2	Standard equipment	3
Braking	3	Body construction	4
Handling/roadholding	3	Paint/exterior finish	4
Driving position	3	Interior finish	4
Instruments/control	2	TOTAL POINTS	64
Visiblity	3		
Heating/ventilation	4	**RATING SCALE**	
Seat comfort	4	5 = Excellent	
Passenger room	3	4 = Very Good	
Ride	3	3 = Average/Acceptable	
Noise	4	2 = Fair	
Exit/entry	3	1 = Poor	

SPECIFICATIONS

	4-door sedan
Wheelbase (in.)	112.7

SPECIFICATIONS

	4-door sedan
Overall length (in.)	205.7
Overall width (in.)	74.2
Overall height (in.)	55.3
Track front (in.)	60.0
Track rear (in.)	59.5
Curb weight (lbs.)	3412[1]
Max. cargo vol. (cu. ft.)	15.6[2]
Fuel tank capacity (gal.)	18.0
Seating capacity	6
Front headroom (in.)	39.3
Front shoulder room (in.)	56.0
Front legroom, max. (in.)	42.5
Rear headroom (in.)	37.7
Rear shoulder room (in.)	55.9
Rear legroom, min. (in.)	36.6

1: Base model
2: Manufacturer's estimate

BODY/CHASSIS

Drivetrain layout: longitudinal front engine/rear-wheel drive. **Suspension front:** independent, lateral non-parallel control arms, transverse torsion bars, telescopic shock absorbers, anti-roll bar. **Suspension rear:** rigid axle, semi-elliptic leaf springs. **Steering:** recirculating ball, power-assisted. **Turns lock-to-lock:** 3.5. **Turn diameter (ft.):** 40.7. **Brakes front:** 10.8-in. discs. **Brakes rear:** 10.0-in. drums. **Construction:** unit

POWERTRAINS

	ohv I-6	ohv V-8
Bore × stroke (in.)	3.40× 4.12	3.91× 3.31

POWERTRAINS

	ohv I-6	ohv V-8
Displacement (liters/cu. in.)	3.7/ 225	5.2/ 318
Compression ratio	8.4:1	8.5:1
Fuel delivery	1bbl.	2bbl.
Net bhp @ rpm	90@ 3600	130@ 4000
Net torque @ rpm (lbs/ft)	165@ 1600	230@ 1600
Availability	S/All	O/All
Final drive ratios		
3-speed automatic	2.94:1	2.94:1[1]

1: 2.26:1 std. Cal., opt. Fed.

KEY bbl. = barrel (carburetor); **bhp** = brake horsepower (advertised); **Cal.** = California only. **Fed.** = Federal/49 state; **FI** = fuel injection; **ohv** = overhead valve; **ohc** = overhead cam; **I** = inline engine; **V** = V engine; **D** = diesel; **T** = turbocharged; **OD** = overdrive transmission; **S** = standard engine; **O** = optional engine.

PRICES

	Retail Price	Dealer Cost	Low Price
DODGE DIPLOMAT			
Salon 4-door sedan	$8248	$7520	$8048
Medallion 4-door sedan	9369	8061	8961
PLYMOUTH GRAN FURY			
Salon 4-door sedan	$8248	$7520	$8020

STANDARD EQUIPMENT (included in above prices):

3.7-liter (225-cid) 1-bbl. six-cylinder engine, 3-speed automatic transmission, power steering, power front-disc/rear-drum brakes, rear bumper guards, space-saving spare tire, whitewall fiberglass-belted radial tires, tinted glass, halogen headlamps, dual horns, AM radio, luxury steering wheel. **Medallion** adds: vinyl roof, remote-control left door mirror, wheel covers, upgraded trim and body sound insulation, upper door frame moldings, trunk dress-up.

OPTIONAL EQUIPMENT:

5.2-liter (318-cid) V-8 2-bbl. (NA Cal.) . . .	$ 225	$ 191	$ 193
Vinyl roof, full, Salons (incl. w/Basic Group)	172	146	148

Prices are accurate at time of printing; subject to manufacturer's change

	Retail Price	Dealer Cost	Low Price
Vinyl bodyside moldings (incl. w/Protection Group)	57	48	49
Tape striping (hood, decklid, bodysides)	109	93	94
Vinyl bench seat, split back w/center armrest, Salons	60	51	52
Light package (incl. w/basic group)			
Salon	147	125	127
Medallion	112	95	96
Basic group			
Salon	1308	1112	1124
Medallion	1101	936	946
Protection group	132	112	114
Air Conditioning (incl. w/basic group)	787	669	676
500-amp. maintenance-free battery	43	37	38
Electronic digital clock	64	54	55
Electric rear-window defroster	138	117	118
Illuminated entry system	75	64	65
Body sound insulation, Salons	43	36	37
Upper door frame moldings	44	37	38
Power Assists			
Power seat, left, Medallion	199	169	171
Power windows (remote-control mirrors req. on Salon)	255	217	220
Power door locks	159	135	137
Power decklid release	40	34	35
Radio equipment			
AM delete (credit)	(56)	(48)	(56)
AM/FM stereo, manual-tune (incl. w/ Basic Group)	109	90	91
AM/FM stereo, electronic-tune			
w/o Basic Group	263	224	227
w/Basic Group	154	131	133
AM/FM stereo electronic-tune w/cassette tape			
w/o Basic Group	402	342	346
w/Basic Group	293	249	252
Conventional spare tire	63	54	55
Automatic speed control	174	148	150
Leather-wrapped steering wheel	53	45	46
Tilt steering column (Intermittent wipers req.)	99	84	85
Power glass sunroof	1041	885	894
Heavy-duty suspension	26	22	23
Trunk dress-up, Salons	54	46	47
Undercoating (incl. w/Basic Group)	41	35	36
Intermittent wipers (incl. w/Basic Group; req. w/tilt wheel)	52	44	45

Prices are accurate at time of printing; subject to manufacturer's change

Dodge Omni & Charger

Dodge Charger 2.2 3-door coupe

WHAT'S NEW FOR '83

Revised drivetrains and a realigned model lineup are this year's news for the L-body front-drive subcompacts from Dodge. The 5-door sedan is still called Omni, but the former 024 coupes are now called Charger. The premium E-type sedan and the stripped Miser versions of both body styles disappear, leaving better-equipped base models, with Omni Custom and Charger 2.2 as the step-up offerings. Later in the year, a new 1.6-liter four imported from Peugeot in France will become the new standard engine for Omni and the base Charger. It replaces the 1.7-liter VW-based unit previously used. The Charger 2.2 retains its domestically built "Trans-4" engine as standard. This now puts out an extra 10 horsepower thanks to revised manifolding, higher compression, and other engineering revisions. The 2.2 is an option in other models, and can be teamed with a new 5-speed overdrive manual gearbox as an alternative to the standard 4-speed.

EVALUATION

Though eclipsed in some ways by more recent U.S. and foreign cars, Omni/Charger have improved through the years, and are still competitive in the small-car field. With the Horizon/Turismo at Plymouth, these were the first American-made front-drive subcompacts, introduced for '78. The new 1.6 Peugeot engine has good track record in Europe. It lacks vigor, but is smooth and economical. The optional 5-speed can only improve mileage with the sprightly 2.2. Charger is basically the same as Omni mechanically, but has less back seat room because of its coupe styling and shorter chassis. Charger 2.2 is a quick little devil, but a noisy one, and its stiff suspension causes lots of jiggling on bad roads. Big deep-dish steering wheel on all models is set too high and close to driver. Pedals on manual-shift cars are awkwardly placed. Coupe models are prone to rattle, especially in hatchback area, and construction quality isn't yet a match for many imports, though it's better than it used to be. Good gas mileage and low prices make these cars worth considering. The Charger 2.2 is a low-bucks street racer with very respectable mileage; lacks refinement though. Major drive-train components and body rust are covered by extended warranty on all Chrysler cars, giving Omni/Charger a leg up on the competition in this respect.

EVALUATION CHECKLIST

(Omni; for Charger see Plymouth Horizon & Turismo.)

Fuel economy	4	Cargo room	4
Driveability	4	Serviceability	5
Acceleration	4	Standard equipment	3
Braking	3	Body construction	3
Handling/roadholding	4	Paint/exterior finish	4
Driving position	3	Interior finish	3
Instruments/control	3	TOTAL POINTS	70
Visiblity	4		
Heating/ventilation	3	**RATING SCALE**	
Seat comfort	3	5 = Excellent	
Passenger room	4	4 = Very Good	
Ride	3	3 = Average/Acceptable	
Noise	3	2 = Fair	
Exit/entry	3	1 = Poor	

SPECIFICATIONS

	Charger 3-door coupe	Omni 5-door sedan
Wheelbase (in.)	96.6	99.1
Overall length (in.)	173.7	164.8
Overall width (in.)	66.7	65.8

SPECIFICATIONS

	Charger 3-door coupe	Omni 5-door sedan
Overall height (in.)	50.8	53.1
Track front (in.)	56.1	56.1
Track rear (in.)	55.6	55.6
Curb weight (lbs.)	2222[1]	2175[1]
Max. cargo vol. (cu. ft.)	10.7/27.3	10.4/27.9
Fuel tank capacity (gal.)	13.0	13.0
Seating capacity	5	5
Front headroom (in.)	37.2	38.0
Front shoulder room (in.)	52.2	51.7
Front legroom, max. (in.)	42.4	42.1
Rear headroom (in.)	34.4	37.1
Rear shoulder room (in.)	50.9	51.5
Rear legroom, min. (in.)	28.7	33.3

1: Base models

BODY/CHASSIS

Drivetrain layout: transverse front engine/front-wheel drive. **Suspension front:** independent, MacPherson struts, lower control arms, coil springs, telescopic shock absorbers, anti-roll bar. **Suspension rear:** semi-independent, beam axle, trailing arms, coil springs, anti-roll bar optional. **Steering:** rack-and-pinion. **Turns lock-to-lock:** 3.6 manual, 2.9 power. **Turn diameter (ft.):** unit. **Brakes front:** 9.0-in. discs. **Brakes rear:** 7.9-in. drums. **Construction:** unit

POWERTRAINS

	ohv I-4	ohc I-4
Bore × stroke (in.)	3.17× 3.07	3.44× 3.62
Displacement (liters/cu. in.)	1.6/ 97.5	2.2/ 135
Compression ratio	8.8:1	9.0:1

POWERTRAINS

	ohv I-4	ohc I-4
Fuel delivery	2bbl.	2bbl.
Net bhp @ rpm	62@ 4800	94@ 5200
Net torque @ rpm (lbs/ft)	83@ 3200	117@ 3200
Availability	S/All[1]	O/All[2]

1: NA Charger 2.2
2: Std. Charger 2.2

Final drive ratios

4-speed OD manual	2.69:1	
5-speed OD manual	2.59:1	2.20:1
3-speed automatic	2.78:1	

KEY bbl. = barrel (carburetor); **bhp** = brake horsepower (advertised); **Cal.** = California only. **Fed.** = Federal/49 state; **FI** = fuel injection; **ohv** = overhead valve; **ohc** = overhead cam; **I** = inline engine; **V** = V engine; **D** = diesel; **T** = turbocharged; **OD** = overdrive transmission; **S** = standard engine; **O** = optional engine.

PRICES

DODGE OMNI & CHARGER	Retail Price	Dealer Cost	Low Price
Omni 5-door sedan	$5841	$5411	$5761
Omni Custom 5-door sedan	6071	5620	6020
Charger 3-door coupe	6379	5836	6236
Charger 2.2 3-door coupe	7303	6668	7168

STANDARD EQUIPMENT (included in above prices):

Omni: 1.6-liter (97-cid) 4-cylinder engine, 4-speed manual transmission, halogen headlamps, full carpeting, quartz clock, dual horns, trip odometer, luggage compartment light, left remote-control door mirror, four-spoke sport steering wheel. **Omni Custom** adds: cargo area carpeting, woodtone instrument panel applique, intermittent wipers, chrome door mirror, deluxe wheel covers, high-back front bucket seats with dual seatback recliners. **Charger** has Omni Custom equipment plus: power liftgate release, sound insulation package, bodyside and rear deck stripes. **Charger 2.2** has Charger equipment, plus: 2.2-liter (135-cid) 4-cylinder engine, 5-speed overdrive manual transmission, rear spoiler, special paint/tape treatment, sport suspension, AM radio, center console.

Prices are accurate at time of printing; subject to manufacturer's change

OPTIONAL EQUIPMENT:

	Retail Price	Dealer Cost	Low Price
2.2-liter (135-cid) 4-cylinder 2-bbl. engine (Std. Charger 2.2)	$ 134	114	116
3-speed automatic transmission	439	373	377
5-speed manual transmission (2.2 engine req.)	75	64	65
Performance axle ratio (5-speed trans. req.)	22	19	20
Vinyl bodyside moldings, black	45	38	39
Light Group			
Charger	62	53	54
Charger 2.2	54	46	47
Omnis	44	37	38
Protection Group			
Chargers	125	106	108
Omnis	181	154	156
Cold Weather Package			
w/o 2.2-liter engine	174	148	150
w/2.2-liter engine.	47	40	41
Two-tone paint			
Charger (NA 2.2)	155	132	134
Omnis	134	114	116
Bright exterior accents, base Charger	64	54	55
Black lower bodyside, paint, Charger 2.2	135	116	118
Air conditioning (tinted glass req. Omni) . .	632	537	543
Center armrest (console req.)	46	39	40
Cargo compartment carpeting, Charger . . .	41	35	36
Cargo compartment carpet & sound insulation, Omni, Charger (Std. Omni Custom, Charger 2.2)	59	50	51
Rallye instrument cluster, Omni	79	67	68
Engine cooling package	141	120	122
Center console			
w/o Light Group	84	71	72
w/Light Group.	76	65	66
Electric rear window defroster.	127	108	110
Tinted glass, Omni (std. Chargers).	90	77	78
Luggage rack, Omni	93	79	80
Power Steering	214	182	184
Radio equipment			
AM, manual tune (std. Charger 2.2) . . .	83	71	72
AM/FM stereo, manual tune			
Charger 2.2.	109	93	94
Others	346	294	297

Prices are accurate at time of printing; subject to manufacturer's change

	Retail Price	Dealer Cost	Low Price
AM/FM stereo electronic tune			
Charger 2.2	263	224	227
Others	346	294	297
AM/FM stereo electronic tune w/cassette tape			
Charger 2.2	402	342	346
Others	485	412	417
Conventional spare tire	63	54	55
Automatic speed control	174	148	150
Rear deck spoiler, Charger	72	61	62
Removeable glass sunroof, Chargers	310	264	267
Heavy-duty suspension, Omnis	34	29	30
Rear tonneau cover, chargers	68	58	59

Dodge 600/ Chrysler E Class

Dodge 600ES 4-door sedan

WHAT'S NEW FOR '83

Dodge's new mid-size front-drive entry is an offshoot of the K-car platform, with a 3-inch longer wheelbase and 10 inches greater length. The companion model in the Chrysler camp is the E Class and (later) the New Yorker. All share the E-body designation and they offer greater passenger and luggage space than the K-cars, richer appointments, and higher prices. The lone body style offered is a 4-door sedan with 6-window side treatment. Of the three models the most interesting is the 600 ES, which Dodge is pitting against European sedans like Audi 4000 and 5000, Volvo GL, and others known for high-caliber road ability. The ES has black

Prices are accurate at time of printing; subject to manufacturer's change

Chrysler E Class 4-door sedan

exterior moldings and a sport handling package, fast-ratio power steering, blackwall Goodyear Eagle GT steel-belted radials, aluminum road wheels, 2.2-liter engine, and 5-speed manual transmission. Automatic is optional on ES, standard on other models. Chrysler's Electronic Voice Alert that uses a simulated male voice to warn the driver of impending doom under the hood is standard on ES and E Class, optional for 600.

EVALUATION

First impressions based on short drives at the Chrysler proving grounds are mostly favorable. A bigger, improved K-car with more room for people and luggage, rich-looking interior and high-quality materials. A good replacement for Chrysler's aging rear-driven sedans, and should be good competition for the GM A-body intermediates. Longer wheelbase gives E-cars more luxurious ride than the K-cars, and it soaks up most bumps easily. Prototype had a surprising amount of tire noise, even with the extra sound insulation added to this car. Capable, reliable Chrysler 2.2 and Mitsubishi 2.6-liter fours have more weight to pull around here, so mileage and performance will be nothing special. Our experience has been that 2.6 with automatic gets only about 20–22 mpg overall. Trendy "talking" dashboard repeats warnings and commands two times, which may lead some drivers to turn the thing off. A complete set of good old-fashioned instruments would be welcome, but are unavailable. Clever—and doubtless relatively inexpensive—adaptation of familiar hardware that gives Chrysler a modern entry at last in the mid-size class. A very nice newcomer, with the added bonus of the company's 5-year/50,000-mile warranty program.

EVALUATION CHECKLIST
(Preliminary)

Fuel economy	3	Cargo room	4
Driveability	4	Serviceability	5
Acceleration	3	Standard equipment	5
Braking	3	Body construction	4
Handling/roadholding	3	Paint/exterior finish	4
Driving position	4	Interior finish	4
Instruments/control	2	TOTAL POINTS	73
Visiblity	4		
Heating/ventilation	4	**RATING SCALE**	
Seat comfort	4	5 = Excellent	
Passenger room	4	4 = Very Good	
Ride	3	3 = Average/Acceptable	
Noise	3	2 = Fair	
Exit/entry	3	1 = Poor	

SPECIFICATIONS

	4-door sedan
Wheelbase (in.)	103.1
Overall length (in.)	185.6
Overall width (in.)	68.3
Overall height (in.)	52.9
Track front (in.)	57.6
Track rear (in.)	57.0
Curb weight (lbs.)	2583[1]
Max. cargo vol. (cu. ft.)	17.1[2]
Fuel tank capacity (gal.)	13.0
Seating capacity	6
Front headroom (in.)	38.5
Front shoulder room (in.)	55.7
Front legroom, max. (in.)	42.2
Rear headroom (in.)	37.5
Rear shoulder room (in.)	56.2
Rear legroom, min. (in.)	36.7

1: Base model   2: Manufacturer's estimate

BODY/CHASSIS

Drivetrain layout: transverse front engine/front-wheel drive.
Suspension front: independent, MacPherson struts, lower A-arms, coil springs, telescopic shock absorbers, anti-roll bar. **Suspension rear:** beam "flex" axle, trailing arms, coil springs, telescopic shock absorbers, anti-roll bar. **Steering:** rack-and-pinion, power-assisted. **Turns lock-to-lock:** 2.5 /3.2. **Turn diameter (ft.):** 35.6. **Brakes front:** 10.1-in. discs. **Brakes rear:** 8.7-in. drums. **Construction:** unit

POWERTRAINS	ohc I-4	ohc I-4
Bore × stroke (in.)	3.44× 3.62	3.59× 3.86
Displacement (liters/cu. in.)	2.2/ 135	2.6/ 156
Compression ratio	9.0:1	8.2:1
Fuel delivery	2bbl.[1]	2bbl.
Net bhp @ rpm	94@ 5200	93@ 4500
Net torque @ rpm (lbs/ft)	117@ 3200	132@ 2500
Availability	S/All	O/All

1: avail. later w/FI; 120 lbs/ft. torque @ 3200 rpm

Final drive ratios

5-speed OD manual[1]	2.57:1	
3-speed automatic	3.02:1	3.02:1

1: 600 ES only; NA others

KEY bbl. = barrel (carburetor); **bhp** = brake horsepower (advertised); **Cal.** = California only. **Fed.** = Federal/49 state; **FI** = fuel injection; **ohv** = overhead valve; **ohc** = overhead cam; **I** = inline engine; **V** = V engine; **D** = diesel; **T** = turbocharged; **OD** = overdrive transmission; **S** = standard engine; **O** = optional engine.

PRICES

DODGE 600	Retail Price	Dealer Cost	Low Price
4-door sedan	$8841	$7611	$8411
ES 4-door sedan	9372	8062	8862

Prices are accurate at time of printing; subject to manufacturer's change

CHRYSLER E CLASS

	Retail Price	Dealer Cost	Low Price
4-door sedan	$9341	$8036	$8936

STANDARD EQUIPMENT (included in above prices):

2.2-liter (135-cid) 4-cylinder engine, 3-speed automatic transmission, power brakes, power steering, remote-locking fuel filler door, electronic digital clock, power decklid release, halogen headlamps, dual horns, message center instrument panel, light group, dual manual door mirrors, AM radio, compact spare tire, luxury wheel covers P185/70R-14 steel belted radial whitewall tires. **ES** adds: 5-speed manual transmission, sport/handling suspension, console, black bumper rubstrips and exterior moldings, electronic voice alert, power door mirrors, aluminum road wheels, raised-black-letter tires.

OPTIONAL EQUIPMENT:

	Retail	Dealer	Low
2.6-liter (156-cid) 4-cylinder engine (auto. trans. req.)	$ 259	$ 220	$ 223
Automatic transmission (std. 600)	439	373	377
Air conditioning	732	622	629
500-amp. battery	43	37	38
Bumper guards, front or rear	28	24	25
Engine cooling package (NA w/AC)	141	120	122
Electric rear window defroster	138	117	119
Tinted glass	105	89	90
Cornering lamps	60	51	52
Electronic voice alert (std. ES)	63	54	55
Illuminated visor vanity mirror	58	49	50
Two-tone paint (NA ES)	170	145	147
Power assists			
Power door locks	170	145	147
Power seat, left or bench	210	179	181
Power windows	255	217	220
Protection package	120	102	104
Radio Equipment			
AM delete (credit)	(56)	(48)	(56)
AM/FM stereo, manual tone	109	93	94
AM/FM stereo, electronic tune	263	224	227
AM/FM stereo, electronic tune w/cassette player	402	342	346
Conventional spare tire	63	54	55
Automatic speed control (intermittent wipers req.)	174	148	150
Leather-wrapped steering wheel	50	42	43
Tilt steering column (intermittent wipers req.)	105	89	90
Sport/handling suspension (std. ES)	55	47	48

Prices are accurate at time of printing; subject to manufacturer's change

	Retail Price	Dealer Cost	Low Price
Electronic travel computer cluster	206	175	177
Trunk dress-up	51	43	44
Wire wheel covers (NA ES)	219	186	188
Cast aluminum road wheels (std. ES)	336	286	289
Intermittent wipers (req. w/auto speed control or tilt steering column).	52	44	45

Ford Escort & EXP

Ford EXP 3-door coupe

WHAT'S NEW FOR '83

The country's best-selling car line comes back for its third model year with two drivetrain changes, a revised GT model, and minor appearance changes. Multiple-port electronic fuel injection is now optional for the Escort and EXP 1.6-liter "CVH" four. A 5-speed manual transmission is available with the EFI engine or the H.O. (High-Output) version introduced in mid-'82. A Fuel-Saver package for Escort with economy 3.04 final drive and wide-ratio 4-speed gearbox is available outside California. All manual-shift models have a standard Volkswagen-like upshift indicator that advises the driver when to change to the next higher gear for greater economy. The GT (available only as a 3-door sedan) gets the fuel-injected engine, 5-speed, TR Performance Suspension and Michelin TRX tires, tuned exhaust, and sporty appearance features as standard. A larger gas tank is adopted for all models, as are all-season steel-belted radials. Last year's base Escort series has been dropped, leaving L models as the low-end offerings. Ford says the '83 models have improved noise, harshness, and vibration control.

EVALUATION

Much improved in '82, the Escort should be an even better car this year with availability of the fuel-injected engine and 5-speed. Similar car sold as Mercury Lynx, so see comments under that listing. Fuel injection could add more refinement and economy to an already thrifty engine. The 5-speed is a definite plus for mileage, as well as better performance in the lower gears. Handling has been improved since 1981, with better control of vertical motion and body sway. TR Performance package and Michelin tires make the GT quite the sporty subcompact, and it could well overshadow 2-seat EXP as the mini-racer of the bunch. The EXP, with its stiff ride, extremely low seating position, and uninspired performance, has never delivered what Ford has promised in its ads. The Escort has always delivered good mileage and hatchback versatility at a very reasonable price. Still lacks refinement in some areas, though, particularly road noise isolation and drivetrain harshness. Test cars we've driven also have been let down by spotty workmanship in places, though. Ford seems to be addressing these problems rapidly. Conclusion: Improved now, and a car we can honestly recommend for value and all-round competence. Best of all, it's American.

EVALUATION CHECKLIST
(Escort; for EXP see Mercury Lynx & LN7)

Fuel economy	4	Cargo room	3
Driveability	4	Serviceability	3
Acceleration	3	Standard equipment	3
Braking	4	Body construction	3
Handling/roadholding	4	Paint/exterior finish	3
Driving position	4	Interior finish	3
Instruments/control	4	TOTAL POINTS	70
Visiblity	4		
Heating/ventilation	4	**RATING SCALE**	
Seat comfort	3	5 = Excellent	
Passenger room	3	4 = Very Good	
Ride	4	3 = Average/Acceptable	
Noise	4	2 = Fair	
Exit/entry	3	1 = Poor	

SPECIFICATIONS

	EXP 3-door coupe	Escort 3-door sedan	Escort 5-door sedan	Escort 5-door wagon
Wheelbase (in.)	94.2	94.2	94.2	94.2
Overall length (in.)	170.3	163.9	163.9	165.0
Overall width (in.)	65.9	65.9	65.9	65.9
Overall height (in.)	50.5	53.3	53.3	53.3
Track front (in.)	54.7	54.7	54.7	54.7
Track rear (in.)	56.0	56.0	56.0	56.0
Curb weight (lbs.)	2156	2016	2078	2117
Max. cargo vol. (cu. ft.)	29.8	26.4	26.1	58.4
Fuel tank capacity (gal.)	13.0	13.0	13.0	13.0
Seating capacity	2	4	4	4
Front headroom (in.)	37.0	38.1	38.1	38.1
Front shoulder room (in.)	51.3	51.4	51.4	51.4
Front legroom, max. (in.)	41.7	41.5	41.5	41.5
Rear headroom (in.)	—	37.4	37.4	38.2
Rear shoulder room (in.)	—	51.7	51.1	51.1
Rear legroom, min. (in.)	—	35.0	35.0	35.0

BODY/CHASSIS

Drivetrain layout: transverse front engine/front-wheel drive.
Suspension front: independent, MacPherson struts, forged lower control arms, coil springs, telescopic shock absorbers, anti-roll-bar. **Suspension rear:** independent, modified Mac-Pherson struts, trailing arms, lower control arms, coil springs, telescopic shock absorbers. **Steering:** rack-and-pinion. **Turns lock-to-lock:** 3.5 manual, 3.0 power. **Turn diameter (ft.):** 35.5. **Brakes front:** 9.3-in. discs. **Brakes rear:** 7.1-in. drums (8.0-in. on wagon, EXP). **Construction:** unit

POWERTRAINS

	ohc I-4	ohc I-4[1]	ohc I-4
Bore × stroke (in.)	3.15× 3.13	3.15× 3.13	3.15× 3.13

POWERTRAINS

	ohc I-4	ohc I-4[1]	ohc I-4
Displacement (liters cu. in.)	1.6/ 98	1.6/ 98	1.6/ 98
Compression ratio	9.0:1	9.0:1	9.5:1
Fuel delivery	2bbl.	2bbl.	FI
Net bhp @ rpm	72@ 5200	80@ 5800	88@ 5400
Net torque @ rpm (lbs/ft)	91@ 3000	88@ 3400	94@ 4200
Availability	S/All	O/All	O/All

1: H.O. engine

Final drive ratios

4-speed OD manual	3.59:1[1]	3.59:1[2]	
5-speed OD manual		3.73:1	3.73:1
3-speed automatic	3.31:1[3]	3.31:1	3.31:1

1: 3.04:1 with "Fuel Saver" package (NA Cal.)
2: Available high-altitude areas only; close-ratio transmission
3: NA EXP

KEY bbl. = barrel (carburetor); **bhp** = brake horsepower (advertised); **Cal.** = California only. **Fed.** = Federal/49 state; **FI** = fuel injection; **ohv** = overhead valve; **ohc** = overhead cam; **I** = inline engine; **V** = V engine; **D** = diesel; **T** = turbocharged; **OD** = overdrive transmission; **S** = standard engine; **O** = optional engine.

PRICES

ESCORT & EXP	Retail Price	Dealer Cost	Low Price
Escort L 3-door sedan	$5639	$5171	$5521
Escort L 5-door sedan	5846	5357	5707
Escort L 5-door wagon.	6052	5543	5893
Escort GL 3-door sedan.	6384	5587	5937
Escort GL 5-door sedan	6601	5773	6123
Escort GL 5-door wagon	6779	5926	6276
Escort GLX 3-door sedan	6771	5919	6269
Escort GLX 5-door sedan	6988	6106	6456
Escort GLX 5-door wagon	7150	6245	6595
Escort GT 3-door sedan	7339	6408	6758
EXP 3-door coupe (base)	6426	5892	6242
EXP 3-door coupe.	7004	6412	6762

Prices are accurate at time of printing; subject to manufacturer's change

STANDARD EQUIPMENT (included in above prices):

Escort L: 1.6-liter (98-cid) 4-cylinder engine, 4-speed manual transmission, AM radio, front disc brakes, cigarette lighter, fold-down rear seatback, hubcaps, vinyl high-back bucket seats, day/night mirror, P155/80R-13 BSW radial tires, halogen headlamps. **L** adds: consolette, cloth seats, color-keyed seatbelts, chrome headlamp bezels and grille, belt moldings, bodyside paint stripe, matte-black rocker panel paint. **GL** adds: deluxe bumper end caps and rub strips, chrome window moldings, vinyl-insert bodyside moldings, chrome hubcaps and trim rings, reclining bucket seats w/GL trim, color-keyed seatbelts, soft-feel steering wheel, remote control liftgate and fuel filler door, load floor carpet, deluxe insulation package. **GLX** adds: dual sport door mirrors, styled-steel wheels w/trim rings, bumper guards, low-back reclining bucket seats, soft vinyl door trim, carpeted lower door panels, console, digital clock, glovebox lock, roof grab handles, light group, upgraded carpet, interval wipers, P165/80R-13 BSW radial tires. **GT** has: base Escort equipment plus black bumpers w/deluxe rub strips and end caps, black grille and headlamp bezels, black exterior moldings, bodyside and rear tape strips, styled-steel wheels w/trim rings, high-back reclining bucket seats, deluxe seatbelts, soft vinyl door trim, soft-feel steering wheel, instrumentation group, console, roof grab handles, handling suspension, TRX tires, & wheels. **EXP:** base model has 1.6-liter (98-cid) engine and 4-speed manual transmission. All others have 1.6-liter (98-cid) H.O. engine and 5-speed manual transmission, and power brakes, electric rear-window defroster, AM radio, intermittent wipers, reclining front bucket seats, full carpeting, halogen headlamps, console, full instrumentation including tachometer and trip odometer, electric remote hatchback release, manual remote-control door mirrors, styled-steel wheels with trim rings, tinted glass, digital clock, cargo cover, auxiliary interior courtesy lighting.

OPTIONAL EQUIPMENT:	Retail Price	Dealer Cost	Low Price
Engines			
1.6-liter HO 4-cylinder 2-bbl..	73	61	62
1.6-liter fuel-injected engine	NA	NA	NA
Transmissions			
5-speed manual (Escort, base EXP). . . .	76	64	65
3-speed automatic (GT, base EXP)	363	305	309
3-speed automatic (other than GT, base EXP)	439	369	373
Air conditioning	624	524	530
Heavy-duty battery	26	22	23
Lower bodyside protection.	68	57	58
Power brakes (std. EXP).	95	80	81
Bumper guards, front or rear	28	24	25
Bumper rub strips.	41	35	36
Digital clock (std. EXP).	57	48	49
Console (std. EXP)	111	93	94
Electric rear-window defroster (std. EXP) . .	124	104	106

Prices are accurate at time of printing; subject to manufacturer's change

	Retail Price	Dealer Cost	Low Price
Engine block heater	18	15	16
Tinted glass	90	76	77
Instrumentation group (std. EXP)	87	73	74
Light group (std. EXP)	43	36	37
Luggage rack	93	78	79
Sport mirrors (std. EXP)	67	56	57
Vinyl-insert bodyside moldings	45	38	39
Metallic glow paint	51	43	44
EXP	146	123	125
Tu-tone paint/tape (L series)	173	145	140
GL, GLX series	134	113	115
Protection group	60	50	51
Radio equipment			
AM delete (credit)	(61)	(51)	(52)
AM/FM	143	120	122
AM/FM stereo (L series)	170	142	144
(except L series)	109	91	92
AM/FM stereo w/cassette tape (L series)	260	218	221
AM/FM stereo w/cassette (except L series)	199	167	169
AM/FM stereo w/8-track (L series)	260	218	221
AM/FM stereo w/8-track (except L series)	199	167	169
Premium sound system	117	98	99
High-back reclining front seats	65	54	55
Low-back reclining front seats	98	82	83
Vinyl seat trim	24	20	21
Leather seat trim (EXP)	144	121	123
Shearling seat trim (EXP)	227	191	193
Open-air flip-up roof			
w/Squire option	217	182	184
Others	310	260	263
Speed control	170	142	144
Squire option, wagons	350	294	297
Power steering	210	176	178
Handling suspension			
L, GL	199	167	169
GLX	41	35	36
Aluminum wheels			
L, GL	383	322	326
GLX, or w/hauling suspension	226	190	192
Opening front vent windows (NA EXP)	60	50	51
Remote-control rear quarter windows	109	91	92
Intermittent wipers (std. EXP)	49	41	42
Rear-window wiper/washer, Escorts	117	98	99

Prices are accurate at time of printing; subject to manufacturer's change

Ford Fairmont Futura/ Mercury Zephyr

Ford Fairmont Futura 2-door coupe

WHAT'S NEW FOR '83

Ford's conventional rear-drive compacts hang on with few changes until they're replaced early next year by the smaller front-drive Ford Tempo/Mercury Topaz. The Fairmont/Zephyr has been a huge sales success since its 1978 debut, and its reliability and simplicity have made it popular as a fleet car and in taxicab service. The same body styles available last year return unchanged. The optional 255-cid V-8 has been dropped. Base engine is still Ford's familiar 2.3-liter overhead-cam four, which now has a new single-barrel carburetor instead of a dual throat unit. The 2.3 also has long-reach spark plugs for faster fuel burning, a redesigned exhaust manifold, and an air conditioning cutoff device to reduce power drain during full-throttle acceleration. The 3.3-liter straight six is the only available power option, and requires automatic. Traction-Lok limited-slip differential is available with optional TR-type tires. A new option on manual-shift cars is an upshift indicator light that informs driver when to change to a higher gear for better fuel economy, a feature introduced by Volkswagen. While Zephyr and Fairmont are scheduled to disappear, their chassis drivetrains, and basic body design live on in the new "down-sized" Mercury Marquis/Ford LTD.

EVALUATION

A solid, reliable, relatively simple car, Fairmont/Zephyr will have to contend again this year with Chrysler's up-to-date K-cars, as well as GM's X-cars. Against these, it seems old hat, but does have its attractions. The main ones are its less complicated rear-drive mechanical layout, sturdy (though not refined) engines, and generally pleasant interior accommodations. Seating is comfortable for up to five, and the deep-well trunk (introduced for '82) enhances utility. Also, goes about its business with relatively little fuss. Ride is mostly good except on closely spaced bumps, which the live rear axle doesn't cope with well. Handling and roadholding are predictable but ordinary. Mileage won't win prizes, but it's still respectable even after six years on the market. We still dislike the 2.3-liter standard four, and recommend you opt for the smoother and more livable six.

EVALUATION CHECKLIST

Fuel economy	3	Cargo room	3
Driveability	3	Serviceability	4
Acceleration	4	Standard equipment	3
Braking	3	Body construction	4
Handling/roadholding	3	Paint/exterior finish	4
Driving position	4	Interior finish	3
Instruments/control	3	TOTAL POINTS	68
Visiblity	4		
Heating/ventilation	4	**RATING SCALE**	
Seat comfort	3	5 = Excellent	
Passenger room	3	4 = Very Good	
Ride	4	3 = Average/Acceptable	
Noise	3	2 = Fair	
Exit/entry	3	1 = Poor	

SPECIFICATIONS

	2-door coupe	2-door sedan	4-door sedan
Wheelbase (in.)	105.5	105.5	105.5
Overall length (in.)	197.4	195.5	195.5
Overall width (in.)	71.0	71.0	71.0
Overall height (in.)	51.7	52.9	52.9
Track front (in.)	56.6	56.6	56.6
Track rear (in.)	57.0	57.0	57.0
Curb weight (lbs.)	2854	2824	2877

SPECIFICATIONS

	2-door coupe	2-door sedan	4-door sedan
Max. cargo vol. (cu. ft.)	16.5	16.7	16.7
Fuel tank capacity (gal.)	16.0[1]	16.0[1]	16.0[1]
Seating capacity	4	5	5
Front headroom (in.)	37.2	38.4	38.4
Front shoulder room (in.)	56.3	56.3	56.3
Front legroom, max. (in.)	41.7	41.7	41.7
Rear headroom (in.)	37.2	37.3	37.3
Rear shoulder room (in.)	57.6	55.6	56.3
Rear legroom, min. (in.)	33.2	35.7	35.7

1: 20-gal. tank opt.

BODY/CHASSIS

Drivetrain layout: longitudinal front engine/rear-wheel drive. **Suspension front:** independent, modified MacPherson struts, lower control arms, coil springs, telescopic shock absorbers, anti-roll-bar. **Suspension rear:** rigid axle, four links, coil springs, telescopic shock absorbers. **Steering:** rack-and-pinion. **Turns lock-to-lock:** 4.1 manual, 3.0 power. **Turn diameter (ft.):** 38.8 **Brakes front:** 10.1-in. discs. **Brakes rear:** 9.0-in. drums. **Construction:** unit

POWERTRAINS

	ohc I-4	ohv I-6
Bore × stroke (in.)	3.78× 3.12	3.68× 3.12
Displacement (liters/cu. in.)	2.3/ 140	3.3/ 200
Compression ratio	9.0:1	8.6:1
Fuel delivery	1bbl.	1bbl.
Net bhp @ rpm[1]	93@ 4600	87@ 3800
Net torque @ rpm (lbs/ft)	128@ 2400	156@ 1800

POWERTRAINS

	ohc I-4	ohv I-6
Availability	S/All	O/All

¹ Preliminary ratings

Final drive ratios

4-speed manual		3.08:1
3-speed automatic	3.08:1	2.73:1

KEY bbl. = barrel (carburetor); **bhp** = brake horsepower (advertised); **Cal.** = California only. **Fed.** = Federal/49 state; **FI** = fuel injection; **ohv** = overhead valve; **ohc** = overhead cam; **I** = inline engine; **V** = V engine; **D** = diesel; **T** = turbocharged; **OD** = overdrive transmission; **S** = standard engine; **O** = optional engine.

PRICES

	Retail Price	Dealer Cost	Low Price
FORD FAIRMONT FUTURA			
2-door sedan...................	$6444	$5651	$6051
4-door sedan...................	6590	5776	6176
2-door coupe...................	6666	5842	6242
MERCURY ZEPHYR			
4-door sedan...................	6545	5749	6149
Z-7 2-door coupe..............	6442	5661	6061
GS 4-door sedan..............	7311	6408	6808
Z-7 GS 2-door coupe..........	7247	6353	6753

STANDARD EQUIPMENT (included in above prices):

2.3-liter (140-cid) 4-cylinder eingine, 4-speed manual transmission w/ floorshift, power brakes, cut-pile carpeting, carpeted lower door panels, woodtone instrument panel and door trim appliqués, right visor vanity mirror, AM radio, low-back front bucket seats, vinyl upholstery, color-keyed seatbelts and 2-spoke steering wheel, dual chrome remote-control door mirrors (left mirror only on 2-door sedan), delux (2-door sedan) or turbine wheel covers, upper bodyside accent stripes (exc. 2-door sedan), deluxe sound package, steel-belted radial tires. **Zephyr GS** adds: tinted rear window, luxury sound package, dual hood accent stripes, luxury carpeting, carpeted trunk, dual illuminated visor vanity mirrors, Flight fron bench seat, luxury cloth-and-vinyl upholstery, luxury 4-spoke steering wheel w/ woodtone appliqué.

OPTIONAL EQUIPMENT:

3.3-liter (200-cid) 6-cylinder engine.....	$ 239	$ 201	$ 204
3-speed automatic transmission.......	439	369	373
Air conditioner...................	724	608	615

Prices are accurate at time of printing; subject to manufacturer's change

	Retail Price	Dealer Cost	Low Price
Traction-Lok axle	95	80	81
Lower bodyside protection.	41	35	36
Electric clock.	35	30	31
Console	191	161	163
Remote decklid release	40	34	35
Interior luxury group, Fairmont	294	247	250
Electric rear-window defroster.	135	114	116
Extended-range fuel tank.	46	39	40
Floorshift (for auto. trans.)	49	41	42
Tinted glass	105	88	89
Illuminated entry system	76	64	65
Instrumentation group	100	84	85
Light group.	55	46	47
Power door locks			
2-doors	120	100	102
4-doors	170	142	144
Rocker panel moldings	33	28	29
Metallic paint.	63	53	54
Two-tone paint.	117	98	99
Appearance protection group	60	50	51
Radio equipment			
AM delete (credit)	(61)	(51)	(52)
AM/FM	59	49	50
AM/FM stereo	109	91	92
AM/FM stereo w/cassette or 8-track tape . . .	199	167	169
Premium sound system	117	98	99
Full or half vinyl roof	152	128	130
Open-air flip-up roof	310	260	263
Power seat	139	117	119
Speed control (incl. luxury steering wheel) . . .	170	142	144
Power steering.	218	183	185
Tilt steering wheel.	105	88	89
Accent stripe	39	33	34
Handling suspension	52	44	45
Cloth & vinyl upholstery	35	30	31
TR-type tires and aluminum wheels	535	450	455
Wire wheel covers.	152	128	130
Styled wheel covers.	66	55	56
Power windows			
2-doors	180	152	154
4-doors	255	214	217
Electric trunklid release.	40	34	35
Opening front vent windows (NA coupes). .	63	53	54
Interval wipers.	49	41	42

Prices are accurate at time of printing; subject to manufacturer's change

Ford LTD/ Mercury Marquis

Ford LTD Brougham 4-door sedan

WHAT'S NEW FOR '83

Familiar names with new sheetmetal and a new size, the LTD and Marquis become mid-size for '83. (Last year's full-size cars continue as the LTD Crown Victoria sedans and Country Squire wagon at Ford and the Grand Marquis at Mercury.) Essentially a reskinned version of last year's Granada/ Cougar, which it replaces, the '83 LTD/Marquis has a claimed drag coefficient of 0.38, very good aerodynamics for a sedan. Only a single series is listed, and includes a 5-door wagon. The chassis is still straight from the Fairmont/Zephyr, but now has gas-pressurized front struts and rear shock absorbers. The engine roster includes a propane-powered version of Ford's 2.3-liter overhead-cam four. The 2.3 gasoline version has a one-barrel carburetor instead of a two-barrel for '83. Optional for the first time in this line is the 3.8-liter V-6, available only with 4-speed overdrive automatic transmission. The dash is borrowed from last year's Thunderbird.

EVALUATION

An updated version of a familiar package, but looks out of date despite the new trimmings. Like their predecessors, these are more four-seaters than five-seaters because of the space-robbing rear-drive layout. The standard instrument cluster looks old-fashioned and provides minimal information. An easy car to drive in a straight line, but marked body roll and overassisted steering result in sloppy handling. With the base four and automatic, the car we tried at Ford's long-lead press show felt underpowered, which doesn't bode well for mileage. This engine did impress us with its smoothness, however. The V-6 car we sampled had adequate acceleration, though it didn't feel much peppier than the four-cylinder. The gas-pressurized shocks offer somewhat better ride control than the mushy Granada/Cougar chassis, though there's still too much front-end float. Wind and road noise were lower than the last Granada we tested. Entry/exit to either front or rear is easy. Smooth and luxurious enough to satisfy big-car fans, but lags behind front-drive competitors from GM and Chrysler in space- and fuel-efficiency and over-the-road poise.

EVALUATION CHECKLIST
(Preliminary)

Fuel economy	3	Cargo room	3
Driveability	4	Serviceability	4
Acceleration	3	Standard equipment	4
Braking	3	Body construction	4
Handling/roadholding	3	Paint/exterior finish	4
Driving position	4	Interior finish	4
Instruments/control	3	TOTAL POINTS	72
Visiblity	4		
Heating/ventilation	4		
Seat comfort	4		
Passenger room	3		
Ride	4		
Noise	4		
Exit/entry	3		

RATING SCALE
5 = Excellent
4 = Very Good
3 = Average/Acceptable
2 = Fair
1 = Poor

SPECIFICATIONS	4-door sedan	5-door wagon
Wheelbase (in.)	105.5	105.5
Overall length (in.)	196.5	196.5
Overall width (in.)	71.0	71.0
Overall height (in.)	53.6	54.3
Track front (in.)	56.6	56.6
Track rear (in.)	57.0	57.0

SPECIFICATIONS

	4-door sedan	5-door wagon
Curb weight (lbs.)	2981	3092
Max. cargo vol. (cu. ft.)	15.1	41.6/75.4
Fuel tank capacity (gal.)	16.0[1]	16.0
Seating capacity	5	5
Front headroom (in.)	38.7	39.1
Front shoulder room (in.)	56.2	56.2
Front legroom, max. (in.)	41.9	41.9
Rear headroom (in.)	37.6	38.4
Rear shoulder room (in.)	56.2	56.2
Rear legroom, min. (in.)	35.9	36.0

1: 20-gal. tank opt.

BODY/CHASSIS

Drivetrain layout: longitudinal front engine/rear-wheel drive. **Suspension front:** independent, modified MacPherson struts, lower control arms, coil springs, gas-pressurized telescopic shock absorbers, anti-roll bar. **Suspension rear:** rigid axle, four links, coil springs, telescopic gas-pressurized shock absorbers. **Steering:** rack-and-pinion. **Turns lock-to-lock:** 3.0 power. **Turn diameter (ft.):** 39.0. **Brakes front:** 10.1-in. discs. **Brakes rear:** 9.0-in. drums (10.0 wagon). **Construction:** unit

POWERTRAINS

	ohc I-4	ohc I-4	ohv I-6	ohv V-6
Bore × stroke (in.)	3.78× 3.12	3.78× 3.12	3.68× 3.12	3.87× 3.44
Displacement (liters cu. in.)	2.3/ 140	2.3/ 140	3.3/ 200	3.8/ 232
Compression ratio	9.0:1	NA	8.6:1	8.7:1
Fuel delivery	1bbl.	—	1bbl.	2bbl.
Net bhp @ rpm*	93@ 4600	NA	87@ 3800	105@ 4000

POWERTRAINS

POWERTRAINS	ohc I-4	ohc I-4	ohv I-6	ohv V-6
Net torque @ rpm* (lbs/ft)	128@ 2400	NA	156@ 1800	181@ 1200
Availability	S/All[1]	O/All[2]	S/All[3]	O/All

*Preliminary ratings 1: NA wagon
2: Requires propane fuel; NA wagon
3: std. wagon, opt. sedan

Final drive ratios

4-speed manual	3.45:1			
3-speed automatic	3.45:1	3.08:1[1]	2.73:1	
4-speed OD automatic				3.08:1[1]

1: 3.45:1 high-altitude areas

KEY bbl. = barrel (carburetor); **bhp** = brake horsepower (advertised); **Cal.** = California only. **Fed.** = Federal/49 state; **FI** = fuel injection; **ohv** = overhead valve; **ohc** = overhead cam; **I** = inline engine; **V** = V engine; **D** = diesel; **T** = turbocharged; **OD** = overdrive transmission; **S** = standard engine; **O** = optional engine.

PRICES

	Retail Price	Dealer Cost	Low Price
FORD LTD			
4-door sedan.	$7777	$6666	7166
Brougham 4-door sedan	8165	6992	7492
5-door wagon	8577	7338	7838
MERCURY MARQUIS			
Marquis 4-door sedan	$7893	$6775	$7275
Marquis Brougham 4-door sedan.	8202	7034	7534
Marquis 5-door wagon	8693	7447	8047
Marquis 5-door wagon w/Brougham Decor option	8974	7683	8283

STANDARD EQUIPMENT (included in above prices):

LTD: 2.3-liter (140-cid) 4-cylinder engine (3.3-liter, 200-cid 6-cylinder with automatic transmission on wagon), 4-speed manual transmission w/ floorshift, power brakes, full carpeting, bench seat, mini-spare tire, AM radio, deluxe radio, deluxe sound package, dual-note horn, remote-control left mirror, color-keyed wheel covers, seatback map, pockets, carpeted lower door panels. **Marquis:** 2.3-liter (140-cid) 4-cylinder engine, 4-speed manual transmission; wagons have 3.3-liter (200-cid) 6-cylinder engine and 3-speed automatic transmission; P185/75R-14 steel belted radial tires, power brakes, dual-note horn, remote-control left mirror, deluxe wheel covers, vinyl door trim, right visor vanity mirror, AM radio, cloth and vinyl

Prices are accurate at time of printing; subject to manufacturer's change

seat trim, full carpeting. **Marquis Brougham** adds: luxury door trim, electronic digital clock, electronic chimes in place of warning buzzer, dual beam dome lamps, illuminated right hand visor vanity mirror, luxury cloth seat trim.

OPTIONAL EQUIPMENT:

	Retail Price	Dealer Cost	Low Price
Engines			
3.3-liter (200-cid) 6-cylinder engine. . . .	$ 239	$ 201	$ 204
3.8-liter (232-cid) V-6			
Sedans.	309	259	262
Wagons	70	58	59
2.3-liter (140-cid) 4-cylinder propane . .	896	753	761
Transmissions			
3-speed automatic	439	369	373
4-speed overdrive automatic (sedans) . .	615	516	522
4-speed overdrive automatic (wagons) . .	176	148	149
Air conditioning, automatic	802	674	681
Air conditioning, manual	724	608	615
Appearance protection group	60	50	51
Traction-Lok limited-slip differential	95	80	81
Heavy-duty battery	26	22	23
Bumper rub strips.	50	42	43
Electronic digital clock	78	66	67
Cold weather group.	77	65	66
Console	77	65	66
Electric rear-window defroster.	135	114	116
Tinted glass	105	88	89
Extended-range fuel tank.	46	39	40
Floorshift, LTD.	49	41	42
Illuminated entry system	76	66	67
Cornering lamps.	60	50	51
Two-way liftgate, wagon	105	88	89
Light group.	38	32	33
Power door locks			
4-door sedans	210	176	178
Wagon	170	142	144
Metallic paint.	63	53	54
Two-tone paint.	117	98	99
Lower bodyside protection.	41	35	36
Electronic instrument cluster	367	308	312
Diagnostic warning lights	54	49	50
Radio equipment			
AM/FM.	59	49	50
AM Delete (credit)	61	51	52
AM/FM stereo	109	91	92
AM/FM electronic stereo	252	212	215
AM/FM stereo w/cassette or 8-track . . .	199	167	169
AM/FM electronic stereo w/cassette. . . .	396	333	337

Prices are accurate at time of printing; subject to manufacturer's change

CONSUMER GUIDE®

	Retail Price	Dealer Cost	Low Price
Vinyl roof, full (NA wagon)	152	128	130
Open-air flip-up roof	310	260	263
Individual seats w/console	61	51	52
Power seats			
single control	207	174	176
dual controls	415	348	352
Speed control	170	142	142
Power steering	218	183	185
Leather-wrapped steering wheel	59	49	50
Tilt steering wheel	105	88	89
Heavy-duty suspension	24	20	21
Trim			
Leather	415	348	352
Vinyl	35	30	31
Power windows	255	214	217
Front vent windows	63	53	54
Interval wipers	49	41	42
Liftgate wiper/washer, wagon	99	83	84
Woodtone exterior, wagon	282	237	240

Ford LTD Crown Victoria/ Mercury Grand Marquis

Ford LTD Crown Victoria 4-door sedan

WHAT'S NEW FOR '83

Ford's venerable full-size lines are back under new names to distinguish them from the new downsized LTD/Marquis. The Crown Victoria 2- and 4-door sedans and 4-door Country Squire wagon are offered in only one trim level; Grand Marquis offers two. The 5.0-liter V-8, teamed with 4-speed overdrive automatic transmission, gains the throttle-body electronic fuel injection previously used only in the big Lincolns. On the outside, all models have new grilles, and sedans get a new taillamp design. Country Squire has revised fake wood bodyside panelling. New options are a remote-locking fuel-filler door and locking wire wheel covers. Base tires have been increased one size to P215/75R-14. Ford is retaining both these lines for big-car buyers who want the traditional American virtues of comfort, quietness and reliability in a roomy, impressive-looking package.

EVALUATION

New just four years ago, these cars still rate in a virtual dead heat overall with the Chevrolet Caprice/Impala. While the Ford can't boast the high mileage figures of the diesel-powered Chevy, they do have better low-end performance when base-engine models are compared. All are similar in passenger accommodation, trunk space, and ride quality, the Fords being perhaps a tad silkier and quieter on the boulevard. Chevy gets the nod for handling, though neither of these cars is meant to be agile. Mileage figures couldn't be closer. In all, the choice of one over the other will probably come down to personal taste and the deal you can get. The Ford is still good value among full-size cars, but the breed is getting rarer, and this series isn't likely to be around that much longer. Size and relative fuel thirst are their greatest shortcomings for the long run. Reliability and durability are among the pluses.

EVALUATION CHECKLIST

Fuel economy	2	Cargo room	4
Driveability	4	Serviceability	3
Acceleration	3	Standard equipment	4
Braking	3	Body construction	4
Handling/roadholding	3	Paint/exterior finish	4
Driving position	3	Interior finish	4
Instruments/control	3	TOTAL POINTS	71
Visiblity	3		
Heating/ventilation	4	**RATING SCALE**	
Seat comfort	4	5 = Excellent	
Passenger room	4	4 = Very Good	
Ride	4	3 = Average/Acceptable	
Noise	4	2 = Fair	
Exit/entry	4	1 = Poor	

SPECIFICATIONS

	2-door sedan	4-door sedan	5-door wagon
Wheelbase (in.)	114.3	114.3	114.3
Overall length (in.)	211.1	211.1	215.0
Overall width (in.)	77.5	77.5	79.3
Overall height (in.)	55.3	55.3	56.8
Track front (in.)	62.2	62.2	62.2
Track rear (in.)	60.0	60.0	60.0
Curb weight (lbs.)	3702	3748	3901
Max. cargo vol. (cu. ft.)	22.4	22.4	89.4
Fuel tank capacity (gal.)	18.0	18.0	18.5
Seating capacity	6	6	6
Front headroom (in.)	37.9	37.9	38.8
Front shoulder room (in.)	61.6	61.6	61.6
Front legroom, max. (in.)	42.1	42.1	42.1
Rear headroom (in.)	37.2	37.2	39.1
Rear shoulder room (in.)	61.0	61.6	61.6
Rear legroom, min. (in.)	40.7	40.7	39.5

BODY/CHASSIS

Drivetrain layout: longitudinal front engine/rear-wheel drive. **Suspension front:** independent; unequal-length upper and lower A-arms, coil springs, telescopic shock absorbers, anti-roll bar. **Suspension rear:** rigid axle, four links, coil springs, telescopic shock absorbers. **Steering:** recirculating ball, power-assisted. **Turns lock-to-lock:** 3.4. **Turn diameter (ft.):** 39.1. **Brakes front:** 11.1-in. discs. **Brakes rear:** 10.0-in. drums (11.0-in. wagon). **Construction:** body-on-frame

POWERTRAINS

	ohv V-8
Bore × stroke (in.)	4.00×3.00
Displacement (liters/cu. in.)	5.0/302

POWERTRAINS

	ohv V-8
Compression ratio	8.3:1
Fuel delivery	FI
Net bhp @ rpm	130@ 3200
Net torque @ rpm (lbs/ft)	240@ 1600
Availability	S/All
Final drive ratios	
4-speed OD automatic	3.08:1¹

1: 3.42:1 high-altitude areas

KEY bbl. = barrel (carburetor); **bhp** = brake horsepower (advertised); **Cal.** = California only. **Fed.** = Federal/49 state; **FI** = fuel injection; **ohv** = overhead valve; **ohc** = overhead cam; **I** = inline engine; **V** = V engine; **D** = diesel; **T** = turbocharged; **OD** = overdrive transmission; **S** = standard engine; **O** = optional engine.

PRICES

FORD LTD CROWN VICTORIA	Retail Price	Dealer Cost	Low Price
Crown Victoria 2-door sedan	$10094	$8635	$9435
Crown Victoria 4-door sedan	10094	8635	9435
Country Squire wagon	10253	8769	9569

STANDARD EQUIPMENT (included in above prices):

5.0 liter (302-cid) fuel injected V-8 engine, 4-speed overdrive automatic transmission, power steering, power brakes, P215/75R-14 WSW steel-belted radial tires (P215/75R-14 on wagons), inflatable spare tire, full carpeting, dual-note horn, sound package, electric clock, deluxe door trim panels, deluxe seatbelts, AM/FM stereo radio.

OPTIONAL EQUIPMENT:

Traction-lok axle.	$ 95	$ 80	$ 81
Automatic temperature air conditioner	802	674	681
Manual-control air conditioner	724	608	615
Autolamp on/off delay system.	73	61	62
Heavy-duty battery	26	22	23
Lower bodyside protection			
Country Squire	52	44	45
Others	39	33	34

Prices are accurate at time of printing; subject to manufacturer's change

	Retail Price	Dealer Cost	Low Price
Bumper rub strips..............	52	44	45
Electronic digital clock	61	51	52
Convenience group			
Sedans w/interior luxury group	95	80	81
Country Squire w/interior luxury group..	106	89	90
Sedans w/out interior group	102	86	87
Country Squire w/out interior group	116	97	98
Electric rear-window defroster.........	135	114	115
Tinted glass	105	88	89
Illuminated entry system............	76	63	64
Interior luxury group			
Crown Victoria 2-door............	838	704	712
Crown Victoria 4-door............	911	765	773
Country Squire	830	698	705
Cornering lamps................	60	50	51
Light group...................	48	40	41
Power lock group			
2-doors w/convenience group	123	103	105
2-doors w/o convenience group	149	125	127
4-doors or wagons w/convenience group	163	137	139
4-doors w/o convenience group	210	176	178
Wagons w/o convenience group	220	184	186
Deluxe luggage rack..............	110	92	93
Vinyl insert bodyside moldings	55	46	47
Metallic glow paint	77	65	66
Tu-tone paint/tape treatment.........	78	66	67
Protection group................	68	57	58
Radio equipment			
AM/FM stereo delete (credit)	(152)	(128)	(130)
AM/FM stereo w/tape	112	94	95
AM/FM stereo search-tune	166	132	134
AM/FM stereo search-tune w/tape	310	260	263
Power seat, single control	210	176	178
Power seats, dual control	420	352	356
Dual-facing rear seats, wagons	167	140	142
Speed control	170	142	144
Leather-wrapped steering wheel	59	49	50
Tilt steering wheel...............	105	88	89
Handling suspension	49	41	42
Heavy-duty suspension............	26	22	23
Conventional spare tire............	63	53	54
Trailer-towing package			
Wagons	200	168	170
Sedans	251	211	214

Prices are accurate at time of printing; subject to manufacturer's change

Trim	Retail Price	Dealer Cost	Low Price
Leather split bench seat	418	351	355
Duraweave vinyl seat	96	81	82
All-vinyl seat	34	29	30
Power windows			
2-doors	180	152	154
Others	255	214	217
Opening front vent windows	63	53	54
Interval wipers	49	41	42

MERCURY GRAND MARQUIS

	Retail Price	Dealer Cost	Low Price
Grand Marquis 2-door sedan	$10654	$9120	$10020
Grand Marquis 4-door sedan	10718	9174	10074
Grand Marquis LS 2-door sedan	11209	9586	10486
Grand Marquis LS 4-door sedan	11273	9640	10540
Colony Park 5-door wagon	10896	9324	10224

STANDARD EQUIPMENT (included in above prices):

5.0-liter (302-cid) fuel injected V-8 engine, 4-speed overdrive automatic transmission, power steering, power brakes, P215/75R-14 WSW steel-belted radial tires, deluxe sound package, rocker panel and wheellip moldings, wheel covers, dual-note horn, flight bench seat, full carpeting, halogen headlamps, AM/FM stereo radio, color-keyed seatbelts, wide lower bodyside moldings, power windows, vinyl roof, deluxe wheel covers, analog clock, left remote-control door mirror, hood/decklid paint stripes, seatbelt warning chimes. **LS** adds: visor vanity mirror, luxury door trim, dual-beam dome lamp, tinted glass. **Colony Park** has Marquis equipment plus 3-way tailgate, power tailgate window, carpeted load floor, heavy-duty frame, woodgrain exterior applique, fold down rear seat, conventional spare tire.

OPTIONAL EQUIPMENT:

	Retail Price	Dealer Cost	Low Price
Automatic air conditioning	$ 802	$ 658	$ 665
Manual air conditioning	724	608	615
Appearance protection group	68	57	58
Traction-Lok limited-slip differential	95	80	81
Autolamp on/off delay system	73	61	62
Heavy-duty battery	26	22	23
Front & rear bumper rub strips	52	44	45
Digital clock	61	50	51
Convenience group			
LS	95	80	81
Grand Marquis	121	101	103
Wagons w/LS decor	106	89	90
Wagons w/o LS decor	116	97	98
Electric rear-window defroster	135	114	116
Tinted glass	105	88	89
LS decor option, Colony Park	555	466	471

Prices are accurate at time of printing; subject to manufacturer's change

CONSUMER GUIDE®

	Retail Price	Dealer Cost	Low Price
Illuminated entry system.	76	64	65
Cornering lamps.	60	50	51
Light group			
Grand Marquis LS and LS decor.	30	26	27
Others	48	40	41
Lock group			
w/convenience group			
2-doors	123	103	105
4-doors & wagons.	170	142	144
w/o convenience group			
2-doors	163	137	139
4-doors	210	176	178
Wagons	220	184	186
Luggage carrier, wagons.	104	87	88
Glamour paint	77	65	66
Two-tone paint.	129	109	111
Lower bodyside protection			
Colony Park.	52	44	45
Sedans.	39	33	34
Radio equipment			
AM/FM stereo delete (credit)	(152)	(128)	(130)
AM/FM stereo w/8-track tape.	112	94	95
AM/FM stereo w/cassette tape	112	94	95
Electronic AM/FM stereo search-tune . . .	166	139	141
Electronic AM/FM stereo search-tune w/			
cassette or 8-track tape.	310	260	263
Power seat, single control	210	176	178
Power seat, dual controls	420	352	356
Dual-facing rear seats, wagons	167	140	142
Speed control	170	142	144
Leather-wrapped steering wheel	59	49	50
Tilt steering wheel.	105	88	89
Handling suspension	49	41	42
Heavy-duty suspension.	26	22	23
Trailer towing package			
Sedans.	251	211	214
Wagons	200	168	170
Trim			
Cloth-trim comfort seats, wagons.	48	40	41
Leather twin-comfort seats	418	351	355
Duraweave bench seats	96	81	82
Tripminder computer	261	219	222
Coach vinyl top	650	546	552
Luxury wheel covers	59	49	50
Vent windows	63	53	54

Prices are accurate at time of printing; subject to manufacturer's change

Ford Mustang/ Mercury Capri

Ford Mustang 5.0 convertible

WHAT'S NEW FOR '83

A flashy new convertible, 4-barrel power for the optional V-8, and a new 5-speed manual transmission and, later, a revived turbocharged four will bolster the image of the original ponycar. Ford's 3.8-liter "Essex" V-6 is added as the step-up option, replacing the 3.3-liter straight six, and the 255-cid V-8 is no longer available. The base 2.3-liter four now has a one-barrel carburetor instead of a two-barrel unit. The 5-speed optional with the 2.3 is the Ford gearbox with its odd U-shaped fourth-fifth shift motion. Later in the year a Borg-Warner 5-speed will be available with the High-Output 5.0 V-8. Also due later is a revised version of Ford's turbo 2.3 with multi-port fuel injection instead of the carburetor previously used on 1979–81 models. Manual shift cars acquire an upshift indicator light as on VWs for more economy-minded drivers. A new grille, headlamp housings, and taillamps alter Mustang's look for '83. Capri gains a large "bubbleback" hatch window and mildly reworked front. The optional handling suspension has heftier anti-sway bars and returned springs and shocks, and is now available without the Michelin TRX tires that were formerly required. The new convertible has a glass rear window, roll-down side windows, and standard power top. It will be offered only in top-line GLX trim.

EVALUATION

You can still order these cars in a variety of flav[...]
difficult to make absolute judgments since equipment varies
with each car. The GT/RS models, among the fastest U.S.
production cars last year, have even more muscle now with
the 4-barrel carb (last year's was a big 2-barrel). The 5-speed
brings with it more closely spaced gear ratios than the
standard wide-ratio 4-speeder, which should also help performance, judging by our brief drives at Ford's summertime
press preview. The revisions to the handling suspension are
an effort to equal the superior roadholding of the Chevy
Camaro/Pontiac Firebird, and it does yield better grip and
handling response, though the GM cars still have the edge.
Milder versions provide decent gas mileage, which the V-8
doesn't, but their handling is of the garden variety with the
standard limp suspension. The 2.3 four has been nasty and
noisy in the past, but it's a little better behaved now and
provides satisfactory, though not satisfying, pickup. The best
choice might be the V-6, which strikes a good performance/
economy balance between the four and V-8. Mustang
doesn't match some imports in overall value, but the snazzy
convertible and rapid GT/RS keep the ponycar tradition
going. Both models offer good accommodation for two and a
well-designed dashboard.

EVALUATION CHECKLIST
(5.0 V-8 model)

Fuel economy	1	Cargo room	3
Driveability	4	Serviceability	3
Acceleration	5	Standard equipment	4
Braking	4	Body construction	4
Handling/roadholding	4	Paint/exterior finish	3
Driving position	3	Interior finish	3
Instruments/control	4	TOTAL POINTS	66
Visiblity	2		
Heating/ventilation	3	**RATING SCALE**	
Seat comfort	4	5 = Excellent	
Passenger room	3	4 = Very Good	
Ride	3	3 = Average/Acceptable	
Noise	3	2 = Fair	
Exit/entry	3	1 = Poor	

PECIFICATIONS

	2-door coupe	3-door coupe	2-door conv.
Wheelbase (in.)	100.4	100.4	100.4
Overall length (in.)	179.1	179.1	179.1
Overall width (in.)	69.1	69.1	69.1
Overall height (in.)	51.9	51.9	51.9
Track front (in.)	56.6	56.6	56.6
Track rear (in.)	57.0	57.0	57.0
Curb weight (lbs.)	2684	2744	NA
Max. cargo vol. (cu. ft.)	10.0	32.5	10.0
Fuel tank capacity (gal.)	15.4	15.4	15.4
Seating capacity	4	4	4
Front headroom (in.)	37.2	37.2	37.2
Front shoulder room (in.)	55.8	55.8	55.8
Front legroom, max. (in.)	41.7	41.7	41.7
Rear headroom (in.)	35.9	35.5	NA
Rear shoulder room (in.)	54.3	54.3	NA
Rear legroom, min. (in.)	29.7	29.7	NA

BODY/CHASSIS

Drivetrain layout: longitudinal front engine/rear-wheel drive. **Suspension front:** independent, modified MacPherson struts, lower control arms, coil springs, telescopic shock absorbers, anti-roll bar. **Suspension rear:** rigid axle, four links, coil springs, telescopic shock absorbers; anti-roll bar optional. **Steering:** rack-and-pinion. **Turns lock-to-lock:** 4.1 manual, 3.0 power. **Turn diameter (ft.):** 37.4. **Brakes front:** 10.1-in. discs. **Brakes rear:** 9.0-in. drums. **Construction:** unit

POWERTRAINS	ohc I-4	ohv V-6	ohv V-8	ohc I-4T
Bore × stroke (in.)	3.78× 3.12	3.87× 3.44	4.00× 3.00	3.78× 3.12

CONSUMER GUIDE®

POWERTRAINS

POWERTRAINS	ohc I-4	ohv V-6	ohv V-8	ohc I-4T
Displacement (liters cu. in.)	2.3/ 140	3.8/ 232	5.0/ 302	2.3/ 140
Compression ratio	9.0:1	8.7:1	8.3:1	NA
Fuel delivery	1bbl.	2bbl.	4bbl.	FI
Net bhp @ rpm[1]	93@ 4600	105@ 4000	176@ 4200	NA
Net torque @ rpm (lbs/ft)[1]	128@ 2400	181@ 1200	247@ 2600	NA
Availability	S/All	O/All	O/All	O/All

[1]Preliminary ratings

Final drive ratios

4-speed manual	3.08:1[1]		3.08:1[3]	
5-speed OD manual	3.45:1[1]		NA	3.45:1
3-speed automatic	3.08:1[2]	2.73:1		

1: 3.45:1 high-altitude areas; NA convertible
2: 3.45:1 Traction-Lok opt.
3: Overdrive transmission

KEY bbl. = barrel (carburetor); **bhp** = brake horsepower (advertised); **Cal.** = California only. **Fed.** = Federal/49 state; **FI** = fuel injection; **ohv** = overhead valve; **ohc** = overhead cam; **I** = inline engine; **V** = V engine; **D** = diesel; **T** = turbocharged; **OD** = overdrive transmission; **S** = standard engine; **O** = optional engine.

PRICES

FORD MUSTANG	Retail Price	Dealer Cost	Low Price
L 2-door coupe	$6727	$6184	$6684
GL 2-door coupe	7264	6377	6877
GL 3-door coupe	7439	6528	7028
GLX 2-door coupe.	7398	6493	6993
GLX 3-door coupe.	7557	6629	7129
GLX convertible	NA	NA	NA
GT 3-door coupe	9328	8152	8952

STANDARD EQUIPMENT (included in above prices):

2.3-liter (140-cid) 4-cylinder engine, 4-speed manual transmission, remote-control left mirror, AM radio, deluxe wheel covers, high-back reclining front bucket seats, carpeting, full instrumentation. **GL** adds: deluxe sound

Prices are accurate at time of printing; subject to manufacturer's change

insulation, black exterior trim, dual bodyside pinstripes, turbine wheel covers, sport steering wheel, low-back reclining bucket seats, upgraded vinyl trim. **GLX** adds: dual bright remote-control door mirrors, luxury-level carpeting, luxury steering wheel, light group, upgraded trim. **GT** has over L equipment: 5.0-liter (302-cid) V-8 engine, wider tires and handling suspension, fog lamps, black dual remote-control door mirrors, cast-aluminum wheels, black exterior treatment, front spoiler, rear spoiler, console w/digital clock, sports blackout interior treatment, GLX seat trim, GL door trim panels.

OPTIONAL EQUIPMENT:

	Retail Price	Dealer Cost	Low Price
Engines			
3.8-liter (232-cid) V-6	$ 309	$ 259	$ 262
5.0-liter (302-cid) H.O. V-8			
Convertible	595	500	505
All others	1343	1128	1140
3-speed automatic transmission	439	369	373
5-speed manual transmission, 4-cylinder . .	124	105	107
Air conditioner	724	608	615
Traction-Lok axle	95	80	81
Lower bodyside protection.	41	35	36
Power brakes	93	78	79
Console	191	161	163
Electric rear-window defroster.	135	114	116
Tinted glass	105	88	89
Light group.	55	46	47
Power lock group	160	134	136
Special tu-tone paint, L series	189	159	161
GL, GLX	150	126	128
Tu-tone paint, lower	116	97	98
Protection group.	60	50	51
Radio equipment			
AM delete (credit)	(61)	(51)	(52)
AM/FM	82	69	(70)
AM/FM stereo.	109	91	92
AM/FM stereo w/cassette tape	199	167	169
Open-air roof.	310	260	263
"T" bar roof	1055	886	895
Sports performance seats	196	165	167
Speed control	170	142	144
Power steering.	202	170	172
Leather-wrapped sport steering wheel	59	49	50
Tilt steering wheel.	105	88	89
Handling suspension	252	212	215
Leather trim			
Cloth trim.	415	348	352
L	29	25	26

	Retail Price	Dealer Cost	Low Price
GL	40	34	35
GLX, GT	57	48	49
Power windows	180	152	154
Interval wipers	49	41	42

MERCURY CAPRI

3-door coupe.	$7556	$6575	$7075
L 3-door coupe	7711	6767	7267
GS 3-door coupe	7914	6941	7441
RS 3-door coupe	9241	8084	8684
Black Magic 3-door coupe	8629	7557	8157

STANDARD EQUIPMENT (included in above prices):

2.3-liter (140-cid) 4-cylinder engine, 4-speed manual transmission, high-back bucket seats, full instrumentation including tachometer, sport steering wheel, color-keyed front and rear bumpers, lighter, full carpeting, day/night mirror, remote-control left mirror, bodyside moldings, P185/75R-14 steel-belted radial tires, semi-styled wheels, halogen headlights, power brakes, AM radio. **GS** adds: right remote-control mirror, sport wheel covers, upgraded interior trim, light group. **RS** has over base equipment: black exterior trim, dual black remote mirrors, rear spoiler, leather-wrapped steering wheel, handling suspension, tape graphics, P205/70R-14 tires, 5.0-liter (302-cid) H.O. V-8.

OPTIONAL EQUIPMENT:

Engines			
3.8-liter (232-cid) V-6	$309	$259	$262
5.0-liter (302-cid) H.O. V-8			
L, GS	1343	1128	1140
Black Magic	866	727	735
3-speed automatic transmission	439	369	373
5-speed manual transmission (4-cyl. engine only)	124	104	106
Air conditioning	724	608	615
Appearance protection group	60	50	51
Traction-Lok axle	95	80	81
Heavy-duty battery	26	22	23
Electric rear-window defroster.	135	114	116
Tinted glass	105	88	89
Light group.	55	46	47
Right remote-control mirror (std. GS)	44	37	38
Rocker panel moldings	33	28	29
Glamour paint	54	45	46
Lower tu-tone paint	78	66	67
Specialty tu-tone paint	137	115	117
Power door lock group	160	134	136

	Retail Price	Dealer Cost	Low Price
Lower bodyside protection.	41	35	36
Radio equipment			
AM delete (credit)	(61)	(51)	(52)
AM/FM	82	69	70
AM/FM stereo.	109	91	92
AM/FM stereo w/cassette tape	199	167	169
Open-air flip-up roof	310	260	263
T-bar roof.	1055	886	895
Sport seats	196	165	167
Speed control	170	142	144
Power steering.	202	170	172
Leather-wrapped steering wheel	59	49	50
Tilt steering wheel.	105	88	89
Handling suspension	252	212	215
Trim			
Base cloth w/vinyl	29	25	26
Accent cloth w/vinyl	40	34	35
Leather/vinyl.	415	348	352
Power windows	180	152	154
Interval wipers.	49	41	42

Ford Thunderbird/ Mercury Cougar

Ford Thunderbird 2-door coupe

WHAT'S NEW FOR '83

A brand-new "aerodynamic" appearance, slightly smaller dimensions, and a sportier image highlight this year's heavily reworked personal-luxury coupes from Ford. The Thunderbird and Mercury's Cougar are still built on the rear-drive "Fox" platform adopted for 1980, but wheelbase has been cut 4.4 inches and overall length and width by some 3 inches. Ford's corporate determination to be the industry leader in low-drag body design has produced sleek new styling with the windshield set at a steeper 60-degree angle. The add-on body trim of previous years has been left on the shelf. Cougar is distinguished by a slightly more vertical grille, a sharply cropped rear roofline, and upswept rear side windows. Both models get a new standard engine, Ford's 3.8-liter "Essex" V-6 (introduced in some '82 lines). At mid-model-year, two other engines are expected for the T-Bird, the fuel-injected version of the 302-cid V-8 as used on the company's big cars and a revived version of the Mustang/Capri 2.3-liter (140-cid) turbocharged four, now with port or multi-point electronic fuel injection. The latter is the heart of a special Turbo Coupe model, with standard 5-speed manual gearbox and specific handling package. Gas-pressurized shock absorbers like those first seen on the '82 Continental are standard for both T-Bird and Cougar. Last year's Thunderbird Town Landau is gone, leaving base and spiffier Heritage models in addition to the Turbo Coupe. Standard Heritage items include digital instrumentation, velour upholstery, and illuminated keyless entry system. The Cougar's XR-7 designation is dropped. Standard for all versions are reclining front seatbacks, full console with storage bin, extended-travel seat tracks, and inboard seatbelt buckles mounted on the seat itself. New-for-'83 options include an emergency kit, locking fuel filler door, and anti-theft alarm system.

EVALUATION

We haven't had a chance to drive the new Thunderbird and Cougar at this writing. However, judging by paper specifications and the prototypes we've looked at, they should be much like their predecessors in driving feel and performance. That means they're still mainly boulevard cruisers. The Turbo Coupe may be an exception because of its turbo four and more youthful chassis settings. Performance with the V-6 should be at least adequate, maybe better than average. We doubt fuel economy will show any significant gain despite the more slippery styling largely because the '83s are only 200 pounds lighter than comparably equipped '82s. The interior layout and appointments are much as before, except that the effect is literally much less sparkling. Rear seating is still tight for adults approaching six feet tall; in fact, it's even tighter now due to a 1.2-inch loss in rear legroom. Base models have restyled and more legible instruments, but you still get only a speedo and fuel gauge. Trunk capacity has been reduced by 3.1 cubic feet, though what's left appears quite useful. The size and weight reductions are laudable, though the differences aren't that great, and the styling is a big improvement.

EVALUATION

New or substantially changed model, and not available for assessment at time of publication.

SPECIFICATIONS	2-door coupe
Wheelbase (in.)	104.0
Overall length (in.)	197.6
Overall width (in.)	71.1
Overall height (in.)	53.2
Track front (in.)	58.1
Track rear (in.)	58.5
Curb weight (lbs.)	3076
Max. cargo vol. (cu. ft.)	14.6[1]
Fuel tank capacity (gal.)	21.0
Seating capacity	4/5
Front headroom (in.)	37.7
Front shoulder room (in.)	56.3
Front legroom, max. (in.)	42.0
Rear headroom (in.)	36.7
Rear shoulder room (in.)	55.2
Rear legroom, min. (in.)	34.3

1: 13.2 cu ft. w/conventional spare tire

BODY/CHASSIS

Drivetrain layout: longitudinal front engine/rear-wheel drive.
Suspension front: independent, modified MacPherson struts, lower control arms, coil springs, gas-pressurized telescopic shock absorbers, anti-roll bar. **Suspension rear:** rigid axle, four links, coil springs, gas-pressurized telescopic shock absorbers with electronic level control, anti-roll bar optional. **Steering:** rack-and-pinion, variable-ratio, power-assisted. **Turns lock-to-lock:** 3.0. **Turn diameter (ft.):** 38.6
Brakes front: 10.1-in. discs. **Brakes rear:** 9.0-in. drums.
Construction: unit

POWERTRAINS	ohv V-6	ohc I-4T
Bore × stroke (in.)	3.87× 3.44	3.78× 3.12
Displacement (liters/cu. in.)	3.8/ 232	2.3/ 140
Compression ratio	8.7:1	NA
Fuel delivery	2bbl.	FI
Net bhp @ rpm[1]	105@ 4000	NA
Net torque @ rpm (lbs/ft)[1]	181@ 1200	NA
Availability	S/All	S/All[2]

[1]*Preliminary ratings*
2: *Turbo coupe only*

Final drive ratios

5-speed OD manual		3.45:1
3-speed automatic	2.47:1[1]	
4-speed OD automatic	3.08:1[2]	

1: *NA high-altitude areas*
2: *3.45:1 high-altitude areas*

KEY bbl. = barrel (carburetor); **bhp** = brake horsepower (advertised); **Cal.** = California only. **Fed.** = Federal/49 state; **FI** = fuel injection; **ohv** = overhead valve; **ohc** = overhead cam; **I** = inline engine; **V** = V engine; **D** = diesel; **T** = turbocharged; **OD** = overdrive transmission; **S** = standard engine; **O** = optional engine.

Prices not available at time of publication.

Honda Accord

Honda Accord 4-door sedan

WHAT'S NEW FOR '83

Completely redesigned last year except for drivetrains, the larger Honda cars are virtually unchanged this season. There is one drivetrain revision, however: a new 4-speed overdrive automatic transmission with lockup torque converter to replace last year's optional 3-speed unit. The standard gearbox remains a 5-speed overdrive manual unit. The '83 Accord switches to P-metric tires, though size is unaltered, on the sedan and hatchback; the fancier LX 3-door retains its non-P-metric Michelin XZX radials. Power steering is now available for the automatic-equipped hatchback. Honda also claims the Accord's flow-through ventilation system has been improved, though we have no details at this writing on precisely what has been done to it.

EVALUATION

Like its Civic sister, the Accord suffers by comparison to its class rivals in two ways: it's comparatively expensive yet it's smaller than most competitors inside and out. Even so, the Accord looks like a bargain next to the underpowered, overweight, and overpriced GM J-cars. Honda's 1.7-liter four is a real gem: smooth-running, quiet (even at indecently high speeds), and responsive. Acceleration is brisk with 5-speed, but tails off markedly with automatic, which may be why Honda has given the '83 a more flexible 4-speed unit.

Mileage is fine with either transmission: we recorded
mpg overall with the automatic in routine running. The
5-speed posted 32 mph in a hard trip down the California
coast. Very capable on the road, with minimal body roll in
hard corners and good sticking power. Optional assisted
steering is light without feeling dead, and makes nipping in
and out of tight spots a snap. The ride strikes a pleasant
balance between sporty firmness and luxury-car softness.
The driving position is comfortable, dash and minor controls
thoughtfully organized. Best of all, the Accord is built with a
level of craftsmanship that wouldn't be out of place in a
Mercedes-Benz. Not so pleasing are the engine's occasional
baulkiness during warmup, limited cabin space for larger
adults, crowded engine bay, and the haughty attitude of
some Honda dealers. And curiously, the Accord lacks certain
optional amenities like a sunroof which most of its rivals offer.
In brief: the competition is catching up, but the Accord still
shines for overall excellence. If only it didn't cost so much.

EVALUATION CHECKLIST

Fuel economy	4	Cargo room	3
Driveability	3	Serviceability	3
Acceleration	4	Standard equipment	4
Braking	4	Body construction	4
Handling/roadholding	4	Paint/exterior finish	4
Driving position	4	Interior finish	5
Instruments/control	4	TOTAL POINTS	74
Visiblity	4		
Heating/ventilation	3	**RATING SCALE**	
Seat comfort	4	5 = Excellent	
Passenger room	2	4 = Very Good	
Ride	4	3 = Average/Acceptable	
Noise	4	2 = Fair	
Exit/entry	3	1 = Poor	

SPECIFICATIONS

	3-door sedan	4-door sedan
Wheelbase (in.)	96.5	96.5
Overall length (in.)	165.8	173.6
Overall width (in.)	65.0	65.0
Overall height (in.)	53.3	54.1

SPECIFICATIONS

	3-door coupe	4-door sedan
Track front (in.)	56.3	56.3
Track rear (in.)	55.9	55.9
Curb weight (lbs.)	2150	2169
Max. cargo vol. (cu. ft.)	NA	NA
Fuel tank capacity (gal.)	15.8	15.8
Seating capacity	4	4
Front headroom (in.)	37.3	38.0
Front shoulder room (in.)	NA	NA
Front legroom, max. (in.)	40.9	40.0
Rear headroom (in.)	35.8	36.6
Rear shoulder room (in.)	NA	NA
Rear legroom, min. (in.)	NA	NA

BODY/CHASSIS

Drivetrain layout: transverse front engine/front-wheel drive.
Suspension front: independent; MacPherson struts, lower lateral arms, coil springs, telescopic shock absorbers, anti-roll bar. **Suspension rear:** MacPherson struts, lower lateral arms, trailing arms, coil springs, telescopic shock absorbers, anti-roll bar. **Steering:** rack-and-pinion, power-assisted. **Turns lock-to-lock:** 3.1. **Turn diameter (ft.):** 31.6. **Brakes front:** 7.5-in. discs. **Brakes rear:** 7.6-in. drums. **Construction:** unit

POWERTRAINS

	ohc I-4
Bore × stroke (in.)	3.03× 3.70
Displacement (liters/cu. in.)	1.7/107
Compression ratio	8.8:1
Fuel delivery	3bbl.
Net bhp @ rpm	75@ 4500

POWERTRAINS	ohc I-4
Net torque @ rpm (lbs/ft)	96@ 3500
Availability	S/All
Final drive ratios	
5-speed OD manual	4.07:1
4-speed OD automatic	3.88:1

KEY bbl. = barrel (carburetor); **bhp** = brake horsepower (advertised); **Cal.** = California only. **Fed.** = Federal/49 state; **FI** = fuel injection; **ohv** = overhead valve; **ohc** = overhead cam; **I** = inline engine; **V** = V engine; **D** = diesel; **T** = turbocharged; **OD** = overdrive transmission; **S** = standard engine; **O** = optional engine.

PRICES

ACCORD	Retail Price	Dealer Cost	Low Price
3-door sedan, 5-speed	$7499	$6349	$6849
3-door sedan, automatic	7999	6770	7270
LX 3-door sedan, 5-speed	8549	7231	7831
LX 3-door sedan, automatic	8849	7483	8083
4-door sedan, 5-speed	8345	7060	7660
4-door sedan, automatic	8645	7312	7912

Note: retail prices include pre-delivery service; add $25 to dealer cost and $30 to retail price for models sold in California and high-altitude areas (emissions-control equipment). Prices shown do not include $169 destination and handling charge. Low prices are estimated; these models customarily sell at or above retail price in most locations. Therefore, readers are urged to shop several dealers to obtain the lowest price.

Honda Civic

WHAT'S NEW FOR '83

The main news concerning Honda's popular front-drive subcompact is a new sporty model, the Civic S, to replace the previous 1500GL. The rest of the lineup is mainly a carryover, except for the high-mileage 5-speed FE (Fuel Economy) 3-door. This now adopts the ratios of the 4-speed manual used in the base Civic, in which fourth is geared at 0.77. The FE's fifth gear is also an overdrive, a tall 0.65 gear.

Prices are accurate at time of printing; subject to manufacturer's change

Honda Civic S 3-door sedan

The Civic S gets a special uprated suspension not shared with other models, as well as standard 165/70SR-13 Michelin radial tires, special front bucket seats, black and red interior trim, and black-finish exterior moldings. Shock absorbers are specially calibrated, too, and there's an anti-roll bar at the rear. One potentially important change involves brakes: all Civics with the larger 1.5-liter engine get standard ventilated front discs instead of the solid-rotor units previously used.

EVALUATION

The unanimous staff choice for value in the crowded minicar market, even though it's one of the most expensive of its kind. Aside from intelligent design that packs maximum interior space into minimum exterior size, the Civic's most impressive aspect is its quality. Plainly put, it's built like a fine Swiss watch, performs with the same precision and smoothness, and gives every indication of being able to withstand the ravages of time and abuse. It's also fun to drive, and you lose little perfomance with the 1300 engine compared to the 1500cc versions. Economy with either is excellent. In our most recent test, the Civic FE delivered an honest 34.6 mpg for our hard-charging drivers in combined city/suburban running. Turn-on-a-dime maneuverability makes the Civic a natural for urban dwellers, yet it's equally at home on the highway where it will cruise without fuss. But no car is perfect. The Civic is quite small, which means a very cramped rear seat especially in the short-wheelbase 3-doors. It's also not lavishly equipped for the money. Speaking of price, Honda dealers know the high demand for their product, and are usually reluctant to discount. Service also varies quite a bit from one outlet to another, and Honda's reputation for good workmanship has been tarnished of late by the much-publicized "rusty fenders" recall. Nevertheless, the Civic is the best-built car in its class, and the best all around, and that's why we again recommend it so highly.

EVALUATION CHECKLIST
(FE (Fuel Economy) model)

Fuel economy	5	Cargo room	2
Driveability	3	Serviceability	4
Acceleration	3	Standard equipment	3
Braking	4	Body construction	4
Handling/roadholding	4	Paint/exterior finish	4
Driving position	3	Interior finish	4
Instruments/control	4	TOTAL POINTS	71
Visiblity	4		
Heating/ventilation	3	**RATING SCALE**	
Seat comfort	4	5 = Excellent	
Passenger room	3	4 = Very Good	
Ride	4	3 = Average/Acceptable	
Noise	3	2 = Fair	
Exit/entry	3	1 = Poor	

SPECIFICATIONS

	3-door sedan	4-door sedan	5-door wagon
Wheelbase (in.)	88.6	91.3	91.3
Overall length (in.)	148.0	161.0	160.8
Overall width (in.)	61.6	61.6	61.6
Overall height (in.)	53.0	53.0	54.1
Track front (in.)	53.5	53.5	53.5
Track rear (in.)	54.3	54.3	54.3
Curb weight (lbs.)	1835	1980	1980
Max. cargo vol. (cu. ft.)	6.9	10.5	27.2
Fuel tank capacity (gal.)	10.8	12.1	10.8
Seating capacity	4	4	4/5
Front headroom (in.)	37.0	37.0	37.0
Front shoulder room (in.)	50.8	50.8	50.8

SPECIFICATIONS

	3-door sedan	4-door sedan	5-door wagon
Front legroom, max. (in.)	40.7	40.7	40.7
Rear headroom (in.)	34.9	35.4	36.4
Rear shoulder room (in.)	50.2	50.8	49.5
Rear legroom, min. (in.)	28.3	30.1	29.7

BODY/CHASSIS

Drivetrain layout: transverse front engine/front-wheel drive. **Suspension front:** independent; MacPherson struts, lower lateral arms, coil springs, telescopic shock absorbers, anti-roll bar. **Suspension rear:** independent; MacPherson struts, lower trailing arms, lower lateral links, coil springs, (parallel leaf springs on wagon), telescopic shock absorbers. **Steering:** rack-and-pinion. **Turns lock-to-lock:** 3.3. **Turn diameter (ft.):** 31.8. **Brakes front:** 7.8-in. (hatchback); 9.0-in. (sedan); 8.1-in. discs (wagon). **Brakes rear:** 7.1-in. (hatchback and sedan); 7.9-in. drums (wagon). **Construction:** unit

POWERTRAINS

	ohc I-4	ohc I-4
Bore × stroke (in.)	2.91× 3.40	2.83× 3.22
Displacement (liters cu. in.)	1.5/ 91	1.3/ 81
Compression ratio	8.8:1	8.8:1
Fuel delivery	3bbl.	3bbl.
Net bhp @ rpm	67@ 5000	62@ 5500
Net torque @ rpm (lb/ft)	79@ 3000	69@ 3000
Avail./Certification	S/All[1]	S/All[2]
Final drive ratios		
4-speed manual		4.07:1
5-speed OD manual	3.88:1	3.72:1[3]

POWERTRAINS	ohc I-4	ohc I-4
3-speed automatic	3.58:1	4.93:1

1 = 1500 only
2 = 1300 only
3 = Available FE model only.
KEY bbl. = barrel (carburetor); **bhp** = brake horsepower (advertised); **Cal.** = California only. **Fed.** = Federal/49 state; **FI** = fuel injection; **ohv** = overhead valve; **ohc** = overhead cam; **I** = inline engine; **V** = V engine; **D** = diesel; **T** = turbocharged; **OD** = overdrive transmission; **S** = standard engine; **O** = optional engine.

PRICES

CIVIC	Retail Price	Dealer Cost	Low Price
1300 3-door sedan, 4-speed	$4899	$4459	$4759
1300 FE 3-door sedan, 5-speed	5999	5149	5499
1500 3-door sedan, 5-speed	5949	5107	5457
1500 3-door sedan, automatic	6149	5277	5627
1500 S 3-door sedan, 5-speed	6399	5489	5839
1500 5-door wagon, 5-speed	6349	5447	5797
1500 5-door wagon, automatic	6549	5617	6017
1500 4-door sedan, 5-speed	6849	5872	6272
1500 4-door sedan, automatic	7049	6042	6442

Note: retail prices include pre-delivery service; add $25 to dealer cost and $30 to retail price for models sold in California and high-altitude areas (emissions-control equipment). Prices shown do not include $169 destination and handling charge. Low prices are estimated; those models customarily sell at or above retail price in most locations. Therefore, readers are urged to shop several dealers to obtain the lowest price.

Imperial

WHAT'S NEW FOR '83

The most expensive, most luxurious model from Chrysler comes back little changed from last year. One exception is that the Frank Sinatra Edition package option has been dropped. Imperial is promoted as a one-price luxury car with no extra-cost options. Buyers have choices in exterior color, upholstery, stereo system, and wheel trim, however. Chrysler calls this a limited-production model, but there also has been limited demand for it despite the long list of standard

Prices are accurate at time of printing; subject to manufacturer's change

Imperial 2-door coupe

features and the trendy neoclassic styling. Powertrain is still the familiar Chrysler 318 V-8 with fuel injection and 3-speed TorqueFlite automatic transmission.

EVALUATION

After a disappointing '81 model year, Imperial sales slipped again in '82. The Imperial is impressive standing still, with its full-house interior and abundant creature comforts. Standard digital instrumentation is futuristic, and the car looks well put together. On the move, however, the Imperial betrays its humble origins. The chassis is the same as that of the Dodge Diplomat and Mirada, Chrysler Cordoba, and Plymouth Gran Fury. The live rear axle thumps and bumps too much for a luxury liner. The standard power steering has almost no feel. With a long nose and excessive body roll in turns, it feels more like an ocean liner. The car does pretty well for all the weight it carries, but the problem is there's just too much of it. The V-8 isn't strong enough for the two-ton curb weight, so performance is weak and mileage low. When you pay more than $20,000 for a car, you're more critical about rattles and looseness, and we spotted too many such items on our last test Imperial. Verdict: doesn't match its competition, Cadillac Seville and Lincoln Continental, in many areas. Surpasses the others, however, with 5-year/50,000-mile powertrain and rust protection.

EVALUATION CHECKLIST

Fuel economy	2	Cargo room	3
Driveability	4	Serviceability	2
Acceleration	2	Standard equipment	5
Braking	3	Body construction	3
Handling/roadholding	3	Paint/exterior finish	5
Driving position	4	Interior finish	4
Instruments/control	3	TOTAL POINTS	68
Visiblity	3		
Heating/ventilation	3	**RATING SCALE**	
Seat comfort	4	5 = Excellent	
Passenger room	3	4 = Very Good	
Ride	3	3 = Average/Acceptable	
Noise	5	2 = Fair	
Exit/entry	4	1 = Poor	

SPECIFICATIONS

	2-door coupe
Wheelbase (in.)	112.7
Overall length (in.)	213.3
Overall width (in.)	72.7
Overall height (in.)	53.2
Track front (in.)	60.0
Track rear (in.)	59.5
Curb weight (lbs.)	4019
Max. cargo vol. (cu. ft.)	16.1[1]
Fuel tank capacity (gal.)	18.0
Seating capacity	5
Front headroom (in.)	37.5
Front shoulder room (in.)	58.0
Front legroom, max. (in.)	43.4
Rear headroom (in.)	36.5
Rear shoulder room (in.)	58.2
Rear legroom, min. (in.)	35.0

1: Manufacturer's estimate

BODY/CHASSIS

Drivetrain layout: longitudinal front engine/rear-wheel drive. **Suspension front:** independent, lateral non-parallel control arms, transverse torsion bars, telescopic shock absorbers, anti-roll bar. **Suspension rear:** rigid axle, semi-elliptic leaf springs, telescopic shock absorbers. **Steering:** recirculating ball, power-assisted. **Turns lock-to-lock:** 3.5. **Turn diameter (ft.):** 40.7. **Brakes front:** 10.8-in. discs. **Brakes rear:** 10.0-in. drums. **Construction:** unit

POWERTRAINS	ohv V-8
Bore × stroke (in.)	3.91×3.31
Displacement (liters/cu. in.)	5.2/318
Compression ratio	8.5:1
Fuel delivery	FI
Net bhp @ rpm	140@ 4000
Net torque @ rpm (lbs/ft)	245@ 2000
Availability	S/All
Final drive ratios	
3-speed automatic	2.24:1

KEY bbl. = barrel (carburetor); **bhp** = brake horsepower (advertised); **Cal.** = California only. **Fed.** = Federal/49 state; **FI** = fuel injection; **ohv** = overhead valve; **ohc** = overhead cam; **I** = inline engine; **V** = V engine; **D** = diesel; **T** = turbocharged; **OD** = overdrive transmission; **S** = standard engine; **O** = optional engine.

PRICES

IMPERIAL	Retail Price	Dealer Cost	Low Price
2-door coupe.	$21846	$18354	$19854

STANDARD EQUIPMENT (included in above prices):

5.2-liter (318-cid) V-8 engine with fuel injection, 3-speed automatic transmission, power steering, power brakes, cruise control, electronic digital instrumentation, power windows, power door locks, automatic climate-control air conditioning, AM/FM stereo radio with six-speaker

Prices are accurate at time of printing; subject to manufacturer's change

premium sound system, electric rear-window defroster, power left and right front seats, dual remote-control door mirrors, deluxe sound insulation, full carpeting including trunk.

Isuzu

Isuzu I-Mark LS 2-door coupe

WHAT'S NEW FOR '83

General Motors' Japanese affiliate is saving its big new-model news for next February. That's when Isuzu will introduce a new high-style four-seat sports coupe. Sold as the Piazza overseas, the new model is dubbed Impulse, and will be a contender in the growing sporty coupe field against the likes of the Toyota Celica Supra, Mitsubishi Starion, Datsun 280-ZX, and, to a lesser extent, the domestic Chevrolet Camaro/Pontiac Firebird and Ford Mustang/Mercury Capri. Styled by Italy's Giorgetto Giugiaro, Impulse is a hatchback based on the rear-drive Isuzu I-Mark, which is a cousin to our Chevrolet Chevette. Features include flush-fit side windows, electronic digital and LED graphic instrumentation, variable-assist power steering, full-house equipment and, possibly, 4-wheel disc brakes. Power is expected to come from a 2.0-liter double-overhead-cam four with computer-controlled engine management system. A 5-speed overdrive manual gearbox will be standard, with 4-speed overdrive electronic-control automatic optional. A four-cylinder diesel, possibly turbocharged, may appear later. Betting is that the base model will carry a sticker price of just under $10,000. Meanwhile, the subcompact I-Mark soldiers on without change following its minor facelift last season. By the end of 1983, Isuzu's full nationwide dealer network should be in place. (Note: comments below are for the I-Mark only.)

EVALUATION

Isuzu's rear-drive subcompact is a very familiar item even though it's been on the U.S. market only a short time. It's basically the 1976–79 Buick/Opel with nicer appointments, a slightly different look, and an available four-cylinder diesel engine. In general, the I-Mark behaves much like a Chevette, no surprise since both stem from GM's T-body "world car" design of the early '70s. However, its larger gasoline engine gives better pickup than the Chevette's, aided by a light, precise manual shift. The Isuzu diesel is no model of refinement, being rough and tiringly noisy, but returns excellent mileage (38 mpg in our most recent test). No matter which engine you get, you'll suffer from the kind of cramped cabin and oddball driving position found in the Chevette. Workmanship, on the other hand, is great. But there's no getting around the advanced age of this design compared to newer small cars. Conclusion: hampered now by the Japanese government's quotas on car exports to the U.S. and by a limited dealer network. Even so, not a standout in any area, and an also-ran in most of them.

EVALUATION CHECKLIST
(I-Mark)

Fuel economy	3	Cargo room	3
Driveability	4	Serviceability	3
Acceleration	4	Standard equipment	3
Braking	4	Body construction	4
Handling/roadholding	3	Paint/exterior finish	4
Driving position	2	Interior finish	4
Instruments/control	3	TOTAL POINTS	67
Visiblity	3		
Heating/ventilation	4	**RATING SCALE**	
Seat comfort	4	5 = Excellent	
Passenger room	2	4 = Very Good	
Ride	3	3 = Average/Acceptable	
Noise	4	2 = Fair	
Exit/entry	3	1 = Poor	

SPECIFICATIONS

	2-door coupe	4-door sedan
Wheelbase (in.)	94.3	94.3
Overall length (in.)	170.7	170.7
Overall width (in.)	61.8	61.8
Overall height (in.)	52.6	53.5
Track front (in.)	51.4	51.4
Track rear (in.)	51.4	51.4
Curb weight (lbs.)	2189[1]	2231[1]
Max. cargo vol. (cu. ft.)	9.8	9.9
Fuel tank capacity (gal.)	13.7	13.7
Seating capacity	4	4
Front headroom (in.)	37.0	37.9
Front shoulder room (in.)	51.1	51.1
Front legroom, max. (in.)	42.0	42.0
Rear headroom (in.)	35.0	36.6
Rear shoulder room (in.)	50.4	50.4
Rear legroom, min. (in.)	30.2	30.9

1: Base models w/gasoline engine

BODY/CHASSIS

Drivetrain layout: longitudinal front engine/rear-wheel drive. **Suspension front:** independent, upper and lower A-arms, coil springs, telescopic shock absorbers, anti-roll bar. **Suspension rear:** rigid axle, three trailing links, torque tube, coil springs, telescopic shock absorbers; anti-roll bar on gas LS models. **Steering:** rack-and-pinion. **Turns lock-to-lock:** 4.7. **Turn diameter (ft.):** 30.1. **Brakes front:** 7.6-in. discs. **Brakes rear:** 9.0-in. drums. **Construction:** unit

POWERTRAINS

	ohc I-4	ohc I-4D
Bore × stroke (in.)	3.31× 3.23	3.31× 3.23

POWERTRAINS

	ohc I-4	ohc I-4D
Displacement (liters/cu. in.)	1.8/ 111	1.8/ 111
Compression ratio	8.5:1	22.0:1
Fuel delivery	2bbl.	FI
Net bhp @ rpm	78@ 4800	51@ 5000
Net torque @ rpm (lbs/ft)	95@ 3000	72@ 3000
Availability	S/All[1]	S/All[2]

1: gasoline models only
2: Diesel models only

Final drive ratios

4-speed manual		3.15:1
5-speed OD manual	3.31:1[1]	3.31:1
3-speed automatic	3.31:1	3.58:1

KEY bbl. = barrel (carburetor); **bhp** = brake horsepower (advertised); **Cal.** = California only. **Fed.** = Federal/49 state; **FI** = fuel injection; **ohv** = overhead valve; **ohc** = overhead cam; **I** = inline engine; **V** = V engine; **D** = diesel; **T** = turbocharged; **OD** = overdrive transmission; **S** = standard engine; **O** = optional engine.

PRICES

ISUZU	Retail Price	Dealer Cost	Low Price
(1982 prices shown; 1983 prices not available at time of publication.)			
I-Mark			
Deluxe 2-door coupe	$5917	$5149	$5549
Deluxe 4-door sedan	6069	5159	5559
LS 2-door coupe	6535	5555	5955
Diesel 2-door coupe	6699	5828	6228
Diesel Deluxe 2-door coupe	7044	5987	6387
Diesel Deluxe 4-door sedan	7194	6115	6615
Diesel LS 2-door coupe	7660	6511	7011

STANDARD EQUIPMENT (included in above prices):

1.8-liter (111-cid) gasoline or diesel engine, 4-speed manual transmission, clock, 2-speed wipers, power brakes, reclining front bucket seats, tinted

Prices are accurate at time of printing; subject to manufacturer's change

CONSUMER GUIDE®

glass, carpeting. **Deluxe** adds: 5-speed manual transmission, electric rear-window defogger, intermittent wipers, console. **LS** adds: dual sport mirrors, bodyside stripes, upgraded trim.

OPTIONAL EQUIPMENT:	Retail Price	Dealer Cost	Low Price
3-speed automatic transmission	$ 297	$ 252	$ 255
Air conditioning	560	476	481
Radio equipment			
AM/FM	90	76	77
AM/FM stereo	216	130	132

Lincoln Continental

Lincoln Continental Givenchy Series 4-door sedan

WHAT'S NEW FOR '83

You'll have to look closely to tell the '82 and '83 versions of Lincoln's bustleback 4-door apart. The one tipoff is a front fender plaque that reads "Electronic Fuel Injection," replacing "Continental" script. This signals adoption of the injected (throttle-body type) version of the 302-cid V-8 previously used only in the senior Lincolns. As before, your one and only transmission is Ford's 4-speed AOD (automatic overdrive) unit with lockup torque converter. Last year's mid-line Signature Series becomes the base Continental for '83, and there's a new Valentino Designer Series model with walnut metallic/ desert tan metallic two-tone paint and cloth or leather interior in desert tan. New to the options slate are a three-channel garage door opener (last year's had only one channel), anti-theft alarm system, and automatic day/night rearview mirror.

EVALUATION

The debut edition of Lincoln's little luxury liner proved to be a much better car than we expected. Its main strengths are excellent noise supression, a smooth engine that starts readily and runs without stumbling, an unobtrusive automatic transmission, and the sort of rolling-boudoir interior decor expected in this class. Loaded with convenience features, some of which we could do without. The standard digital instrumentation is an example; it provides little constant information on what's happening to the engine, most of which is left to warning lights. Ride isn't as mushy as on most U.S. plushmobiles, though wavy roads bring out unsettling nose bobbing. Mileage is dreadful (13.8 mpg in our test). Don't expect miracles on the fuel-injected '83 because the main problem here is heft. Acceleration turned out to be surprisingly brisk despite that, and the Conti will scoot around corners with more agility than you'd expect. Legroom is somewhat limited all-around, and the rear compartment feels confined because of the broad rear roof pillars that also hinder over-the-shoulder vision. We were appalled at the misaligned exterior trim on our test car. This is what Ford means by "Quality is Job 1?" Still, a better buy than Seville or Imperial, in our view. Appeal is now bolstered by a 36-month/36,000-mile warranty on scheduled and non-scheduled maintenance. Protection is free for the first third of this, after which a $50 deductible applies.

EVALUATION CHECKLIST

Fuel economy	1	Cargo room	4
Driveability	4	Serviceability	3
Acceleration	4	Standard equipment	5
Braking	3	Body construction	4
Handling/roadholding	3	Paint/exterior finish	3
Driving position	4	Interior finish	4
Instruments/control	3	TOTAL POINTS	72
Visiblity	3		
Heating/ventilation	4	**RATING SCALE**	
Seat comfort	4	5 = Excellent	
Passenger room	3	4 = Very Good	
Ride	4	3 = Average/Acceptable	
Noise	5	2 = Fair	
Exit/entry	4	1 = Poor	

SPECIFICATIONS

	4-door sedan
Wheelbase (in.)	108.6
Overall length (in.)	201.2
Overall width (in.)	73.6
Overall height (in.)	54.8
Track front (in.)	58.4
Track rear (in.)	59.0
Curb weight (lbs.)	3680[1]
Max. cargo vol. (cu. ft.)	15.0
Fuel tank capacity (gal.)	22.0
Seating capacity	6
Front headroom (in.)	38.5
Front shoulder room (in.)	57.9
Front legroom, max. (in.)	42.8
Rear headroom (in.)	37.7
Rear shoulder room (in.)	57.9
Rear legroom, min. (in.)	37.2

1: manufacturer's estimate

BODY/CHASSIS

Drivetrain layout: longitudinal front engine/rear-wheel drive. **Suspension front:** independent; modified MacPherson struts, lower control arms, coil springs, gas-pressurized telescopic shock absorbers, anti-roll bar. **Suspension rear:** rigid axle, four links, coil springs, gas-pressurized shock absorbers. **Steering:** rack-and-pinion variable-ratio, power-assisted. **Turns lock-to-lock:** 3.1 **Turn diameter (ft.):** 42.6 **Brakes front:** 10.9-in. discs. **Brakes rear:** 11.3-in. discs. **Construction:** unit

POWERTRAINS

	ohv V-8
Bore × stroke (in.)	4.00× 3.00

POWERTRAINS

	ohv V-8
Displacement (liters/cu. in.)	5.0/ 302
Compression ratio	8.3:1
Fuel delivery	FI
Net bhp @ rpm	130@ 3200
Net torque @ rpm (lbs/ft)	240@ 1600
Availability	S/All
Final drive ratios	
4-speed OD automatic	3.08:1[1]

1:3.42:1 high-altitude areas; 3.27:1 w/Traction-Lok

KEY bbl. = barrel (carburetor); **bhp** = brake horsepower (advertised); **Cal.** = California only. **Fed.** = Federal/49 state; **FI** = fuel injectoin; **ohv** = overhead valve; **ohc** = overhead cam; **I** = inline engine; **V** = V engine; **D** = diesel; **T** = turbocharged; **OD** = overdrive transmission; **S** = standard engine; **O** = optional engine.

PRICES

CONTINENTAL	Retail Price	Dealer Cost	Low Price
4-door sedan.	$20985	$17701	$19701
Valentino Series 4-door sedan	22576	19022	21022
Givenchy Series 4-door sedan.	22576	19022	21022

STANDARD EQUIPMENT (included in above prices):

5.0-liter (302-cid) V-8 engine, 4-speed overdrive automatic transmission, power steering, 4-wheel power disc brakes, power door locks, power windows, power antenna, power dual heated door mirrors, tilt steering wheel, speed control, illuminated entry system, headlight convenience group, tinted glass, interval wipers, cornering lamps, automatic temperature control air conditioning, Twin-Comfort lounge front seat, AM/FM stereo search-tune radio w/six speakers and premium sound system. **Designer Series** adds: dual-shade paint, narrow upper bodyside moldings, coach lamps, wire-spoke aluminum wheels, unique seat treatment w/choice of luxury cloth or leather upholstery, leather-wrapped steering wheel, luxury cloth door inserts.

Prices are accurate at time of printing; subject to manufacturer's change

OPTIONAL EQUIPMENT:	Retail Price	Dealer Cost	Low Price
Keyless entry system	$ 89	$ 74	$ 75
Dual illuminated visor vanity mirrors.	149	124	126
Vinyl-insert bodyside moldings	64	53	54
Power glass moonroof	1289	1070	1081
Paint			
Moondust	263	218	221
Two-tone, base model.	320	265	268
AM/FM electronic stereo radio w/8-track or cassette tape	170	141	143
Leather-wrapped steering wheel, base model	99	82	83
Leather trim	551	457	462
Anti-theft alarm system.	185	154	156
Garage door opener.	140	116	118
Auto dim elec rearview mirror	89	74	75
Coach lamps	88	73	74
Brushed aluminum upper body moldings . .	74	61	62
Conventional spare tire	97	81	82

Lincoln Mark VI & Town Car

Lincoln Mark VI Bill Blass Series 2-door coupe

WHAT'S NEW FOR '83

The senior Lincolns again are mostly carryovers this year, with only minor changes to standard and optional features. The Givenchy Designer Series has been discontinued for the Mark VI. Last year's drivetrain, the fuel-injected 302-cid V-8 and 4-speed automatic overdrive transmission, is still the only one available. All models have a new all-electronic AM/FM stereo search radio as standard equipment. New options include an automatic dimming day/night rearview mirror, anti-theft alarm system, garage door opener with three channels (last year's was one channel), and locking wire wheel covers. Carriage Roof, aping the top-up look of a convertible, is available for Town Car and the 4-door Mark.

EVALUATION

Mark VI and Lincoln sedan are very close to the Cadillac DeVille/Fleetwood in virtually every area, except the Cadillacs offer an optional diesel engine for those who want better mileage. For most buyers in this price bracket, mileage won't be that important, though. Lincoln has a slight edge in performance with the 302 V-8 over the smaller, less proven Cadillac aluminum V-8. The Lincolns are also a little quieter and seem assembled with greater care, judging by owner reports we've received. Interiors are tastefully trimmed if you're into velour, though the amount of chrome is still excessive. Ride is extremely quiet, but wavy roads cause lots of up and down body motion. The trunk is deep and large, and has a low load lip. Rear entry on the 2-door Mark is tight, as is the rear seat, which is a disappointment on such a large car. Big and thirsty by any standards, even if you can afford one. Also overdecorated and conspicuous. Okay for extroverted high rollers; impractical for most others.

EVALUATION CHECKLIST

Fuel economy	2	Cargo room	4
Driveability	4	Serviceability	3
Acceleration	3	Standard equipment	5
Braking	3	Body construction	5
Handling/roadholding	3	Paint/exterior finish	4
Driving position	4	Interior finish	4
Instruments/control	3	TOTAL POINTS	74
Visiblity	3		
Heating/ventilation	4	**RATING SCALE**	
Seat comfort	5	5 = Excellent	
Passenger room	4	4 = Very Good	
Ride	4	3 = Average/Acceptable	
Noise	4	2 = Fair	
Exit/entry	3	1 = Poor	

SPECIFICATIONS

	2-door coupe	4-door sedan
Wheelbase (in.)	114.3	117.3
Overall length (in.)	216.0	219.0
Overall width (in.)	78.1	78.1
Overall height (in.)	55.2	56.1
Track front (in.)	62.2	62.2
Track rear (in.)	60.0	60.0
Curb weight (lbs.)	4004	4062[1]/ 4105
Max. cargo vol. (cu. ft.)	22.4	22.4
Fuel tank capacity (gal.)	18.0	18.0
Seating capacity	6	6
Front headroom (in.)	38.0	39.0
Front shoulder room (in.)	60.7	60.7
Front legroom, max. (in.)	43.5	43.5
Rear headroom (in.)	37.9	38.2
Rear shoulder room (in.)	60.9	60.7
Rear legroom, min. (in.)	36.7	42.1

1: Town Car/Mark VI

BODY/CHASSIS

Drivetrain layout: longitudinal front engine/rear-wheel drive. **Suspension front:** independent, unequal-length upper and lower A-arms, coil springs, telescopic shock absorbers, anti-roll bar. **Suspension rear:** rigid axle, four links, coil springs, telescopic shock absorbers, **Steering:** recirculating ball, power-assisted. **Turns lock-to-lock:** 3.4. **Turn diameter (ft.):** 40.0. **Brakes front:** 11.1-in. discs. **Brakes rear:** 10.0-in. drums. **Construction:** body-on-frame

POWERTRAINS	ohv V-8
Bore × stroke (in.)	4.00× 3.00

POWERTRAINS

	ohv V-8
Displacement (liters/cu. in.)	5.0/302
Compression ratio	8.3:1
Fuel delivery	FI
Net bhp @ rpm	130@3200
Net torque @ rpm (lbs/ft)	240@1600
Availability	S/All
Final drive ratios	
4-speed OD automatic	3.08:1[1]

1: 3.42:1 high-altitude areas and w/Traction-Lok

KEY bbl. = barrel (carburetor); **bhp** = brake horsepower (advertised); **Cal.** = California only. **Fed.** = Federal/49 state; **FI** = fuel injectoin; **ohv** = overhead valve; **ohc** = overhead cam; **I** = inline engine; **V** = V engine; **D** = diesel; **T** = turbocharged; **OD** = overdrive transmission; **S** = standard engine; **O** = optional engine.

PRICES

LINCOLN TOWN CAR	Retail Price	Dealer Cost	Low Price
4-door sedan	$16923	$14299	$16299
Signature Series 4-door sedan	18265	15412	17412
Cartier Edition 4-door sedan	19601	16521	18521
MARK VI			
2-door coupe	$20229	$17091	$19091
4-door sedan	20717	17495	19494
Signature Series 2-door coupe	23124	19494	21494
Signature Series 4-door sedan	23612	19898	21898
Bill Blass Series 2-door coupe	24533	20663	22663
Pucci Series 4-door sedan	24407	20558	22558

STANDARD EQUIPMENT (included in above prices):

Town Car: 5.0-liter (302-cid) V-8 engine with fuel injection, 4-speed overdrive automatic transmission, power brakes, power steering, power windows, automatic temperature control air conditioning, tinted glass; AM/FM search-tune radio w/power antenna, digital clock, remote decklid release, WSW steel-belted radial tires, remote-control left door mirror,

Prices are accurate at time of printing; subject to manufacturer's change

cornering lamps, luxury wheel covers, vinyl roof. **Mark VI** adds: electronic instrument display, padded vinyl roof, 6-way twin-comfort lounge seats, power door locks, speed control, tilt steering wheel, interval wipers. **Mark VI Signature** adds: color-keyed turbine-spoke aluminum wheels, 6-way power leather or cloth seats w/recliners, intermittent wipers, keyless entry system, premium sound system, tilt steering wheel, headlamp convenience group, remote-control right door mirror, garage door opener, landau vinyl roof, defroster group, speed control, illuminated visor vanity mirrors.

OPTIONAL EQUIPMENT:

	Retail Price	Dealer Cost	Low Price
Traction-Lok limited-slip differential	$ 96	$ 80	$ 81
Defroster group (std. Signature)	160	133	135
Dual exhausts	83	69	70
Garage door opener (std. Signature)	140	116	118
Headlamp convenience group	178	148	150
Illuminated entry system	77	64	65
Electronic instrument panel, Town Car	804	667	674
Electronic instrument panel delete (credit)	(804)	(667)	(674)
Garage door opener	140	116	118
Anti-theft alarm system	185	154	156
Keyless entry system	165	137	139
Power glass moonroof	1289	1070	1081
Dual-shade paint	320	265	268
Moondust paint	263	218	221
Lower bodyside protection	40	33	34
Radio equipment			
AM/FM electronic stereo w/8-track tape	170	141	143
AM/FM electronic stereo w/cassette tape	170	141	143
40 ch. CB w/power antenna	356	295	298
Premium sound system	194	161	163
Carriage roof	1069	887	896
Coach roof, Mark VI 2-door	381	317	321
Coach roof, Mark VI 4-door	294	244	247
Coach roof, Town Car	343	285	288
Twin-comfort power seat w/passenger recliner, Town Car & Mark VI	302	251	254
Twin-comfort power seat w/dual recliner, Signature & Cartier	54	45	46
Leather wrapped steering wheel	99	82	83
Speed control, Town Car	188	156	158
Tilt steering wheel, Town Car	96	80	81
Leather interior trim, Mark VI	551	457	462
Leather interior trim, Signature	459	381	385
Leather interior trim, Town Car	521	432	437
Interval wipers, Town Car	60	50	51
Puncture resistant tires	139	116	118

Prices are accurate at time of printing; subject to manufacturer's change

Mazda GLC

Mazda GLC Sport 4-door sedan

WHAT'S NEW FOR '83

Having recently passed the 1-million mark in unit production, Mazda's front-drive minicar comes in for a few detail mechanical and cosmetic revisions this year. Most significant is a new feedback carburetor linked to an oxygen sensor in the exhaust manifold to provide more precise control of the air/fuel mixture. Mazda claims a small mileage improvement as a result, and the '83 EPA city figure for the 5-speed model is up by 1 mpg to 36. A clutch cable damper has been added to reduce transmission noise. New to the lineup is a Sport version of the notchback 4-door as a companion to the 3-door model. Both have a beefed-up suspension with front and rear anti-roll bars and specially calibrated shock absorbers, plus upgraded interior trim. The GLC's standard reclining front seat backrests get a new angle adjustment mechanism with finer settings, and a lumbar support adjuster has been added for Sport models and Custom L sedans. New extra-cost equipment includes power steering and, for Sport models only, power door locks and an electric sliding sunroof made of heavy-gauge tinted plastic. The rear-drive 5-door wagon, the sole holdover from the original GLC line, returns unchanged except for the engine modifications. Most of Mazda's 1983 activity centers on the all-new front-drive replacement for the familiar 626, the company's largest U.S.-market offering.

EVALUATION

Last tested by us in 4-door sedan form, the GLC is an appealing car at an appealing price. Our real-world mileage worked out to 32.9 mpg, which confirmed last year's 35-mpg EPA city rating. Engine delivers adequate pickup, but feels and sounds harsh going up through gears. Tire roar and some exhaust-induced body resonance mar refinement in highway driving. Easy to whirl around in tight spaces, aided by superb outward vision, small outer dimensions, and a high seating position. Deceptively spacious interior will hold four adults in reasonable comfort on medium-length journeys. Ride will seem too firm for some, especially over sharp bumps. Logical, well-arranged dash of modern design; good major control relationships. Sedan's trunk borders on the cavernous, and the split-back rear seat can be flopped down to increase load space as on the hatchbacks. GLC feels structurally less solid than Honda's Civic, and there's some evidence of cost-cutting in the grade of interior trim used. Against this, price is very competitive, and reliability/ durability so far appears very good. Opinion: not our top choice this year, but a serious contender for your hard-earned dollars as an economical, all-purpose small car.

EVALUATION CHECKLIST

Fuel economy	5	Cargo room	4
Driveability	4	Serviceability	4
Acceleration	3	Standard equipment	3
Braking	3	Body construction	4
Handling/roadholding	4	Paint/exterior finish	4
Driving position	4	Interior finish	3
Instruments/control	3	TOTAL POINTS	72
Visiblity	5		
Heating/ventilation	4	**RATING SCALE**	
Seat comfort	3	5 = Excellent	
Passenger room	3	4 = Very Good	
Ride	3	3 = Average/Acceptable	
Noise	3	2 = Fair	
Exit/entry	3	1 = Poor	

SPECIFICATIONS	3-door sedan	4-door sedan	5-door sedan	5-door wagon
Wheelbase (in.)	93.1	93.1	93.1	91.1

SPECIFICATIONS	3-door sedan	4-door sedan	5-door sedan	5-door wagon
Overall length (in.)	159.1	166.8	159.1	165.4
Overall width (in.)	64.2	64.2	64.2	62.8
Overall height (in.)	54.1	54.1	54.1	56.3
Track front (in.)	54.7	54.7	54.7	51.0
Track rear (in.)	54.9	54.9	54.9	51.6
Curb weight (lbs.)	1890[1]	1935[1]	1935[1]	2130[1]
Max. cargo vol. (cu. ft.)	10.2[2]	13.6	10.2[2]	57.2[3]
Fuel tank capacity (gal.)	11.1	11.1	11.1	11.9
Seating capacity	5	5	5	5
Front headroom (in.)	37.9	37.9	37.9	38.6
Front shoulder room (in.)	52.1	52.1	52.1	51.6
Front legroom, max. (in.)	41.5	41.5	41.5	40.6
Rear headroom (in.)	37.0	37.0	37.0	37.0
Rear shoulder room (in.)	52.1	52.1	52.1	51.6
Rear legroom, min. (in.)	34.5	34.5	34.5	31.1

1: Base models
2: w/rear seat up
3: w/rear seat down

BODY/CHASSIS

Drivetrain layout: transverse front engine/front-wheel drive (longitudinal front engine/rear-wheel drive wagon). **Suspension front:** independent, MacPherson struts, lower A-arms, variable rate coil springs, telescopic shock absorbers (MacPherson struts, lower A-arms, coil springs, anti-roll bar on wagon). **Suspension rear:** independent, MacPherson struts, twin transverse trailing links, variable-rate coil springs, telescopic shock absorbers, anti-roll bar (rigid axle, semi-elliptic leaf springs on wagon). **Steering:** rack-and-pinion (recirculating ball on wagon). **Turns lock-to-lock:** 3.6. **Turn diameter (ft.):** 30.2 (28.8 wagon). **Brakes front:** 8.9-in. discs. (9.0-in. wagon). **Brakes rear:** 7.1-in. drums (7.9-in. wagon). **Construction:** unit

POWERTRAINS	ohc I-4
Bore × stroke (in.)	3.03× 3.15
Displacement (liters/cu. in.)	1.5/ 91
Compression ratio	9.0:1
Fuel delivery	2661.
Net bhp @ rpm	68@ 5000
Net torque @ rpm (lbs/ft)	82@ 3000
Availability	S/All
Final drive ratios	
4-speed manual	3.85:1[1]
5-speed OD manual	3.85:1[1]
3-speed automatic	3.63:1[2]

1: 3.73:1 wagon
2: 3.91:1 wagon

KEY bbl. = barrel (carburetor); **bhp** = brake horsepower (advertised); **Cal.** = California only. **Fed.** = Federal/49 state; **FI** = fuel injection; **ohv** = overhead valve; **ohc** = overhead cam; **I** = inline engine; **V** = V engine; **D** = diesel; **T** = turbocharged; **OD** = overdrive transmission; **S** = standard engine; **O** = optional engine.

PRICES

GLC	Retail Price	Dealer Cost	Low Price
3-door sedan, 4-speed	$5295	$4862	$5162
Custom 3-door sedan, 5-speed	5695	5050	5400
Custom L 3-door sedan, 5-speed.	6095	5402	5752
Sport 3-door sedan, 5-speed	6545	5897	6297
Custom 4-door sedan, 5-speed	6245	5533	5933
Custom L 4-door sedan, 5-speed.	6745	5973	6373
Sport 4-door sedan, 5-speed	7145	6324	6824
Deluxe 5-door wagon, 5-speed	6245	5533	5933

STANDARD EQUIPMENT (included in above prices):

1.5-liter (91-cid) 4-cylinder engine, transmission as above, remote-control left mirror, electric rear-window defroster, reclining front bucket seats,

Prices are accurate at time of printing; subject to manufacturer's change

power brakes, locking fuel-filler door, bodyside protection moldings, fold-down rear seatback, trip odometer, vinyl upholstery. **Custom** adds: tinted glass, chrome bumpers and exterior moldings, full door trim with armrests, carpeting, split-back fold-down rear seat, dual sunvisors, passenger assist handles, woodgrain dash trim, cigarette lighter, choice of cloth or vinyl upholstery. **Custom L** adds: remote hatch/trunklid release, rear-window wiper/washer (except 4-doors), cargo area light, front door pockets, intermittent wipers, quartz clock, soft-grip steering wheel, vanity mirror. **Sport** adds: upgraded wheels and tires, blackout exterior moldings and grille treatment, halogen headlamps, remote-control right door mirror, 4-spoke soft-grip steering wheel, adjustable steering column, driver's seat tilt adjuster, front seatback pockets, tachometer, rear-seat headrests, dual horns.

OPTIONAL EQUIPMENT:	Retail Price	Dealer Cost	Low Price
Air conditioning			
All exc. wagon	$ 590	$ 442	$ 447
Wagon	540	431	436
AM/FM full-control stereo radio (NA			
wagon)	270	192	193
Sunroof, Custom L & Sport only	265	226	229
Power steering, Custom L & Sport 4-doors			
only	180	153	155
Automatic transmission (NA base			
3-door)	290	265	268
Cruise control (NA wagon)	200	150	152
Aluminum wheels, Sport models only	245	196	198
Electric sunroof & power door locks, Sport			
4-door only	500	426	431

Mazda RX-7

WHAT'S NEW FOR '83

The big news from Toyo Kogyo this year is the new front-drive successor to the three-year-old rear-drive 626 series. It will debut toward the end of calendar 1982. Accordingly, Mazda has only touched up its rotary-engine RX-7 sports car for '83. These minor modifications consist of standard maintenance-free (sealed) battery, a removable roof panel as standard for the two upper models (GS and GSL), easier-to-read markings for heating/ventilation controls, and upgraded sound systems, again for the upper two models. All RX-7s also come in for redesigned seats with more cushion support, and a lumbar support adjuster.

Prices are accurate at time of printing; subject to manufacturer's change

CONSUMER GUIDE®

Mazda RX-7 GSL 2-door coupe

EVALUATION

An extremely well-designed and snappy 2-seater, and still the best sports car value around, in our opinion. High-winding rotary engine has earned its stripes for reliability/durability, with a much lower than average repair incidence than for some piston engines. Takes corners like a go kart except in the rain, when the rear end can slide readily under sudden power application. Steering becomes heavy at parking pace, is pleasant on the move. First-class placement of major and minor controls, but cockpit is snug for those approaching six-foot height. Mazda's usual thorough and tidy assembly, but door panels look decidedly low-buck. Equipment level is high, even on the standard model. Mileage puts a damper on our enthusiasm—we failed to break 20 mpg in admittedly spirited city/suburban driving. If you can live with that, the RX-7 is the easiest of all the 2-seaters to live with.

EVALUATION CHECKLIST

Fuel economy	2	Cargo room	3
Driveability	3	Serviceability	4
Acceleration	4	Standard equipment	4
Braking	4	Body construction	5
Handling/roadholding	4	Paint/exterior finish	5
Driving position	4	Interior finish	4
Instruments/control	5	TOTAL POINTS	75
Visiblity	4		
Heating/ventilation	3	**RATING SCALE**	
Seat comfort	4	5 = Excellent	
Passenger room	2	4 = Very Good	
Ride	4	3 = Average/Acceptable	
Noise	4	2 = Fair	
Exit/entry	3	1 = Poor	

SPECIFICATIONS

	2-door coupe
Wheelbase (in.)	95.3
Overall length (in.)	170.1
Overall width (in.)	65.7
Overall height (in.)	49.6
Track front (in.)	55.9
Track rear (in.)	55.1
Curb weight (lbs.)	2345[1]
Max. cargo vol. (cu. ft.)	17.0
Fuel tank capacity (gal.)	16.6
Seating capacity	2
Front headroom (in.)	37.2
Front shoulder room (in.)	51.4
Front legroom, max. (in.)	41.5

1: w/manual transmission

BODY/CHASSIS

Drivetrain layout: longitudinal front engine/rear-wheel drive. **Suspension front:** independent, MacPherson struts, lower lateral links, compliance struts, coil springs, telescopic shock absorbers, anti-roll bar. **Suspension rear:** rigid axle, lower trailing links, upper angled links, Watt linkage, coil springs, telescopic shock absorbers, anti-roll bar. **Steering:** recirculating ball, variable-ratio. **Turns lock-to-lock:** 3.7. **Turn diameter (ft.):** 31.5. **Brakes front:** 8.9-in. discs. **Brakes rear:** 7.9-in. drums (9.3-in. discs GSL model). **Construction:** unit

POWERTRAINS

	2-rotor wankel
Chamber volume (cc/cu. in.)	573/ 35
Displacement (liters/cu. in.)	1.1/ 70

POWERTRAINS	2-rotor wankel
Compression ratio	9.4:1
Fuel delivery	2bbl.
Net bhp @ rpm	100@ 6000
Net torque @ rpm (lbs/ft)	105@ 4000
Availability	S/All
Final drive ratios	
5-speed OD manual	3.91:1
3-speed automatic	3.91:1

KEY bbl. = barrel (carburetor); **bhp** = brake horsepower (advertised); **Cal.** = California only. **Fed.** = Federal/49 state; **FI** = fuel injectoin; **ohv** = overhead valve; **ohc** = overhead cam; **I** = inline engine; **V** = V engine; **D** = diesel; **T** = turbocharged; **OD** = overdrive transmission; **S** = standard engine; **O** = optional engine.

PRICES

RX-7	Retail Price	Dealer Cost	Low Price
S 2-door coupe	$ 9695	$ 8499	$ 9399
GS 2-door coupe	10595	9176	10076
GSL 2-door coupe.	12195	10479	11479

STANDARD EQUIPMENT (included in above prices):

1.1-liter (70-cid) rotary engine, 5-speed manual transmission, power brakes, tinted glass, electric rear-window defroster, intermittent wipers, full carpeting, reclining front bucket seats, quartz clock, full instrumentation including tachometer, front air dam, lockable fuel-filler door with remote release, full cut-pile carpeting, center console, concealed storage bins, bodyside protection moldings, styled-steel wheels. **GS** adds: AM/FM stereo radio with power antenna, halogen headlamps, remote hatch release, dual remote-control door mirrors, 4-spoke sports steering wheel, interior light package, luggage hold-down straps, driver's footrest, console storage compartment and armrest. **GSL** adds: aluminum wheels, tilt sunroof, cruise control, rear-window wiper/washer, limited-slip differential, rear disc brakes, 4-speaker system, digital clock, power windows, cloth door trim.

OPTIONAL EQUIPMENT

3-speed automatic transmission (NA S) . . .	$ 355	$ 302	$ 306

Prices are accurate at time of printing; subject to manufacturer's change

	Retail Price	Dealer Cost	Low Price
Air conditioning	630	473	478
Aluminum wheels & lift-out sunroof, GS only (std. GSL)	650	520	526
Leather Package, GSL only	650	520	526
Aluminum wheels & 185/70SR-13 tires, S only.	420	336	340
Cruise control (std. GSL)	200	150	152
AM/FM stereo radio, S	320	229	232

Mercedes-Benz W123-Series

Mercedes-Benz 300D Turbodiesel 4-door sedan

WHAT'S NEW FOR '83

After standardizing on turbodiesel power for its smaller models except the least expensive 240D sedan, Mercedes-Benz makes only detail alterations this year. (The W123 designation is the factory's internal code for this body group.) The 240D retains its normally aspirated four-cylinder diesel, the 300-series sedan, coupe, and wagon continue with a turbocharged five-cylinder engine. All except the coupe and wagon receive improved door deals, redesigned windshield post moldings, and additional moldings on the rear extractor vents all to reduce wind noise. Sedans have reshaped rear seats, and all four models get hollowed out front seatbacks to open up more rear kneeroom. Other alterations include a return to "realistic" speedometer markings following repeal of the federal 85-mph speedometer rule, standard electric remote-control right door mirror, more steeply angled front seat headrests that interfere less with rear vision, twin lighted vanity mirrors, a front courtesy light delay switch, and rear seat courtesy light switches for all but the coupe.

EVALUATION

These smaller Mercedes are all meticulously crafted, exceptionally well-engineered cars. Though large by today's standards and cumbersome in close-quarters maneuvering, all offer genuine 5-passenger seating, a comfortable driving position, logically arranged dash and minor controls, and a satisfying precision that implies years of faithful, reliable service. All also have first-rate handling and roadholding, abetted by what is perhaps the best power steering system around. In fact, most owners are unlikely to approach, let alone exceed, the high dynamic capabilities of this chassis in normal driving. Drawbacks are few: the ride is firmer than many may find comfortable, and some ill-mannered thumping can get through. Seats are also firm, almost park-bench hard, and interior furnishings look austere in view of the high price. Mercedes parts and service costs are much higher than for other makes, but then if you're worried about that you're not a serious Mercedes buyer. If you can afford one, we envy you.

EVALUATION CHECKLIST
(300D Turbodiesel sedan)

Fuel economy	4	Cargo room	3
Driveability	4	Serviceability	3
Acceleration	4	Standard equipment	5
Braking	4	Body construction	5
Handling/roadholding	5	Paint/exterior finish	5
Driving position	4	Interior finish	4
Instruments/control	4	TOTAL POINTS	80
Visiblity	5		
Heating/ventilation	4	**RATING SCALE**	
Seat comfort	3	5 = Excellent	
Passenger room	4	4 = Very Good	
Ride	3	3 = Average/Acceptable	
Noise	3	2 = Fair	
Exit/entry	4	1 = Poor	

SPECIFICATIONS

	300CD 2-door coupe	300D 4-door sedan	300TD 5-door wagon	240D 4-door sedan
Wheelbase (in.)	106.7	110.0	110.0	110.0
Overall length (in.)	187.5	190.9	190.9	190.9
Overall width (in.)	70.3	70.3	70.3	70.3
Overall height (in.)	54.9	56.6	58.7	56.6
Track front (in.)	58.6	58.6	58.6	58.6
Track rear (in.)	56.9	56.9	57.2	56.9
Curb weight (lbs.)	3585	3585	3780	3130
Max. cargo vol. (cu. ft.)	12.6	12.6	41.1/ 73.9	12.6
Fuel tank capacity (gal.)	23.9	23.9	21.4	19.7
Seating capacity	5	5	5	5
Front head-room (in.)	37.8	38.3	38.4	38.3
Front shoulder room (in.)	55.3	56.0	56.0	56.0
Front legroom, max. (in.)	41.9	41.9	41.9	41.9
Rear headroom (in.)	36.4	37.3	37.5	37.3
Rear shoulder room (in.)	54.1	55.7	55.5	55.7
Rear legroom, min. (in.)	30.3	33.5	34.8	33.5

BODY/CHASSIS

Drivetrain layout: longitudinal front engine/rear-wheel drive.
Suspension front: independent, upper and lower A-arms,
coil springs, gas-pressurized telescopic shock absorbers,
anti-roll bar. **Suspension rear:** independent, "diagonal
pivot" axle (semi-trailing arms), coil springs, gas-pressurized
telescopic shock absorbers, anti-roll bar. **Steering:** recirculating ball, power-assisted. **Turns lock-to-lock:** 3.2. **Turn
diameter (ft.):** 37.0. **Brakes front:** 11.0-in. discs. **Brakes
rear:** 11.0-in. discs. **Construction:** unit

POWERTRAINS

	ohc I-4D	ohc I-5TD
Bore × stroke (in.)	3.58× 3.64	3.58× 3.64
Displacement (liters/cu. in.)	2.4/ 146	3.0/ 183
Compression ratio	21.0:1	21.5:1
Fuel delivery	FI	FI
Net bhp @ rpm	67@ 4000	120@ 4350
Net torque @ rpm (lbs/ft)	97@ 2400	170@ 2400
Availability	S/All[1]	S/All[2]

1: 240 D only
2: 300D, 300CD, 300TD only

Final drive ratios

4-speed manual	3.69:1	
4-speed automatic	3.69:1	3.07:1

KEY bbl. = barrel (carburetor); **bhp** = brake horsepower (advertised); **Cal.** = California only. **Fed.** = Federal/49 state; **FI** = fuel injectoin; **ohv** = overhead valve; **ohc** = overhead cam; **I** = inline engine; **V** = V engine; **D** = diesel; **T** = turbocharged; **OD** = overdrive transmission; **S** = standard engine; **O** = optional engine.

PRICES

MERCEDES-BENZ W123 Series	Retail Price	Dealer Cost	Low Price*
(1982 prices shown; 1983 prices not available at time of publication.)			
240D 4-door sedan, 4-speed	$21858	$17846	$19846
240D 4-door sedan, automatic	23158	18526	20526
300D Turbodiesel 4-door sedan, automatic			
. . . .	29698	23758	26758
300CD Turbodiesel 2-door coupe, automatic	32836	26269	29269
300TD Turbodiesel 5-door wagon, automatic	32933	26346	29346

*estimated; these models customarily sell at or above retail in most locations.

Prices are accurate at time of printing; subject to manufacturer's change

STANDARD EQUIPMENT (included in above prices):

240D: 2.4-liter (146-cid) 4-cylinder diesel engine, 4-speed manual or 4-speed overdrive automatic transmission as above, power all-disc brakes, AM/FM stereo radio with cassette player, central locking system, electric rear window defroster, halogen headlamps, fog lamps, front bucket seats with reclining backrests, driver's seat height adjuster, front center folding armrest, automatic antenna with height adjuster, passenger visor vanity mirror, cruise control (automatic transmission only), power steering, tinted glass, parcel nets on front seatbacks, full carpeting, MB-Tex vinyl upholstery and door trim, air conditioning, light-alloy wheels with wheel covers, front door map pockets, intermittent wipers. **300D and 300CD Turbodiesel** add: 3.0-liter (183-cid) 5-cylinder turbocharged diesel engine, 4-speed overdrive automatic transmission, power windows, automatic climate control air conditioning system, forged light-alloy wheels, combination tachometer and quartz analog clock. **300TD Turbodiesel wagon** adds: right door mirror, split-back fold-down rear seat, rear window wiper/washer.

OPTIONAL EQUIPMENT:	Retail Price	Dealer Cost	Low Price
Rear seat headrests	$ 214	$ 171	$ 195
Metallic paint, solid color	673	538	575
Cargo area partition net & cargo cover, 300TD only	333	266	300
Electronically tuned AM/FM stereo radio w/ cassette player	443	354	395
Seat options			
Heated front seat (each).	188	150	160
Fold-down third seat, 300TD only	834	667	735
Leather upholstery	1083	866	950
Velour upholstery	1073	858	940
Sunroof			
Manual	657	526	585
Electric (NA 300TD)	829	663	740
Forged light-alloy wheels, 240D	537	430	490
Power windows, 240D (std. others)	711	619	675

Mercedes-Benz S-Series

WHAT'S NEW FOR '83

The four models in the senior S-class Mercedes-Benz line come in for even fewer changes than their smaller W123 running mates. The quartet again consists of the 300SD turbodiesel sedan and a gasoline trio powered by the all-aluminum 3.8-liter (234-cid) V-8 introduced two years ago, the two-seat 380SL roadster, 4-seat 380SEC coupe, and

Prices are accurate at time of printing; subject to manufacturer's change

Mercedes-Benz 380SEC 2-door coupe

long-wheelbase 380SEL sedan. All but the SL are based on the W126 platform, also new for '81. The roadster is a holdover from the previous W116-series design. For '83, the V-8's ignition system and electronic idle speed control have been modified to yield a claimed 5.8 percent improvement in EPA city fuel economy (up to 18 mpg). Engine response from upper-range speeds is also said to be improved. Aside from a revised color palette, other changes are confined to a new speedometer with mph markings above the now-discontinued federal 85-mph maximum, standard electric remote-control right door mirror, and reshaped front seat headrests. V-8 models have an extra "B" position on the automatic transmission shift quadrant that allows manual selection of first gear for additional engine braking when going down steep inclines.

EVALUATION

The 300SD and 380SEL and SEC are all magnificent cars—beautifully crafted, painstakingly engineered, highly refined, satisfying to drive. The all-independent suspension of the new W126 chassis gives a marvelously controlled and quiet ride, aided by solid body construction and gobs of sound insulation that keep noise from all sources to library levels. Despite its 5.5-inch shorter wheelbase, the 300SD gives away little interior room to the SEL. The more compact SEC coupe disappoints for rear seat space relative to its overall size, its entry/exit is more restricted than in the sedans, and front headroom is skimpy for six-footers. All are big, and clumsy in close-quarters maneuvers. By contrast, they're remarkably agile in tight low-speed turns and high-speed sweepers, complemented by properly weighted power steering with plenty of feel. Seats are wonderfully supportive, and adjust every way but sideways. The driving position is high and upright, controls properly spaced for long-distance comfort, minor controls convenient to operate. And the quality of materials and assembly is evident to the eye and touch. The V-8 suffers an annoying hesitation on moving off, but is deliciously smooth and adequately peppy. Unhappily, its gas consumption is piggish (15.8 mpg overall in our test of the SEC). The 300SD gave us 24.1 overall—not terrific for a "smoker" engine, but reasonable considering the size and weight. By comparison, the SL roadster comes off less well. Our test car's brakes were too heavy, pulled to the left in hard stops, and squealed annoyingly. Seats are harder than in other Mercedes, and the driving position less happy. Not as much fun to drive as the smaller W123 cars for some reason, perhaps indicating this oldest of Mercedes' current production models is overdue for replacement.

EVALUATION CHECKLIST
(380SEC)

Fuel economy	2	Cargo room	4
Driveability	4	Serviceability	3
Acceleration	4	Standard equipment	5
Braking	5	Body construction	5
Handling/roadholding	4	Paint/exterior finish	5
Driving position	4	Interior finish	5
Instruments/control	4	TOTAL POINTS	80
Visiblity	3		
Heating/ventilation	4	**RATING SCALE**	
Seat comfort	5	5 = Excellent	
Passenger room	3	4 = Very Good	
Ride	5	3 = Average/Acceptable	
Noise	3	2 = Fair	
Exit/entry	3	1 = Poor	

SPECIFICATIONS	380SL 2-door coupe	380SEC 2-door coupe	300SD 4-door sedan	380SEL 4-door sedan
Wheelbase (in.)	96.9	112.2	115.6	121.1

CONSUMER GUIDE®

SPECIFICATIONS	380SL 2-door coupe	380SEC 2-door coupe	300SD 4-door sedan	380SEL 4-door sedan
Overall length (in.)	182.3	199.2	202.6	208.1
Overall width (in.)	70.5	72.0	71.7	71.7
Overall height (in.)	50.8	55.4	56.3	56.7
Track front (in.)	57.2	60.8	60.8	60.8
Track rear (in.)	56.7	59.7	59.7	59.7
Curb weight (lbs.)	3640	3760	3780	3780
Max. cargo vol. (cu. ft.)	6.6	14.9	15.2	15.2
Fuel tank capacity (gal).	25.5	27.1	23.6	27.1
Seating capacity	2	5	5	5
Front headroom (in.)	36.5	37.8	38.5	38.6
Front shoulder room (in.)	51.6	57.2	56.2	56.2
Front legroom, max. (in.)	42.2	41.9	41.9	41.9
Rear headroom (in.)	—	36.7	37.1	37.2
Rear shoulder room (in.)	—	54.2	55.7	55.7
Rear legroom, min. (in.)	—	30.6	34.4	39.6

BODY/CHASSIS

Drivetrain layout: longitudinal front engine/rear-wheel drive. **Suspension front:** independent, upper and lower A-arms, coil springs, gas-pressurized telescopic shock absorbers, anti-roll bar. **Suspension rear:** independent, "diagonal pivot" axle (semi-trailing arms), coil springs, gas-pressurized telescopic shock absorbers, anti-roll bar. **Steering:** recirculating ball, variable-ratio power-assist. **Turns lock-to-lock:** 2.9. **Turn diameter (ft.):** 34.4 SL, 38.1 SEC, 39.0 SD, 40.6 SEL. **Brakes front:** 11.0-in. discs. **Brakes rear:** 11.0-in. discs. **Construction:** unit

POWERTRAINS

	ohc I-5TD	ohc V-8
Bore × stroke (in.)	3.58× 3.64	3.46× 3.11
Displacement (liters/cu. in.)	3.0/ 183	3.8/ 234
Compression ratio	21.5:1	8.3:1
Fuel delivery	FI	FI
Net bhp @ rpm	120@ 4350	155@ 4750
Net torque @ rpm (lbs/ft)	170@ 2400	196@ 2750
Availability	S/All[1]	S/All[2]

1: 300 SD only
2: 380 SL, 380 SEL, 380 SEC only

Final drive ratios

4-speed automatic	3.07:1	2.47:1

KEY bbl. = barrel (carburetor); **bhp** = brake horsepower (advertised); **Cal.** = California only. **Fed.** = Federal/49 state; **FI** = fuel injection; **ohv** = overhead valve; **ohc** = overhead cam; **I** = inline engine; **V** = V engine; **D** = diesel; **T** = turbocharged; **OD** = overdrive transmission; **S** = standard engine; **O** = optional engine.

PRICES

MERCEDES-BENZ S-Series	Retail Price	Dealer Cost	Low Price*
(1982 prices shown; 1983 prices not available at time of publication.)			
300SD Turbodiesel 4-door sedan	$36830	$29464	$33464*
380SEL 4-door sedan	46433	37146	42146
380SEC 2-door coupe	51956	41565	46565
380SL 2-seat coupe/roadster	41733	33386	37386

*estimated; these models customarily sell at or above retail in most locations.

STANDARD EQUIPMENT (included in above prices):

300SD: 3.0-liter (183-cid) 5-cylinder tubocharged diesel engine, 4-speed overdrive automatic transmission, power all-disc brakes, power steering, power windows, automatic climate-control air conditioning, electronically tuned AM/FM stereo radio with cassette player, central locking system, electric rear window defroster, halogen headlamps, fog lamps, front bucket seats with eight-way power adjustment, folding center front armrest,

Prices are accurate at time of printing; subject to manufacturer's change

automatic antenna with height adjuster, illuminated dual visor vanity mirrors, cruise control, tinted glass, parcel nets on front seatbacks, rear reading lamps, full carpeting including trunk, light-alloy wheels, front door map pockets, intermittent wipers, dual remote-control door mirrors (electrically adjustable on right), combination tachometer and quartz analog clock. **380SEL** adds: 3.8-liter (234-cid) gasoline V-8 engine with electronic fuel injection, power rear seat adjuster, choice of leather or velour upholstery and interior trim. **380SEC** has 380SEL equipment, but deletes rear reading lamps and power rear seat adjuster. **380SL** has 380SEL equipment, but deletes electric right mirror for manual mirror, deletes parcel nets, deletes power seat control for two-position manual height adjuster, and deletes standard interior trim for MB-Tex vinyl upholstery.

OPTIONAL EQUIPMENT:	Retail Price	Dealer Cost	Low Price
Rear seat headrests (NA 380SL)	$ 214	$ 171	$ 195
Metallic paint			
Solid color.	N/C	N/C	N/C
Two-tone, SL only	N/C	N/C	N/C
Seat options			
Heated front seat (each).	188	150	160
Heated rear seat, sedans	375	300	340
Leather upholstery (N/C 380SEL, SEC)			
300SD	1124	899	1000
380SL	853	682	775
Velour upholstery (N/C 380SEL, SEC),			
300SD	1117	894	975
Electric sliding sunroof (NA 380SL)			
380SEC	974	779	865
Others	829	663	740

Mercury Lynx & LN7

WHAT'S NEW FOR '83

Mercury's versions of the "world car" front-drive subcompacts get the same mechanical revisions as Escort. Lynx, L-M Division's top seller, has a simplified model lineup, a new grille, and revised interior trim. The base model has been dropped, and the lowest price Lynx is now the L. The GL series has been discontinued. The two-seat LN7 coupe now has the H.O. (High-Output) version of 1.6-liter CVH four as standard, plus 5-speed manual transmission. Electronic fuel injection is optional on all models. Manual-shift models add an indicator light that shows the driver when to shift to a higher gear for better fuel economy. A high-mpg model with

Prices are accurate at time of printing; subject to manufacturer's change

Mercury LN7 3-door coupe

economy gearing is available outside California. A remote-control locking fuel filler door is now standard on all but the L series and the heat/defrost blower fan has an extra (fourth) speed. Fuel tank capacity has been increased to 13 gallons on all models. The reworked Lynx RS 3-door includes the fuel-injected engine, 5-speed, TR sport suspension and wheels, and Michelin TRX tires. Full-width cloth seat trim is standard, and hatchback models have a removable rear package shelf.

EVALUATION

The CVH engine was retuned for '82, and produced better mileage and quicker acceleration. Suspension was also improved to reduce the "world cars'" floaty ride. Our overall impression of the '82 Escort/Lynx was much more favorable as a result. (See comments under Escort.) The 5-door sedan added to the line last year is much easier for a family to live with than the 3-door. Escort/Lynx makes good use of interior space, but short wheelbase limits room for adults in the rear. Hatchback practicality is diminished somewhat by a rear seat that doesn't lay flat when folded down and a high liftover to the cargo deck. Like its EXP sibling, the two-seat LN7 has a harsh, choppy ride, a low seating position that impedes visibility, and more drivetrain harshness and noise than we find tolerable. LN7/EXP has never delivered impressive performance, and ends up being an unrefined stab at a sports car. Quality control has been a sore spot, though Ford promises to do a better job of smoothing the rough edges. Lynx is nearly the same as Escort, but sells at a higher price.

EVALUATION CHECKLIST
(LN7; for Lynx see Ford Escort & EXP)

Fuel economy 4	Cargo room 4
Driveability 4	Serviceability 3
Acceleration 3	Standard equipment 4
Braking 3	Body construction 4
Handling/roadholding 4	Paint/exterior finish 4
Driving position 2	Interior finish 3
Instruments/control 3	TOTAL POINTS 66
Visiblity 3	
Heating/ventilation 4	**RATING SCALE**
Seat comfort 4	5 = Excellent
Passenger room 2	4 = Very Good
Ride 3	3 = Average/Acceptable
Noise 2	2 = Fair
Exit/entry 3	1 = Poor

SPECIFICATIONS	LN7 3-door coupe	Lynx 3-door sedan	Lynx 5-door sedan	Lynx 5-door wagon
Wheelbase (in.)	94.2	94.2	94.2	94.2
Overall length (in.)	170.3	163.9	163.9	165.0
Overall width (in.)	65.9	65.9	65.9	65.9
Overall height (in.)	50.5	53.3	53.3	53.3
Track front (in.)	54.7	54.7	54.7	54.7
Track rear (in.)	56.0	56.0	56.0	56.0
Curb weight (lbs.)	2156	2016	2078	2117
Max. cargo vol. (cu. ft.)	29.8	26.4	26.1	58.4
Fuel tank capacity (gal.)	13.0	13.0	13.0	13.0
Seating capacity	2	4	4	4
Front headroom (in.)	37.0	38.1	38.1	38.1
Front shoulder room (in.)	51.3	51.4	51.4	51.4
Front legroom, max. (in.)	41.7	41.5	41.5	41.5
Rear headroom (in.)	—	37.4	37.4	38.2
Rear shoulder room (in.)	—	51.7	51.1	51.1
Rear legroom, min. (in.)	—	35.0	35.0	35.0

BODY/CHASSIS

Drivetrain layout: transverse front engine/front-wheel drive. **Suspension front:** independent, MacPherson struts, forged lower control arms, coil springs, telescopic shock absorbers, anti-roll bar. **Suspension rear:** independent, modified Mac-Pherson struts, trailing arms, lower control arms, coil springs, telescopic shock absorbers. **Steering:** rack-and-pinion. **Turns lock-to-lock:** 3.5 manual, 3.0 power. **Turn diameter (ft.):** 35.5. **Brakes front:** 9.3-in. discs. **Brakes rear:** 7.1-in. drums (8.0-in. on wagon, EXP). **Construction:** unit

POWERTRAINS	ohc I-4	ohc I-4[1]	ohc I-4
Bore × stroke (in.)	3.15× 3.13	3.15× 3.13	3.15× 3.13
Displacement (liters/cu. in.)	1.6/ 98	1.6/ 98	1.6/ 98
Compression ratio	9.0:1	9.0:1	9.5:1
Fuel delivery	2bbl.	2bbl.	FI
Net bhp @ rpm*	72@ 5200	80@ 5800	88@ 5400
Net torque @ rpm (lbs/ft)*	91@ 3000	88@ 3400	94@ 4200
Availability	S/All	O/All	O/All

*Preliminary ratings 1:H.O. engine

Final drive ratios

4-speed OD manual	3.59:1[1]	3.59:1[2]	
5-speed OD manual		3.73:1	3.73:1
3-speed automatic	3.31:1[3]	3.31:1	3.31:1

1: 3.04:1 with "Fuel Saver" package (NA Cal.)
2: Available high-altitude area only; close-ratio transmission
3: NA LN7

KEY bbl. = barrel (carburetor); **bhp** = brake horsepower (advertised); **Cal.** = California only. **Fed.** = Federal/49 state; **FI** = fuel injectoin; **ohv** = overhead valve; **ohc** = overhead cam; **I** = inline engine; **V** = V engine; **D** = diesel; **T** = turbocharged; **OD** = overdrive transmission; **S** = standard engine; **O** = optional engine.

PRICES

MERCURY LYNX/LN7

	Retail Price	Dealer Cost	Low Price
Lynx L 3-door sedan	$5751	$5284	$5634
Lynx L 5-door sedan	5958	5460	5810
Lynx L 5-door wagon	6166	5657	6007
Lynx GS 3-door sedan	6476	5678	6028
Lynx GS 5-door sedan	6693	5864	6214
Lynx GS 5-door wagon	6872	6018	6368
Lynx LS 3-door sedan	7529	6583	6983
Lynx LS 5-door sedan	7746	6770	7170
Lynx LS 5-door wagon	7909	6910	7310
Lynx RS 3-door sedan	7370	6446	6846
LN7 3-door coupe	7398	6781	7181
LN7 Sport 3-door hatchback coupe	8084	7076	7576
LN7 Grand Sport 3-door hatchback coupe	8465	7403	7903
LN7 RS 3-door hatchback coupe	8765	7661	8161

STANDARD EQUIPMENT (included in above prices):

LN7 has 1.6-liter (98-cid) H.O. 4-cylinder engine, 5-speed manual transmission, power brakes, electric rear-window defroster, AM radio, intermittent wipers, reclining front bucket seats, full carpeting, halogen headlamps, console, full instrumentation including tachometer and trip odometer, electric remote hatchback release, manual remote-control door mirrors, styled-steel wheels with trim rings, tinted glass, digital clock, cargo cover, auxiliary interior courtesy lighting. **Lynx** has 1.6-liter (98-cid) 4-cylinder engine, 4-speed manual transmission, AM radio, front disc brakes, cigarette lighter, fold-down rear seat-back, hubcaps, cloth high-back bucket seats, day/night mirror, P165/80R13 BSW radial tires, halogen headlamps. **GS** adds: deluxe bumper end caps and rub strips, chrome window moldings, vinyl-insert bodyside moldings, chrome hubcaps & trim rings, reclining bucket seats w/GL trim, color-keyed seatbelts, soft-feel steering wheel, consolette, load floor carpet, deluxe insulation package. **LS** adds: dual sport mirrors, styled-steel wheels w/trim rings, bumper guards, low-back reclining bucket seats, soft-vinyl door trim panels w/carpeted lower portion, console, digital clock, glovebox lock, roof grab handles, light group, upgraded carpeting, interval wipers, electric rear defroster, cargo cover, AM/FM stereo radio. **RS** has base Lynx equipment plus fuel-injected 1.6 engine, 5-speed manual transmission, black bumpers w/deluxe rub strips and end caps, black grille and headlamp bezels, black exterior moldings, bodyside and rear tape stripes, fog lamps, airdam, styled-steel wheels w/trim rings, soft-feel steering wheel, instrumentation group, console, roof grab handles, handling suspension, deluxe insulation, TRX radial tires.

Prices are accurate at time of printing; subject to manufacturer's change

OPTIONAL EQUIPMENT:

	Retail Price	Dealer Cost	Low Price
Engines			
1.6-liter (98-cid) H.O. engine	$ 73	$ 61	$ 62
1.6-liter (98-cid) fuel injected engine	367	308	312
5-speed manual transmission	76	64	65
3-speed automatic transmission			
RS, LN7	363	305	309
All others	439	369	373
Air conditioning	624	524	530
Heavy-duty battery (std. LN7)	26	22	23
Lower bodyside protection	68	57	58
Power brakes (std. LN7)	95	80	81
Digital clock	57	48	49
Console	111	93	94
Electric rear window defroster	124	104	106
Engine block heater	18	15	16
Tinted glass (std. LN7)	90	76	77
Instrumentation group	87	73	74
Light group	43	36	37
Luggage rack	93	78	79
Protection group	60	50	51
Radio equipment			
AM/FM ex. LS	82	69	70
AM/FM stereo (std. LS)	109	91	92
AM/FM stereo w/cassette or 8-track			
Lynx LS	90	76	77
Others	199	167	169
Reclining front seatbacks, Lynx L	65	54	55
Low-back reclining bucket seats, Lynx L	98	82	83
Vinyl seat trim	24	20	21
Open-air flip-up roof			
w/villager option, wagon	217	182	184
other	310	260	263
Speed control	170	142	144
Villager option, wagons	316	265	268
Power steering	210	176	178
Handling suspension			
Lynx L, GS	145	122	124
LS	41	35	36
TR performance suspension	41	35	36
Leather trim, LN7	144	121	123
Shearing & Leather trim, LN7	227	191	193
Opening front vent windows, Lynx	60	50	51
Remote-control rear quarter windows, Lynx	109	91	92
Intermittent wipers (std. LN7)	49	41	42
Rear window wiper/washer	117	98	99

Prices are accurate at time of printing; subject to manufacturer's change

CONSUMER GUIDE®

	Retail Price	Deal[er] Cos[t]	
TR performance pkg w/ steel wheels			
L, GS	313	263	266
TR performance pkg w/aluminum wheels			
L, GS	515	432	437
LS	185	156	158
RS	201	169	171

Mitsubishi Cordia & Tredia

Mitsubishi Cordia LS 3-door coupe

WHAT'S NEW FOR '83

Yet another Japanese make enters the U.S. market under its own banner this year with two entries in the growing field of front-drive small cars. The Cordia hatchback coupe and Tredia notchback sedan come from Mitsubishi Motors Corporation, which has been selling cars here under the Dodge and Plymouth labels since the early '70s. Though they look considerably different, Cordia and Tredia share basic mechanicals and chassis design, and both borrow some components from the familiar Dodge/Plymouth Colt minicars. Only one engine is listed for both, a gasoline four with MMC's patented Silent Shaft feature. There are three trim and equipment levels in each line, base, L, and LS. The latter two have a standard "4+4" dual-range manual transmission. Three-speed automatic is optional for both.

Prices are accurate at time of printing; subject to manufacturer's change

EVALUATION

Both these newcomers make a good first impression. The Tredia's styling is innocuous, which may prove a sales handicap. The Cordia is sleek yet practical thanks to its hatchback tail and splitback rear seat, but its load lip is high and outright cargo volume not all that generous. Plus points in both are the smooth and peppy engine, better-than-average off-the-line pickup, crisp handling, easy maneuverability, robust construction, and fairly complete equipment. Minus points are limited cabin space owing to the small external size and projected mileage that's good but not great. Front headroom in both is marginal for adults. Back seat space is tight, too, especially in the sloped-roof Cordia where rear legroom is virtually nonexistent with the front seats all the way back. The digital dash in the Cordia LS is entertaining, and legible even in bright sunlight. Unfortunately, LCDs lose intensity with age, which would require replacing the whole cluster in about five years, an expensive nuisance. Apparent assembly and finish on both are very good, and MMC products have a good reputation for reliability and sturdiness. One initial drawback common to all three new MMC models (including the sporty Starion described elsewhere) is that there are only 70 dealers to provide parts and service, though that will surely change. In all, pleasant, capable small cars with good equipment and, in the Cordia's case, some intriguing features.

EVALUATION CHECKLIST
(Preliminary)

Fuel economy	3	Cargo room	3
Driveability	4	Serviceability	3
Acceleration	4	Standard equipment	4
Braking	4	Body construction	4
Handling/roadholding	4	Paint/exterior finish	4
Driving position	4	Interior finish	4
Instruments/control	4	TOTAL POINTS	70
Visiblity	3		
Heating/ventilation	3	**RATING SCALE**	
Seat comfort	4	5 = Excellent	
Passenger room	2	4 = Very Good	
Ride	3	3 = Average/Acceptable	
Noise	3	2 = Fair	
Exit/entry	3	1 = Poor	

SPECIFICATIONS

	3-door coupe	4-door sedan
Wheelbase (in.)	96.3	96.3
Overall length (in.)	173.0	172.4
Overall width (in.)	65.4	65.4
Overall height (in.)	51.6	53.7
Track front (in.)	55.5	55.5
Track rear (in.)	54.1	54.1
Curb weight (lbs.)	2182[1]	2205[1]
Max. cargo vol. (cu. ft.)	NA	NA
Fuel tank capacity (gal.)	13.2	13.2
Seating capacity	4	4
Front headroom (in.)	36.8	37.7
Front shoulder room (in.)	52.8	52.8
Front legroom, max. (in.)	41.3	40.9
Rear headroom (in.)	35.6	36.5
Rear shoulder room (in.)	50.0	52.8
Rear legroom, min. (in.)	30.3	34.2

1: Base model

BODY/CHASSIS

Drivetrain layout: transverse front engine/front-wheel drive.
Suspension front: independent, MacPherson struts, lateral control arms, compliance struts, coil springs, telescopic shock absorbers, anti-roll bar. **Suspension rear:** independent, trailing arms, coil springs, telescopic shock absorbers. **Steering:** rack-and-pinion. **Turns lock-to-lock:** NA. **Turn diameter (ft.):** 32.1. **Brakes front:** 9.6-in. discs. **Brakes rear:** 8.0-in. drums. **Construction:** unit

POWERTRAINS

	ohc I-4
Bore × stroke (in.)	3.17× 3.46

POWERTRAINS	ohc I-4
Displacement (liters/cu. in.)	1.8/ 110
Compression ratio	8.5:1
Fuel delivery	2bbl.
Net bhp @ rpm[1]	82@ 5000
Net torque @ rpm (lbs/ft)[1]	93@ 3000
Availability	S/All

[1]Preliminary ratings

Final drive ratios

4 × 2 - speed manual	3.47:1
5-speed OD manual	2.57:1
3-speed automatic	2.80:1

KEY bbl. = barrel (carburetor); **bhp** = brake horsepower (advertised); **Cal.** = California only. **Fed.** = Federal/49 state; **FI** = fuel injection; **ohv** = overhead valve; **ohc** = overhead cam; **I** = inline engine; **V** = V engine; **D** = diesel; **T** = turbocharged; **OD** = overdrive transmission; **S** = standard engine; **O** = optional engine.

Prices not available at time of publication.

Mitsubishi Starion

WHAT'S NEW FOR '83

Due to go on sale by the time you read this, Starion is a new rear-drive sports-luxury contender from an established Japanese automaker selling here under its own name for the first time. This shapely 2+2 hatchback is based on Dodge Challenger/Plymouth Sapporo running gear and chassis pieces. It's powered by a new turbocharged version of Mitsubishi's well-known 2.6-liter "balancer" four, but with electronic throttle-body fuel injection. Starion is offered in base and LS models. The latter comes with air conditioning, six-way adjustable front seats, digital instrumentation, and

Mitsubishi Starion LS Turbo 2-door coupe

eight-speaker sound system to justify its higher price. Standard on both models are power steering and all-disc brakes, electric windows, alloy wheels, and variable-intermittent wipers. Options include a "Technical Performance Package" with electronic anti-skid control for the rear brakes, a first for the U.S. market. Starion is seen as competing with the likes of the Datsun 280-ZX, Mazda RX-7, Toyota Celica Supra, Porsche 944 and, eventually, the all-new 1983 Chevrolet Corvette. Comments here are based on driving impressions formed at an advance press showing at Laguna Seca Raceway in California.

EVALUATION

Our experience with the Starion has been limited so far, so take our evaluation here with the proverbial grain of salt. In general, this is a competent "boulevard sports car" with fine performance and plenty of showroom appeal because of its full-house equipment. Off the line, Starion feels very strong and smooth, without the annoying "step" transition from negative to positive turbo boost. We'd guesstimate 0–60 mph acceleration on the order of 8.5 seconds, which is good going. Handling is mostly neat and clean, but the power recirculating-ball steering lacks precision. It was hard to judge quietness or ride at our test-track drive, but the Starion is certainly no worse in these areas than, say, the Porsche 944 or Mazda RX-7. The cockpit is snug, maybe too much so for larger grownups, and only kids need seriously consider riding in back for any length of time. Mileage will likely be nothing special; the company claims only 21 mpg. Interesting new upper-class sporty coupe, but small cabin and lack of automatic transmission may limit sales appeal. We'll pass final judgment after we've conducted a full road test.

EVALUATION CHECKLIST
(Preliminary)

Fuel economy	2	Cargo room	3
Driveability	4	Serviceability	3
Acceleration	4	Standard equipment	5
Braking	4	Body construction	4
Handling/roadholding	4	Paint/exterior finish	4
Driving position	3	Interior finish	4
Instruments/control	4	TOTAL POINTS	70
Visiblity	3		
Heating/ventilation	4	**RATING SCALE**	
Seat comfort	4	5 = Excellent	
Passenger room	2	4 = Very Good	
Ride	3	3 = Average/Acceptable	
Noise	3	2 = Fair	
Exit/entry	3	1 = Poor	

SPECIFICATIONS

	2-door coupe
Wheelbase (in.)	95.9
Overall length (in.)	173.2
Overall width (in.)	66.3
Overall height (in.)	51.8
Track front (in.)	54.9
Track rear (in.)	55.1
Curb weight (lbs.)	2820
Max. cargo vol. (cu. ft.)	NA
Fuel tank capacity (gal.)	20.0
Seating capacity	4
Front headroom (in.)	36.7
Front shoulder room (in.)	52.4
Front legroom, max. (in.)	41.1
Rear headroom (in.)	35.5

SPECIFICATIONS	2-door coupe
Rear shoulder room (in.)	51.1
Rear legroom, min. (in.)	30.7

1: Base model

BODY/CHASSIS

Drivetrain layout: longitudinal front engine/rear-wheel drive.
Suspension front: independent, MacPherson struts, lower lateral arms, tensions rods, coil springs, gas-filled telescopic shock absorbers, anti-roll bar. **Suspension rear:** semi-independent, semi-trailing arms, transverse arms, torque tube, coil spring struts, gas-filled telescopic shock absorbers, anti-roll bar. **Steering:** recirculating ball, power-assisted. **Turns lock-to-lock:** NA **Turn diameter (ft.):** NA **Brakes front:** 10.0-in. discs. **Brakes rear:** 9.7-in. drums. **Construction:** unit

POWERTRAINS	ohc I-4T
Bore × stroke (in.)	3.59× 3.86
Displacement (liters/cu. in.)	2.6/ 156
Compression ratio	7.0:1
Fuel delivery	FI
Net bhp @ rpm[1]	145@ 5000
Net torque @ rpm (lbs/ft)[1]	185@ 2500
Availability	S/All

[1]*Preliminary ratings*

Final drive ratios

5-speed OD manual	3.54:1

KEY bbl. = barrel (carburetor); **bhp** = brake horsepower (advertised); **Cal.** = California only. **Fed.** = Federal/49 state; **FI** = fuel injectoin; **ohv** = overhead valve; **ohc** = overhead cam; **I** = inline engine; **V** = V engine; **D** = diesel; **T** = turbocharged; **OD** = overdrive transmission; **S** = standard engine; **O** = optional engine.

Oldsmobile Cutlass Ciera

Oldsmobile Cutlass Ciera LS 2-door coupe

WHAT'S NEW FOR '83

Oldsmobile's front-drive mid-size, introduced last January as part of GM A-car fleet, has revised rear-end moldings and taillamps as its only appearance changes for '83. The base coupe and sedan have been dropped, leaving the LS and Brougham models from last year. Engine choices are the same as before, and only 3-speed automatic transmission is available (something that applies to all A-cars). At mid-year a 4-speed overdrive automatic will be added as an option. New for Ciera is a sporty ES package option patterned after the Omega ES model but without its 2.8-liter H.O. V-6. Other new options are exterior opera lamps and an electronic instrument cluster.

EVALUATION

Pleasant, capable offshoot of the X-car design and a good example of a contemporary sedan. Interior space equals that of the bigger rear-drive Cutlass Supreme, yet Ciera generally yields better fuel economy because of lower weight. Either gas engine returns decent mileage, though they aren't at the top of the class. The gas engines deliver subdued performance. Acceleration is adequate for most situations, but without many thrills. The diesel V-6 gives admirable acceleration for its breed and doesn't have the loud, rough idle some diesels are noted for. It's a good alternative for those seeking maximum mileage, though it comes at a much higher price. Ride with the standard suspension is definitely in the Olds tradition, with soft springing that allows the front end to bob noticeably on even slightly wavy roads. That problem can be fixed by ordering the upgraded suspension, which doesn't hurt ride. We like the upright driving position, adequate trunk room, and high overall comfort. Recent models we've tried, however, have suffered from indifferent workmanship; one diesel car was delivered with a leaking power steering system, a problem that necessitates replacing the entire steering rack, a costly repair job. Despite modern design and front-drive advantages, it's hard to convince many people that Ciera is a big improvement over the more popular Cutlass Supreme, though an improvement it certainly is.

EVALUATION CHECKLIST

Fuel economy	3	Cargo room	3
Driveability	4	Serviceability	2
Acceleration	3	Standard equipment	3
Braking	4	Body construction	4
Handling/roadholding	4	Paint/exterior finish	3
Driving position	4	Interior finish	3
Instruments/control	3	TOTAL POINTS	69
Visiblity	4		
Heating/ventilation	4	**RATING SCALE**	
Seat comfort	4	5 = Excellent	
Passenger room	4	4 = Very Good	
Ride	3	3 = Average/Acceptable	
Noise	4	2 = Fair	
Exit/entry	3	1 = Poor	

SPECIFICATIONS	2-door coupe	4-door sedan
Wheelbase (in.)	104.9	104.9
Overall length (in.)	188.4	188.4
Overall width (in.)	69.5	69.5
Overall height (in.)	55.1	55.1
Track front (in.)	58.7	58.7

SPECIFICATIONS

	2-door coupe	4-door sedan
Track rear (in.)	57.0	57.0
Curb weight (lbs.)	2659	2678
Max. cargo vol. (cu. ft.)	16.0	16.0
Fuel tank capacity (gal.)	15.7[1]	15.7[1]
Seating capacity	5	5
Front headroom (in.)	38.6	38.6
Front shoulder room (in.)	56.2	56.2
Front legroom, max. (in.)	42.1	42.1
Rear headroom (in.)	37.9	38.0
Rear shoulder room (in.)	57.0	56.2
Rear legroom, min. (in.)	35.8	36.4

1: 17.0 w/diesel engine

BODY/CHASSIS

Drivetrain layout: transverse front engine/front-wheel drive.
Suspension front: independent, MacPherson struts, lower control arms, coil springs, telescopic shock absorbers, anti-roll bar. **Suspension rear:** beam "twist" axle with integral anti-roll bar, trailing arms, panhard rod, coil springs, telescopic shock absorbers. **Steering:** rack-and-pinion, power-assisted. **Turns lock-to-lock:** 3.1. **Turn diameter (ft.):** 38.1. **Brakes front:** 9.7-in. discs (10.2 w/Diesel engine). **Brakes rear:** 8.9-in. drums. **Construction:** unit

POWERTRAINS

	ohv I-4	ohv V-6	ohv V-6D
Bore × stroke (in.)	4.00× 3.00	3.80× 2.66	4.06× 3.39
Displacement (liters/cu. in.)	2.5/ 151	3.0/ 181	4.3/ 262
Compression ratio	8.2:1	8.45:1	22.8:1
Fuel delivery	FI	2bbl.	FI

POWERTRAINS	ohv I-4	ohv V-6	ohv V-6D
Net bhp @ rpm	82@ 5200	110@ 4800	85@ 3600
Net torque @ rpm (lbs/ft)	132@ 2800	145@ 2600	165@ 1600
Availability	S/All	O/All	O/All
Final drive ratios			
3-speed automatic	2.39:1[1]	2.53:1[2]	2.39:1

1: 2.84:1 high-altitude areas
2: 2.97:1 high-altitude areas

KEY bbl. = barrel (carburetor); **bhp** = brake horsepower (advertised); **Cal.** = California only. **Fed.** = Federal/49 state; **FI** = fuel injectoin; **ohv** = overhead valve; **ohc** = overhead cam; **I** = inline engine; **V** = V engine; **D** = diesel; **T** = turbocharged; **OD** = overdrive transmission; **S** = standard engine; **O** = optional engine.

PRICES

CUTLASS CIERA	Retail Price	Dealer Cost	Low Price
LS 2-door coupe	$8703	$7512	$8012
LS 4-door sedan.	8892	7675	8175
Brougham 2-door coupe	9183	7926	8525
Brougham 4-door sedan	9385	8100	8700

STANDARD EQUIPMENT (included in above prices):

2.5-liter (151-cid) fuel-injected 4-cylinder engine, 3-speed automatic transmission, power brakes, power steering, AM radio, full carpeting, P185/80R-13 fiberglass-belted radial tires.

OPTIONAL EQUIPMENT:

Engines			
3.0-liter (181-cid) V-6	$ 150	$ 128	$ 130
4.3-liter (262-cid) diesel V-6	500	425	430
Air conditioning	725	616	623
Heavy-duty battery			
Gasoline engines	25	21	22
Diesel engine	50	43	44
Center console (w/shift lever)	100	85	86
Center console (w/o shift lever)	80	68	69
Heavy-duty cooling system	30	26	27
High-capacity heavy-duty cooling system			
w/air conditioning	40	34	35

Prices are accurate at time of printing; subject to manufacturer's change

	Retail Price	Dealer Cost	Low Price
w/out air conditioning	70	60	61
Cruise control	170	145	147
Electric rear window defroster	135	115	117
Power door locks			
Coupes	120	102	104
Sedans	170	145	147
ES package			
LS	897	763	771
Brougham	752	639	646
Tinted glass	105	89	90
Engine block heater	19	16	17
Engine block & fuel line heater, diesel	49	42	43
Rallye instrument cluster	142	121	123
Dome/reading lamp	30	26	27
Halogen high beam headlamps	10	9	9
Radio equipment			
AM delete (credit)	(56)	(48)	(49)
AM/FM ETR stereo	138	117	119
AM/FM ETR stereo w/digital clock	177	150	152
AM/FM ETR stereo w/cassette & digital clock	455	387	391
CB (add to above prices)	275	234	237
Dual front & rear speakers (incl. w/ stereo)	30	26	27
Dual extended range rear speakers	25	21	22
Power antenna	60	51	52
Tri-band power antenna	100	85	86
Power left seat	210	179	181
Power bench seat	210	179	181
Reclining bucket seats (each), exc. base	147	125	127
Reclining passenger's seat	45	38	39
45/45 divided front seat, LS	133	113	115
Sport steering wheel	50	43	44
Tilt steering wheel	105	89	90
Flip-open glass sunroof	295	251	254
Automatic level control	165	140	142
Firm ride & handling package	30	26	27
Landau vinyl top	215	183	185
Trailer towing wiring harness	30	26	27
Leather upholstery Brougham	364	309	313
Deluxe trunk trim	40	34	35
Power trunklid release	40	34	35
Power windows			
Coupes	180	153	155
Sedans	280	217	220
Intermittent wipers	49	42	43

Prices are accurate at time of printing; subject to manufacturer's change

Oldsmobile Cutlass Supreme

Oldsmobile Cutlass Supreme Brougham 2-door coupe

WHAT'S NEW FOR '83

While Oldsmobile concentrates on promoting its slower-selling lines like Cutlass Ciera and Firenza, buyers keep flocking to the Cutlass Supreme, which ranked as the second best-selling domestic in the 1982 model year. That formula is little changed this year, with the same six models, minor grille revisions, and one fewer engine option as the highlights. Coupes now have a rectangular-pattern grille insert with vertical bars; sedans and wagons share a square-pattern insert. The sportiest of the three coupes, the Calais, gains black-painted headlamp doors, amber parking lamp lenses, and standard color-keyed paint stripe. The Hurst/Olds muscle car from the '60s returns as a limited-production option package for the Calais.

EVALUATION

Swanky looks and well-rounded design make Cutlass a consistent best-seller. Front seat room and comfort rate high, and ride and general refinement are just what many buyers seek. All Cutlasses without suspension upgrades have the usual pillowy soft Detroit ride and modest handling and roadholding limits. Coupes sacrifice some rear legroom for their sportier looks, but gain a little trunk space. Interior decor ranges from tasteful to overdone, depending on model and trim. The diesel engines are your best bet for mileage since neither gas engine is very fuel efficient in these cars. The penalties of the diesel are high initial cost, slower acceleration (though not as slow as you might think), and a poor repair record in the case of the V-8. Stylish and well mannered, Cutlass will probably remain one of America's best-liked cars until Olds decides to discontinue this line. And given the way it keeps selling, that day might be a long way off.

EVALUATION CHECKLIST

Fuel economy	3	Cargo room	3
Driveability	3	Serviceability	3
Acceleration	3	Standard equipment	3
Braking	3	Body construction	4
Handling/roadholding	3	Paint/exterior finish	4
Driving position	4	Interior finish	4
Instruments/control	3	TOTAL POINTS	68
Visiblity	3		
Heating/ventilation	4	**RATING SCALE**	
Seat comfort	4	5 = Excellent	
Passenger room	3	4 = Very Good	
Ride	4	3 = Average/Acceptable	
Noise	4	2 = Fair	
Exit/entry	3	1 = Poor	

SPECIFICATIONS

	2-door coupe	4-door sedan	4-door wagon
Wheelbase (in.)	108.1	108.1	108.1
Overall length (in.)	200.0	200.4	200.4
Overall width (in.)	71.6	71.9	71.8
Overall height (in.)	55.6	56.6	56.9
Track front (in.)	58.5	58.5	58.5
Track rear (in.)	57.7	57.7	57.7
Curb weight (lbs.)	3231	3292	3433
Max. cargo vol. (cu. ft.)	16.8	16.3	71.8
Fuel tank capacity (gal.)	18.1[1]	18.1[1]	18.2
Seating capacity	5	5	5

SPECIFICATIONS

	2-door coupe	4-door sedan	4-door wagon
Front headroom (in.)	37.9	38.7	38.8
Front shoulder room (in.)	56.6	56.7	56.7
Front legroom, max. (in.)	42.8	42.8	42.8
Rear headroom (in.)	38.1	37.8	38.8
Rear shoulder room (in.)	55.9	57.1	57.1
Rear legroom, min. (in.)	36.3	38.0	35.5

1: 19.8 gal. w/diesel engine

BODY/CHASSIS

Drivetrain layout: longitudinal front engine/rear-wheel drive. **Suspension front:** independent, unequal-length upper and lower A-arms, coil springs, telescopic shock absorbers, anti-roll bar. **Suspension rear:** rigid axle, four links, control arms, coil springs, telescopic shock absorbers; anti-roll bar optional. **Steering:** recirculating ball, power-assisted. **Turns lock-to-lock:** 3.6. (V-8s), 4.1 (V-6s). **Turn diameter (ft.):** 38.2 coupe, 37.3 others. **Brakes front:** 10.5-in. discs. **Brakes Rear:** 9.5-in. drums. **Construction:** body-on-frame

POWER-TRAINS	ohv V-6	ohv V-6D	ohv V-8	ohv V-8D	ohv V-8
Bore × stroke (in.)	3.80× 3.40	4.06× 3.39	3.80× 3.39	4.06× 3.39	3.80× 3.39
Displacement (liters/cu. in.)	3.8/ 231	4.3/ 262	5.0/ 307	5.7/ 350	5.0/ 307
Compression ratio	8.0:1	22.5:1	8.0:1	22.5:1	9.0:1
Fuel delivery	2bbl.	FI	4bbl.	FI	4bbl.
Net bhp @ rpm	110@ 3800	85@ 3600	140@ 3600	105@ 3200	180@ 4400
Net torque @ rpm (lbs/ft)	190@ 1600	165@ 1600	240@ 1600	200@ 1600	245@ 3200
Availability	S/All	O/All	O/All	O/All	S/All[1]

1: Std. Hurst/Olds; NA others

POWER-TRAINS	ohv V-6	ohv V-6	ohv V-8	ohv V-8D	ohv V-8
Final drive ratios					
3-speed automatic	2.41:1[1]	2.41:1[2]	2.41:1[3]	2.29:1[4]	
4-speed automatic					3.73:1

1: 3.08:1, 3.23:1 opt.; 2.73:1 std. wagon
2: 2.56:1 high-altitude areas
3: 2.56:1 opt.; 2.29:1 std. wagon
4: 2.73:1 opt.; 2.29:1 std. wagon

KEY bbl. = barrel (carburetor); **bhp** = brake horsepower (advertised); **Cal.** = California only. **Fed.** = Federal/49 state; **FI** = fuel injectoin; **ohv** = overhead valve; **ohc** = overhead cam; **I** = inline engine; **V** = V engine; **D** = diesel; **T** = turbocharged; **OD** = overdrive transmission; **S** = standard engine; **O** = optional engine.

PRICES

CUTLASS SUPREME	Retail Price	Dealer Cost	Low Price
2-door coupe.	$8950	7725	8525
4-door sedan.	9103	7857	8857
Brougham 2-door coupe	9589	8277	9077
Brougham 4-door sedan	9719	8389	9189
Calais 2-door coupe.	9848	8500	9300
Cruiser 4-door wagon	9381	8097	8897

STANDARD EQUIPMENT (included in above prices):

3.8-liter (231-cid) V-6 engine, 3-speed automatic transmission, BSW glass-belted radial tires, full carpeting, day/night mirror, bench seat, power brakes, power steering. **Brougham** adds: custom sport bench seat, upgraded interior and exterior trim. **Calais** adds: steel-belted radial tires, custom sport steering wheel with padded rim, stand-up hood ornament, special wheel discs, ride and handling suspension, reclining front contour seats, full instrumentation.

OPTIONAL EQUIPMENT:

Engines			
4.3-liter (262-cid) diesel V-6	$ 500	$ 425	$ 430
5.0-liter (307-cid) V-8 4-bbl.	225	191	192
5.7-liter (350-cid) diesel V-8	700	595	601
Four-season air conditioning	725	616	623
Rear window air deflector, wagons.	40	34	35
Astroroof, coupes only	895	761	769
Limited-slip differential	95	81	82

Prices are accurate at time of printing; subject to manufacturer's change

CONSUMER GUIDE®

	Retail Price	Dealer Cost	Low Price
Heavy-duty battery			
w/gasoline engine	25	21	22
w/diesel engine (2)	50	43	44
Electric clock	35	30	31
Electric digital clock	60	51	52
Console	100	85	86
Convenience group (std. Brougham)			
Base coupe, sedan	57	48	49
Wagons	50	43	44
Calais coupe.	42	36	37
High-capacity cooling system			
w/air conditioning	40	34	35
w/o air conditioning	70	60	61
Hurst/Olds package	1997	1696	1713
High-capacity radiator	30	26	27
Cruise control	170	145	147
Electric rear-window defroster.	135	115	117
Engine block heater	19	16	17
Gauge package (standard Calais)	142	121	123
Tinted glass	105	89	90
Lamp monitor	77	65	66
Power door locks			
Coupes	120	102	104
Sedans, wagons	170	145	147
Locks, tire storage, rear quarter storage			
Wagon	57	48	49
Luggage rack, wagon	125	106	108
Radio equipment			
AM	112	95	96
AM/FM stereo	198	168	170
AM/FM stereo w/cassette tape	298	253	256
AM/FM ETR stereo w/digital clock &			
cassette	555	472	477
Removable glass roof panel, coupes	825	701	709
Full vinyl roof (NA wagons)	155	132	134
Full padded vinyl roof, sedans	240	204	207
Landau vinyl roof, coupes	240	204	207
Contour bucket seats	57	48	49
Power seat, 6-way			
Left bucket (NA Broughams, wagon) . . .	210	179	181
Divided bench (NA Calais, Cruiser)	133	113	115
Bench, ex. base Supreme.	210	179	181
Manual seatback recliner			
Cruiser, Brougham	70	60	61
Custom sport steering wheel (NA Calais) . .	50	43	44
Tilt-away steering wheel	105	89	90

Prices are accurate at time of printing; subject to manufacturer's change

	Retail Price	Dealer Cost	Low Price
Firm ride & handling package			
Sedans, coupes (ex. Calais)	49	42	43
Calais, wagons	30	26	27
Power tailgate release, wagon.	40	34	35
Custom leather seating, Brougham.	364	309	313
Power trunklid release (NA wagons)	40	34	35
Deluxe trunk trim	60	51	52
Power windows			
2-doors or front only	180	153	155
4-doors	255	217	220
Pulse wiper system	49	42	43
Woodgrain applique, wagon.	275	234	237

Oldsmobile Delta 88 & 98

Oldsmobile Delta 88 Royale 2-door coupe

WHAT'S NEW FOR '83

The big Oldsmobiles return almost unchanged from last year. The smaller Delta 88 series has a new grille design with horizontal bars; the larger 98 also has a revised grille. The 4.3-liter gas V-8 available as an option on 88s last year is discontinued. Both cars posted sales gains in '82 (the 88 ranked among the 10 best-selling domestics), indicating there are still plenty of big-car fans. GM is expected to field a new family of smaller front-drive replacements starting with the '84 model year. The new full-size fleet reportedly will be based on a stretched version of the X-car platform, and will have unit construction instead of the present separate body/chassis. The new big cars should be longer than the current A-car sedans such as the Cutlass Ciera.

Prices are accurate at time of printing; subject to manufacturer's change

EVALUATION

When 88/98 and GM's other big cars were downsized for 1977, they looked fairly small compared to their outsize predecessors. Now they seem as large and out of proportion as the old models did back then. Still good sellers, though, these Oldsmobiles are as good as big cars come. Both offer full 6-passenger room and comfort, the smooth ride typical of the breed, quiet cruising ability, and large trunks. The Ninety-Eight isn't far behind Cadillac in the luxury it provides. You pay for the size in mileage, which is poor by today's standards but not out of line for the class. The exception is the diesel engine, which can give respectable mileage with a corresponding loss in acceleration and passing power. The big diesel has had persistent reliability problems, however, particularly with clogged fuel injectors and faulty fuel pumps. Clumsy to move around in tight spots, and not very agile. The soft suspension also permits a good deal of float and front-end plunge over wavy surfaces, and the rear axle can patter uncomfortably over washboard surfaces. Too much car for our taste, but a good choice if king-size comfort is what you crave.

EVALUATION CHECKLIST

Fuel economy	2	Cargo room	4
Driveability	4	Serviceability	3
Acceleration	3	Standard equipment	4
Braking	4	Body construction	4
Handling/roadholding	3	Paint/exterior finish	4
Driving position	3	Interior finish	4
Instruments/control	3	TOTAL POINTS	74
Visiblity	3		
Heating/ventilation	4	**RATING SCALE**	
Seat comfort	4	5 = Excellent	
Passenger room	5	4 = Very Good	
Ride	4	3 = Average/Acceptable	
Noise	5	2 = Fair	
Exit/entry	4	1 = Poor	

SPECIFICATIONS	98 2-door and 4-door	88 2-door and 4-door	Delta 88 5-door wagon
Wheelbase (in.)	119.0	116.0	116.0

SPECIFICATIONS

	98 2-door and 4-door	88 2-door and 4-door	Delta 88 5-door wagon
Overall length (in.)	221.1	218.1	220.3
Overall width (in.)	76.3	76.3	79.8
Overall height (in.)	58.0	57.5	59.1
Track front (in.)	61.7	61.7	62.1
Track rear (in.)	60.7	60.7	64.1
Curb weight (lbs.)[1]	3842	3572	4026
Max. cargo vol. (cu. ft.)	20.5	20.8	87.2
Fuel tank capacity (gal.)	25.0[1]	25.0[1]	22.0
Seating capacity	6	6	6
Front headroom (in.)	39.5	39.5	39.6
Front shoulder room (in.)	59.6	60.6	60.6
Front legroom, max. (in.)	42.2	42.2	42.2
Rear headroom (in.)	38.1	38.2	39.3
Rear shoulder room (in.)	59.8	60.5	60.5
Rear legroom, min. (in.)	41.7	38.9	37.8

1: 26.0 gal. w/diesel engine

BODY/CHASSIS

Drivetrain layout: longitudinal front engine/rear-wheel drive. **Suspension front:** independent, unequal-length upper and lower A-arms, coil springs, telescopic shock absorbers, anti-roll bar. **Suspension rear:** rigid axle, four links, coil springs, telescopic shock absorbers, anti-roll bar. **Steering:** recirculating ball, power-assisted. **Turns lock-to-lock:** 4.1 88, 4.0 98, 3.5 wagon. **Turn diameter (ft.):** 39.1 88, 40.0 98. **Brakes front:** 11.0-in. discs. 88, 11.9-in. 98, wagon. **Brakes rear:** 9.5-in. drums 88, 11.0 98, wagon. **Construction:** body-on-frame

POWERTRAINS

	ohv V-6	ohv V-6	ohv V-8	ohv V-8D
Bore × stroke (in.)	3.80× 3.40	3.97× 3.40	3.80× 3.39	4.06× 3.39
Displacement (liters/cu. in.)	3.8/ 231	4.1/ 252	5.0/ 307	5.7/ 350
Compression ratio	8.0:1	8.0:1	8.0:1	22.5:1
Fuel delivery	2bbl.	4bbl.	4bbl.	FI
Net bhp @ rpm	110@ 3800	125@ 4000	140@ 3600	105@ 3200
Net torque @ rpm (lbs/ft)	190@ 1600	205@ 2000	240@ 1600	200@ 1600
Availability	S/All[1]	S/All[2]	O/All[3]	O/All[4]

1: std. Delta 88s; NA 98, wagon
2: std. 98; NA Delta 88, wagon
3: std. wagon; opt. others. Avail. only w/4-speed transmission on 98s.
4: avail. only w/4-speed transmission on 98s.

Final drive ratios

	ohv V-6	ohv V-6	ohv V-8	ohv V-8D
3-speed automatic	2.73:1[1]		2.41:1[2]	2.41:1
4-speed OD automatic		3.23:1	2.73:1[2]	2.93:1

1: 3.23:1 opt. 2: 3.08:1, 3.23:1 opt. exc. Cal.

KEY bbl. = barrel (carburetor); **bhp** = brake horsepower (advertised); **Cal.** = California only. **Fed.** = Federal/49 state; **FI** = fuel injection; **ohv** = overhead valve; **ohc** = overhead cam; **I** = inline engine; **V** = V engine; **D** = diesel; **T** = turbocharged; **OD** = overdrive transmission; **S** = standard engine; **O** = optional engine.

PRICES

98/DELTA 88	Retail Price	Dealer Cost	Low Price
Delta 88 4-door sedan	$ 9084	$ 7841	$ 8641
Delta 88 Royale 2-door coupe.	9202	7943	8743
Delta 88 Royale 4-door sedan.	9363	8082	8882
Delta 88 Royale Brougham 2-door coupe . .	9671	8348	9248
Delta 88 Royale Brougham 4-door sedan . .	9762	8426	9326
Custom Cruiser 5-door wagon	10083	8704	9604
Ninety-Eight 2-door Regency coupe	12943	11171	12171
Ninety-Eight 4-door Regency sedan	13120	11324	12324
Ninety-Eight Regency Brougham sedan . . .	14170	12230	13230

Prices are accurate at time of printing; subject to manufacturer's change

STANDARD EQUIPMENT (included in above prices):

Delta 88 has: 3.8-liter (231-cid) V-6 engine, 3-speed automatic transmission, power steering, power brakes, ashtray and dome lights, deluxe steering wheel, full carpeting, carpeted lower door panels, wheel covers, glass-belted radial tires. **Delta 88 Royale** adds: custom sport front bench seat, velour upholstery, glovebox lamp, reading/dome lamp, door-pull straps, bodyside moldings. **Delta 88 Royale Brougham** adds: opera lamps (coupe), divided front seat with individual controls, lamp convenience package, visor vanity mirror, seatbelt chimes. **Custom Cruiser** has: Delta 88 equipment plus 5.0-liter (307-cid) V-8 engine, 3-way tailgate, velour or vinyl interior, 4-speed overdrive automatic transmission. **Ninety-Eight** has: 4.1-liter (252-cid) V-6 engine, 4-speed overdrive automatic transmission, power steering, power brakes, power windows, power driver seat, electric clock, front & rear fold-down center armrests, front ashtray lamp, glovebox and courtesy lamps, steel-belted radial tires, air conditioning, tinted glass, loose-cushion-look interior, velour upholstery, divided front seat w/dual controls, digital clock, door courtesy lamps, front seatback pouches.

OPTIONAL EQUIPMENT:

Engines	Retail Price	Dealer Cost	Low Price
5.0-liter (307-cid) V-8, Delta 88 (except			
wagon)	$ 225	$ 191	$193
98	75	64	65
5.7-liter (350-cid) V-8 diesel	700	595	601
4-speed overdrive transmission (Delta 88,			
exc. wagon)	175	149	151
Four-season air conditioning (std. 98)	725	616	623
Tempmatic air conditioning, 98	55	47	48
Others	780	663	670
Astroroof	1195	1016	1027
Limited-slip differential	95	81	82
High-capacity battery			
w/gas engine	25	21	22
w/diesel engine (2)	50	43	44
Rear bumper step, wagon	25	21	22
Electric digital clock, Delta 88	96	82	83
98	36	31	32
High-capacity cooling system w/air			
conditioning	40	34	35
w/o air conditioning	70	60	61
High-capacity radiator	30	26	27
Cruise control	170	145	147
Electric rear-window defroster	135	115	117
California emission system			
w/gasoline engine	NA	NA	NA
w/diesel engine	NA	NA	NA
Diesel engine block/fuel line heater	49	42	43

Prices are accurate at time of printing; subject to manufacturer's change

	Retail Price	Dealer Cost	Low Price
Tinted glass (std. 98).	105	89	91
Halogen high-beam headlamps	10	8	9
Illumination package	75	64	65
Cornering lamps.	60	51	52
Automatic load-leveling system	165	140	142
Power door locks			
2-doors	120	102	104
4-doors (ex. wagon).	170	145	147
Wagon	220	187	189
Automatic door locks, 98	80	68	69
Luggage carrier, roof, wagon	150	128	130
Radio equipment			
AM (NA 98)	112	95	96
AM/FM stereo (NA 98)	198	168	170
AM/FM stereo w/cassette tape			
98	100	85	86
Others	298	253	256
AM/FM stero electronic tune			
w/digital clock, 98	165	140	142
AM/FM stereo electronic tune			
w/digital clock & cassette tape			
98	318	270	273
Delta 88	555	472	477
Wagon	530	451	456
Reminder package.	40	34	35
Full vinyl roof			
Delta 88s	180	153	155
Full vinyl roof, padded (NA Delta 88s)	240	204	207
Landau vinyl roof	215	183	185
Power seat, 6-way	210	179	181
Manual seatback recliner.	70	60	61
Divided front seat			
Delta 88 Royale.	133	113	115
Wagon	174	148	150
Third seat, wagon.	220	187	189
Tilt steering wheel.	105	89	90
(Standard 98 Regency Brougham sedan)			
Tilt & telescopic steering wheel.	160	136	138
98 Regency Brougham sedan	55	47	48
Firm ride suspension			
Delta 88	49	42	43
Wagon, 98	30	26	27
Trailer wiring harness, 5-wire	30	26	27
Custom leather trim, 98	379	322	326
Trip odometer	16	14	15

Prices are accurate at time of printing; subject to manufacturer's change

	Retail Price	Dealer Cost	Low Price
Power trunk release.	40	34	35
Twilight sentinel	60	51	52
Power windows			
Delta 88 2-door.	180	153	155
Delta 88 4-door, wagon.	255	217	220
Pulse wiper system	49	42	43
Bodyside vinyl woodgrain applique,			
wagon	290	247	250

Oldsmobile Toronado

Oldsmobile Toronado Brougham 2-door coupe

WHAT'S NEW FOR '83

Oldsmobile's front-drive personal-luxury coupe is a virtual carryover except for a pricey new optional sound system jointly developed by GM's Delco Electronics Division and the Bose Corporation. It consists of an electronically tuned radio/cassette main unit with Dolby noise reduction. Each of the four speakers has its own tuned enclosure with built-in 25-watt amplifier, and two equalizer circuits in the receiver individually adjust response of the front and rear speakers, allowing the system to be tailored to the car in which it is installed. The Delco/Bose system is also available on this year's Buick Riviera and the Cadillac Eldorado and Seville.

EVALUATION

Little changed since the first 1979 model in this current series. Front-wheel drive alone does not make a paragon of engineering efficiency—Toronado is too big and heavy for that. However, it gets around surprisingly well considering its

Prices are accurate at time of printing; subject to manufacturer's change

heft, mainly because of the sophisticated all-independent suspension. Front-drive pulling power also helps. Ride is butter-smooth on all but the roughest roads, yet cornering response is poised and stable, providing you don't ask the car to do things it was never intended to do. What it does best is transport four people in opulent peace over long distances on the highway. Cabin comfort is high, though the rear seat area feels closed in because of the formal-look roof. That also hampers the driver's view over the shoulder, especially when parking or changing lanes. Acceleration is merely adequate with either gas engine. The diesel seems downright slow, but returns more acceptable mpg figures. Continuing complaints of clogged diesel fuel injectors, though, makes this engine our third choice if we were considering a Toronado. About the only buyers who should consider this car are well-to-do types who won't mind (and can afford) its high purchase price and relative thirst.

EVALUATION CHECKLIST

Fuel economy	3	Cargo room	3
Driveability	4	Serviceability	2
Acceleration	3	Standard equipment	4
Braking	3	Body construction	4
Handling/roadholding	3	Paint/exterior finish	4
Driving position	4	Interior finish	4
Instruments/control	3	TOTAL POINTS	68
Visiblity	3		
Heating/ventilation	4	**RATING SCALE**	
Seat comfort	4	5 = Excellent	
Passenger room	3	4 = Very Good	
Ride	3	3 = Average/Acceptable	
Noise	4	2 = Fair	
Exit/entry	3	1 = Poor	

SPECIFICATIONS

	2-door coupe
Wheelbase (in.)	114.0
Overall length (in.)	206.0
Overall width (in.)	71.4
Overall height (in.)	55.2
Track front (in.)	59.3

SPECIFICATIONS

	2-door coupe
Track rear (in.)	60.0
Curb weight (lbs.)	3695
Max. cargo vol. (cu. ft.)	15.2
Fuel tank capacity (gal.)	21.1[1]
Seating capacity	5
Front headroom (in.)	37.9
Front shoulder room (in.)	56.6
Front legroom, max. (in.)	42.8
Rear headroom (in.)	37.9
Rear shoulder room (in.)	55.9
Rear legroom, min. (in.)	38.9

1: 22.8 w/diesel engine

BODY/CHASSIS

Drivetrain layout: longitudinal front engine/front-wheel drive. **Suspension front:** independent, torsion bars, unequal-length upper and lower control arms, telescopic shock absorbers, anti-roll bar. **Suspension rear:** independent, semi-trailing arms, coil springs, telescopic shock absorbers with electronic level control, anti-roll bar. **Steering:** recirculating ball, power-assisted. **Turns lock-to-lock:** 3.0. **Turn diameter (ft.):** 39.9. **Brakes front:** 10.5-in. discs. **Brakes rear:** 9.5-in. drums (10.5-in. discs opt.). **Construction:** body-on-frame

POWERTRAINS

	ohv V-6	ohv V-8	ohv V-8D
Bore × stroke (in.)	3.97× 3.40	3.80× 3.39	4.06× 3.39
Displacement (liters/cu. in.)	4.1/ 252	5.0/ 307	5.7/ 350
Compression ratio	8.0:1	8.0:1	22.5:1
Fuel delivery	4bbl.	4bbl.	FI

POWERTRAINS	ohv V-6	ohv V-8	ohv V-8D
Net bhp @ rpm	125@ 4000	140@ 3600	105@ 3200
Net torque @ rpm (lbs/ft)	205@ 2000	240@ 1600	200@ 1600
Availability	S/All	O/All	O/All
Final drive ratios			
4-speed OD automatic	3.15:1	2.73:1	2.93:1

KEY **bbl.** = barrel (carburetor); **bhp** = brake horsepower (advertised); **Cal.** = California only. **Fed.** = Federal/49 state; **FI** = fuel injection; **ohv** = overhead valve; **ohc** = overhead cam; **I** = inline engine; **V** = V engine; **D** = diesel; **T** = turbocharged; **OD** = overdrive transmission; **S** = standard engine; **O** = optional engine.

PRICES

TORONADO	Retail Price	Dealer Cost	Low Price
Brougham 2-door coupe	$15252	$13164	$14664

STANDARD EQUIPMENT (included in above prices):

4.1-liter (252-cid) V-6 engine, 4-speed automatic transmission, power steering, power brakes, power windows, air conditioning, AM/FM stereo radio w/power antenna, power door locks, power seat, automatic level control, tinted glass, deluxe carpeting, dual remote-control mirrors, halogen headlamps, digital clock, cornering lamps, cruise control.

OPTIONAL EQUIPMENT:

5.0-liter (307-cid) V-8 engine	$ 75	$ 64	$ 65
5.7-liter (350-cid) diesel V-8 engine	700	595	601
Tempmatic air conditioning	55	47	48
Astroroof, electric, glass.	1195	1016	1028
Automatic door locks	80	68	69
Electric rear-window defroster.	135	115	117
Engine block heater	19	16	17
Engine block & fuel line heater	49	42	43
Instrument panel cluster	44	37	38
Power seat, 6-way passenger.	210	179	181
Power seat, 6-way driver w/memory.	185	157	159
Power seat recliner, passenger	145	123	125
Seatback recliner, L. or R	70	60	61
Radio equipment			
AM/FM stereo delete (credit)	(230)	(196)	(198)

Prices are accurate at time of printing; subject to manufacturer's change

	Retail Price	Dealer Cost	Low Price
AM/FM stereo ETR w/digital clock & cassette and Bose speakers	895	761	769
AM/FM stereo ETR w/digital clock & cassette	328	279	281
Reminder package.	56	48	49
Custom sport steering wheel	50	43	44
Tilt & telescope steering wheel	55	47	48
Firm ride & handling suspension	49	42	43
Twilight sentinel	60	51	52
Exterior opera lamps	77	65	66
Reading lamps.	50	43	44
Illumination package	75	64	65
Theft deterrent system	165	140	142
Power trunklid release	40	34	35
Landau vinyl roof	240	204	207
Leather seat trim	384	326	330
Pulse wiper system	49	42	43
Simulated wire wheel discs	189	161	163
Puncture sealing tires.	176	149	151

Plymouth Horizon & Turismo

Plymouth Horizon 5-door sedan

WHAT'S NEW FOR '83

A new engine, new transmission, and new name are the
story for Plymouth's front-drive subcompacts, which parallel
the Dodge Omni/Charger. The new engine is a 1.6-liter four
built by Peugeot in France. It replaces the 1.7-liter VW-based

unit that had been the base mill, and will be phased in during the model year. The new transmission is a 5-speed overdrive manual (actually a fifth gear tacked on to Chrysler's 4-speed) with longer legs for better economy and more relaxed highway cruising. It's optional with both engines. The new name is Turismo, which now graces the coupe versions that used to be called TC3. The five-door Horizon sedans will be available in base and Custom price levels. The Miser coupes and sedans have been discontinued. The Turismo will be offered in base form and in high-performance Turismo 2.2 trim, the latter with 5-speed gearbox, sport suspension and exhaust, and racier exterior. The 2.2 engine has modified intake and exhaust manifolds, cylinder head and exhaust systems and a higher compression ratio for more horsepower (up by 10) and torque.

EVALUATION

The coupe and sedan are based on the same floorpan, though the sedan has a longer wheelbase and is shorter overall while it's the other way round on the coupe. Since they share running gear, they're much alike. Both offer good mileage, and are available for a reasonable price. The 1.6 Peugeot engine has had many years of service in Europe, and should be at least as reliable and economical as the engine it's replacing if not more so. With hatchback styling, both are practical, though the sedan is more so because of its greater rear seat room. The rear seat in the coupe is useful only for carrying children or groceries. Both are agile enough to make average drivers look good in close-quarters maneuvers. The Turismo 2.2 with its performance gearing is awfully quick for an engine that's known more for economy and durability than acceleration. You don't sacrifice much mileage with the sporty model, either. The difference is in the ride: it's much choppier and harder to live with on broken pavement than with the standard suspension. Driving position isn't too good in either coupe or sedan because of the large, high mounted steering wheel, low-set seats, and awkward pedal placement. Quality control is not up to Japanese standards, and the coupes especially are prone to rattle. Attractive prices and good reliability are pluses, as is the 5-year/50,000-mile warranty on powertrain components and body rust.

EVALUATION CHECKLIST

(Turismo; for Horizon see Dodge Omni & Charger)

Fuel economy	3	Cargo room	4
Driveability	3	Serviceability	5
Acceleration	4	Standard equipment	3
Braking	3	Body construction	4
Handling/roadholding	4	Paint/exterior finish	3
Driving position	3	Interior finish	3
Instruments/control	3	TOTAL POINTS	64
Visiblity	3		
Heating/ventilation	3	**RATING SCALE**	
Seat comfort	3	5 = Excellent	
Passenger room	3	4 = Very Good	
Ride	2	3 = Average/Acceptable	
Noise	2	2 = Fair	
Exit/entry	3	1 = Poor	

SPECIFICATIONS

	Turismo 3-door coupe	Horizon 5-door sedan
Wheelbase (in.)	96.6	99.1
Overall length (in.)	173.7	164.8
Overall width (in.)	66.7	65.8
Overall height (in.)	50.8	53.1
Track front (in.)	56.1	56.1
Track rear (in.)	55.6	55.6
Curb weight (lbs.)	2222¹	2175¹
Max. cargo vol. (cu. ft.)	10.7/ 27.3	10.4/ 27.9
Fuel tank capacity (gal.)	13.0	13.0
Seating capacity	5	5
Front headroom (in.)	37.2	38.0
Front shoulder room (in.)	52.2	51.7
Front legroom, max. (in.)	42.4	42.1
Rear headroom (in.)	34.4	37.1
Rear shoulder room (in.)	50.9	51.5

SPECIFICATIONS

	Turismo 3-door coupe	Horizon 5-door sedan
Rear legroom, min. (in.)	28.7	33.3

1: Base models

BODY/CHASSIS

Drivetrain layout: transverse front engine/front-wheel drive. **Suspension front:** independent, MacPherson struts, lower control arms, coil springs, telescopic shock absorbers, anti-roll bar. **Suspension rear:** semi-independent, beam axle, trailing arms, coil springs; anti-roll bar optional. **Steering:** rack-and-pinion. **Turns lock-to-lock:** 3.6 manual, 2.9 power. **Turn diameter (ft.):** 34.5. **Brakes front:** 9.0-in. discs. **Brakes rear:** 7.9-in. drums. **Construction:** unit

POWERTRAINS

	ohv I-4	ohc I-4
Bore × stroke (in.)	3.17× 3.07	3.44× 3.62
Displacement (liters/cu. in.)	1.6/ 97.5	2.2/ 135
Compression ratio	8.8:1	9.0:1
Fuel delivery	2bbl.	2bbl.
Net bhp @ rpm	62@ 4800	94@ 5200
Net torque @ rpm (lbs/ft)	83@ 3200	117@ 3200
Availability	S/All¹	O/All²

1: NA Turismo 2.2   2: std. Turismo 2.2

Final drive ratios

4-speed OD manual	2.69:1	
5-speed OD manual	2.59:1	2.20:1
3-speed automatic		2.78:1

KEY bbl. = barrel (carburetor); **bhp** = brake horsepower (advertised); **Cal.** = California only. **Fed.** = Federal/49 state; **FI** = fuel injection; **ohv** = overhead valve; **ohc** = overhead cam; **I** = inline engine; **V** = V engine; **D** = diesel; **T** = turbocharged; **OD** = overdrive transmission; **S** = standard engine; **O** = optional engine.

PRICES

PLYMOUTH HORIZON & TURISMO	Retail Price	Dealer Cost	Low Price
Horizon 5-door sedan.	$5841	$5411	$5761
Horizon Custom 5-door sedan	6071	5620	6020
Turismo 3-door coupe	6379	5836	6236
Turismo 2.2 3-door coupe.	7303	6668	7168

OPTIONAL EQUIPMENT:

	Retail Price	Dealer Cost	Low Price
2.2-liter (135-cid) 4-cylinder 2-bbl. engine (std. Turismo 2.2)	134	114	116
3-speed automatic transmission	439	373	377
5-speed manual transmission (2.2 engine req.)	75	64	65
Performance axle ratio (5-speed trans. req.)	22	19	20
Vinyl bodyside moldings, black	45	38	39
Light Group			
Turismo	62	53	54
Turismo 2.2.	54	46	47
Horizons	44	37	38
Protection Group			
Turismos.	125	106	108
Horizons	181	154	156
Cold Weather Package	174	147	149
Two-tone paint			
Turismo (NA 2.2)	155	132	134
Horizons	134	114	116
Bright exterior accents, base Turismo	64	54	55
Air conditioning (tinted glass req. Horizon)	632	537	543
Center armrest (console req.).	46	39	40
Cargo compartment carpeting, Turismo . . .	41	35	36
Cargo compartment dress-up & sound insulation, Horizon, Turismo (std. Horizon Custom, Turismo 2.2).	59	50	51
Rallye instrument cluster, Horizon	79	67	68
Engine cooling package	141	120	122
Center console			
w/o Light Group	84	71	72
w/Light Group.	76	65	66
Electric rear window defroster.	127	108	110
Tinted glass, Horizon (std. Turismos)	90	76	77
Luggage rack, Horizon	93	79	80
Power steering.	214	182	184

Prices are accurate at time of printing; subject to manufacturer's change

Radio equipment	Retail Price	Dealer Cost	Low Price
AM, manual-tune (std. Turismo 2.2)			
AM/FM stereo, manual-tune	83	71	72
Turismo 2.2.	109	93	94
Others	192	163	165
AM/FM stereo electronic-tune			
Turismo 2.2.	263	224	227
Others	346	294	297
AM/FM stereo, electronic-tune w/cassette tape			
Turismo 2.2.	402	342	346
Others	485	412	417
Conventional spare tire	63	54	55
Automatic speed control	174	148	150
Rear deck spoiler, Turismo (std. 2.2)	72	61	62
Removable glass sunroof, Turismos	310	263	266
Heavy-duty suspension, Horizons	34	29	30
Rear tonneau cover, Turismos	68	58	59
Rear window wiper/washer, Horizons	117	99	100

Pontiac Bonneville & Grand Prix

Pontiac Bonneville Brougham 4-door sedan

WHAT'S NEW FOR '83

Now the largest cars in the Pontiac tribe, the rear-drive G-body Bonneville sedan and wagon and the personal-luxury Grand Prix coupe are little changed from last year. The 4.1-liter Buick-built V-6 is scratched from the options chart in favor of the familiar Chevrolet 305-cid V-8. Olds-mobile's 350-cid diesel V-8 returns, but its cutdown 4.3-liter V-6 derivative, which was listed for '82, apparently does not.

Prices are accurate at time of printing; subject to manufacturer's change

Base power remains Buick's ubiquitous 3.8-liter gas V-6. The only available transmission is still a 3-speed automatic with lockup torque converter clutch.

EVALUATION

As before, there's little to choose between these Pontiacs and the equivalent Buick Regal, Olds Cutlass, and Chevy Malibu/Monte Carlo for performance, economy, or passenger space. All are smooth-riding, pleasantly appointed cars of reasonable proportions, with decent handling, middling mileage, and adequate acceleration. As with other GM cars that offer it, we're leery of the diesel V-8 option because owner complaints of poor drivability and frequent servicing continue to crop up. Either gasoline engine is a much better bet for long-term durability, and both have a slightly better than average repair record.

EVALUATION CHECKLIST

Fuel economy	3	Cargo room	3
Driveability	4	Serviceability	3
Acceleration	3	Standard equipment	3
Braking	3	Body construction	4
Handling/roadholding	3	Paint/exterior finish	3
Driving position	4	Interior finish	4
Instruments/control	3	TOTAL POINTS	65
Visiblity	3		
Heating/ventilation	4	**RATING SCALE**	
Seat comfort	3	5 = Excellent	
Passenger room	3	4 = Very Good	
Ride	3	3 = Average/Acceptable	
Noise	3	2 = Fair	
Exit/entry	3	1 = Poor	

SPECIFICATIONS	Grand Prix 2-door coupe	Bonneville 4-door sedan	4-door wagon
Wheelbase (in.)	108.1	108.1	108.1
Overall length (in.)	201.9	200.0	200.8
Overall width (in.)	72.1	72.0	72.6
Overall height (in.)	55.7	56.6	56.9

SPECIFICATIONS

	Grand Prix 2-door coupe	Bonneville 4-door sedan	4-door wagon
Track front (in.)	58.5	58.5	58.5
Track rear (in.)	57.8	57.8	57.8
Curb weight (lbs.)	3261[1]	3217[1]	3278[1]
Max. cargo vol. (cu. ft.)	16.2	16.6	71.8
Fuel tank capacity (gal.)	17.5[2]	17.5[2]	18.3[2]
Seating capacity	5	5	5
Front headroom (in.)	37.6	38.5	38.8
Front shoulder room (in.)	56.1	56.5	57.1
Front legroom, max. (in.)	42.8	42.8	42.8
Rear headroom (in.)	37.8	37.6	38.8
Rear shoulder room (in.)	55.9	57.1	57.1
Rear legroom, min. (in.)	36.3	38.0	35.5

1: Base model
2: 19.8 gal. w/Diesel engines

BODY/CHASSIS

Drivetrain layout: longitudinal front engine/rear-wheel drive. **Suspension front:** independent, unequal-length upper and lower A-arms, coil springs, telescopic shock absorbers, anti-roll bar. **Suspension rear:** rigid axle, four links, control arms, coil springs, telescopic shock absorbers, anti-roll bar optional. **Steering:** recirculating ball, power-assisted. **Turns lock-to-lock:** 3.3. **Turn diameter (ft.):** 37.6. **Brakes front:** 10.5-in. discs. **Brakes rear:** 9.5-in. drums. **Construction:** body-on-frame

POWERTRAINS

	ohv V-6	ohv V-8	ohv V-8D
Bore × stroke (in.)	3.80× 3.40	3.74× 3.48	4.06× 3.39
Displacement (liters/cu. in.)	3.8/ 231	5.0/ 305	5.7/ 350
Compression ratio	8.0:1	8.6:1	22.1:1

POWERTRAINS

	ohv V-6	ohv V-8	ohv V-8D
Fuel delivery	2bbl.	2bbl.	FI
Net bhp @ rpm	110@ 3800	150@ 4000	105@ 3200
Net torque @ rpm (lbs/ft)	190@ 1600	240@ 2400	200@ 1600
Availability	S/All	O/All	O/All
Final drive ratios			
3-speed automatic	2.41:1[1]	2.73:1[2]	3.23:1[3]

1: 2.73:1 on wagon
2: 2.29:1 Grand prix, 3.08:1 wagon
3: 2.73:1 Grand Prix, 2.41:1 wagon

KEY bbl. = barrel (carburetor); **bhp** = brake horsepower (advertised); **Cal.** = California only. **Fed.** = Federal/49 state; **FI** = fuel injection; **ohv** = overhead valve; **ohc** = overhead cam; **I** = inline engine; **V** = V engine; **D** = diesel; **T** = turbocharged; **OD** = overdrive transmission; **S** = standard engine; **O** = optional engine.

PRICES

	Retail Price	Dealer Cost	Low Price
GRAND PRIX			
2-door coupe...................	$8698	$7508	$8108
LJ 2-door coupe...............	9166	7912	8512
Brougham 2-door coupe	9781	8442	9042
BONNEVILLE			
4-door sedan.................	$8899	$7681	$8281
4-door wagon	9112	7865	8465
Brougham 4-door sedan	9399	8113	8713

STANDARD EQUIPMENT (included in above prices):

3.8-liter (231-cid) V-6 engine, 3-speed automatic transmission, power brakes, power steering, notchback front seat, deluxe wheel covers, full carpeting. **Grand Prix LJ** adds: custom seatbelts, additional acoustical insulation, sport mirrors (left remote control), wide rocker panel moldings, windowsill & hood rear edge moldings, velour seat trim, luxury-cushion steering wheel, deluxe wheel covers. **Grand Prix Brougham** adds: upgraded trim, 60/40 notchback front seat w/cloth trim. **Bonneville Brougham** has in addition to base equipment: front door courtesy lamps, 60/40 notchback front bench seat, luxury-cushion steering wheel, upgraded trim.

Prices are accurate at time of printing; subject to manufacturer's change

OPTIONAL EQUIPMENT:	Retail Price	Dealer Cost	Low Price
Engines			
5.0-liter (307-cid) V-8 4-bbl.	$ 225	$ 191	$ 193
5.7-liter (350-cid) diesel V-8	799	679	686
Custom air conditioning	725	616	623
70-amp. alternator w/o rear defroster, air conditioning, or cold-weather group	51	43	44
Limited-slip differential	95	81	82
Heavy-duty battery, w/o cold-weather group, ex. diesel.	25	21	22
Heavy-duty battery, diesel engine (2) . . .	50	43	44
Custom seatbelts, Base Grand Prix.	26	22	23
Brougham Landau Package, Grand Prix . . .	549	467	472
Front or rear bumper guards	26	22	23
Digital clock	35	30	31
Cold-weather group delete w/diesel (credit) .	(99)	(84)	(85)
Cruise control	170	145	147
Remote decklid release.	40	34	35
Electric rear-window defroster.	135	115	117
Power door locks			
Grand Prix	120	102	104
Bonneville	170	145	147
Rallye instrument cluster (inc. trip odometer & tachometer.	153	130	132
Tinted glass	105	89	90
Hatch roof, Grand Prix			
w/o Brougham Landau Pkg.	861	732	740
w/Brougham Landau Pkg.	825	701	709
Halogen high-beam headlamps	10	9	9
Additional sound insulation, Grand Prix . . .	40	34	35
Cornering lamps.	68	58	59
Dome/reading lamp, Grand Prix	23	20	21
Door courtesy lamps	45	38	39
Roof luggage carrier, wagon	125	106	108
Luggage compartment trim	50	43	44
Radio equipment			
AM	112	95	96
AM/FM stereo.	208	177	179
AM/FM stereo w/cassette	308	262	265
AM/FM stereo ETR w/cassette & digital clock	501	426	431
AM/FM ETR stereo w/digital clock	348	296	299
6-way power driver seat	210	179	181
60/40 power driver & passenger seat	420	357	361
Notchback 60/40 seat			
Ex. Broughams.	133	113	115

Prices are accurate at time of printing; subject to manufacturer's change

	Retail Price	Dealer Cost	Low Price
Brougham (leather)	475	404	409
Bucket seats w/console.	287	244	247
Reclining front passenger seat	60	51	52
Super-lift rear shocks.	64	54	55
Luxury-cushion steering wheel (std. Brougham & LJ).	26	22	23
Tilt steering wheel.	105	89	90
Power glass sunroof	895	761	769
Heavy-duty springs	16	14	15
Power tailgate release, wagons	40	34	35
Full vinyl top (ex. wagons)	155	132	134
Padded vinyl top (ex. wagons)	240	204	207
Trailer light cable, 5-wire	27	23	24
Custom trim group, wagon	376	320	324
Power windows (std. Brougham Landau)			
Coupes.	180	153	155
Sedans, wagons	255	217	220
Controlled-cycle wipers.	49	42	43
Wagon bodyside woodgrain applique	283	241	244

Pontiac Firebird

Pontiac Firebird S/E 2-door coupe

WHAT'S NEW FOR '83

On the market only since last winter, Pontiac's third-generation ponycar comes in for more alterations than half-year models usually get the following fall. Most concern drivetrains. A new integral-rail shift mechanism replaces last year's cable linkage on the wide-ratio 4-speed manual gearbox, which remains standard on the base Firebird with

Prices are accurate at time of printing; subject to manufacturer's change

standard 2.5-liter four-cylinder engine. New this year is a close-ratio 5-speed overdrive manual, which becomes standard for the mid-line Firebird S/E and the base Trans Am. The S/E is still powered by the Chevy 2.8-liter 60-degree V-6, but the '83 has the H.O. (High-Output) version that, interestingly enough, is not offered in the equivalent Camaro Berlinetta. Also new is a 4-speed overdrive automatic as standard for the injected Trans Am and optional for all other engines. A split-back folding rear seat is a new no-cost extra for S/E, and comes with a special custom trim option on the base Firebird and Trans Am. Optional for all are Lear/Siegler multi-adjustable buckets with lumbar support, movable cushion bolsters, and reclining backrests.

EVALUATION

One of 1982's sales bright spots, due primarily to stunning looks. How you assess the Firebird depends on which model you're talking about. Our road test experience has so far been limited to the Trans Am with automatic and standard carbureted V-8. It's a mover (10.8 seconds in our 0–60 mph clocking) but also a shaker, with a stiff ride, lots of tire rumble, and occasional loud rear-end thump over big bumps and ruts. The tradeoff is super handling and flat cornering behavior. The power steering has good feel most of the time, but becomes vague away from the straight-ahead and is overassisted. A brief drive in the '83 S/E revealed the extra power of the H.O. V-6 makes a real difference in driving satisfaction. This model and the base coupe feel much lighter on their feet than the V-8 cars and have a much more comfortable ride. Noise levels are disappointingly high on all models in hard acceleration. The new Firebird is still big and heavy for a sporty coupe, so don't expect great mileage even with the standard four. The best we got with our T/A was 18.1 mpg, though admittedly that was 1 mpg over the EPA estimate. Common to all models are long, heavy doors that make entry/exit a challenge in tight spots (especially to the rear), minimal front headroom for tall adults, a well-organized dash (better than Camaro's), a snug driving position with properly spaced major controls, and a back seat that's useless for anything but toddlers or groceries. There's not much luggage room, either, though the fold-down back seat and hatchback tail let two carry a good amount with them on a long trip.

EVALUATION CHECKLIST
(Trans Am)

Fuel economy	2	Cargo room	2
Driveability	4	Serviceability	3
Acceleration	4	Standard equipment	4
Braking	4	Body construction	4
Handling/roadholding	5	Paint/exterior finish	4
Driving position	4	Interior finish	3
Instruments/control	4	TOTAL POINTS	68
Visiblity	3		
Heating/ventilation	4	**RATING SCALE**	
Seat comfort	4	5 = Excellent	
Passenger room	2	4 = Very Good	
Ride	3	3 = Average/Acceptable	
Noise	2	2 = Fair	
Exit/entry	3	1 = Poor	

SPECIFICATIONS

	2-door coupe
Wheelbase (in.)	101.0
Overall length (in.)	189.8
Overall width (in.)	72.6
Overall height (in.)	50.7
Track front (in.)	60.7
Track rear (in.)	61.6
Curb weight (lbs.)[1]	2973[1]
Max. cargo vol. (cu. ft.)	31.9
Fuel tank capacity (gal.)	16.0
Seating capacity	4
Front headroom (in.)	37.0
Front shoulder room (in.)	57.7
Front legroom, max. (in.)	43.0
Rear headroom (in.)	35.6
Rear shoulder room (in.)	56.2
Rear legroom, min. (in.)	28.6

1: average all models w/base equipment

BODY/CHASSIS

Drivetrain layout: longitudinal front engine/rear-wheel drive. **Suspension front:** independent, modified MacPherson struts, lower control arms, coil springs, telescopic shock absorbers, anti-roll bar. **Suspension rear:** rigid axle, torque tube, longitudinal control arms, coil springs, Panhard rod, telescopic shock absorbers, anti-roll bar. **Steering:** recirculating ball, power-assisted. **Turns lock-to-lock:** 2.8. **Turn diameter (ft.):** 36.7. **Brakes front:** 10.5-in. discs. **Brakes rear:** 9.5-in. drums (discs opt.). **Construction:** unit

POWERTRAINS	ohv I-4	ohv V-6	ohv V-6	ohv V-8	ohv V-8
Bore × stroke (in.)	4.00× 3.00	3.50× 2.99	3.50× 2.99	3.74× 3.48	3.74× 3.48
Displacement (liters/cu. in.)	2.5/ 151	2.8/ 173	2.8/ 173	5.0/ 305	5.0/ 305
Compression ratio	8.2:1	8.42:1	8.94:1	8.6:1	9.5:1
Fuel delivery	FI	2bbl.	2bbl.	4bbl.	FI
Net bhp @ rpm	90@ 4000	112@ 5100	135@ 5400	150@ 4000	175@ 4200
Net torque @ rpm (lbs/ft)	132@ 2800	148@ 2400	145@ 2400	240@ 2400	250@ 2800
Availability	S/All[1]	O/All[2]	S/All[3]	S/All[4]	/All[5]

1: std. base; opt. SE; NA Trans Am
2: opt. base only
3: std. S/E; NA base, Trans Am
4: std. Trans Am; opt. base, S/E
5: opt. Trans Am only

Final drive ratios

4-speed manual	3.42:1				
5-speed OD manual	3.73:1	3.73:1	3.73:1	3.23:1	
3-speed automatic	3.08:1	3.08:1			
4-speed OD automatic	3.23:1		3.23:1	2.93:1	2.93:1

KEY bbl. = barrel (carburetor); **bhp** = brake horsepower (advertised); **Cal.** = California only. **Fed.** = Federal/49 state; **FI** = fuel injectoin; **ohv** = overhead valve; **ohc** = overhead cam; **I** = inline engine; **V** = V engine; **D** = diesel; **T** = turbocharged; **OD** = overdrive transmission; **S** = standard engine; **O** = optional engine.

PRICES

PONTIAC FIREBIRD	Retail Price	Dealer Cost	Low Price
2-door coupe	$ 8399	$7502	$ 8350
Trans Am 2-door coupe	10396	9285	10395
S/E 2-door coupe	10322	9219	10320

STANDARD EQUIPMENT (included in above prices):

2.5-liter (151-cid) 4-cylinder engine with electronic fuel injection, 4-speed manual transmission, power steering, power brakes, center console, full carpeting, reclining front bucket seats, fold-down rear seatback, electrically retracting quartz-halogen headlamps, dual outside mirrors, Formula steering wheel. **Trans AM** adds: 5.0-liter (305-cid) V-8 engine, black-finish exterior accents, front fender air extractors, wheel opening flares, sport mirrors with left remote, rear spoiler, turbo-cast aluminum wheels, full instrumentation, special suspension. **S/E** adds over base Firebird: 2.8-liter (173-cid) V-6 engine, black finish exterior accents, body color bodyside moldings, lockable fuel filler door, sport mirrors with left remote, rear window wiper/washer, body color turbo-cast aluminum wheels, extra acoustical insulation, electric hatch release, full instrumentation, "Viscount" upholstery, special suspension, luxury interior.

OPTIONAL EQUIPMENT:

Engines

2.5-liter (151-cid) 4-cyl., S/E (credit). . . $	(300) $	(255) $	(255)
2.8-liter (173-cid) V-6, base Firebird . . .	150	128	130
5.0-liter (350-cid) V-8 (std. Trans Am)			
Base Firebird (NA w/man. trans.)	375	320	324
S/E w/Auto. Trans. or Spl. Perf. Pkg. .	50	43	44
S/E w/Man. Trans. or Spl. Perf. Pkg. .	75	64	65
5.0-liter (305-cid) V-8w/"Cross-Fire"			
fuel injection (incl. spl. handling pkg.,			
limited-slip differential, sport hood, 4-			
wheel disc brakes, dual exhausts)			
Trans Am w/o Recaro Trans Am Pkg.	858	729	737
Trans Am w/Recaro Trans Am Pkg. .	NC	NC	NC
Transmissions			
5-speed manual			
Base Firebird	125	106	108
Others	NC	NC	NC
3-speed automatic			
Base Firebird	425	361	365

Prices are accurate at time of printing; subject to manufacturer's change

	Retail Price	Dealer Cost	Low Price
S/E	195	166	168
4-speed Automatic			
Base Firebird	525	446	451
Trans Am, S.E	295	251	254
Air conditioning (tinted glass required) . . .	725	616	623
Heavy-duty battery	25	21	22
Limited-slip differential, w/o 4-wheel disc brakes	95	81	82
4-wheel disc brakes (incl. limited-slip differential) (NA base Firebird)	274	233	236
Cruise control	170	145	147
Cargo cover	64	54	55
Remote-control hatch release (std. S/E) . . .	40	34	35
Electric rear-window defroster.	135	115	117
Engine block heater, 4-cyl. only	18	15	16
Custom exterior group, base Firebird . . .	112	95	96
Locking fuel-filler door (std. S/E)	11	9	10
Rally gauge cluster, base Firebird	150	128	130
Tinted glass	105	89	90
Removable glass roof panels (incl. w/ Recaro Trans Am Pkg.)	825	701	709
Power door locks	120	102	104
6-way power driver's seat	210	179	181
Power windows	180	153	155
Heavy-duty Radiator	70	60	61
Radio equipment (stereos include extended-range sound system)			
AM	112	95	96
AM (incl. digital clock)	151	128	130
AM/FM stereo ETR	248	211	214
AM/FM ETR stereo w/cassette tape & clock	387	329	333
AM/FM ETR stereo w/digital readout & clock	287	244	247
AM/FM ETR stereo w/cassette, seek & scan, clock & graphic equalizer	590	502	508
Recaro Trans Am Package			
w/Std. V-8	3160	2686	2713
w/Cross-Fire V-8	3610	3069	3100
Cloth bucket seats (ex. S/E)	30	26	27
Special Performance Pkg.			
Trans Am w/o opt. V-8 or Recaro Pkg. .	408	347	351
S/E	408	347	351
Rear spoiler (std. Trans Am)	70	60	61
Sunshield louvered rear window	210	179	181
Tilt steering wheel			

Prices are accurate at time of printing; subject to manufacturer's change

CONSUMER GUIDE®

	Retail Price	Dealer Cost	Low Price
Luxury trim group			
Base Firebird, cloth or vinyl	349	297	300
Base Firebird, leather	1294	1100	1111
Trans AM w/o Recaro Pkg., cloth or vinyl	349	297	300
Trans Am w/o Recaro Pk., leather	1294	1100	1111
S/E, leather	945	803	812
Rear window wiper/washer (std. S/E)	120	102	104
Intermittent wipers	49	42	43

Pontiac Phoenix

Pontiac Phoenix SJ 2-door sedan

WHAT'S NEW FOR '83

A minor exterior trim rehash and a little interior spiffing up highlight the otherwise unchanged '83 version of Pontiac's X-car. The front-drive compact Phoenix retains the model lineup, basic design, and standard and optional equipment from last year. All models get a new split, horizontal-bar grille flanked by parking lamps now mounted inboard of the headlamps. Taillights are also restyled, and there's greater use of black instead of chrome for exterior moldings. The instrument cluster has been redesigned slightly, and base models get a revised full-width bench seat.

EVALUATION

Like its X-car siblings, Phoenix is as appealing as ever because of its manageable size, ample passenger space, and successful ride/handling compromise. It's also pleasant to drive and easy to live with. Not so easy to take is the

CONSUMER GUIDE®

continuing history of mechanical troubles and worrisome recalls that have plagued the X-car quartet since its early-1979 introduction (for further comments, see Buick Skylark and Chevrolet Citation).

EVALUATION CHECKLIST

Fuel economy 3	Cargo room. 4
Driveability. 4	Serviceability 2
Acceleration. 3	Standard equipment. 3
Braking 4	Body construction 4
Handling/roadholding 4	Paint/exterior finish 4
Driving position 4	Interior finish 4
Instruments/control. 3	TOTAL POINTS 69
Visiblity 4	
Heating/ventilation 4	**RATING SCALE**
Seat comfort 3	5 = Excellent
Passenger room 3	4 = Very Good
Ride 3	3 = Average/Acceptable
Noise 4	2 = Fair
Exit/entry. 3	1 = Poor

SPECIFICATIONS

	2-door sedan	5-door sedan
Wheelbase (in.)	104.9	104.9
Overall length (in.)	182.1	183.1
Overall width (in.)	69.0	69.1
Overall height (in.)	53.5	53.4
Track front (in.)	58.7	58.7
Track rear (in.)	57.0	57.0
Curb weight (lbs.)	2473	2531
Max. cargo vol. (cu. ft.)	13.9	41.3
Fuel tank capacity (gal.)	14.6	14.6
Seating capacity	5	5
Front headroom (in.)	38.2	38.1
Front shoulder room (in.)	56.2	56.0
Front legroom, max. (in.)	42.2	42.2
Rear headroom (in.)	37.4	37.4

SPECIFICATIONS

	2-door sedan	5-door sedan
Rear shoulder room (in.)	56.3	56.1
Rear legroom, min. (in.)	34.5	35.5

BODY/CHASSIS

Drivetrain layout: transverse front engine/front-wheel drive. **Suspension front:** independent, MacPherson struts, lower control arms, coils springs, telescopic shock absorbers, anti-roll bar. **Suspension rear:** beam "twist" axle with integral anti-roll bar, trailing arms, Panhard rod, coil springs, telescopic shock absorbers. **Steering:** rack-and-pinion (power-assisted on SJ). **Turns lock-to-lock:** 3.5 manual, 3.1 power. **Turn diameter (ft.):** 38.3. **Brakes front:** 9.7-in. discs. **Brakes rear:** 7.9-in. drums. **Construction:** unit

POWERTRAINS

	ohv I-4	ohv V-6	ohv V-6
Bore × stroke (in.)	4.00× 3.00	3.50× 2.99	3.50× 2.99
Displacement (liters/cu. in.)	2.5/ 151	2.8/ 173	2.8/ 173
Compression ratio	8.2:1	8.42:1	8.94:1
Fuel delivery	FI	2bbl.	2bbl.
Net bhp @ rpm	90@ 4000	112@ 5100	135@ 5400
Net torque @ rpm (lbs/ft)	132@ 2800	148@ 2400	145@ 2400
Availability	S/All	O/All[1]	S/All[2]

1: NA SJ   2:H.O. engine. Std. SJ, NA others

Final drive ratios

4-speed OD manual	3.32:1	3.32:1	3.06:1
3-speed automatic	3.32:1	3.32:1	3.06:1

KEY bbl. = barrel (carburetor); **bhp** = brake horsepower (advertised); **Cal.** = California only. **Fed.** = Federal/49 state; **FI** = fuel injecton; **ohv** = overhead valve; **ohc** = overhead cam; **I** = inline engine; **V** = V engine; **D** = diesel; **T** = turbocharged; **OD** = overdrive transmission; **S** = standard engine; **O** = optional engine.

PHOENIX	Retail Price	Dealer Cost	Low Price
2-door sedan	$6942	$6198	$6698
5-door sedan	7087	6330	6830
LJ 2-door sedan	7489	6689	7189
LJ 5-door sedan	7698	6875	7375
SJ 2-door sedan	8861	7914	8514
SJ 5-door sedan	8948	7992	8692

STANDARD EQUIPMENT (included in above prices):

2.5-liter (151-cid) 4-cylinder engine with fuel injection, 4-speed manual transmission, front disc brakes, bench seat, carpeting, AM radio, lighter, deluxe-cushion steering wheel, narrow rocker panel moldings (hatchback), wheel opening moldings (hatchback), P185/80R-13 glass-belted radial tires. **LJ** adds: dual horns, additional sound insulation, upgraded trim. **SJ** adds: hood ornament & windsplit molding, wide rocker panel moldings, roof drip moldings, wheel covers, notchback front seat, carpeted lower door trim, color-keyed steering wheel, deluxe seatbelts, cargo cover, sport mirrors (left remote), power steering, two-tone paint package, 2.8-liter (173-cid) HO V-6 engine.

OPTIONAL EQUIPMENT:

Engines			
2.8-liter (173-cid) V-6	$ 150	$ 128	$ 130
3-speed automatic transmission	425	361	365
Air conditioning	725	616	623
Heavy-duty battery	25	21	22
Electric clock	35	30	31
Heavy-duty cooling			
w/o air conditioning	70	60	61
w/o air conditioning	40	34	35
Console	100	85	86
Cruise Master cruise control	170	145	147
Rear window defogger	135	115	117
Power door locks			
2-doors	120	102	104
4-doors	170	145	147
Engine block heater	18	15	16
85-amp. generator	85	72	73
Tinted glass	105	89	90
Special instrumentation	48	41	42
Designer accent paint	210	179	181
Radio equipment			
AM delete (credit)	(56)	(48)	(48)

Prices are accurate at time of printing; subject to manufacturer's change

	Retail Price	Dealer Cost	Low Price
AM/FM ETR stereo basic feature w/o clock	138	117	119
Above w/clock	177	150	152
AM/FM ETR stereo full feature	302	257	260
AM/FM stereo basic feature w/cassette . .	277	235	238
AM/FM ETR stereo w/cassette & graphic equalizer	505	429	434
Seat recliner, passenger or driver (each) . .	45	38	39
Power seat	210	179	181
Superlift rear shock absorbers	68	58	59
Sport steering wheel	50	43	44
Tilt steering wheel	105	89	90
Sunroof, Vista-Vent	295	251	254
Rally tuned suspension (NA SJ)	50	43	44
Vinyl top			
Landau, padded (coupes)	215	183	185
Long	155	132	134
Electric trunk release	40	34	35
Power windows			
Coupes	180	153	155
Sedans	255	217	220
Intermittent wiper system	49	42	43

Pontiac 2000

Pontiac 2000 LE 4-door sedan and 5-door wagon

WHAT'S NEW FOR '83

A new standard drivetrain and revised equipment lists are the tonic Pontiac hopes will spark sales for its version of GM's slow-selling front-drive J-car. Replacing last year's overhead-valve Chevy-built four is an overhead-cam unit built by GM's subsidiary in Brazil and designed by Opel in Germany. The new engine has about the same displacement as the previous one, but has electronic throttle-body fuel injection instead of a carburetor and a cast aluminum cylinder head instead of cast iron. The 2000 (formerly J2000) also has a new standard transmission, the 5-speed overdrive manual gearbox supplied by Isuzu, being offered as an extra-cost item at other GM divisions. The model lineup is expanded with an LE version of the 5-door J-wagon and a sporty SE hatchback. Coming next spring is a new convertible model, actually a conversion carried out by the American Sunroof Company. To be called Sunbird, the new 2000 ragtop will have up-level interior, power steering, and handling package as standard.

EVALUATION

Poor pickup and shocking sticker prices hurt J-car sales in the 1982 model year, and the '83 Pontiac 2000 is typical of the remedial steps GM is trying to make these small cars more salable. Compared with this year's 2.0-liter Chevy four, the new ohc engine spins more readily and perhaps more smoothly. As the output figures suggest, there's little to choose between the two for acceleration either from standstill or midrange speeds. Where the ohc may have an edge is in greater responsiveness and shift smoothness with automatic. Compared with last year's 4-speed J2000, the '83 5-speed is perceptibly quicker, but 0–60 mph times are still on the wrong side of 15 seconds so don't expect to win any impromptu drag races. Assessment: getting better, but still looks expensive for what it offers.

EVALUATION CHECKLIST

Fuel economy	4	Cargo room	3
Driveability	3	Serviceability	3
Acceleration	3	Standard equipment	3
Braking	3	Body construction	4
Handling/roadholding	3	Paint/exterior finish	4
Driving position	3	Interior finish	4
Instruments/control	3	TOTAL POINTS	69
Visiblity	4		
Heating/ventilation	4	**RATING SCALE**	
Seat comfort	3	5 = Excellent	
Passenger room	3	4 = Very Good	
Ride	4	3 = Average/Acceptable	
Noise	4	2 = Fair	
Exit/entry	3	1 = Poor	

SPECIFICATIONS	3-door coupe	2-door sedan	4-door sedan	5-door wagon
Wheelbase (in.)	101.2	101.2	101.2	101.2
Overall length (in.)	173.6	173.6	175.9	175.9
Overall width (in.)	68.6	68.6	68.6	68.6
Overall height (in.)	51.9	53.5	54.8	54.8
Track front (in.)	55.5	55.5	55.5	55.5
Track rear (in.)	55.1	55.1	55.1	55.1
Curb weight (lbs.)	2413[1]	2353[1]	2412[1]	2487[1]
Max. cargo vol. (cu. ft.)	38.5	12.6	13.5	64.4
Fuel tank capacity (gal.)	14.0	14.0	14.0	14.0
Seating capacity	5	5	5	5
Front headroom (in.)	37.6	37.7	38.5	38.3
Front shoulder room (in.)	53.7	53.7	53.7	53.7
Front legroom, max. (in.)	42.2	42.1	42.2	42.1
Rear headroom (in.)	36.5	36.5	37.8	38.7
Rear shoulder room (in.)	52.5	52.5	53.7	53.7
Rear legroom, min. (in.)	30.9	31.2	34.3	33.1

1: base models

BODY/CHASSIS

Drivetrain layout: transverse front engine/front-wheel drive. **Suspension front:** independent, MacPherson struts, lower control arms, coil springs, telescopic shock absorbers, anti-roll bar. **Suspension rear:** semi-independent, beam axle, trailing arms, coil springs, telescopic shock absorbers, anti-roll bar optional. **Steering:** rack-and-pinion. **Turns lock-to-lock:** 4.0 manual, 2.9 power. **Turn diameter (ft.):** 34.7. **Brakes front:** 9.7-in. discs. **Brakes rear:** 7.9-in. drums. **Construction:** unit

POWERTRAINS

	ohc I-4	ohv I-4
Bore × stroke (in.)	3.34× 3.13	3.50× 3.15

POWERTRAINS	ohc I-4	ohv I-4
Displacement (liters/cu. in.)	1.8/ 111	2.0/ 121
Compression ratio	9.0:1	9.3:1
Fuel delivery	FI	FI
Net bhp @ rpm	84@ 5200	86@ 4900
Net torque @ rpm (lbs/ft)	102@ 2800	110@ 3000
Availability	S/All	O/All

: NA S/E model

Final drive ratios		
4-speed OD manual		3.19:1
5-speed OD manual	3.83:1	
3-speed automatic	3.18:1	3.18:1

KEY bbl. = barrel (carburetor); **bhp** = brake horsepower (advertised); **Cal.** = California only. **Fed.** = Federal/49 state; **FI** = fuel injection; **ohv** = overhead valve; **ohc** = overhead cam; **I** = inline engine; **V** = V engine; **D** = diesel; **T** = turbocharged; **OD** = overdrive transmission; **S** = standard engine; **O** = optional engine.

PRICES

PONTIAC 2000	Retail Price	Dealer Cost	Low Price
2-door sedan...................	$6499	$5803	$6203
4-door sedan...................	6621	5913	6313
3-door coupe..................	6809	6081	6581
5-door wagon	6926	6186	6686
LE 2-door sedan	7020	6270	6770
LE 4-door sedan..............	7194	6425	6925
LE 5-door Wagon	7497	6696	7296
SE 3-door coupe	8393	7496	8096

STANDARD EQUIPMENT (included in above prices):

1.8-liter (112-cid) 4-cylinder engine, 5-speed manual transmission, power brakes, reclining front bucket seats, locking fuel-filler door, swing-out rear quarter windows (exc. wagon, 4-door sedans), cigarette lighter, full carpeting, console, fold-down rear seatback (except sedans), remote hatch/trunklid/tailgate release, trip odometer. **LE** adds: wheel trim rings, AM

Prices are accurate at time of printing; subject to manufacturer's change

radio, upgraded trim. **SE** adds: full instrumentation, sport mirrors, power steering.

OPTIONAL EQUIPMENT:	Retail Price	Dealer Cost	Low Price
2.0-liter 4-cyl. engine (credit)	$ (50)	$ (43)	$ (43)
Air conditioning	625	531	537
3-speed automatic transmission	320	272	275
4-spd. manual trans. (credit)	(75)	(64)	(64)
Heavy-duty battery	25	21	22
Cargo area cover (ex. sedans)	80	51	52
Cruise control	170	145	147
Electric rear-window defroster.	125	106	108
Power door locks			
Coupe, 2-door	120	102	104
4-door, wagon	170	145	147
Custom exterior group	86	73	74
Rallye gauges (NA SE)	62	53	54
Rallye gauges with tachometer			
SE.	NC	NC	NC
Others	140	119	121
Tinted glass	90	77	78
Handling package	48	41	42
Halogen headlamps	10	9	10
Additional sound insulation	43	37	38
Lamp group	44	37	38
Luggage carrier	98	83	84
Heavy-duty radiator			
w/o air conditioning	70	60	61
w/air conditioning	40	34	35
Radio equipment			
AM delete (credit) (NA 2000).	(56)	(48)	(48)
AM, base	112	95	96
AM w/clock			
Base	151	128	130
LE, SE	39	33	34
AM/FM ETR stereo			
Base	248	211	214
LE, SE	148	126	128
AM/FM ETR stereo w/clock			
Base 2000.	287	244	247
LE, SE	187	159	161
AM/FM stereo w/cassette & clock			
Base 2000.	387	329	333
LE, SE	287	244	247
AM/FM ETR stereo w/cassette, seek & scan, graphic equalizer, clock			
Base	590	502	508
LE, SE	490	417	422

Prices are accurate at time of printing; subject to manufacturer's change

CONSUMER GUIDE®

	Retail Price	Dealer Cost	Low Price
Lear-Siegler Bucket Seats, LE,SE.	400	340	344
Power seat	210	179	181
Rear spoiler, coupe	70	60	61
Power steering (std. SE)	199	169	171
Formula steering wheel.	65	55	56
Tilt steering wheel.	99	84	85
Sunroof	295	251	254
Cloth interior trim	30	26	27
Custom trim group			
Coupe, sedan	249	212	215
Hatchback, wagon	299	254	257
Power windows			
Coupe, 2-door sedan	120	102	104
4-door, wagon	170	145	147
Controlled cycle wipers.	49	42	43
Rear wiper/washer, coupe & wagon	117	99	101

Pontiac 6000

Pontiac 6000 STE 4-door sedan

WHAT'S NEW FOR '83

Launched in January 1982 as one of GM's front-drive A-body intermediates, the Pontiac 6000 gets a new line leader and a couple of new options for its first full model year. Topping the '83 lineup is the STE (Special Touring Edition), a specially equipped 4-door intended as an American challenge to upmarket European sedans like the Audi 5000. It's powered by the H.O. (High-Output) version of the Chevrolet 60-degree V-6, an exclusive in the A-body family. STE also gets a Honda-like "Driver Information Center" and a roadside emergency kit packed in a genuine-leather pouch, all standard. Production will be limited to between 16,000 and

Prices are accurate at time of printing; subject to manufacturer's change

18,000 units. Each will get special handling during assembly and a final pre-delivery inspection and road test. Other 6000s are little changed except for revised interior trim and "high interest" instrument panel markings. Cast aluminum sport wheels similar to the STE's standard issue are a new option, as is an upgraded suspension (Y99) with bigger wheels and tires, faster power steering, and specific bushings, spring and shock rates, and track bar.

EVALUATION

By a small margin, our staff's pick as the best buy in the intermediate field this year. Though ostensibly similar to its A-body siblings (Buick Century, Chevrolet Celebrity, Oldsmobile Cutlass Ciera), the 6000 offers slightly crisper handling, more responsive steering, and a firmer ride that's still very supple and absorbent. All this reflects Pontiac's particular approach to blending corporate components, one of the few areas where GM's various divisions have any freedom any more. We also like the 6000's more restrained use of brightwork inside and out compared with the Ciera or Century. Brief exposure to the new STE model at GM's summertime long-lead press show reveals this is the closest thing to a genuine European sports sedan ever to come from Detroit, and at $13,500 it's priced smack in the middle of Audi/Volvo territory. As for the standard 6000s, the bouquets and brickbats we've mentioned for the other A-cars apply here.

EVALUATION CHECKLIST

Fuel economy	2	Cargo room	3
Driveability	3	Serviceability	2
Acceleration	3	Standard equipment	3
Braking	3	Body construction	5
Handling/roadholding	4	Paint/exterior finish	4
Driving position	4	Interior finish	4
Instruments/control	3	TOTAL POINTS	70
Visiblity	4		
Heating/ventilation	4	**RATING SCALE**	
Seat comfort	4	5 = Excellent	
Passenger room	4	4 = Very Good	
Ride	4	3 = Average/Acceptable	
Noise	4	2 = Fair	
Exit/entry	3	1 = Poor	

SPECIFICATIONS

	2-door coupe	4-door sedan
Wheelbase (in.)	104.9	104.9
Overall length (in.)	188.7	188.7
Overall width (in.)	68.2	68.2
Overall height (in.)	54.8	54.8
Track front (in.)	58.7	58.7
Track rear (in.)	57.0	57.0
Curb weight (lbs.)	2599[1]	2717[1]
Max. cargo vol. (cu. ft.)	16.2	16.2
Fuel tank capacity (gal.)	15.7[2]	15.7[2]
Seating capacity	5	5
Front headroom (in.)	38.6	38.6
Front shoulder room (in.)	56.3	56.2
Front legroom, max. (in.)	42.2	42.2
Rear headroom (in.)	38.0	38.0
Rear shoulder room (in.)	57.0	56.2
Rear legroom, min. (in.)	35.7	36.4

1: Base models   2: 16.4 w/gas V-6, 16.6 w/Diesel V-6

BODY/CHASSIS

Drivetrain layout: transverse front engine/front-wheel drive. **Suspension front:** independent, MacPherson struts, lower control arms, coil springs, telescopic shock absorbers, anti-roll bar. **Suspension rear:** beam "twist" axle with integral anti-roll bar, trailing arms, panhard rod, coil springs, telescopic shock absorbers. **Steering:** rack-and-pinion, power-assisted. **Turns lock-to-lock:** 3.1. **Turn diameter (ft.):** 36.9. **Brakes front:** 9.7-in. discs. **Brakes rear:** 8.9-in. drums. **Construction:** unit

POWERTRAINS

	ohv I-4	ohv V-6	ohv V-6	ohv V-6D
Bore × stroke (in.)	4.00× 3.00	3.50× 2.99	3.50× 2.99	4.06× 3.99

POWERTRAINS

	ohv I-4	ohv V-6	ohv V-6	ohv V-6D
Displacement (liters/cu. in.)	2.5/ 151	2.8/ 173	2.8/ 173	4.3/ 262
Compression ratio	8.2:1	8.42:1	8.94:1	21.6:1
Fuel delivery	FI	2bbl.	2bbl.	FI
Net bhp @ rpm	90@ 4000	112@ 5100	135@ 4000	85@ 3600
Net torque @ rpm (lbs/ft)	132@ 2800	148@ 2400	145@ 2400	165@ 1600
Availability	S/All²	O/All²	S/All¹	O/All²

1: H.O. engine std. STE only; NA others
2: NA STE

Final drive ratios

3-speed automatic	2.39:1¹	2.39:1¹	3.33:1	2.39:1¹

1: 2.84:1 high-altitude areas

KEY bbl. = barrel (carburetor); **bhp** = brake horsepower (advertised); **Cal.** = California only. **Fed.** = Federal/49 state; **FI** = fuel injection; **ohv** = overhead valve; **ohc** = overhead cam; **I** = inline engine; **V** = V engine; **D** = diesel; **T** = turbocharged; **OD** = overdrive transmission; **S** = standard engine; **O** = optional engine.

PRICES

PONTIAC 6000	Retail Price	Dealer Cost	Low Price
2-door coupe.	$ 8399	$ 7249	7849
4-door sedan.	8569	7396	7996
LE 2-door coupe.	8837	7627	8527
LE 4-door sedan.	8984	7754	8654
STE 4-door sedan	13572	11714	12814

STANDARD EQUIPMENT (included in above prices):

2.5-liter (151-cid) fuel-injected 4-cylinder engine, 3-speed automatic transmission, power brakes, power steering, AM radio, full carpeting, 185/80R-13 fiberglass-belted radial tires. **LE** adds: digital clock, dual horns, cloth upholstery, custom wheel covers with trim rings, locking fuel filler door. **STE** adds: 2.8-liter H.O. V-6, air conditioning, cruise control, remote trunk lid release, electric rear defogger, driver information center, emergency kit, dual outlet exhaust, tinted glass, fog lamps and halogen headlamps, lamp group, electric outside remote mirrors, power door locks, power windows, AM/FM ETR stereo radio w/clock & cassette, 45/45 split front seat

Prices are accurate at time of printing; subject to manufacturer's change

w/reclining feature, handling and ride suspension, electronic ride control, cast aluminum wheels.

OPTIONAL EQUIPMENT:

	Retail Price	Dealer Cost	Low Price
Engines			
2.8-liter (173-cid) V-6	$150	$128	$130
4.3-liter (262-cid) diesel V-6	599	509	515
Air conditioning	725	616	623
Heavy-duty battery			
Gas engines w/o cold weather group . . .	25	21	22
Diesel engine	50	43	44
Digital clock (std. LE)	39	33	34
Cold-weather group (std. w/diesel eng.) . .	43	37	38
Center console			
w/divided front seat	100	85	86
Heavy-duty cooling system			
w/o air conditioning	70	60	61
w/ air conditioning	40	34	35
Cruise control	170	145	147
Remote trunklid release	40	34	35
Electric rear window defroster.	135	115	117
Power door locks			
Coupes.	120	102	104
Sedans.	170	145	147
Locking fuel filler door (std. LE)	11	9	10
Rally gauge cluster (incl. trip odometer) . .	70	60	61
Tinted glass	105	89	90
Halogen high beam headlamps	10	9	9
Radio equipment			
AM delete (credit)			
Base	(56)	(48)	(49)
LE (deletes digital clock)	(39)	(33)	(34)
AM/FM ETR stereo	148	126	128
AM/FM ETR stereo			
Base (incl. digital clock)	287	244	247
LE.	248	196	198
AM/FM ETR stereo			
Base (incl. digital clock)	187	159	161
AM/FM ETR stereo w/cassette			
and graphic equalizer			
Base (incl. digital clock)	490	417	422
LE	451	384	388
Dual front & rear speakers			
(std. w/stereo)	40	34	35
Seats			
Cloth base.	28	24	25
Buckets w/seatback recliners & console,			
Base	257	218	221

Prices are accurate at time of printing; subject to manufacturer's change

	Retail Price	Dealer Cost	Low Price
45/45 split bench, LE	133	113	115
Passenger reclining seatback	45	38	39
Dual reclining seatbacks.	90	77	78
6-way power seat	210	179	181
Formula steering wheel.	45	38	39
Tilt steering wheel.	105	89	90
Bodyside striping	40	34	35
Flip-open glass sunroof	295	251	254
Suspension equipment			
Electronic ride control	165	140	142
Superlift rear shock absorbers	64	54	55
Heavy-duty springs	16	14	15
Power windows			
Coupes.	180	153	155
Sedans.	255	217	220
Intermittent wipers	49	42	43

Renault Alliance

Renault Alliance DL 2-door sedan

WHAT'S NEW FOR '83

The first new product to emerge from the American Motors/
Renault alliance, this front-drive small car is essentially the
European Renault 9 re-engineered for the U.S. market by
AMC. Built by AMC at its Kenosha, Wisconsin factory,
Alliance is offered in 2- and 4-door sedan body styles,

Prices are accurate at time of printing; subject to manufacturer's change

CONSUMER GUIDE®

both notchbacks, in four trim levels. It's powered by a fuel-injected derivative of the familiar 1.4-liter overhead-valve four from the smaller Renault Le Car, but mounted transversely hooked to a 4-speed transaxle is standard in base and L models, a 5-speed overdrive gearbox is standard on DL and Limited versions, and electronically controlled 3-speed automatic is an across-the-board extra. There's a full range of big-car options listed, including power steering, cruise control, and leather upholstery.

EVALUATION

At this writing, we're completing our first tests of the Alliance, and this car has thoroughly charmed our staff. Frankly, we hadn't expected that, because past Renaults have both amused and amazed us with their eccentric design details, buzzy operation, and erratic workmanship. Yet the Alliance is thoroughly conventional and follows modern small-car design practice. Though the engine is on the small side even for the minicar class, it provides decent pickup thanks to the car's low weight. Acceleration is adequate with automatic and almost lively with manual transmission. The engine is also a smooth runner and fairly quiet below 4000 rpm. Ride is impressively absorbent, particularly for a lightweight short-wheelbase car, one of the good things about the Alliance's French heritage. Handling is nimble and body roll, though noticeable, is far better controlled than in past Renaults. Cabin space is good for the overall size, but despite AMC's claims only four grownups (not five) can ride in real comfort, due mainly to lack of back seat width. The pedestal front seat mounts are a logical solution to the problem of finding usable rear footroom in such a small car. Headroom is limited for six-footers front and back but legroom is decent, and those in back don't have to scrunch up like sardines to fit. Dash and minor controls are straightforward and simple to use. Outward visibility is excellent, and combines with the small size and tight turning circle to make parking a breeze. It's too early to predict durability/reliability, but assembly on the cars we've seen so far appears better than average (close to Japanese standards, in fact), though the doors seem tinny and the door locks flimsy. Verdict: an unexpectedly capable newcomer. Should be just the shot in the arm AMC so desperately needs, but faces a field of formidable rivals.

EVALUATION CHECKLIST

Fuel economy 4
Driveability 4
Acceleration 3
Braking 3
Handling/roadholding 4
Driving position 4
Instruments/control 3
Visiblity 4
Heating/ventilation 4
Seat comfort 4
Passenger room 3
Ride 5
Noise 4
Exit/entry 3

Cargo room 2
Serviceability 4
Standard equipment 3
Body construction 3
Paint/exterior finish 3
Interior finish 4
TOTAL POINTS 71

RATING SCALE
5 = Excellent
4 = Very Good
3 = Average/Acceptable
2 = Fair
1 = Poor

SPECIFICATIONS

	2-door sedan	4-door sedan
Wheelbase (in.)	97.8	97.8
Overall length (in.)	163.8	163.8
Overall width (in.)	65.0	65.0
Overall height (in.)	54.5	54.5
Track front (in.)	55.2	55.2
Track rear (in.)	52.8	52.8
Curb weight (lbs.)	1945[1]	1980[1]
Max. cargo vol. (cu. ft.)	12.8[2]	12.8[2]
Fuel tank capacity (gal.)	12.5	12.5
Seating capacity	5	5
Front headroom (in.)	37.1	37.1
Front shoulder room (in.)	52.6	52.6
Front legroom, max. (in.)	40.8	40.8
Rear headroom (in.)	37.0	37.0
Rear shoulder room (in.)	51.0	51.7
Rear legroom, min. (in.)	38.4	38.4

1: Base models
2: Manufacturer's estimate

BODY/CHASSIS

Drivetrain layout: transverse front engine/front-wheel drive. **Suspension front:** independent, MacPherson struts, coil springs, telescopic shock absorbers, anti-roll bar. **Suspension rear:** independent, trailing arms, transverse torsion bars, telescopic shock absorbers, anti-roll bars. **Steering:** rack-and-pinion. **Turns lock-to-lock:** NA. **Turn diameter (ft.):** NA. **Brakes front:** 9.4-in. discs. **Brakes rear:** 8.0-in. drums. **Construction:** unit

POWERTRAINS	ohv I-4
Bore × stroke (in.)	2.99× 3.03
Displacement (liters/cu. in.)	1.4/ 85
Compression ratio	8.8:1
Fuel delivery	FI
Net bhp @ rpm	62@ 4200[1]
Net torque @ rpm (lbs/ft)	75@ 2500
Availability	S/All

1: estimated

Final drive ratios	
4-speed manual	3.29:1
5-speed OD manual	3.87:1
3-speed automatic	3.56:1

KEY **bbl.** = barrel (carburetor); **bhp** = brake horsepower (advertised); **Cal.** = California only. **Fed.** = Federal/49 state; **FI** = fuel injection; **ohv** = overhead valve; **ohc** = overhead cam; **I** = inline engine; **V** = V engine; **D** = diesel; **T** = turbocharged; **OD** = overdrive transmission; **S** = standard engine; **O** = optional engine.

PRICES

ALLIANCE	Retail Price	Dealer Cost	Low Price
2-door sedan.	$5595	5147	$5497

Prices are accurate at time of printing; subject to manufacturer's change

	Retail Price	Dealer Cost	Low Price
L 2-door sedan	6020	5298	5648
L 4-door sedan	6270	5518	5918
DL 2-door sedan	6665	5856	6256
DL 4-door sedan	6905	6076	6576
Limited 4-door sedan	7470	6574	7075

STANDARD EQUIPMENT (included in above prices):

1.4-liter 4-cylinder fuel injected engine, 4-speed manual transmission, power brakes, bucket seats, styled steel wheels, body side moldings. **DL** adds: 5-speed manual transmission, remote left mirror, reclining seats, cloth seat trim, digital clock, tinted glass, extra insulation, tachometer, **Limited** adds: luxury seat & door trim, rear center armrest, light group, visibility group, luxury wheel covers, halogen headlamps.

OPTIONAL EQUIPMENT:

Transmissions			
5-speed manual, L	$ 155	$ 129	$ 131
Automatic, base, L	412	342	346
Air conditioning	651	540	546
Air conditioning pkg. (For dealer inst. air cond.)	99	82	83
Heavy-duty battery	26	22	23
Quartz digital clock, L	49	41	42
Cold climate group			
w/o air cond.	57	47	48
w/air cond.	10	8	9
Heavy duty cooling	67	56	57
Cruise control	161	134	136
Elec. rear window defroster	124	103	105
Power door locks			
2-door DL	110	91	92
4-door DL, Limited	157	130	132
Tinted glass, base, L	85	71	72
Halogen headlamps, L, DL	20	17	18
Extra quiet insulation pkg., L	62	52	53
Keyless entry syst., DL, Limited	72	60	61
Light group	46	38	39
Metallic paint			
L	62	52	53
DL, Limited	NC	NC	NC
Two-tone paint, L, DL, Limited	134	111	113
Protection group (NA base sdn.)			
Incl. door edge guards	52	43	44
w/o door edge guards	39	32	33
Radio equipment			
AM	62	68	69

Prices are accurate at time of printing; subject to manufacturer's change

	Retail Price	Dealer Cost	Low Price
AM/FM	130	108	110
AM/FM stereo (NA base)	191	159	161
AM/FM stereo ETR w/cassette (NA base).	465	386	390
Left inst. panel speaker	28	23	24
Power steering.	196	163	165
Leather steering wheel (NA base).	60	50	51
Systems sentry (NA base)	98	81	82
Tachometer, L	82	68	69
Trim/seats			
Fabric buckets, L	30	25	26
Leather buckets, Limited	413	343	346
Visibility group			
L	160	133	135
DL	129	107	109
Intermittent wipers, L, DL (std. Ltd)	50	42	43
Power windows/door locks			
2-door DL	280	232	235
4-door DL, Limited.	328	272	275

Renault Fuego & 18i

Renault Fuego 2-door coupe

WHAT'S NEW FOR '83

There's little to report on the largest models in Renault's U.S. lineup. Introduced here last spring, the normally aspirated and turbocharged Fuego coupes receive simplified two-stalk steering column controls for lights and wiper/washer functions, replacing last year's three-stalk arrangement. There are also two new options, the "infrawave" remote electronic door lock system offered on the new Alliance and electric remote-control door mirrors. Both are available separately or as part of a Convenience Group that also includes power windows and door locks. Other standard and optional equipment is unchanged, as are drivetrains, chassis, and trim. Launched in the U.S. for the 1981 model year, the 18i sedan and wagon also get the new column stalk arrangement, plus a numerically lower final drive ratio (3.44:1 versus 3.78:1 last year) for a longer stride on the highway and better fuel economy. The base-trim versions are scratched, and the former 5-speed overdrive manual gearbox option moves over to the standard equipment column. Though they look considerably different outside, Fuego and 18i share the same floorpan, dashboard, drivetrains, and mechanical layout, though only Fuego is available with the turbo version of Renault's long-lived 1.6-liter overhead-valve four.

EVALUATION

Despite sharing certain components and design features, these are two very different animals. In turbo form the Fuego is loads of fun. It offers satisfying acceleration, particularly from mid-range speeds, together with gratifying mileage (nearly 27 mpg in our hands). Typically French suspension is soft and supple, so ride is pleasantly smooth yet handling deceptively good, aided in large measure by this model's sticky Michelin TRX tires. The slick shape is distinctive, eye-catching, and helps minimize wind roar. This plus good mechanical and road noise suppression add up to a refined highway cruiser. Irritations are a vague and rubbery shift linkage, spongy brakes that squeal too easily, and restricted over-the-shoulder visibility. The cabin is tastefully trimmed in high-grade materials and feels plush, but seats are set so high off the floor that headroom is very limited for even medium-size adults. Rear entry/exit is clumsy, as is loading heavy cargo over the high rear sill. The underhood area is crowded, and engine cooling seems marginal. By contrast, the 18i is simply undistinguished. It's let down by an irritating exhaust boom and general mechanical harshness that betrays the advanced age of this Renault engine. Acceleration is only adequate with manual shift, mediocre with automatic.

Workmanship seems more slap-dash than on German or Japanese competitors, and the leather interior trim on the last 18i wagon we drove didn't look like it should cost what it does. In brief: the 18i is a deservedly slow seller, being too ordinary in too many areas. The Fuego is doing much better, which only shows that styling and zip still count for something even in today's depressed auto market.

EVALUATION CHECKLIST
(Fuego Turbo)

Fuel economy	4	Cargo room	3
Driveability	3	Serviceability	3
Acceleration	4	Standard equipment	4
Braking	3	Body construction	4
Handling/roadholding	4	Paint/exterior finish	4
Driving position	3	Interior finish	4
Instruments/control	3	TOTAL POINTS	70
Visiblity	3		
Heating/ventilation	3	**RATING SCALE**	
Seat comfort	4	5 = Excellent	
Passenger room	3	4 = Very Good	
Ride	4	3 = Average/Acceptable	
Noise	4	2 = Fair	
Exit/entry	3	1 = Poor	

SPECIFICATIONS

	Fuego 2-door coupe	18i 4-door sedan	18i 5-door wagon
Wheelbase (in.)	96.1	96.1	96.1
Overall length (in.)	176.8	178.7	181.5
Overall width (in.)	66.6	66.5	66.5
Overall height (in.)	50.5	55.3	55.2
Track front (in.)	56.4	55.7	55.7
Track rear (in.)	53.0	53.4	53.4
Curb weight (lbs.)	2379	2261	2426
Max. cargo vol. (cu. ft.)	13.8/ 33.8	11.9	35.0/ 65.0
Fuel tank capacity (gal.)	14.8	14.0	15.0
Seating capacity	4	5	5

SPECIFICATIONS

	Fuego 2-door coupe	18i 4-door sedan	18i 5-door wagon
Front headroom (in.)	36.4	37.4	37.4
Front shoulder room (in.)	56.1	54.9	54.9
Front legroom, max. (in.)	41.6	41.3	41.3
Rear headroom (in.)	35.8	36.2	36.8
Rear shoulder room (in.)	54.1	53.9	53.9
Rear legroom, min. (in.)	30.2	32.6	32.6

BODY/CHASSIS

Drivetrain layout: longitudinal front engine/front-wheel drive. **Suspension front:** independent, lower A-arms, upper transverse arms, upper reaction arms, coil springs, telescopic shock absorbers, anti-roll bar. **Suspension rear:** beam axle, A-shaped control bracket and lateral trailing arms on Fuego, four links on 18i, coil springs, telescopic shock absorbers, anti-roll bar. **Steering:** rack-and-pinion, variable power assist. **Turns lock-to-lock:** 2.8. **Turn diameter (ft.):** 33.8/35.7 18i/Fuego. **Brakes front:** 9.4-in. discs. **Brakes rear:** 9.0-in. drums. **Construction:** unit

POWERTRAINS

	ohv I-4	ohv I-4T
Bore × stroke (in.)	3.10× 3.30	3.03× 3.30
Displacement (liters/cu. in.)	1.6/ 100.5	1.6/ 95.5
Compression ratio	8.6:1	8.0:1
Fuel delivery	FI	FI
Net bhp @ rpm	81.5@ 5500	107@ 5500
Net torque @ rpm (lbs/ft)	86@ 2500	120@ 2500
Availability	S/All[1]	S/All[2]

1: NA Fuego Turbo   2: Fuego Turbo only

POWERTRAINS

	ohv I-4	I-4 T
Final drive ratios		
5-speed OD manual	3.44:1	3.78:1
3-speed automatic	3.44:1	

KEY bbl. = barrel (carburetor); **bhp** = brake horsepower (advertised); **Cal.** = California only. **Fed.** = Federal/49 state; **FI** = fuel injectoin; **ohv** = overhead valve; **ohc** = overhead cam; **I** = inline engine; **V** = V engine; **D** = diesel; **T** = turbocharged; **OD** = overdrive transmission; **S** = standard engine; **O** = optional engine.

PRICES

18i & FUEGO	Retail Price	Dealer Cost	Low Price
18i Deluxe 4-door sedan	$8395	$7136	$7736
18i Deluxe 5-door wagon	8855	7527	8127
Fuego 2-door coupe	8695	7391	7991
Fuego Turbo 2-door coupe	11095	9431	10331

STANDARD EQUIPMENT (included in above prices):

18i: 1.6-liter (100-cid) fuel-injected 4-cylinder engine, 5-speed overdrive manual transmission, front bucket seats w/reclining backrests, cloth upholstery and interior trim, full color-keyed carpeting including cargo area, analog clock, courtesy lights, center console, intermittent windshield wipers, padded steering wheel, tachometer and oil level gauge, trip odometer, passenger visor vanity mirror, styled wheel covers, AM/FM stereo radio w/2 speakers, electric rear window defroster, extra-quiet insulation package, power steering, power brakes, rear window wiper/washer (wagon), tinted glass. **Fuego** adds: digital clock, split-back rear seat, adjustable steering column, leather-wrapped steering wheel, 4-speaker sound system, left remote-control door mirror, remote liftgate release, **Fuego Turbo** adds: 1.6-liter (100-cid) fuel-injected 4-cylinder turbocharged engine, aluminum wheels, Michelin TRX tires, Visibility Group, air conditioning, front floormats, special exterior striping.

OPTIONAL EQUIPMENT

Air conditioning (std. Fuego Turbo)	$ 640	$ 531	$ 540
3-speed automatic transmission (NA Fuego Turbo)	365	303	307
Cruise control (auto. trans. req.)	170	141	143
Cast aluminum wheels, 18i	360	299	302
Cast aluminum wheels, Fuego (incl. Michelin TRX tires)	440	365	369
Convenience Group 18i	375	311	315

Prices are accurate at time of printing; subject to manufacturer's change

	Retail Price	Dealer Cost	Low Price
Fuego, Fuego Turbo	525	436	541
Front floormats (std. Fuego Turbo)	30	25	26
AM/FM stereo radio w/cassette player	149	124	126
Roof rack, 18i wagon only.	115	95	96
Metallic paint.	135	112	114
Touring Interior	645	535	541
Deluxe vinyl seats, 18i wagon.	26	22	23
Electric fold-back vinyl sunroof, Fuego, Fuego Turbo.	425	353	358
Visibility group, Fuego only	140	116	118

Saab

Saab 900 Turbo 3-door sedan

WHAT'S NEW FOR '83

Sweden's front-wheel-drive pioneer makes mostly minor refinements to its 900 lineup this year. All models get extra running lights either side of the grille to supplement the parking/side marker units at the outer ends of the nose. Also common to all '83 Saabs are asbestos-free pads for the all-disc brake system, said to improve braking performance under all driving conditions. Front pads are of the semi-metallic type; those at the rear are made of an organic material. Outboard rear seat passengers now have three-point shoulder/lap belts like those in the front compartment. A conventional lap belt remains for the center position. On non-turbo models the exhaust gas recirculation system previously used for emissions control has been deleted through closer engine calibrations. Saab claims improved drivability

Prices are accurate at time of printing; subject to manufacturer's change

and slightly better mileage with no increase in tailpipe pollutants as a result. The top-line 900 Turbo returns with the APC (Automatic Performance Control) system introduced during the '82 season. This continuously adjusts turbo boost in response to information from various engine sensors to account for the quality of fuel being used, and yields a slight gain in torque compared to the earlier non-APC engine. Turbo and 900S models get electric front windows and a central locking system for doors and trunklid as new standard items.

EVALUATION

Entertaining and pleasant to drive, thanks to properly weighted and geared power steering plus a competent front-drive chassis. Nimble through turns, and hangs on well despite more body roll than we'd like. Never feels clumsy in city traffic, and is easy to maneuver in tight spots. Ride can be thumpy on the Turbo, firm but comfortable on other models. Roof styling leaves shallow windows, and right-rear vision is hampered by thick roof pillars and the front seat headrests. Tail is invisible, so backing up demands caution. Fairly quiet in hard acceleration. Manual models are relaxed in fifth gear on the highway. Turbo has exhilarating performance, spoiled by turbo lag that is much more pronounced with automatic transmission. With manual shift, the non-turbo 900 is unexpectedly lively (we clocked 13.5 seconds in the 0–60 mph test). High-set driver's seat helps you feel in charge, but some of our testers don't like the steering wheel/pedals spacing. Front cabin has adequate stretch-out room for adults, and the firm seats are comfortable. Rear headroom is tight for taller persons as is legroom unless the front seats are moved up some. Dash organizes all minor controls neatly and puts them close at hand, but wheel rim can obscure parts of the gauges. Rear seat folds up station wagon style for great cargo room. Saabs are a bit heavy, but even so our APC Turbo returned 22.4 mpg, which isn't bad considering the available performance. In our experience, the unblown models do 2–3 mpg better if you're careful with your right foot. Limited dealer network, so getting parts and service can be a trial. Bottom line: capable all-rounder with a personality you either like or you don't. Not outrageously priced all things considered, but not cheap to maintain.

EVALUATION CHECKLIST
(APC Turbo)

Fuel economy	4	Cargo room	5
Driveability	3	Serviceability	3
Acceleration	4	Standard equipment	4
Braking	4	Body construction	5
Handling/roadholding	4	Paint/exterior finish	5
Driving position	4	Interior finish	3
Instruments/control	4	TOTAL POINTS	76
Visiblity	3		
Heating/ventilation	4		
Seat comfort	4		
Passenger room	3		
Ride	3		
Noise	3		
Exit/entry	4		

RATING SCALE
5 = Excellent
4 = Very Good
3 = Average/Acceptable
2 = Fair
1 = Poor

SPECIFICATIONS

	3-door sedan	4-door sedan
Wheelbase (in.)	99.1	99.1
Overall length (in.)	187.6	187.6
Overall width (in.)	66.5	66.5
Overall height (in.)	55.9	55.9
Track front (in.)	56.3	56.3
Track rear (in.)	56.7	56.7
Curb weight (lbs.)	2600[1]	2640[1]
Max. cargo vol. (cu. ft.)	21.3/ 56.5	21.8
Fuel tank capacity (gal.)	16.6	16.6
Seating capacity	5	5
Front headroom (in.)	36.8[2]	36.8[2]
Front shoulder room (in.)	52.2	53.0
Front legroom, max. (in.)	41.7	41.7
Rear headroom (in.)	37.4	37.4
Rear shoulder room (in.)	53.3	54.5
Rear legroom, min. (in.)	36.2	36.2

1: Base model   2: with sunroof

BODY/CHASSIS

Drivetrain layout: longitudinal front engine/front-wheel drive. **Suspension front:** independent, transverse A-arms, pivot-mounted coil springs, telescopic shock absorbers (gas-pressurized on Turbo). **Suspension rear:** tubular beam axle, trailing arms, panhard rod, coil springs, telescopic shock absorbers (gas-pressurized on Turbo). **Steering:** rack-and-pinion, power-assisted. **Turns lock-to-lock:** 3.6. **Turn diameter (ft.):** 33.8. **Brakes front:** 11.0-in. discs. **Brakes rear:** 10.6-in. discs. **Construction:** unit

POWERTRAINS	ohc I-4	ohc I-4T
Bore × stroke (in.)	3.54× 3.07	3.54× 3.07
Displacement (liters/cu. in.)	2.0/ 121	2.0/ 121
Compression ratio	9.25:1	8.5:1
Fuel delivery	FI	FI
Net bhp @ rpm	110@ 5250	135@ 4800
Net torque @ rpm (lbs/ft)	119@ 3500	160–172 @3500
Availability	S/All[1]	S/All[2]

1: 900, 900S only   2: 900 Turbo only

Final drive ratios		
5-speed OD manual	3.67:1	3.67:1
3-speed automatic	3.67:1	3.67:1

KEY bbl. = barrel (carburetor); **bhp** = brake horsepower (advertised); **Cal.** = California only. **Fed.** = Federal/49 state; **FI** = fuel injection; **ohv** = overhead valve; **ohc** = overhead cam; **I** = inline engine; **V** = V engine; **D** = diesel; **T** = turbocharged; **OD** = overdrive transmission; **S** = standard engine; **O** = optional engine.

PRICES

SAAB	Retail Price
(dealer cost and low price not available at time of publication)	
3-door sedan.	$10750

Prices are accurate at time of printing; subject to manufacturer's change

	Retail Price
4-door sedan	11050
S 3-door sedan	13550
S 4-door sedan	13950
Turbo 3-door sedan	16510
Turbo 4-door sedan	16910

STANDARD EQUIPMENT (included in above prices):

2.0-liter (120-cid) 4-cylinder fuel-injected engine, 5-speed overdrive manual transmission, power steering, power brakes, clock, tachometer, trip odometer, electric rear-window defroster, intermittent wipers, tinted glass, driver's seat tilt/height adjuster, full carpeting, reclining front bucket seats, fold-down rear seat AM/FM stereo radio. **S** adds: electrically heated front seats, fold-down rear center armrest, manual sunroof. **Turbo** adds: air conditioning, halogen headlamps, electric remote-control door mirrors, front door power windows (4-door), front and rear spoilers (3-door), turbocharged engine, uprated suspension and tires.

OPTIONAL EQUIPMENT:

3-speed automatic transmission	$ 370.
Metallic or special black paint	350.

Subaru

Subaru DL (left) and GL 4-door sedans

WHAT'S NEW FOR '83

Running gear revisions and several new options are listed for this year's lineup of front-drive and 4wd passenger cars from Fuji Heavy Industries of Japan. Both the 1.6-liter and 1.8-liter versions of the water-cooled, horizontally opposed Subaru four gain an extra two horsepower and, on automatic-equipped models, American-made hydraulic valve lifters.

Prices are accurate at time of printing; subject to manufacturer's change

Torque output is unchanged. A lockup torque converter is now specified for the automatic for less converter slippage that wastes fuel. In the Subaru system the lockup is effective in all forward gears. The self-shift transmission is extended to the 4wd hatchbacks and wagons for the first time. A new extra-cost item for some GL models is digital instrumentation combined with a trip computer, the latter really a fancy clock that can measure the vehicle's mileage range for the fuel remaining. Also new is what the importer calls an "on-board computer diagnostic system," which signals if part of the engine's emissions control system is malfunctioning. Most DL models get a standard AM/FM radio this year, and a 4-speaker system is now included on the more expensive GL offerings. Styling, dimensions, chassis, and basic mechanicals are reruns.

EVALUATION

Published reports of inept workmanship resulting in costly, time-consuming owner repairs make us seriously doubt Subaru's ad slogan, "inexpensive, and built to stay that way." Specific complaints concern cooling system problems and, on 4wd models, faulty universal joints. The importer is apparently reluctant to acknowledge such problems or to aid customers, who frequently find parts hard to get and dealers less than sympathetic. All we can add is, let the buyer beware. In some respects, Subarus are built down to a price, and seem a notch below other Japanese cars in construction quality and the type of interior materials used. Too bad, because these are well-equipped cars appealing to those looking for a complete car at a rock-bottom price. Dull performance, but good fuel economy from harsh 1.8-liter engine. Mileage could be better, though; our last test Subaru, the 5-speed GL 4-door, returned a lackluster 26.5 mpg overall. All-independent suspension gives a firm but not bouncy ride, though big bumps and dips are felt. Braking marred by premature rear-wheel lockup in panic stops and a fair degree of nosedive. Tire noise resonates through the body on coarsely paved roads. Easy to whirl around in traffic, though manual steering is heavy for parking. Outward vision poses no problems. Interior is too small for four large adults, and fore/aft front seat travel could be usefully longer. Good major control spacings, but dash is high relative to seat and steering wheel. Dash is neatly organized, but has too many separate panels that give it a slight jukebox look. Notchback sedans have fold-down split rear seatbacks that extend the load platform from the rather puny trunk. Repair record used to be very good, but we wonder about that now. Judgment: let down by crude-sounding, low-suds engine and the look of some materials. Won't be good choice for reliable, practical transportation until durability/reliability bugs are squashed.

EVALUATION CHECKLIST

Fuel economy	4	Cargo room	3
Driveability	3	Serviceability	4
Acceleration	3	Standard equipment	3
Braking	3	Body construction	3
Handling/roadholding	4	Paint/exterior finish	4
Driving position	3	Interior finish	4
Instruments/control	4	TOTAL POINTS	68
Visiblity	4		
Heating/ventilation	3	**RATING SCALE**	
Seat comfort	3	5 = Excellent	
Passenger room	3	4 = Very Good	
Ride	4	3 = Average/Acceptable	
Noise	3	2 = Fair	
Exit/entry	3	1 = Poor	

SPECIFICATIONS[1]	2-door hardtop	3-door sedan	4-door sedan	5-door wagon
Wheelbase (in.)	96.9	93.7	96.9	96.7
Overall length (in.)	168.1	157.9	168.1	169.3
Overall width (in.)	63.6	63.6	63.6	63.6
Overall height (in.)	53.7	53.7	53.7	54.7
Track front (in.)	52.4	52.4	52.4	52.5
Track rear (in.)	53.0	53.0	53.0	53.0
Curb weight (lbs.)	2110[2]	2050[2]	2130[2]	2250[2]
Max. cargo vol. (cu. ft.)	13.0	NA	13.0	NA
Fuel tank capacity (gal.)	15.8	13.2	15.8	15.8
Seating capacity	5	4	5	5
Front headroom (in.)	36.0	36.2	36.0	36.0

SPECIFICATIONS[1]	2-door coupe	3-door sedan	4-door sedan	5-door wagon
Front shoulder room (in.)	51.0	51.0	51.0	51.0
Front legroom, max. (in.)	40.0	39.3	40.0	40.0
Rear headroom (in.)	32.5	36.6	NA	NA
Rear shoulder room (in.)	50.0	50.0	50.0	50.0
Rear legroom, min. (in.)	NA	30.2	NA	NA

1: Some dimensions vary slightly depending on model
2: Base models

BODY/CHASSIS

Drivetrain layout: longitudinal front engine/front-wheel drive (four-wheel drive on 4WD models). **Suspension front:** independent, MacPherson struts, lower lateral arms, compliance struts, coil springs, telescopic shock absorbers, anti-roll bar. **Suspension rear:** independent, semi-trailing arms, longitudinal torsion bars, telescopic shock absorbers. **Steering:** rack-and-pinion. **Turns lock-to-lock:** 3.8. **Turn diameter (ft.):** 31.6. **Brakes front:** 7.2-in. discs. **Brakes rear:** 7.1-in. drums. **Construction:** unit

POWERTRAINS	ohv flat-4	ohv flat-4
Bore × stroke (in.)	3.62×2.36	3.62×2.64
Displacement (liters/cu. in.)	1.6/97	1.8/109
Compression ratio	9.0:1	8.7:1
Fuel delivery	2bbl.	2bbl.
Net bhp @ rpm	69@4800	73@4400
Net torque @ rpm (lbs/ft)	86@2800	94@2400
Availability	S/All[1]	S/All[2]

1: NA on 4WD models
2: std. 4WD models

POWERTRAINS	ohv flat-4	ohv flat-4
Final drive ratios		
4×2-speed OD manual[1]		3.89:1
4-speed manual	3.70:1	
5-speed OD manual	3.70:1	3.70:1
3-speed automatic[2]		3.70:1

1: 4WD models only
2: NA w/1.6 liter engine

KEY bbl. = barrel (carburetor); **bhp** = brake horsepower (advertised); **Cal.** = California only. **Fed.** = Federal/49 state; **FI** = fuel injectoin; **ohv** = overhead valve; **ohc** = overhead cam; **I** = inline engine; **V** = V engine; **D** = diesel; **T** = turbocharged; **OD** = overdrive transmission; **S** = standard engine; **O** = optional engine.

Prices not available at time of publication.

Toyota Celica & Celica Supra

Toyota Celica Supra 3-door coupe

WHAT'S NEW FOR '83

Brand-new last year, Toyota's sporty coupe duo comes in for a few mechanical refinements aimed at better performance and enhanced mileage. As before, the four-cylinder Celica notchback and hatchback and the six-cylinder Supra hatchback share basic body structure from the cowl back, but differ in engine, frontal styling, the notchback's rear-end appearance, equipment and, of course, price. In the Celica line, the GT-S option package introduced for mid-'82 becomes a regular model, and is now offered in both body styles. It's intended as a low-cost alternative to the Supra, and shares that model's independent rear suspension, wider wheels and tires, sports front bucket seats, and black fender flares. Other Celicas retain their familiar four-link live axle rear suspension. All models except the base manual-transmission ST notchback acquire electronic fuel injection this year, which yields a gain of 9 bhp. Supra's twin-cam six goes up by 5 bhp thanks to adoption of platinum-tipped spark plugs and the microprocessor injection control. The optional 4-speed overdrive automatic transmission now incorporates Toyota's multi-mode ECT system described in the Cressida report. A shorter final drive ratio is now specified with the standard 5-speed gearbox for better low-end getaway. New standard features this year include rear "sunshade" spoiler and headlamp washers. The luxury L-type gets revised cloth upholstery as standard.

EVALUATION

Lots of flash and standard equipment plus a good performance/economy compromise made both these models sales winners in '82. Both suffer the usual sporty coupe problems of clumsy access to a very cramped rear seat area, limited cargo room (especially the Celica notchbacks), marginal front head clearance for taller adults, and only fair underhood access. As you'd expect, the Supra is quick, but returns decent mileage all things considered (we logged 19 mpg; the '82 EPA city rating was 21). It also corners flat with minimal body roll, aided by high-geared power-assisted steering with good feel and boost that decreases with speed for better control, a good point for safety. With its all-independent suspension, the Supra also steps over bumps with more composure than the live-axle Celica, which reacts more sharply to tar strips and the like, and also heels over more in hard cornering. Like most big fours, the Celica's engine lacks finesse at higher rpm. Mileage is okay but not great: 22 mpg in our test. The Supra is our choice as the best buy among sporty coupes, besting even its four-cylinder running mate, which suffers only by comparison.

EVALUATION CHECKLIST
(Celica Supra)

Fuel economy	3	Cargo room	4
Driveability	5	Serviceability	2
Acceleration	4	Standard equipment	5
Braking	3	Body construction	5
Handling/roadholding	4	Paint/exterior finish	5
Driving position	5	Interior finish	5
Instruments/control	4	TOTAL POINTS	80
Visiblity	4		
Heating/ventilation	4	**RATING SCALE**	
Seat comfort	4	5 = Excellent	
Passenger room	3	4 = Very Good	
Ride	4	3 = Average/Acceptable	
Noise	4	2 = Fair	
Exit/entry	3	1 = Poor	

SPECIFICATIONS	Celica 2-door coupe	Celica 3-door coupe	Celica Supra 3-door coupe
Wheelbase (in.)	98.4	98.4	103.0
Overall length (in.)	176.2	176.6	183.5
Overall width (in.)	65.5[1]	65.5[1]	67.7[4]
Overall height (in.)	52.0	52.0	52.0
Track front (in.)	54.9	54.9[2]	57.9[5]
Track rear (in.)	53.7	53.7[2]	56.7[5]
Curb weight (lbs.)	2496[3]	2566[3]	2970[3]
Max. cargo vol. (cu. ft.)	10.6	25.8	21.0
Fuel tank capacity (gal.)	16.1	16.1	16.1
Seating capacity	4	4	4
Front headroom (in.)	37.4	37.4	37.4
Front shoulder room (in.)	53.3	53.3	53.3
Front legroom, max. (in.)	43.0	43.0	43.0
Rear headroom (in.)	37.0	35.6	35.6
Rear shoulder room (in.)	52.1	52.1	52.1
Rear legroom, min. (in.)	25.4	25.4	25.4

1: 67.7 in. GT-S   4: 66.3 L-Type
2: 56.5/56.5 GT-S   5: 56.3/55.1 L-Type
3: Base models

BODY/CHASSIS

Drivetrain layout: longitudinal front engine/rear-wheel drive.
Suspension front: independent, MacPherson struts, offset
coil springs, lower control arms, telescopic shock absorbers,
anti-roll bar. **Suspension rear:** rigid axle, four trailing links,
lateral track bar, telescopic shock absorbers, anti-roll bar.
Celica GT-S and Supra have independent semi-trailing arms,
coil springs, telescopic shock absorbers, anti-roll bar. **Steering:** rack-and-pinion (variable power-assist on Supra). **Turns
lock-to-lock:** 3.8 manual, 3.1 power. **Turn diameter (ft.):**
32.8/35.4 Celica/Supra. **Brakes front:** 10.1-in. discs. **Brakes
rear:** 9.0-in. drums (10.4-in discs Supra). **Construction:** unit

POWERTRAINS

	ohc I-4	ohc I-6
Bore × stroke (in.)	3.62× 3.50	3.27× 3.35
Displacement (liters/cu. in.)	2.4/ 144	2.8/ 168
Compression ratio	9.0:1	8.8:1
Fuel delivery	FI	FI
Net bhp @ rpm	105@ 4800	150@ 5200
Net torque @ rpm (lbs/ft)	137@ 2800	159@ 4400
Availability	S/All[1]	S/All[2]

1: Celica; NA Supra
2: Supra only

Final drive ratios

5-speed OD manual	3.42:1	4.10:1[1]
4-speed OD automatic	3.58:1	4.10:1

1: 3.73:1 L-Type

KEY bbl. = barrel (carburetor); **bhp** = brake horsepower (advertised); **Cal.** = California
only. **Fed.** = Federal/49 state; **FI** = fuel injectoin; **ohv** = overhead valve; **ohc** = overhead
cam; **I** = inline engine; **V** = V engine; **D** = diesel; **T** = turbocharged; **OD** = overdrive
transmission; **S** = standard engine; **O** = optional engine.

PRICES

TOYOTA CELICA/CELICA SUPRA	Retail Price	Dealer Cost	Low Price
Celica ST 2-door coupe, 5-speed	$7299	$6241	$6741
Celica GT 2-door coupe, automatic.	9039	7683	8483
Celica GT 2-door coupe, 5-speed.	8599	7309	7909
Celica GT 3-door coupe, automatic.	9389	7981	8681
Celica GT 3-door coupe, 5-speed.	8949	7607	8407
Celica GT-S 2-door coupe, 5-speed	9969	8424	9224
Celica GT-S 3-door coupe, 5-speed	10319	8720	9620
Supra L-Type 3-door coupe, 5-speed	14148	11601	13601
Supra L-Type 3-door coupe, automatic . . .	14748	12093	14093
Supra 3-door coupe, 5-speed	15398	12626	14626
Supra 3-door coupe, automatic.	15998	13118	15118

STANDARD EQUIPMENT (included in above prices):

Celica: 2.4-liter (134-cid) 4-cylinder engine, transmission as above, power brakes, styled-steel wheels, wheel trim rings (ex. ST), retractable headlamps, left door mirror, tachometer and trip odometer, electric rear-window defroster, tinted glass with windshield sunshade band, analog quartz clock, reclining front bucket seats, center console, full carpeting. **Celica GT** adds: halogen headlamps, 6-position tilt steering wheel, remote trunklid/hatch release, remote fuel-filler door release, digital clock, height-adjustable driver's seat with lumbar support adjuster, cloth upholstery, split fold-down rear seatback, electronic AM/FM stereo radio, oil pressure gauge and voltmeter. **GT-S** adds: Supra-type independent rear suspension, 225/60HR-14 RBL tires, aluminum alloy wheels, multi-adjustable sport front bucket seats, black fender flares. **Supra** has: 2.8-liter (168-cid) 6-cylinder engine with fuel injection, transmission as above, variable-assist power steering, independent rear suspension, limited-slip differential (except L-Type), 4-wheel power disc brakes, aluminum-alloy wheels, pop-up headlamps with halogen elements, foglamps, dual electric remote-control door mirrors, rear-window wiper/washer with intermittent control, full instrumentation including tachometer and trip odometer, cruise control, leather-wrapped steering wheel, tilt steering wheel, intermittent wipers, automatic temperature control air conditioning, electric rear-window defroster, tinted glass with windshield sunshade band, digital quartz clock, center console, hatch and fuel-filler door releases, power windows, power door locks, reclining front bucket seats with driver's height and lumbar support adjuster (Performance has Sport Seats with 8-way adjustment), cloth upholstery, full carpeting. AM/FM stereo radio with five speakers.

OPTIONAL EQUIPMENT:

Air conditioning, Celica.	630	504	509
Power steering, Celica	195	166	168

Prices are accurate at time of printing; subject to manufacturer's change

CONSUMER GUIDE®

	Retail Price	Dealer Cost	
Cruise control, Celica.............	135	108	110
Electric sunroof	460	368	372
AM/FM stereo radio w/5 speakers, Celica ..	315	189	191
Cassette tape player & amp/equalizer	440	308	312
Two-tone package, Celica	470	376	380
Rear-window wiper/washer, Celica 3-door	85	70	71
Leather package, Supra	430	344	348
Rear-window sunshade, Supra	120	96	98
Two-tone paint................	130	104	106
Black package, Celica............	1050	828	837
Aluminum wheels, Celica	320	256	259
Digital instrumentation with trip computer, Supra L-Type only	470	376	380
Power Package, Celica	395	316	320
Black paint	70	44	45

Toyota Corolla

Toyota Corolla SR-5 3-door Sport Coupe

WHAT'S NEW FOR '83

Still the best-seller in the Toyota stable, the conventional rear-drive Corolla comes in for a smaller engine and a switch in steering. Replacing last year's 1.8-liter overhead-valve four is a 1.6-liter overhead-cam unit producing the same 70 horsepower and 8 lbs/ft less torque. The Corolla's recirculating-ball steering gear now gives way to the more precise rack-and-pinion type, and power assist is available on all models except the base 2-door sedan. The model lineup stays the same, and all models come in for what Toyota terms "several interior upgrades."

Prices are accurate at time of printing; subject to manufacturer's change

EVALUATION

An orthodox rear-drive economy car, average in most ways, better than average in a few. Small size and light steering effort combine with good outward vision and handy turning circle to make light work of parking and city traffic. Road manners are nothing special, with a bit too much body roll and a simply located rear axle that can hop slightly if the corners are bumpy. Ride is okay, subject to the expected for/aft pitching and sharp vertical bounce expected in a light live-axle small car. Braking effort needs better front/rear proportioning; rear end can hop in hard, anchors-out stops. Like most cars in this size group, Corolla has limited rear seat room for adults. Front seat room is adequate without being particularly generous. Seat comfort not a strong point. Sedans lack fold-down back seat, but most other models have it. Simple, sturdy drivetrain is easy to work on. Not amply endowed with standard features or plush materials except for the SR-5s, but very good workmanship is a Toyota hallmark. This year's new ohc engine may prove to be smoother and more refined than the somewhat growly 1.8 it replaces, and should return similar fuel economy (our last Corolla sipped gas at the miserly rate of 29 mpg overall). Verdict: a safe bet for reliability and mileage, and fine value despite its conventional engineering.

EVALUATION CHECKLIST

Fuel economy	4	Cargo room	3
Driveability	3	Serviceability	4
Acceleration	3	Standard equipment	4
Braking	3	Body construction	4
Handling/roadholding	4	Paint/exterior finish	4
Driving position	4	Interior finish	3
Instruments/control	4	TOTAL POINTS	71
Visiblity	5		
Heating/ventilation	4		

RATING SCALE

Seat comfort	3	5 = Excellent
Passenger room	3	4 = Very Good
Ride	3	3 = Average/Acceptable
Noise	3	2 = Fair
Exit/entry	3	1 = Poor

SPECIFI-CATIONS	2-door hardtop	3-door Sport Coupe	3-door Lftbk.	2/4-door sedan	5-door wagon
Wheelbase (in.)	94.5	94.5	94.5	94.5	94.5
Overall length (in.)	168.3	168.3	168.3	166.3	168.9
Overall width (in.)	64.0	64.0	64.0	63.4	63.4
Overall height (in.)	50.8	50.8	50.8	53.0	53.0
Track front	52.8	52.8	52.8	52.1	52.1
Track rear (in.)	53.0	53.0	53.0	52.4	52.4
Curb weight (lbs.)	2178	NA	NA	2166	NA
Max. cargo vol. (cu. ft.)	9.5	11.3/ 24.5	11.5/ 24.6	10.7	19.4 55.6
Fuel tank capacity (gal.)	13.2	13.2	13.2	13.2	13.2
Seating capacity	4	4	4	5	5
Front head-room (in.)[1]	36.7	36.7	36.6	37.8	37.4
Front shoulder room (in.)	51.5	51.5	51.5	51.8	51.8
Front legroom, max. (in.)	41.6	41.6	41.6	42.1	42.1
Rear head-room (in.)	35.7	35.0	35.7	36.6	35.9
Rear shoulder room (in.)	50.2	50.0	50.2	51.7	51.9
Rear legroom, min. (in.)	29.7	29.7	29.7	30.8	30.0

1: without sunroof

BODY/CHASSIS

Drivetrain layout: longitudinal front engine/rear-wheel drive.
Suspension front: independent, MacPherson struts, lower

lateral arms, offset coil springs, telescopic shock absorbers, anti-roll bar. **Suspension rear:** rigid axle, four trailing links, Panhard rod, coil springs (leaf springs on wagon), anti-roll bar on SR5 hardtop and Sport Coupe. **Steering:** recirculating ball. **Turns lock-to-lock:** 3.8. **Turn diameter (ft.):** 33.5. **Brakes front:** 8.9-in. discs. **Brakes rear:** 9.0-in. drums. **Construction:** unit

POWERTRAINS

	ohc I-4
Bore × stroke (in.)	3.94× 3.03
Displacement (liters/cu. in.)	1.6/ 97
Compression ratio	9.0:1
Fuel delivery	2bbl.
Net bhp @ rpm	70@ 4800
Net torque @ rpm (lbs/ft)	85@ 2800
Availability	S/All
Final drive ratios	
4-speed manual	3.31:1
5-speed OD manual	3.58:1
3-speed automatic	3.73:1
4-speed OD automatic	3.91:1

KEY bbl. = barrel (carburetor); **bhp** = brake horsepower (advertised); **Cal.** = California only. **Fed.** = Federal/49 state; **FI** = fuel injectoin; **ohv** = overhead valve; **ohc** = overhead cam; **I** = inline engine; **V** = V engine; **D** = diesel; **T** = turbocharged; **OD** = overdrive transmission; **S** = standard engine; **O** = optional engine.

PRICES

TOYOTA COROLLA	Retail Price	Dealer Cost	Low Price
Standard 2-door sedan, 4-speed	$5448	$4713	$5213
Deluxe 2-door sedan, 5-speed	6018	5175	5675
Deluxe 2-door sedan, automatic	6318	5433	5933
Deluxe 4-door sedan, 5-speed	6138	5279	5779

Prices are accurate at time of printing; subject to manufacturer's change

	Retail Price	Dealer Cost	Low Price
Deluxe 4-door sedan, automatic	6438	5537	6037
Deluxe 3-door Liftback coupe, automatic . .	6718	5777	6177
Deluxe 5-door wagon, 5-speed	6508	5597	6097
Deluxe 5-door wagon, automatic	6808	5855	6355
SR5 2-door hardtop, 5-speed	7248	6212	6712
SR5 2-door hardtop, automatic	7688	6589	7089
SR5 3-door sport coupe, 5-speed	7308	6263	6763
SR5 3-door Liftback coupe, 5-speed	7208	6177	6677

STANDARD EQUIPMENT (included in above prices):

1.8-liter (108-cid) 4-cylinder engine, transmission as above, power brakes.
Deluxe adds: reclining front bucket seats, trip odometer, mist-cycle wipers, full carpeting, electric rear-window defroster, bodyside protection moldings, digital quartz clock, tinted glass, flip-out rear side windows (2-door sedan), fold-down rear seat (wagon) with split back on Liftback, remote hatch release (Liftback), swivelling radio mount (Liftback/Hardtop). **SR5** adds: full instrumentation with tachometer, intermittent wipers, AM/FM stereo radio, rear deck cargo cover (except hardtop).

OPTIONAL EQUIPMENT:

Air conditioning	$610	$488	$494
Electric rear-window defroster, Standard . .	70	58	59
Cold-weather kit (NA std. 2-door)	50	43	44
High-altitude/cold-weather kit (ex. Standard)	70	63	64
Cold-weather kit and rear-window defroster, Standard only	85	73	74
Flip-up sunroof, ...	285	228	231
Power steering.	185	158	160
Cloth upholstery	30	25	26
Woodgrain package, wagon	240	206	209
Rear-window wiper/washer	90	74	75
AM/FM stereo radio	250	150	152
AM/FM stereo radio w/cassette, SR5 exc. hardtop.	140	98	100
AM/FM stereo radio w/cassette and 4 speakers, SR5 hardtop	170	119	121
Black package, SR5s	985	776	784
Two-tone paint.	130	104	106
Sport package	540	432	437
Electric rear-window defroster.	80	66	67
Black sport package, SR-5 5-speed hardtop only.	1250	988	998
Black sport package, SR5 5-speed sport coupe only.	1340	1062	1073

Prices are accurate at time of printing; subject to manufacturer's change

Toyota Cressida

Toyota Cressida 4-door sedan

WHAT'S NEW FOR '83

Toyota's luxury liner gets its most extensive changes since
the current design appeared two years ago. The Cressida
now adopts the twin-cam cylinder head from the Celica
Supra for its 2.8-liter inline six. This bumps rated horsepower
from 116 bhp on last year's single-cam engine to 143 bhp.
Also shared with this year's Supra is microprocessor control
for the electronic fuel injection system. There's a choice of
transmissions for the first time, either the 4-speed overdrive
automatic from '82 or a 5-speed overdrive manual. The latter
also comes from the Supra, and pulls a standard limited-slip
differential. The automatic, which is standard on the wagon,
is now called ECT for electronically controlled transmission.
This denotes three driving modes—performance, economy,
and normal—from which the driver can select depending on
conditions. Sedan models now get the same independent
rear suspension introduced on the '82 Supra, plus rear disc
brakes. The wagon retains its four-link live axle arrangement,
but gets a larger-diameter anti-roll bar. Styling changes
consist of a modestly altered grille and taillamps plus semi-
concealed wipers. Inside, the front bucket seats have been
reshaped to open up more rear kneeroom, according to
Toyota. Supra's optional digital instrumentation is now available for Cressida, too, as is a new "Black Package" that
includes the manual transmission and leather upholstery.

EVALUATION

Toyota's answer to the Datsun Maxima. Both represent the Japanese concept of a conventionally engineered luxury car equipped for U.S. customers. Size pits Cressida against U.S. compact/mid-size models, yet the Toyota is heavier and has decidedly inferior fuel economy. Usable rear seat space comparable to that of GM's G-body cars or the new Ford LTD/Mercury Marquis, but headroom is restricted for taller adults front and back. Smooth straight six and unobtrusive automatic transmission plus well-sealed cabin make for very relaxed running. Ride is soft but floaty over crests, handling soggy in tight low-speed turns. In fact, the Cressida ranks a notch below the not-too-inspired Maxima when it comes to roadability. Sumptuous cabin appointments matched by thorough attention to detail assembly. Driving position and outward vision okay. Dash design more restrained than Maxima's, and trunk space is better, too. Underhood layout is tidy, but complexities of injection and emissions plumbing will deter home mechanics. Not unreasonably priced considering all the standard features but you can get similar equipment and the same room for less money elsewhere. Viewpoint: lacks the verve of an Audi, but has appeal for those interested in luxury on a smaller scale. Twin-cam engine, independent rear end, and new manual gearbox may give the '83 a more sporting flavor, though. We look forward to trying it.

EVALUATION CHECKLIST

Fuel economy	3	Cargo room	3
Driveability	4	Serviceability	3
Acceleration	3	Standard equipment	5
Braking	3	Body construction	5
Handling/roadholding	3	Paint/exterior finish	5
Driving position	3	Interior finish	5
Instruments/control	4	TOTAL POINTS	76
Visiblity	4		
Heating/ventilation	4	**RATING SCALE**	
Seat comfort	4	5 = Excellent	
Passenger room	3	4 = Very Good	
Ride	4	3 = Average/Acceptable	
Noise	4	2 = Fair	
Exit/entry	4	1 = Poor	

SPECIFICATIONS

	4-door sedan	5-door wagon
Wheelbase (in.)	104.1	104.1
Overall length (in.)	186.2	186.6
Overall width (in.)	66.5	66.5
Overall height (in.)	54.3	55.5
Track front (in.)	54.7	54.7
Track rear (in.)	54.9	54.5
Curb weight (lbs.)	3020[1]	3007[1]
Max. cargo vol. (cu. ft.)	12.4	37.3/ 67.3
Fuel tank capacity (gal.)	17.2	17.2
Seating capacity	5	5
Front headroom (in.)	38.3	37.9
Front shoulder room (in.)	NA	NA
Front legroom, max. (in.)	42.7	42.7
Rear headroom (in.)	39.4	37.6
Rear shoulder room (in.)	NA	NA
Rear legroom, min. (in.)	32	31.1

1: with 4-speed overdrive automatic transmission

BODY/CHASSIS

Drivetrain layout: longitudinal front engine/rear-wheel drive. **Suspension front:** independent, MacPherson struts, offset coil springs, lower control arms, telescopic shock absorbers, anti-roll bar. **Suspension rear:** independent, semi-trailing arms, coil springs, telescopic shock absorbers, anti-roll bar (sedan); rigid axle, four trailing links, Panhard rod, coil springs, telescopic shock absorbers. **Steering:** recirculating ball, power-assisted. **Turns lock-to-lock:** 3.3. **Turn diameter (ft.):** 38.1. **Brakes front:** 10.4-in. discs. **Brakes rear:** 10.0-in. discs sedan, 9.0-in. drums wagon. **Construction:** unit

POWERTRAINS

	ohc I-6
Bore × stroke (in.)	3.27× 3.27
Displacement (liters/cu. in.)	2.8/ 168
Compression ratio	8.8:1
Fuel delivery	FI
Net bhp @ rpm	143@ 5200
Net torque @ rpm (lbs/ft)	154@ 4400
Availability	S/All
Final drive ratios	
5-speed OD manual	3.73:1
4-speed OD automatic	4.10:1[1]

1: std. wagon

KEY bbl. = barrel (carburetor); **bhp** = brake horsepower (advertised); **Cal.** = California only. **Fed.** = Federal/49 state; **FI** = fuel injecton; **ohv** = overhead valve; **ohc** = overhead cam; **I** = inline engine; **V** = V engine; **D** = diesel; **T** = turbocharged; **OD** = overdrive transmission; **S** = standard engine; **O** = optional engine.

PRICES

TOYOTA CRESSIDA	Retail Price	Dealer Cost	Low Price
4-door sedan, 5-speed	$13169	$10799	$11999
4-door sedan, automatic	13569	11127	12327
5-door wagon, automatic	13729	11258	12458

STANDARD EQUIPMENT (included in above prices): 2.8-liter (168-cid) 6-cylinder engine w/electronic fuel injection, 5-speed overdrive manual or 4-speed overdrive automatic transmission as above, power steering, power brakes, cruise control, auto-temp. air conditioning, rear-window defroster, AM/FM stereo radio w/power antenna, intermittent wipers, cruise control, aluminum-alloy wheels, tinted glass, power door locks and windows, halogen high-beam headlamps, velour upholstery.

OPTIONAL EQUIPMENT	Retail Price	Dealer Cost	Low Price
Power sunroof	$460	$368	$372

Prices are accurate at time of printing; subject to manufacturer's change

	Retail Price	Dealer Cost	Low Price
Cassette player and amp/equalizer	440	308	312
Leather package	480	384	388
Two-tone paint package	220	176	178
Digital display & trip computer	470	376	380
Black package	550	428	433

Toyota Starlet

Toyota Starlet 3-door sedan

WHAT'S NEW FOR '83

The emphasis is on greater fuel efficiency in this year's edition of the littlest Toyota. The rear-drive Starlet was the EPA fuel economy champ in its debut year of 1981, but was beaten by the Honda Civic FE and the Dodge/Plymouth Colt among '82s. For 1983, Toyota re-profiles the Starlet's nose and front fenders for a claimed reduction in fuel-wasting aerodynamic drag. Also new is electronic fuel injection with microprocessor control for the 1.3-liter four-cylinder engine. In what would seem to be a retrograde move, the 5-speed overdrive manual gearbox previously specified has been made an option on all but California cars. Replacing it is a 4-speed manual. With either gearbox there's a taller 2.93:1 final drive versus 3.15:1 last year, presumably for fewer engine revs at highway speeds. Toyota also claims improved acceleration and torque in second and third gears for the 4-speed Starlet. Other alterations are a deeper rear hatch door for easier access to the cargo bay compared with the previous lift-up back window, and cloth seat inserts and

Prices are accurate at time of printing; subject to manufacturer's change

cargo area carpeting are added as standard. The 4-speed model with optional air conditioning comes with an extra "Economy" setting that cycles the compressor for a shorter time span, another gas-saving measure.

EVALUATION

We may have fewer criticisms of the Starlet now that Toyota has addressed some of the shortcomings in its three-quarter-scale Chevette. In particular, the interior should be less stark and plasticky, cargo access easier with the deeper back door, and performance perhaps better than before. As for the rest of it, this will remain primarily a high-mileage commuter car, a role it fills admirably well. Our overall mpg for a 60/40 mix of hard city/highway driving worked out to 36 mpg, and a spot check showed a phenomenal 52 on the highway. Small and light, so maneuverability is as you'd expect. Nips in and out of tight spots with ease, aided by pleasantly direct steering and clear outward vision. Despite a simple suspension and rear drive, handling is agile, and panic braking causes no unwanted rear-axle hop. Ride is not so hot, a function of the fairly stiff springing and petite 90.6-inch wheelbase. Rear drive isn't the best way to make use of available interior space within a given package size, and the cabin is indeed cramped. Toyota's usual top-notch construction quality combined with engineering simplicity imply troublefree service over many years.

EVALUATION CHECKLIST

Fuel economy	5	Cargo room	2
Driveability	4	Serviceability	4
Acceleration	3	Standard equipment	3
Braking	5	Body construction	4
Handling/roadholding	4	Paint/exterior finish	4
Driving position	3	Interior finish	4
Instruments/control	3	TOTAL POINTS	69
Visiblity	4		
Heating/ventilation	4	**RATING SCALE**	
Seat comfort	2	5 = Excellent	
Passenger room	2	4 = Very Good	
Ride	3	3 = Average/Acceptable	
Noise	3	2 = Fair	
Exit/entry	3	1 = Poor	

SPECIFICATIONS

	3-door sedan
Wheelbase (in.)	90.6
Overall length (in.)	153.5
Overall width (in.)	60.0
Overall height (in.)	54.3
Track front (in.)	50.8
Track rear (in.)	50.2
Curb weight (lbs.)	1755
Max. cargo vol. (cu. ft.)	6.0/23.7
Fuel tank capacity (gal.)	10.6
Seating capacity	4
Front headroom (in.)	37.3
Front shoulder room (in.)	50.0
Front legroom, max. (in.)	40.9
Rear headroom (in.)	36.0
Rear shoulder room (in.)	49.5
Rear legroom, min. (in.)	29.1

BODY/CHASSIS

Drivetrain layout: longitudinal front engine/rear-wheel drive. **Suspension front:** independent, MacPherson struts, lower A-arms, offset coil springs, telescopic shock absorbers, integral anti-roll bar. **Suspension rear:** rigid axle, four trailing links, lower control arms, coil springs, telescopic shock absorbers. **Steering:** rack-and-pinion. **Turns lock-to-lock:** 3.1. **Turn diameter (ft.):** 30.2. **Brakes front:** 8.9-in. discs. **Brakes rear:** 7.9-in. drums. **Construction:** unit

POWERTRAINS

	ohv I-4
Bore × stroke (in.)	2.95×2.87

POWERTRAINS

	ohv I-4
Displacement (liters/cu. in.)	1.3/ 79
Compression ratio	9.5:1
Fuel delivery	FI
Net bhp @ rpm	58@ 4200
Net torque @ rpm (lbs/ft)	74@ 3400
Availability	S/All
Final drive ratios	
4-speed manual	2.93:1
5-speed OD manual[1]	2.93:1

1: limited availability; Fed. only

KEY bbl. = barrel (carburetor); **bhp** = brake horsepower (advertised); **Cal.** = California only. **Fed.** = Federal/49 state; **FI** = fuel injection; **ohv** = overhead valve; **ohc** = overhead cam; **I** = inline engine; **V** = V engine; **D** = diesel; **T** = turbocharged; **OD** = overdrive transmission; **S** = standard engine; **O** = optional engine.

PRICES

	Retail Price	Dealer Cost	Low Price
TOYOTA STARLET			
3-door sedan, 4-speed	$5798	$4986	$5286
3-door sedan, 5-speed	5838	5021	5371

STANDARD EQUIPMENT (included in above prices):

1.3-liter (79-cid) 4-cylinder engine, 5-speed overdrive manual transmission, power brakes, styled-steel wheels, full carpeting, fold-down rear seatback, reclining front bucket seats, electric rear-window defroster, tinted glass, tachometer, flip-out rear-quarter windows, locking fuel-filler door, cigarette lighter, trip odometer, mist-cycle wipers, day/night rearview mirror.

OPTIONAL EQUIPMENT:

Air conditioning	$580	$469	$475
Cold-weather kit	50	43	44
AM/FM stereo radio	250	150	152
AM/FM stereo radio w/cassette	375	238	241
Rear-window wiper/washer	90	74	75

Prices are accurate at time of printing; subject to manufacturer's change

Toyota Tercel

Toyota Tercel SR-5 3-door sedan

WHAT'S NEW FOR '83

Virtually all-new except for running gear, Toyota's front-drive
subcompact is fully restyled, gets a different rear suspension,
and picks up additional comfort and convenience features.
No longer bearing the Corolla name, the '83 Tercel line also
includes a new 4wd 5-door wagon. All front-drive models are
now hatchback sedans, offered as a 3-door in base, Deluxe,
or sporty SR-5 guise as well as a Deluxe 5-door. Styling is
more angular and modern, if boxy in the econocar fashion.
Despite a 2.7-inch shorter wheelbase, the new Tercel is
claimed to provide more interior space, due partly to a more
compact rear suspension system. This consists of MacPherson struts and twin lower links with offset conical coil springs.
The front MacPherson-strut suspension is as before, but
there's a 2.1-inch increase in track, and the rack-and-pinion
steering has been modified to give a three-foot tighter turning
circle. Powertrains are a repeat, except that the optional
3-speed automatic now incorporates an overdrive top gear.
New optional items include twin remote control door mirrors,
four-way tilt front seats, digital clock, variable-assist power
steering, and sliding steel sunroof. The 4wd wagon uses the
1.5-liter Tercel engine hooked to a 6-speed manual gearbox
with an ultra-low bottom ratio for use in 4wd. This obviates
the need for a separate transfer case. In the 2wd mode, the
gearbox functions like a normal 5-speed. The wagon has its
own four-link live-axle rear suspension and distinctive high-
built body design.

EVALUATION

We haven't driven any of the new Tercels yet, so we'll wait until we can before drawing any firm conclusions. The previous Tercel sold well here despite dumpy styling. The 4wd wagon looks interesting, and provides the first direct competition for Subaru in the pint-size off-road market. It's in a strong position for sure, given Toyota's enviable and long-standing overall repair record and huge dealer network. We look forward to testing both front- and all-wheel-drive Tercels soon.

EVALUATION CHECKLIST

New or substantially changed model, and not available for assessment at time of publication.

SPECIFICATIONS	3-door sedan	5-door sedan	5-door wagon
Wheelbase (in.)	95.7	95.7	95.7
Overall length (in.)	158.7	158.7	169.7
Overall width (in.)	63.6	63.6	63.6
Overall height (in.)	54.5	54.5	59.1
Track front (in.)	54.5	54.5	54.3
Track rear (in.)	53.9	53.9	53.1
Curb weight (lbs.)	1985[1]	1985[1]	2230[1]
Fuel tank capacity (gal.)	11.9	11.9	13.2
Seating capacity	5	5	5
Front headroom (in.)	38.1	38.1	40.2
Front legroom, max. (in.)	42.1	42.1	42.1
Rear headroom (in.)	37.1	37.1	39.4
Rear legroom, min. (in.)	31.8	31.8	33.9

1: Base model

BODY/CHASSIS

Drivetrain layout: longitudinal front engine/front-wheel drive (4WD on wagon). **Suspension front:** independent, Macherson struts, offset coil springs, integral anti-roll bar, telescopic shock absorbers, **Suspension rear:** independent, MacPherson struts, double lower lateral links, offset coil springs, telescopic shock absorbers. Wagon has rigid axle, four trailing links, coil springs, telescopic shock absorbers, anti-roll bar **Steering:** rack-and-pinion. **Turns lock-to-lock:** NA. **Turn diameter (ft.):** NA. **Brakes front:** discs. **Brakes rear:** drums. **Construction:** unit

POWERTRAINS

	ohc I-4
Bore × stroke (in.)	3.05× 3.03
Displacement (liters/cu. in.)	1.5/ 88
Compression ratio	9.0:1
Fuel delivery	2bb1.
Net bhp @ rpm	62@ 4800
Net torque @ rpm (lbs/ft)	76@ 2800
Availability	S/All
Final drive ratios	
4-speed manual	3.15:1
5-speed OD manual	3.58:1
6-speed OD manual	3.73:1¹
3-speed automatic	3.58:1

1: 4WD wagon only

KEY bbl. = barrel (carburetor); **bhp** = brake horsepower (advertised); **Cal.** = California only. **Fed.** = Federal/49 state; **FI** = fuel injectoin; **ohv** = overhead valve; **ohc** = overhead cam; **I** = inline engine; **V** = V engine; **D** = diesel; **T** = turbocharged; **OD** = overdrive transmission; **S** = standard engine; **O** = optional engine.

PRICES

TOYOTA TERCEL	Retail Price	Dealer Cost	Low Price
Standard 3-door sedan, 4-speed	$4998	$4573	$4873
Deluxe 3-door sedan, 5-speed	5898	5072	5422

Prices are accurate at time of printing; subject to manufacturer's change

	Retail Price	Dealer Cost	Low Price
Deluxe 3-door sedan, automatic	6198	5330	5680
Deluxe 5-door sedan, 5-speed	6058	5210	5560
Deluxe 5-door sedan, automatic	6358	5468	5818
SR5 3-door sedan, 5-speed	6618	5672	6072
Deluxe 4WD 5-door wagon, 6-speed.	7398	6288	6788
SR5 4WD 5-door wagon, 6-speed	8148	6885	7385

STANDARD EQUIPMENT (included in above prices):

1.5-liter (89-cid) four-cylinder engine, transmission as above, split fold-down rear seatback, dual-access cargo area cover, reclining front bucket seats, vinyl upholstery and interior trim, full carpeting (except Standard 2-door). **SR-5 sedan** adds: cloth upholstery, dual remote-control door mirrors, AM/FM stereo radio w/4 speakers, 4-way tilt front seats, digital clock, tachometer, wide bodyside moldings, upgraded wheels and tires. **4wd wagon** adds: 4-wheel-drive. **SR-5 4wd wagon** adds: multi-adjustable contour front seats, molded two-tone door panels, inclinometer gauge.

OPTIONAL EQUIPMENT:

Cargo area cover	40	33	34
AM/FM stereo radio w/cassette tape			
Deluxe	375	238	242
SR5.	140	98	99
AM/FM stereo radio, Deluxe 4WD	280	168	170
Air conditioning	580	469	474
Rear window wiper/washer	90	74	75
Electric sunroof	460	368	372
Black package	1005	799	817
Power steering.	185	158	160
Cloth upholstery (std. SR5)	30	25	26
Tire package	120	96	97
Two-tone paint.	150	120	122

Volkswagen Quantum

WHAT'S NEW FOR '83

After getting off to a late start for the 1982 model year, Volkswagen's successor to the old Dasher at the top of its lineup is predictably little changed this year. However, there will be two extra engine choices for the front-drive Quantum in '83. One is a four-cylinder turbocharged diesel based on the familiar 1.6-liter normally aspirated unit used in the smaller Rabbit/Jetta. Coming later on is a 2.2-liter fuel-

Prices are accurate at time of printing; subject to manufacturer's change

Volkswagen Quantum GL 4-door sedan

injected inline five, basically the unit used in the base Audi
5000. Returning as base equipment for the 4-door sedan,
3-door fastback coupe and 5-door wagon is VW's fuel-
injected 1.7-liter gasoline four. Standard gearbox remains a
5-speed overdrive manual, and 3-speed automatic is optional
with both engines. The automatic used with the turbodiesel is
VW/Audi's recently introduced "E-Mode" transmission. This
features a special "economy" position in which drive from the
engine is disconnected whenever the accelerator pedal is
released. The purpose of this is to cut mechanical drag that
brings down fuel economy.

EVALUATION

Tested by us in 3-door coupe form, the Quantum impresses
with its eager character, roomy interior, and high degree of
ride comfort. The standard power steering gives quick direc-
tional response, though both road feel and self-centering
could be better. Cornering is stable and predictable, spoiled
only by a little more body roll than we prefer. Ride is a little
floaty over large humpback ridges, but is otherwise well-
damped and absorbent. Unhappily, Quantum driving was
spoiled on our test car by notchy shift action and annoying
cold-start stumble and stutter. Acceleration with manual shift
wasn't spectacular (13.5 seconds in our 0–60 mph runs), and
our mileage result was suspiciously low (17.6 mpg versus a
28-mpg EPA city rating). The interior will seat four adults in
comfort, five with a bit of squeezing. Seats are well-shaped,
not too hard, and are covered in a nice tweedy cloth. Pedals,
steering wheel and shifter are properly spaced and minor
switches handy, but the temperature and fuel gauges are
small and difficult to read; nighttime dash illumination needs
to be stronger. VW's upshift reminder light is a laudable idea

for more economical driving habits, though it may annoy some. Solid construction and generally tidy fit and finish, though interior materials are sturdy rather than plush. Coupe offers hatchback convenience, low load sill, and fine cargo room. Wagon is even better. The notchback sedan also scores well for trunk space. Bottom line: Well-rounded, roomy, practical, and fun to drive, but rather expensive, especially compared with most Japanese rivals.

EVALUATION CHECKLIST

Fuel economy	3	Cargo room	4
Driveability	3	Serviceability	3
Acceleration	3	Standard equipment	3
Braking	4	Body construction	4
Handling/roadholding	4	Paint/exterior finish	4
Driving position	4	Interior finish	4
Instruments/control	3	TOTAL POINTS	72
Visiblity	4		
Heating/ventilation	4	**RATING SCALE**	
Seat comfort	4	5 = Excellent	
Passenger room	4	4 = Very Good	
Ride	4	3 = Average/Acceptable	
Noise	3	2 = Fair	
Exit/entry	3	1 = Poor	

SPECIFICATIONS

	3-door coupe	4-door sedan	5-door wagon
Wheelbase (in.)	100.4	100.4	100.4
Overall length (in.)	178.2	180.2	183.1
Overall width (in.)	66.9	66.9	66.9
Overall height (in.)	55.1	55.1	55.1
Track front (in.)	55.7	55.7	55.7
Track rear (in.)	56.0	56.0	56.0
Curb weight (lbs.)	2469	2513	2535
Max. cargo vol. (cu. ft.)	20.7	12.0	38.5/64.7
Fuel tank capacity (gal.)	15.8	15.8	15.8
Seating capacity	5	5	5

SPECIFICATIONS

	3-door coupe	4-door sedan	5-door wagon
Front headroom (in.)	38.2	38.1	38.1
Front shoulder room (in.)	53.5	53.5	53.5
Front legroom, max. (in.)	42.3	42.3	42.3
Rear headroom (in.)	37.4	37.6	37.8
Rear shoulder room (in.)	54.1	54.3	54.3
Rear legroom, min. (in.)	32.6	32.8	32.6

BODY/CHASSIS

Drivetrain layout: longitudinal front engine/front-wheel drive. **Suspension front:** independent, MacPherson struts, lower A-arms, coil springs, telescopic shock absorbers, anti-roll bar. **Suspension rear:** beam twist axle with anti-roll function, coil springs, telescopic shock absorbers. **Steering:** rack-and-pinion, power-assisted. **Turns lock-to-lock:** 3.4. **Turn diameter (ft.):** 31.5. **Brakes front:** 9.4-in. discs. **Brakes rear:** 7.9-in. drums. **Construction:** unit

POWERTRAINS

	ohc I-4	ohc I-4TD
Bore × stroke (in.)	3.13× 3.40	3.01× 3.40
Displacement (liters/cu. in.)	1.7/ 105	1.6/ 97
Compression ratio	8.2:1	23.0:1
Fuel delivery	FI	FI
Net bhp @ rpm	74@ 5000	52@ 4800
Net torque @ rpm (lbs/ft)	89@ 3000	72@ 2000
Availability	S/All	O/All
Final drive ratios		
5-speed OD manual	4.11.1	4.11:1
3-speed automatic	3.73:1	NA

KEY bbl. = barrel (carburetor); bhp = brake horsepower (advertised); Cal. = California only. Fed. = Federal/49 state; FI = fuel injectoin; ohv = overhead valve; ohc = overhead cam; I = inline engine; V = V engine; D = diesel; T = turbocharged; OD = overdrive transmission; S = standard engine; O = optional engine.

PRICES

VOLKSWAGEN QUANTUM	Retail Price	Dealer Cost	Low Price
(1982 prices shown; 1983 prices not available at time of publication)			
3-door coupe, 5-speed	$10,250	$8794	$9694
3-door coupe, automatic	10,655	9149	9949
GL 3-door coupe, 5-speed	11000	9435	10335
GL 3-door coupe, automatic	11405	9790	10690
4-door sedan, 5-speed	10550	9049	9849
4-door sedan, automatic	10955	9404	10204
GL 4-door sedan, 5-speed	11350	9733	10733
GL 4-door sedan, automatic	11755	9888	10888
5-door wagon, 5-speed	10950	9393	10293
5-door wagon, automatic	11355	9748	10748
GL 5-door wagon, 5-speed	11750	10077	11077
GL 5-door wagon, automatic	12155	10432	11432

Note: Prices shown do not include $270 destination charge.

STANDARD EQUIPMENT (included in above prices):

1.7-liter (105-cid) fuel-injected 4-cylinder engine, 5-speed overdrive manual or 3-speed automatic transmission as above, full carpeting, quartz clock, electric rear window defroster, front bucket seats w/reclining backrests, tinted glass, halogen headlamps, dual remote-control door mirrors, visor vanity mirror, lockable fuel filler cap, bodyside protection moldings, padded steering wheel, light-alloy wheels, trip odometer. **GL** adds: cruise control, power door locks, adjustable rear headrests, dual electric remote-control door mirrors, illuminated visor vanity mirror, power windows.

OPTIONAL EQUIPMENT :

Air conditioning	$690	$552	$558
Cruise control delete, GL (credit)	(150)	(126)	(128)
Leatherette interior trim, wagons	70	56	57
Metallic paint	125	105	107
AM/FM stereo radio w/cassette player (incl. 4-speakers & power antenna)	640	512	518
Speakers, antenna, suppression pkg.	275	220	223
Electric sunroof	350	294	297
Alloy wheels (std. GL)	375	300	304

Prices are accurate at time of printing; subject to manufacturer's change

Volkswagen Rabbit & Jetta

Volkswagen Jetta 4-door sedan

WHAT'S NEW FOR '83

Volkswagen is pinning its hopes on a rearranged model lineup and a new engine option to bolster the appeal of its aging front-drive Rabbit, which suffered a near 50-percent drop in sales during the '82 model year. The German-made Jetta, notchback companion to the American-built Rabbit hatchbacks, also gets the new engine, but otherwise stays the same. That engine is a turbocharged derivative of the well-known VW 1.6-liter diesel four, which continues in normally aspirated form as an option for both lines. A new top-line GL series multiplies offerings in the Rabbit hutch. Answering enthusiast calls for a U.S. version of the Golf GTi, the sportiest of the European Rabbits, VW debuts a sporty Rabbit 3-door this year, featuring a 1.8-liter enlargement of the fuel-injected 1.7-liter gasoline four. Standard Rabbit GTi equipment includes close-ratio 5-speed gearbox, wider wheels and tires, beefed-up chassis, black-finish exterior trim, flared wheel wells, sport steering and front seats, special instrumentation, and tuned exhaust system. The base Rabbit L series is now powered by the carbureted VW gas four (not available in California). LS and GL models get the fuel-injected 1.7.

CONSUMER GUIDE®

EVALUATION CHECKLIST
(Jetta Diesel)

Fuel economy	5	Cargo room	4
Driveability	4	Serviceability	4
Acceleration	3	Standard equipment	3
Braking	3	Body construction	4
Handling/roadholding	4	Paint/exterior finish	4
Driving position	3	Interior finish	3
Instruments/control	3	TOTAL POINTS	72
Visiblity	5		
Heating/ventilation	4	**RATING SCALE**	
Seat comfort	3	5 = Excellent	
Passenger room	3	4 = Very Good	
Ride	4	3 = Average/Acceptable	
Noise	3	2 = Fair	
Exit/entry	3	1 = Poor	

EVALUATION

We look forward to driving the new GTi and the turbodiesel models. However, bad publicity about VW engines makes us wonder whether the '83s will be any more reliable than earlier cars. Be advised that excessive oil consumption, oil leaks, and premature valvetrain wear have been documented, something to keep in mind. Apart from that major weakness, both these cars are still good buys, though not the best value for money anymore. Biggest plus points for both Rabbit and Jetta are good interior space utilization (though the back seat is cramped for adults with the front seats all the way back), fine assembly quality, good all-around vision, and nimbleness. The American Rabbits don't handle as well as the German-built ones used to, a point the imported Jetta proves. Earns average marks for noise, though both engines run smoothly. The diesel in particular is clattery at idle and in low-speed driving. Interior decor in lower-priced Rabbits can look cold and uninviting next to the Jetta, and workmanship seems a bit off, too. Sparse instrumentation and slightly awkward sit-up-and-beg driving posture, but mostly comfortable passenger accommodations in both. Ride firm, but jolts only over really big bumps and heaves. Rabbit has hatchback versatility, Jetta has deceptively large trunk. Service access easy as pie with the diesel, okay on gas models. Diesel mileage is astounding: our test Jetta returned an actual 46.8 overall. Performance isn't too good, though. Service can be costly. Once the standard of minicar design, but eclipsed in space and fuel efficiency by some newer competitors. Still recommended, with reservations.

SPECIFICATIONS	Jetta 2-door sedan	Rabbit 3-door sedan	Jetta 4-door sedan	Rabbit 5-door sedan
Wheelbase (in.)	94.5	94.5	94.5	94.5
Overall length (in.)	167.8	155.3	167.8	155.3
Overall width (in.)	63.4	63.4	63.4	63.4
Overall height (in.)	55.5	55.5	55.5	55.5
Track front (in.)	54.7	54.7	54.7	54.7
Track rear (in.)	53.1	53.1	53.1	53.1
Curb weight (lbs.)	2025[1]	1920[1]	2025[1]	1920[1]
Max. cargo vol. (cu. ft.)	13.0	14.0/ 22.6	13.0	14.0/ 22.6
Fuel tank capacity (gal.)	10.6	10.0	10.6	10.0
Seating capacity	4	4	4	4
Front headroom (in.)	37.2	37.2	37.2	37.2
Front shoulder room (in.)	50.9	52.0	50.9	52.0
Front legroom, max. (in.)	38.7	39.7	38.7	39.7
Rear headroom (in.)	36.1	36.1	36.1	36.1
Rear shoulder room (in.)	52.2	52.2	52.2	52.2
Rear legroom, min. (in.)	32.6	32.2	32.6	32.2

1: Base models

BODY/CHASSIS

Drivetrain layout: transverse front engine/front-wheel drive. **Suspension front:** independent, MacPherson struts, lower A-arms, coil springs, telescopic shock absorbers. **Suspension rear:** beam axle, trailing arms, coil springs, telescopic shock absorbers; anti-roll bar on Jetta. **Steering:** rack-and-pinion. **Turns lock-to-lock:** 3.9. **Turn diameter (ft.):** 31.2. **Brakes front:** 9.4-in. discs. **Brakes rear:** 7.1-in. drums. **Construction:** unit

POWERTRAINS	ohc I-4	ohc I-4	ohc I-4	ohc I-4D	ohc I-4TD
Bore × stroke (in.)	3.13× 3.40	3.13× 3.40	3.19× 3.40	3.01× 3.40	3.01× 3.40
Displacement (liters/cu. in.)	1.7/ 105	1.7/ 105	1.8/ 110	1.6/ 97	1.6 97
Compression ratio	8.2:1	8.2:1	8.5:1	23.0:1	23.0:1
Fuel delivery	2bbl.	FI	FI	FI	FI
Net bhp @ rpm	NA	74@ 5000	90@ 5000	52@ 4800	68@ 4500
Net torque @ rpm (lbs/ft)	NA	90@ 3000	100@ 3000	72@ 2000	98@ 3000
Availability	S/Fed.	O/Fed[1]	S/All[2]	O/All[3]	O/All[3]

1: Std. Cal. Rabbit; Std. all for Jetta
2: Rabbit GTi only
3: NA Jetta

Final drive ratios

4-speed OD manual	3.89:1	3.89:1			
5-speed OD manual	3.89:1	3.89:1	3.94:1	4.11:1	4.11:1
3-speed automatic	3.56:1	3.56:1			

KEY bbl. = barrel (carburetor); **bhp** = brake horsepower (advertised); **Cal.** = California only. **Fed.** = Federal/49 state; **FI** = fuel injection; **ohv** = overhead valve; **ohc** = overhead cam; **I** = inline engine; **V** = V engine; **D** = diesel; **T** = turbocharged; **OD** = overdrive transmission; **S** = standard engine; **O** = optional engine.

PRICES

VOLKSWAGEN RABBIT & JETTA	Retail Price	Dealer Cost	Low Price

(1982 prices shown; 1983 prices not available at time of publication).

RABBIT

3-door sedan, 4-speed	$5990	$5541	$5941
L 3-door sedan, 4-speed	6615	5719	6119
L 3-door sedan, 5-speed	6820	5891	6291
L 3-door sedan, automatic	6995	6054	6554
L 3-door sedan, 4-speed (carburetor)	6390	5528	5928
L Diesel 3-door sedan, 4-speed	7140	6165	6665

Prices are accurate at time of printing; subject to manufacturer's change

	Retail Price	Dealer Cost	Low Price
L Diesel 3-door sedan, 5-speed	7345	6337	6837
L Diesel 3-door sedan, automatic	7610	6590	7090
LS 3-door sedan, 4-speed	7065	6035	6535
LS 3-door sedan, 5-speed	7270	6207	6707
LS 3-door sedan, automatic	7590	6481	6981
LS Diesel 3-door sedan, 4-speed	7590	6481	6981
LS Diesel 3-door sedan, 5-speed	7795	6653	7153
LS Diesel 3-door sedan, automatic	8060	6906	7406
L 5-door sedan, 4-speed	6825	5900	6300
L 5-door sedan, 5-speed	7030	6072	6572
L 5-door sedan, automatic	7205	6235	6735
L 5-door sedan, 4-speed (carburetor)	6600	5709	6109
L Diesel 5-door sedan, 4-speed	7350	6346	6846
L Diesel 5-door sedan, 5-speed	7555	6518	7018
L Diesel 5-door sedan, automatic	7820	6771	7271
LS 5-door sedan, 4-speed	7275	6216	6716
LS 5-door sedan, 5-speed	7480	6338	6838
LS 5-door sedan, automatic	7655	6551	7051
LS Diesel 5-door sedan, 4-speed	7800	6662	7162
LS Diesel 5-door sedan, 5-speed	8005	6834	7334
LS Diesel 5-door sedan, automatic	8270	7087	7687
2-door convertible, 5-speed	10595	9195	9995
2-door convertible, automatic	11000	9550	10350

JETTA

	Retail Price	Dealer Cost	Low Price
2-door sedan, 5-speed	8375	7233	7833
2-door sedan, automatic	8780	7588	8388
Diesel 2-door sedan, 5-speed	9020	7781	8581
Diesel 2-door sedan, automatic	9515	8226	9026
4-door sedan, 5-speed	8595	7420	8020
4-door sedan, automatic	9000	7775	8575
Diesel 4-door sedan, 5-speed	9240	7968	8768
Diesel 4-door sedan, automatic	9735	8413	9213

STANDARD EQUIPMENT (included in above prices):

Rabbit has 1.7-liter (105-cid) 4-cylinder engine with carburetor or fuel injection (Diesel models have 1.6-liter, 98-cid 4-cylinder diesel engine), 4-speed or 5-speed overdrive manual or 3-speed automatic transmission as above, power brakes. **L** adds: bright exterior moldings, reclining front seats, fold-down rear seat, luggage compartment cover, trip odometer, engine coolant gauge, quartz clock, tinted glass bodyside protection moldings. **LS** adds: opening front vent windows, dual remote-control door mirrors, full wheel covers, woodgrain instrument panel applique, cigarette lighter, rear ashtray, intermittent wipers. **S** model adds: red accent striping, blackout exterior moldings, black front spoiler and wheellip flares, upgraded wheels

Prices are accurate at time of printing; subject to manufacturer's change

and tires, full instrumentation including tachometer, sport steering wheel, map pockets, deluxe interior light package. **Convertible** adds: floor console, integral roll bar, passenger vanity mirror, lockable fuel filler cap, dual-tone horn, digital clock, padded steering wheel, carpeted lower door panels. **Jetta** has: 1.7-liter (105-cid) 4-cylinder engine with fuel injection, 5-speed overdrive manual or 3-speed automatic transmission as above, power brakes, electric rear-window defroster, dual remote-control door mirrors, AM/FM stereo radio, intermittent wipers, reclining front bucket seats, quartz clock, trip odometer, lockable fuel filler cap, floor console, tinted glass, woodgrain instrument panel applique, full carpeting, padded steering wheel. **Jetta Diesel** adds: 1.6-liter (98-cid) 4-cylinder diesel engine.

OPTIONAL EQUIPMENT

	Retail Price	Dealer Cost	Low Price
Air conditioning			
Rabbit (exc. base, conv.).	$630	$504	$510
Jetta, Rabbit conv.	690	552	558
65-amp. alternator, Rabbit (exc. conv.) . . .	55	44	45
Custom Value Package, base Rabbit 3-door			
and 5-door L models only	225	180	182
California Emission Control, Rabbit (exc.			
conv)	65	65	65
California warranty, Jetta, Rabbit exc. S . .	285	285	285
Electric rear window defroster, base Rabbit			
3-door only	95	76	77
Tinted glass, base Rabbit 3-door	65	52	53
Engine preheater, Rabbit (exc. conv.)	20	16	17
Heavy-duty cooling system, Rabbit (exc.			
conv., S, base).	75	60	61
Heavy-duty heater, Rabbit (exc. conv.) . . .	70	59	60
Heavy-duty package, Rabbit Diesel models			
only	120	96	97
Floormats, F&R, Rabbit (exc. conv.)	25	20	20
Special instrumentation, Rabbit (NA base,			
std. conv., S).	120	96	97
Leatherette upholstery, Rabbit L & LS. . . .	70	56	57
Metallic paint (exc. base 3-door), Rabbit . .	1250	105	107
Passive restraint system, Rabbit L, Black			
Tie, Jetta (std. LS).	70	59	60
Passive restraint system delete (credit),			
Rabbit LS only	(50)	(43)	(43)
AM/FM radio, Rabbit (exc. base 3-door,			
conv.)	155	80	81
AM/FM stereo radio, Rabbit (exc. conv.,			
base 3-door, std. Jetta).	230	130	132
AM/FM stereo radio w/cassette player,			
Rabbit (exc. conv., base 3-door)	330	205	208
Jetta	525	420	425

Prices are accurate at time of printing; subject to manufacturer's change

	Retail Price	Dealer Cost	Low Price
Dual rear speakers w/balance control (for stereo radios)	60	48	49
Power steering, Rabbit (exc. conv., base)	195	164	166
Sport steering wheel, Convertible (std. Rabbit S)	50	40	41
Sport seats, Convertible (std. Rabbit S) . . .	195	156	158
Manual sunroof, Rabbit (exc. conv., base 3-door)	265	223	226
Jetta	280	235	238
Rear window wiper/washer, Rabbit (exc. conv., base)	115	97	98

Volkswagen Scirocco

Volkswagen Scirocco GL 3-door coupe

WHAT'S NEW FOR '83

Volkswagen's second-generation front-drive sporty coupe debuted last season, and continues unchanged. As before, the Scirocco uses the Rabbit/Jetta chassis and running gear, but has its own special low-slung body. Unlike other VW models, it's not offered with an optional diesel engine.

EVALUATION

A little roomier and softer-riding than its predecessor, but not very practical for more than two because of extremely limited back seat space. Feels quite lively by seat of the pants, an impression enhanced by a sporty exhaust note that proves tiresome on long highway trips. Tire rumble over coarse

Prices are accurate at time of printing; subject to manufacturer's change

pavement is also an aggravation, but wind noise is well-controlled. Our observed mileage worked out to 24.3 mpg, not quite up to the EPA's suggested 28-mpg city rating, but not bad for a sporty coupe. Excessively high steering effort makes parking and close-quarters maneuvering a chore, and visibility through the big hatchback window is cluttered by the rear spoiler and gaudy "Scirocco" decal. Delightful to drive once on the move, however, with lots of handling agility, good traction, and only modest body lean. A vague linkage on our test car hampered fast shifts and made it easy to wrong-slot, especially into or out of fifth. Low-slung driving position will feel cramped for larger persons, and the low build hinders entry/exit. Front headroom is minimal for the tall, though there's ample fore/aft seat travel to accommodate lanky legs. Fine steering wheel/pedals/shifter placement, but nearly vertical wheel can interfere with right leg movement. Ride is firm without being harsh, complemented by properly sprung front seats that locate the body securely in hard cornering. Trunk space is good for a 2+2, but a high liftover makes for back strain when loading heavy cargo. Interior decor is businesslike in the German manner, may be too austere for some. Radio and some minor controls could be more conveniently sited. Decent heat/vent system apart from noisy blower fan. Service access okay, workmanship generally tight and neat. Our view: Outshines rivals like the four-banger Toyota Celica and Datsun 200-SX on the road, but less practical as an all-rounder. A well-made driver's car.

EVALUATION CHECKLIST

Fuel economy	4	Cargo room	3
Driveability	3	Serviceability	3
Acceleration	4	Standard equipment	3
Braking	3	Body construction	4
Handling/roadholding	4	Paint/exterior finish	3
Driving position	4	Interior finish	3
Instruments/control	3	TOTAL POINTS	65
Visiblity	3		
Heating/ventilation	3	**RATING SCALE**	
Seat comfort	3	5 = Excellent	
Passenger room	2	4 = Very Good	
Ride	4	3 = Average/Acceptable	
Noise	3	2 = Fair	
Exit/entry	3	1 = Poor	

SPECIFICATIONS

	3-door coupe
Wheelbase (in.)	94.5
Overall length (in.)	165.7
Overall width (in.)	64.0
Overall height (in.)	51.4
Track front (in.)	54.7
Track rear (in.)	53.5
Curb weight (lbs.)	2159
Max. cargo vol. (cu. ft.)	18.0/ 23.7
Fuel tank capacity (gal.)	10.6
Seating capacity	4
Front headroom (in.)	36.6
Front shoulder room (in.)	53.5
Front legroom, max. (in.)	39.0
Rear headroom (in.)	34.0
Rear shoulder room (in.)	52.8
Rear legroom, min. (in.)	30.3

BODY/CHASSIS

Drivetrain layout: transverse front engine/front-wheel drive. **Suspension front:** independent, MacPherson struts, lower A-arms, coil springs, telescopic shock absorbers, Suspension rear: beam axle with anti-roll function, trailing arms, coil springs, telescopic shock absorbers, anti-roll bar. **Steering:** rack-and-pinion. **Turns lock-to-lock:** 3.9. **Turn diameter (ft.):** 31.2. **Brakes front:** 9.4-in. discs. **Brakes rear:** 7.1-in. drums. **Construction:** unit

POWERTRAINS

	ohc I-4
Bore × stroke (in.)	3.13× 3.40

POWERTRAINS	ohc I-4
Displacement (liters/cu. in.)	1.7/ 105
Compression ratio	8.2:1
Fuel delivery	FI
Net bhp @ rpm	74@ 5000
Net torque @ rpm (lbs/ft)	90@ 3000
Availability	S/All
Final drive ratios	
5-speed OD manual	3.89:1
3-speed automatic	3.56:1

KEY bbl. = barrel (carburetor); **bhp** = brake horsepower (advertised); **Cal.** = California only. **Fed.** = Federal/49 state; **FI** = fuel injection; **ohv** = overhead valve; **ohc** = overhead cam; **I** = inline engine; **V** = V engine; **D** = diesel; **T** = turbocharged; **OD** = overdrive transmission; **S** = standard engine; **O** = optional engine.

PRICES

VOLKSWAGEN SCIROCCO	Retail Price	Dealer Cost	Low Price
(1982 prices shown; 1983 prices not available at time of publication.)			
3-door coupe, 5-speed	$10150	$8658	$9658
3-door coupe, automatic	10555	9013	10013

Note: Prices shown do not include $270 destination charge

STANDARD EQUIPMENT (included in above prices):

1.7-liter (105-cid) fuel-injected 4-cylinder engine, 5-speed overdrive manual or 3-speed automatic transmission as above, power brakes, full carpeting, digital clock, electric rear window defroster, tinted glass, halogen headlamps, oil temperature gauge, tachometer, remote-control left door mirror, AM/FM stereo radio w/cassette player, sport front bucket seats w/reclining backrests and height cushion height adjuster, front and rear spoilers, 4-spoke sport steering wheel, **GL** adds: power antenna, power windows, dual electric remote-control door mirrors.

OPTIONAL EQUIPMENT:

Air conditioning	$690	$552	$558

Prices are accurate at time of printing; subject to manufacturer's change

	Retail Price	Dealer Cost	Low Price
Metallic paint	125	105	107
Sunroof	350	294	297
Rear window wiper/washer	125	105	107

Volvo

Volvo 760 GLE 4-door sedan

WHAT'S NEW FOR '83

The first new Volvo model since the mid-'60s arrives this year
at the top of the Swedish automaker's U.S. lineup. The new
760-series, offered only as a 4-door sedan, should be on sale
around the time you read this. Replacing last year's 200-
series GLE sedan, the 760 is powered by that model's
light-alloy gasoline V-6 mated to the 4-speed overdrive
automatic transmission introduced on some '82 Volvos. Later
a turbocharged version of the 2.4-liter Volkswagen-built
six-cylinder diesel will be available, offered with a choice of
either 3-speed automatic or Volvo's 4-speed-plus-overdrive
manual gearbox. The 760 boasts angular, upright lines not
unlike that of GM's A-body intermediates and a respectably
low 0.40 coefficient of drag. As Volvo's new flagship,
the 760 will list at just under $20,000 (exact prices were not
available at press time). The rest of the Volvo line returns
much as before. All the 200-series models gain lighter
European-style bumpers that fit more closely to the body.
The normally aspirated gasoline four has been given a bore
and compression boost for a claimed 9 percent gain in
horsepower and 13 percent more torque. The turbocharged

Prices are accurate at time of printing; subject to manufacturer's change

gasoline four retains last year's 2.1-liter displacement. The unblown diesel six is still available, but now only with the upper level GL trim. Body style offerings remain the same. (Note: comments below are for the 1982 200-series models.)

EVALUATION

Roomy, practical, and solid as a rock. All the familiar 200-series Volvos have the old-fashioned, boxy body that gives comfortably upright seating, good outward vision, and ample passenger space all-round. Sedans have decent trunk space; wagon cargo bay is cavernous. Firm, supportive seats sit high off the floor. Easy to park (though Volvos no longer look as small as they used to) thanks to light, accurate power steering, standard on all models. Handling and road-holding only average, but hold no unpleasant surprises. The GLT is an exception, because of its stiffer suspension and grippier tires. However, ride is thumpier and noisier, a tradeoff that won't appeal to most buyers. All models have all-disc brakes that are powerful and reassuring. Good control layout and commanding driving position, too, but we dislike the way the radio is buried just above the transmission hump in front of the shifter. Performance and mileage depend on engine. The turbo four is very stong low down, but feels harsh and has a boomy exhaust. The diesel six is hard pressed to provide much pickup off the line, but it's fine for

EVALUATION CHECKLIST
(200-Series GL model)

Fuel economy	3	Cargo room	3
Driveability	5	Serviceability	3
Acceleration	3	Standard equipment	4
Braking	4	Body construction	5
Handling/roadholding	3	Paint/exterior finish	4
Driving position	4	Interior finish	4
Instruments/control	4	TOTAL POINTS	78
Visiblity	5		
Heating/ventilation	4	**RATING SCALE**	
Seat comfort	4	5 = Excellent	
Passenger room	4	4 = Very Good	
Ride	4	3 = Average/Acceptable	
Noise	4	2 = Fair	
Exit/entry	4	1 = Poor	

the highway. The standard four is the best of the bunch. It's smooth-revving, tolerably quiet, and surprisingly muscular. With it, mileage isn't great, mostly due to high curb weight, so the diesel is the pennypincher's choice. All Volvos are a bit expensive, but still good value. Our favorite remains the four-cylinder gasoline GL—elegantly understated inside and out, loaded with standard features, and delightful to drive. We recommend it. We haven't driven the new 760 at this writing, but would predict performance and fuel economy with the V-6 will be much like that of the old GLE. The turbodiesel should be better on both counts.

SPECIFICATIONS

	760 4-door sedan	2-door sedan	4-door sedan	5-door wagon
Wheelbase (in.)	109.1	104.3	104.3	104.3
Overall length (in.)	188.4	188.5	188.5	188.5
Overall width (in.)	68.9	67.3	67.3	67.3
Overall height (in.)	55.5	57.5	57.5	57.5
Track front (in.)	57.5	56.3	56.3	56.3
Track rear (in.)	57.5	53.5	53.5	53.5
Curb weight (lbs.)	2996	2926[1]	2957[1]	3079[1]
Max. cargo vol. (cu. ft.)	15.2	13.9	13.9	41.1/76.0
Fuel tank capacity (gal.)	NA	15.8	15.8	15.8
Seating capacity	5	5	5	5
Front headroom (in.)	38.2	37.4	37.4	37.4
Front shoulder room (in.)	55.9	54.3	55.3	55.3
Front legroom, max. (in.)	40.5	39.8	39.8	39.8
Rear headroom (in.)	36.6	36.3	36.3	36.8
Rear shoulder room (in.)	55.9	53.1	54.1	54.1
Rear legroom, min. (in.)	36.1	36.8	36.8	36.8

1: DL 4-cyl. models

BODY/CHASSIS

Drivetrain layout: longitudinal front engine/rear-wheel drive. **Suspension front:** independent; MacPherson struts, lower A-arms, coil springs (eccentrically mounted on 760-series), telescopic shock absorbers, (gas-pressurized on 760-series), anti-roll-bar. **Suspension rear:** rigid axle, four trailing arms, Panhard rod, coil springs, telescopic shock absorbers, anti-roll bar; rigid axle, two trailing arms, wishbone subframe bracket, Panhard rod, coil springs, gas-pressurized shock absorbers with self-levelling (760-series). **Steering:** rack-and-pinion, power-assisted. **Turns lock-to-lock:** 3.5. **Turn diameter (ft.):** 32.2. **Brakes front:** 10.2-in. discs. **Brakes rear:** 11.1-in. discs. **Construction:** unit

POWERTRAINS	ohc I-4	ohc I-4T	ohc I-6D	ohc I-4TD	ohc V-6
Bore × stroke (in.)	3.78× 3.15	3.62× 3.15	3.01× 3.40	3.01× 3.40	3.58× 2.87
Displacement (liters cu. in.)	2.3/ 141	2.1/ 130	2.4/ 145	2.4/ 145	2.8/ 174
Compression ratio	10.3:1	7.5:1	23.0:1	23.0:1	8.8:1
Fueld delivery	FI	FI	FI	FI	FI
Net bhp @ rpm	107@ 5400	127@ 5400	76@ 4800	106@ 4800	130@ 5500
Net torque @ rpm (lbs/ft)	127@ 3500	150@ 3750	98@ 2800	139@ 2400	153@ 2750
Availabiltiy	S/All	S/All[1]	S/All[2]	S/All[3]	S/All[3]

1: GLT Turbo only
2: Diesel models only
3: 760 series only

Final drive ratios

4-speed manual w/OD	3.31:1	3.73:1	3.54:1	3.54:1	
3-speed automatic				3.15:1	
4-speed automatic w/OD	3.73:1	3.91:1	3.31:1		3.54:1

PRICES

VOLVO

	Retail Price
DL 2-door sedan	$10650
DL 4-door sedan	11085
DL 5-door wagon	11585
GL 4-door sedan	14495
GL 5-door wagon	14995
GLT 2-door sedan	16050
GLT 4-door sedan	16360
GLT 5-door wagon	16860
Diesel 4-door sedan	14980
Diesel 5-door wagon	15740
760 4-door sedan, V-6	18785
760 4-door sedan, turbodiesel	19595

Note: Above prices do not include $295 destination charge.

STANDARD EQUIPMENT (included in above prices):

DL: 2.3-liter (141-cid) 4-cylinder engine with fuel injection, 4-speed-plus-overdrive manual transmission, 4-wheel power disc brakes, tinted glass, full carpeting, electric rear window defroster, halogen headlamps, electric clock, reclining front bucket seats, intermittent wipers, remote-control left door mirror (dual mirrors on wagon), rear window wiper/washer with intermittent control (wagon), molded front door pockets, central locking system (exc. 2-door). **GL** adds: air conditioning, power antenna, power windows, electric sliding steel sunroof (sedans), full instrumentation including tachometer and oil pressure and voltmeter gauges (except with diesel engine), heated driver's seat, power door locks, velour upholstery (leather on wagon), delay-timer courtesy lights. **Diesel** models have GL equipment plus 2.4-liter (145-cid) 6-cylinder diesel engine. **GLT** adds: dual electric remote-control door mirrors, uprated suspension, alloy wheels, front spoiler, 2.1-liter (130-cid) turbocharged 4-cylinder engine with fuel injection, premium tires.

OPTIONAL EQUIPMENT

4-speed overdrive automatic transmission	
DL, GL, GLT	$390
Diesel	260
Lambda Sond emissions control system (req. on GLT models)	137
LH Lambda emissions control system (req. DL, GL gasoline models)	158
Leather upholstery, GL, GLT models only	590
California extended diesel warranty	325